ULTRAMAN

EIICHI SHIMIZU × TOMOHIRO SHIMOGUCHI

1

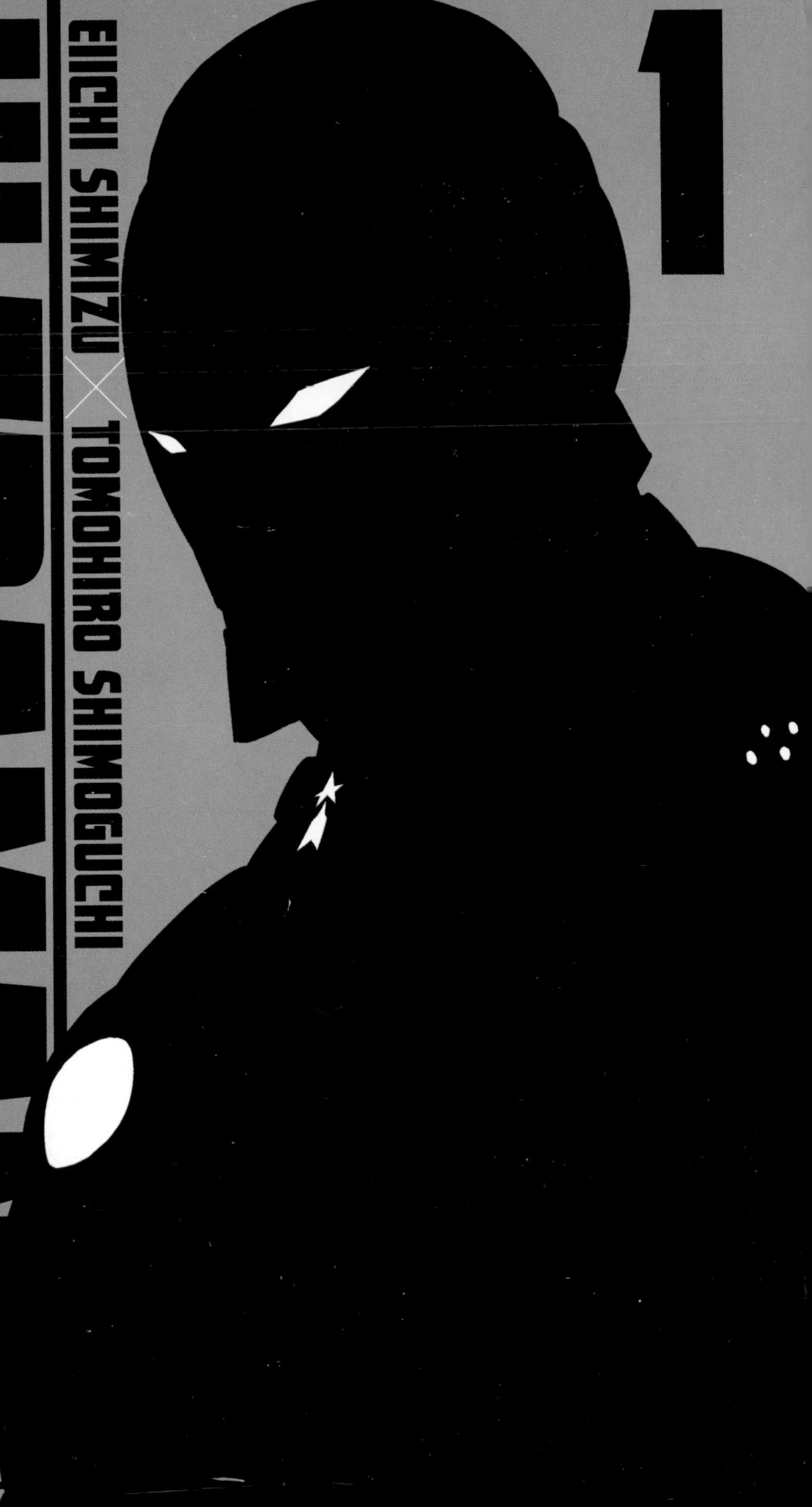

THIS IS T
BEGINNIN
OF A NEW AC

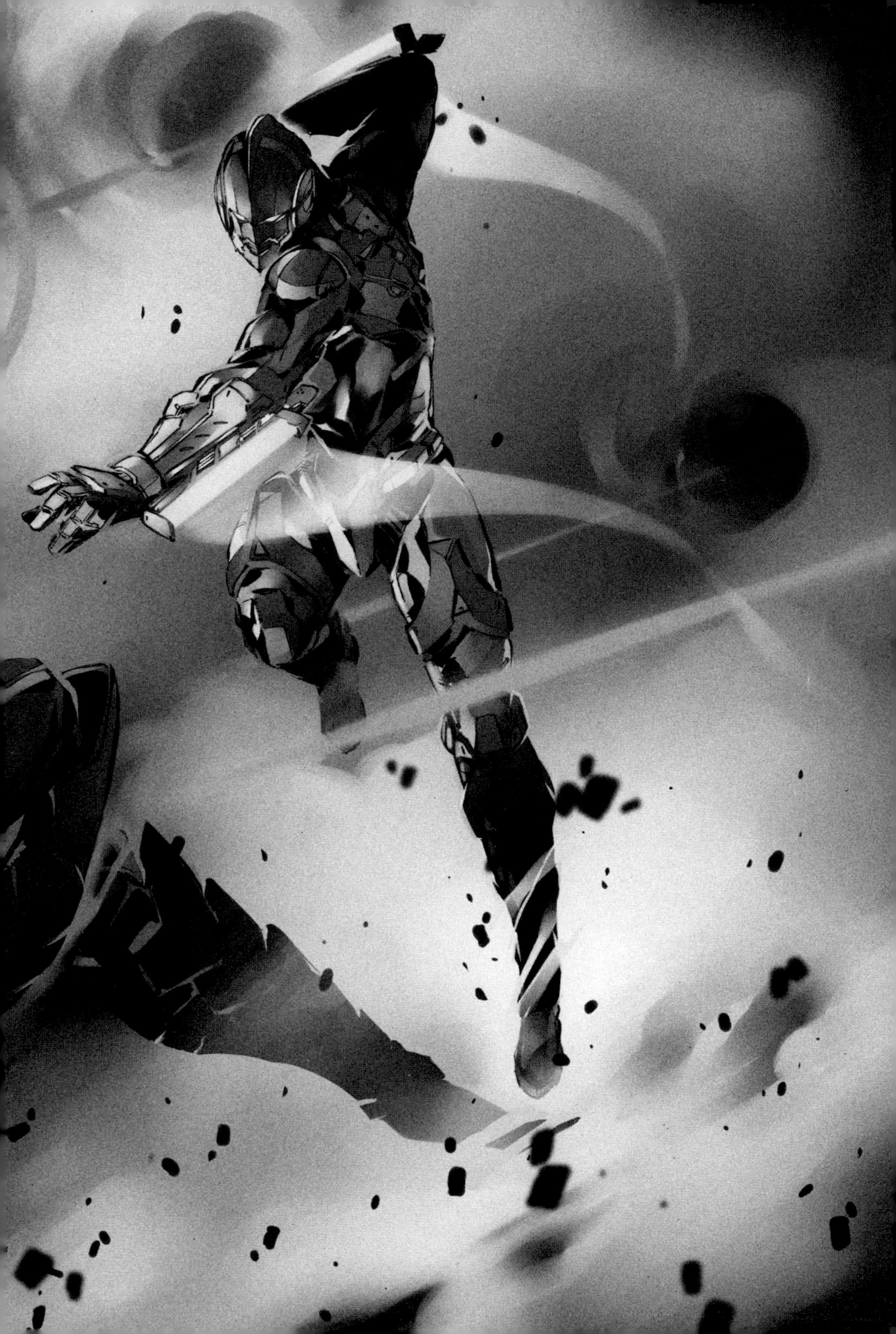

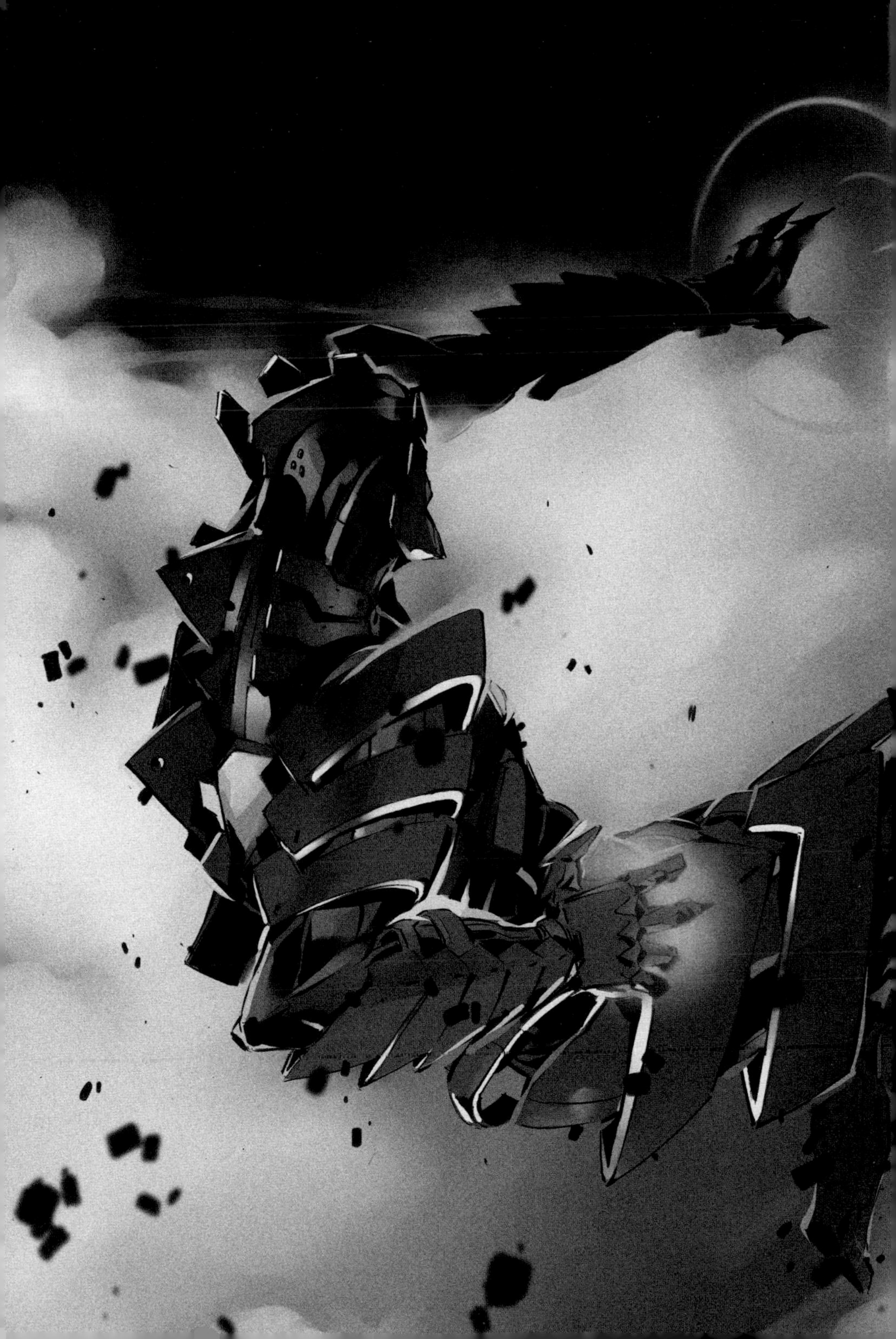

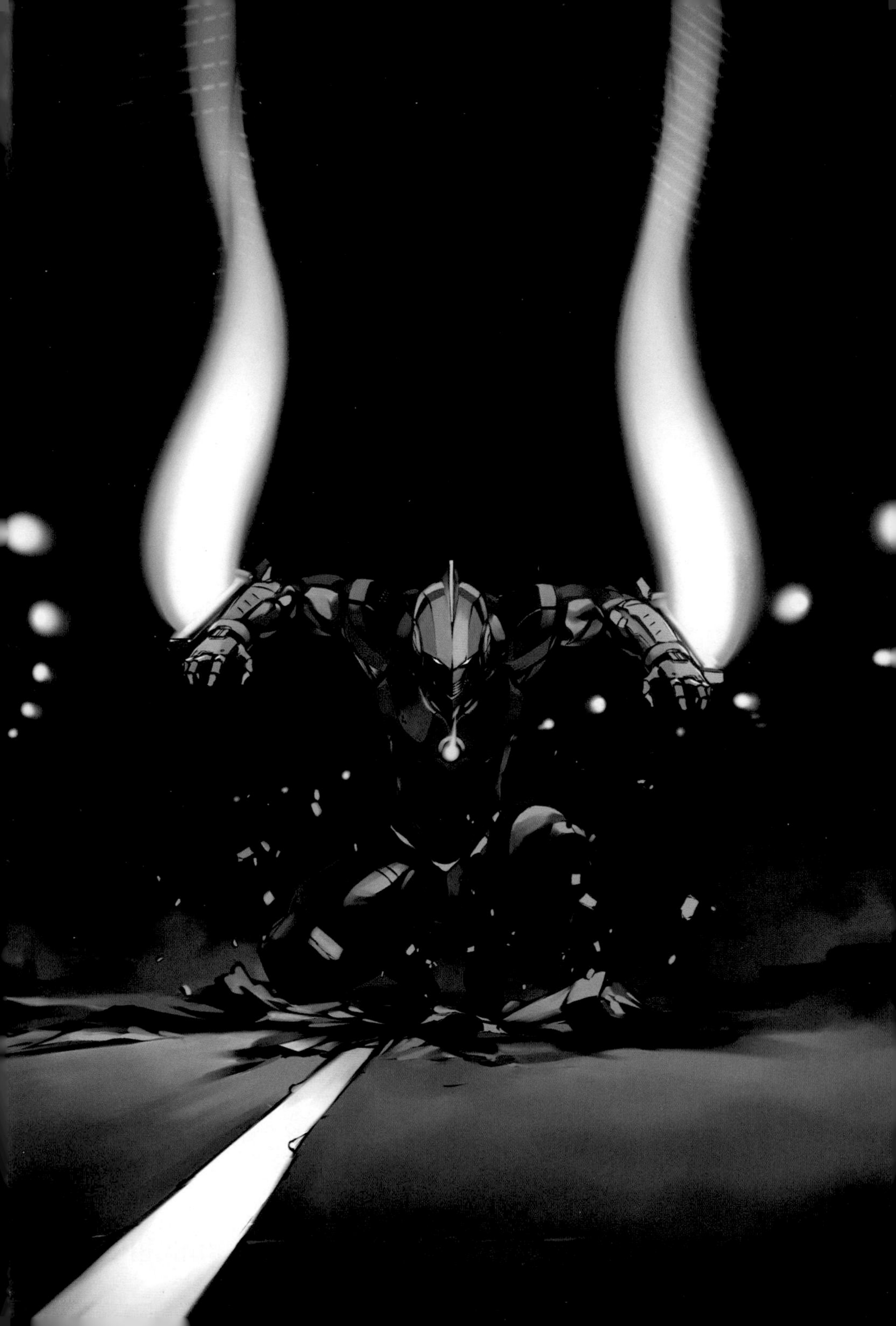

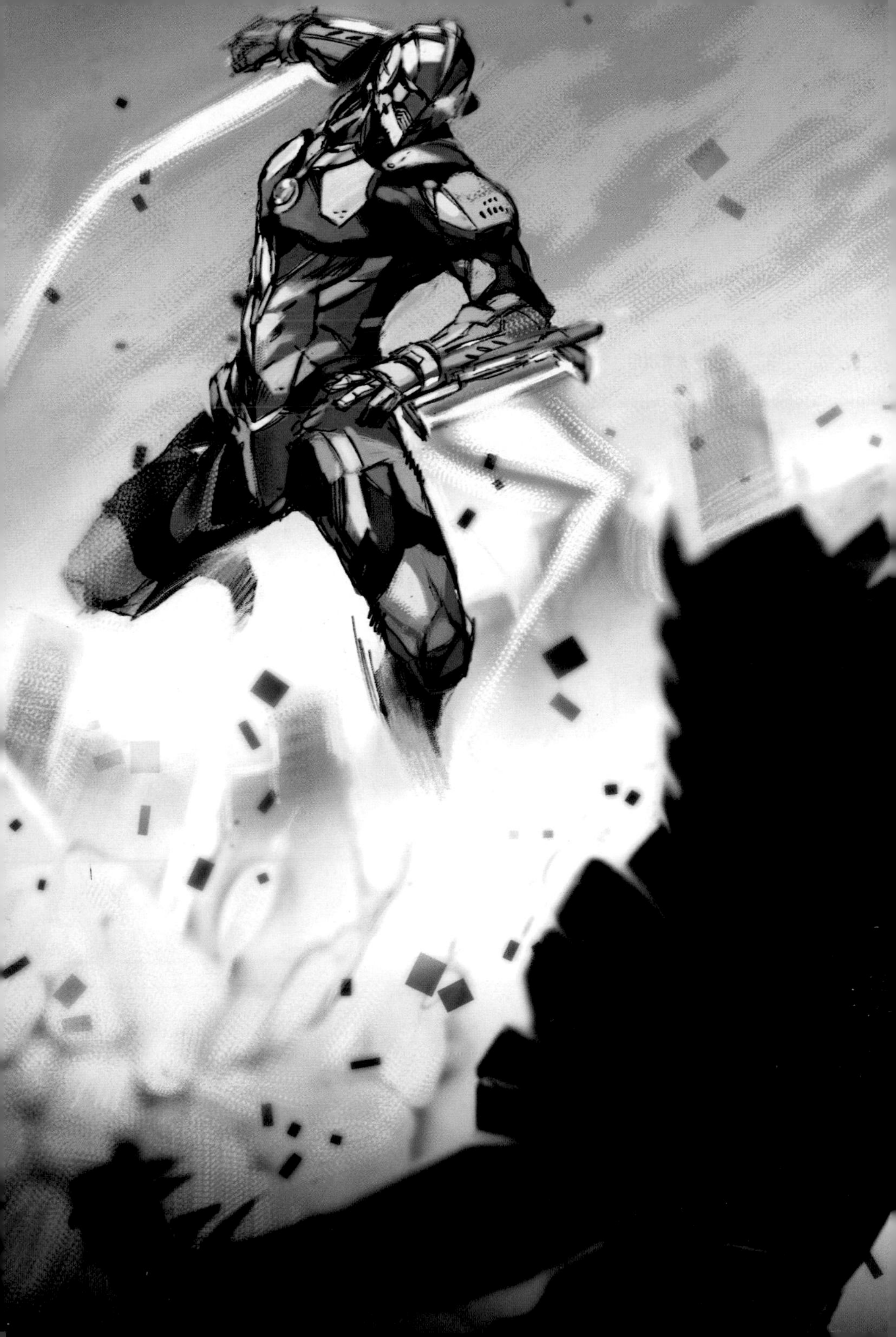

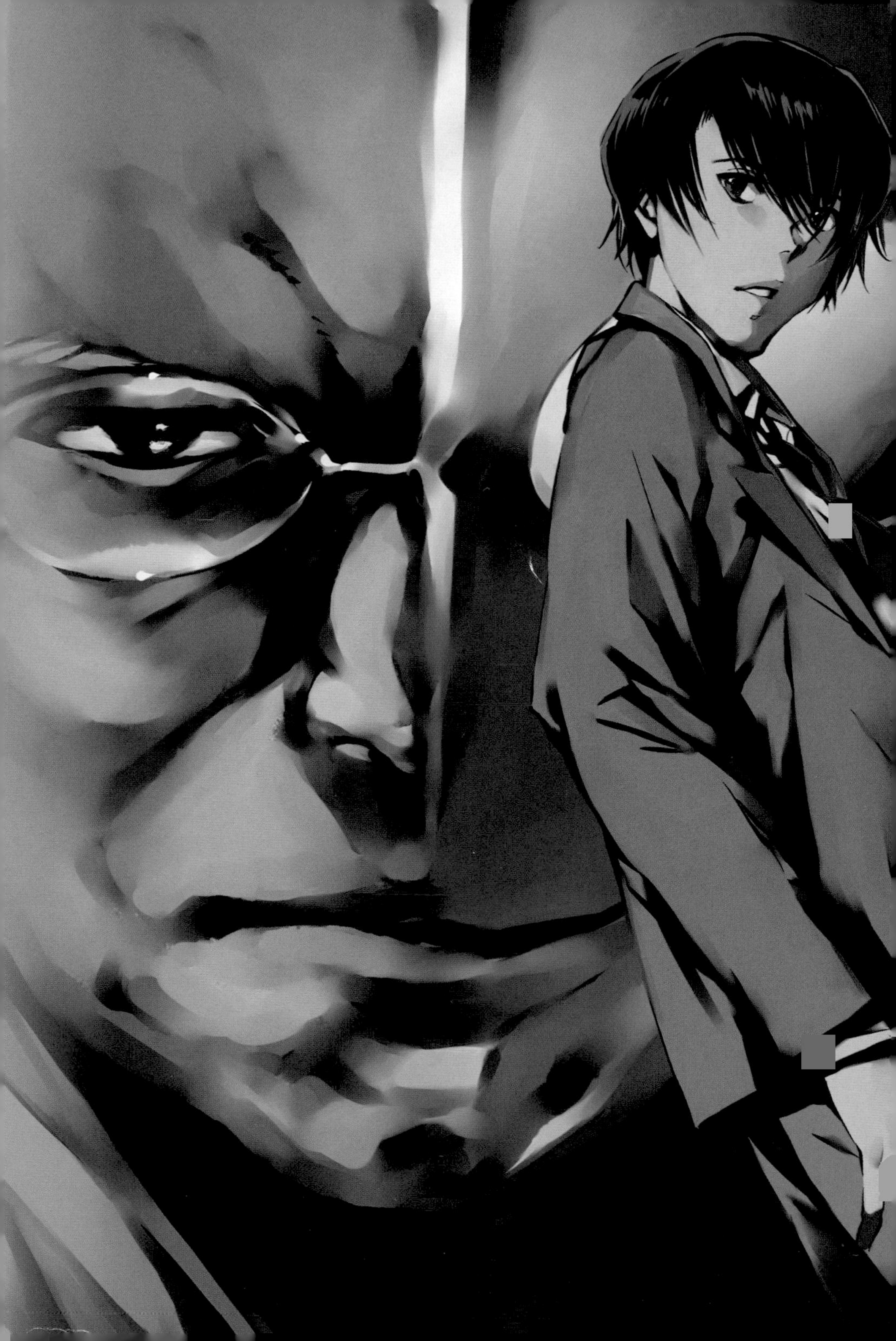

FREE FROM ALIEN AGGRESSION, THE EARTH WAS NOW PEACEFUL.

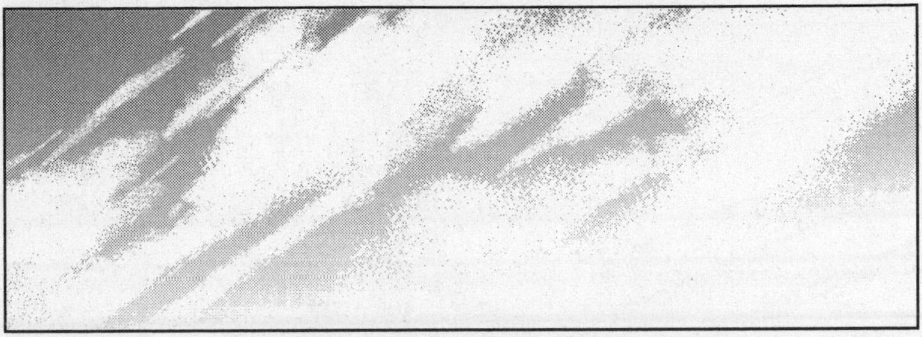

THOUGH HUMAN CONFLICTS CONTINUED, HUMANITY ITSELF FACED NO MORE THREATS FROM EXTRA-TERRESTRIAL INVADERS.

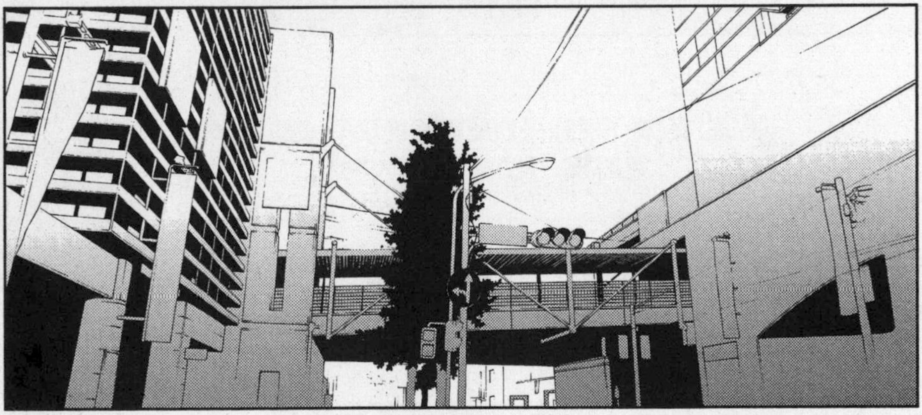

SEVERAL DECADES LATER...

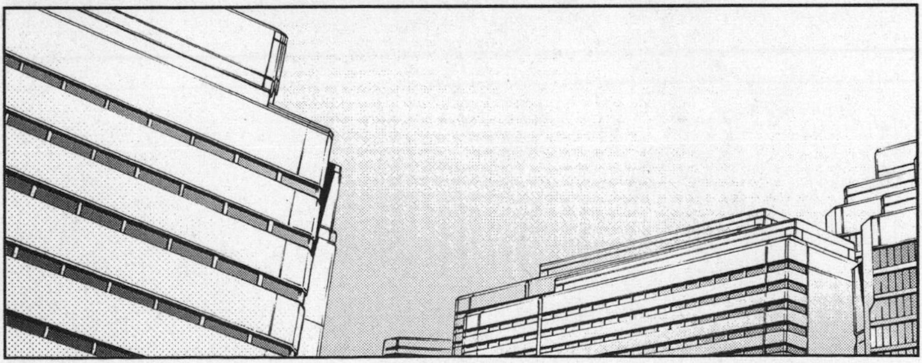

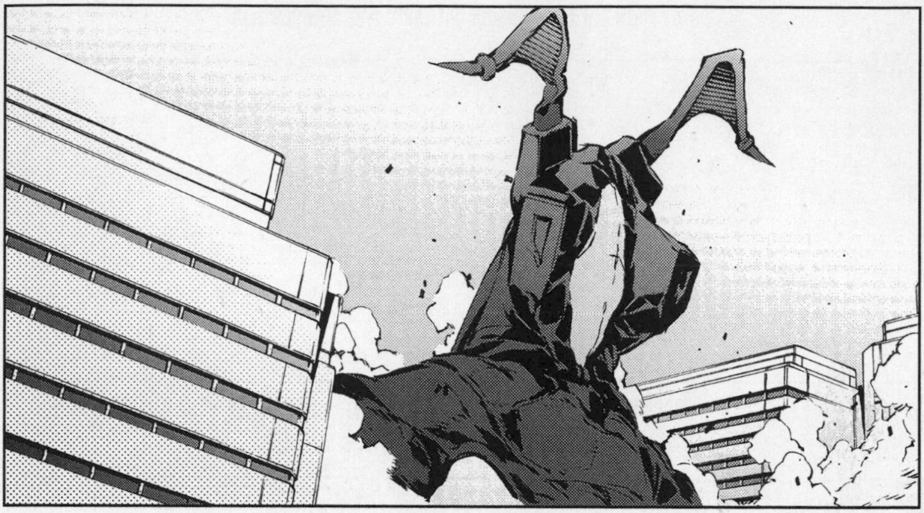

THIS TALE BEGINS YEARS AFTER THE GIANT OF LIGHT—ALSO KNOWN AS ULTRAMAN—BECAME ONLY A MEMORY...

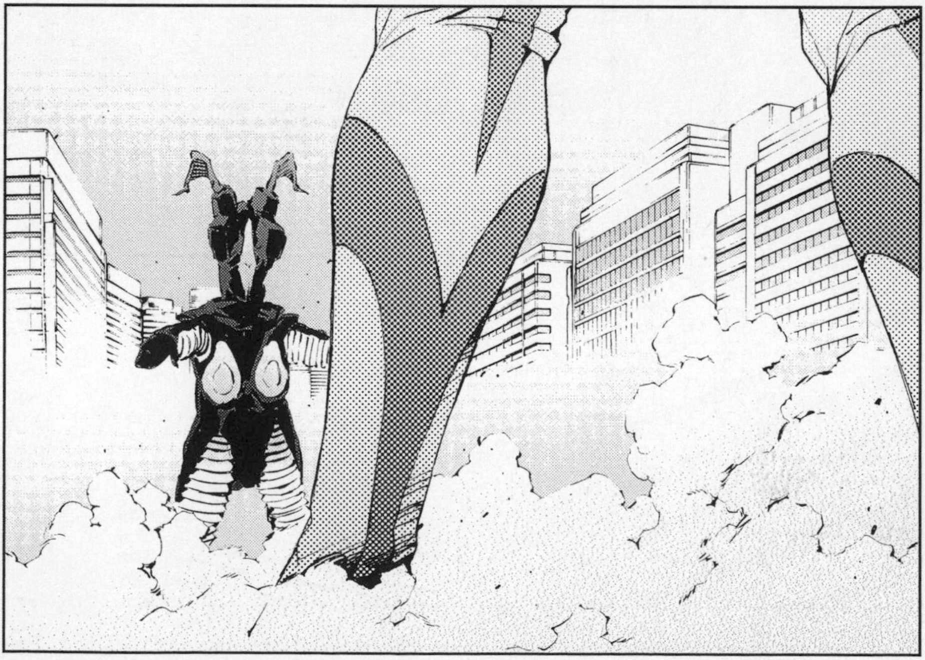

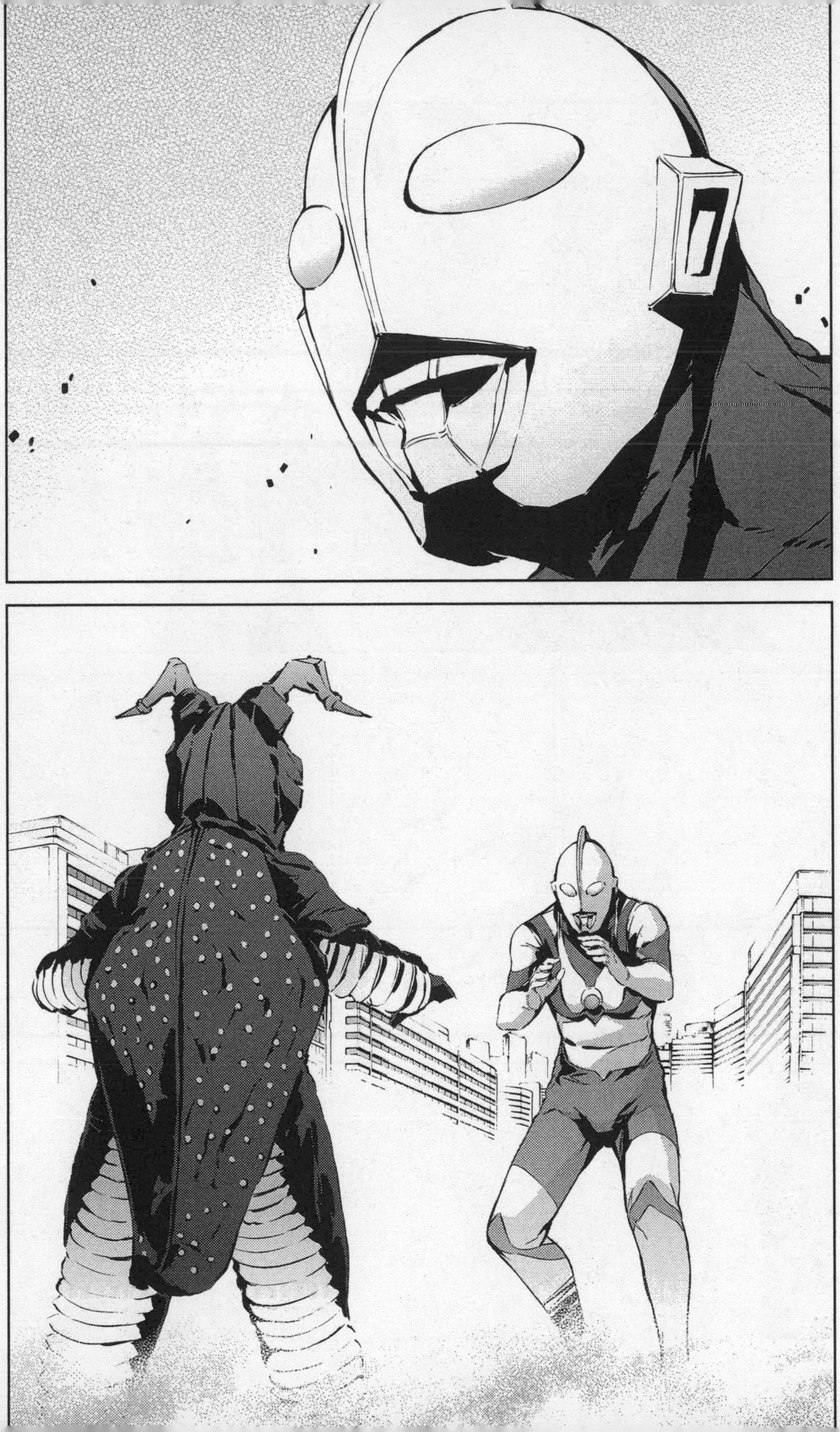

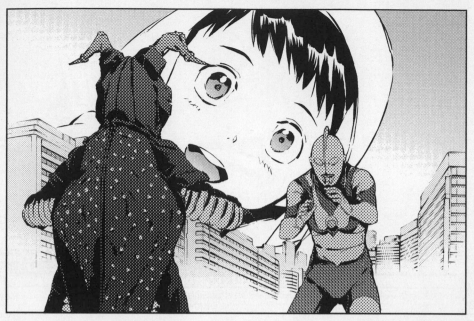

AS
YOU
CAN
SEE...

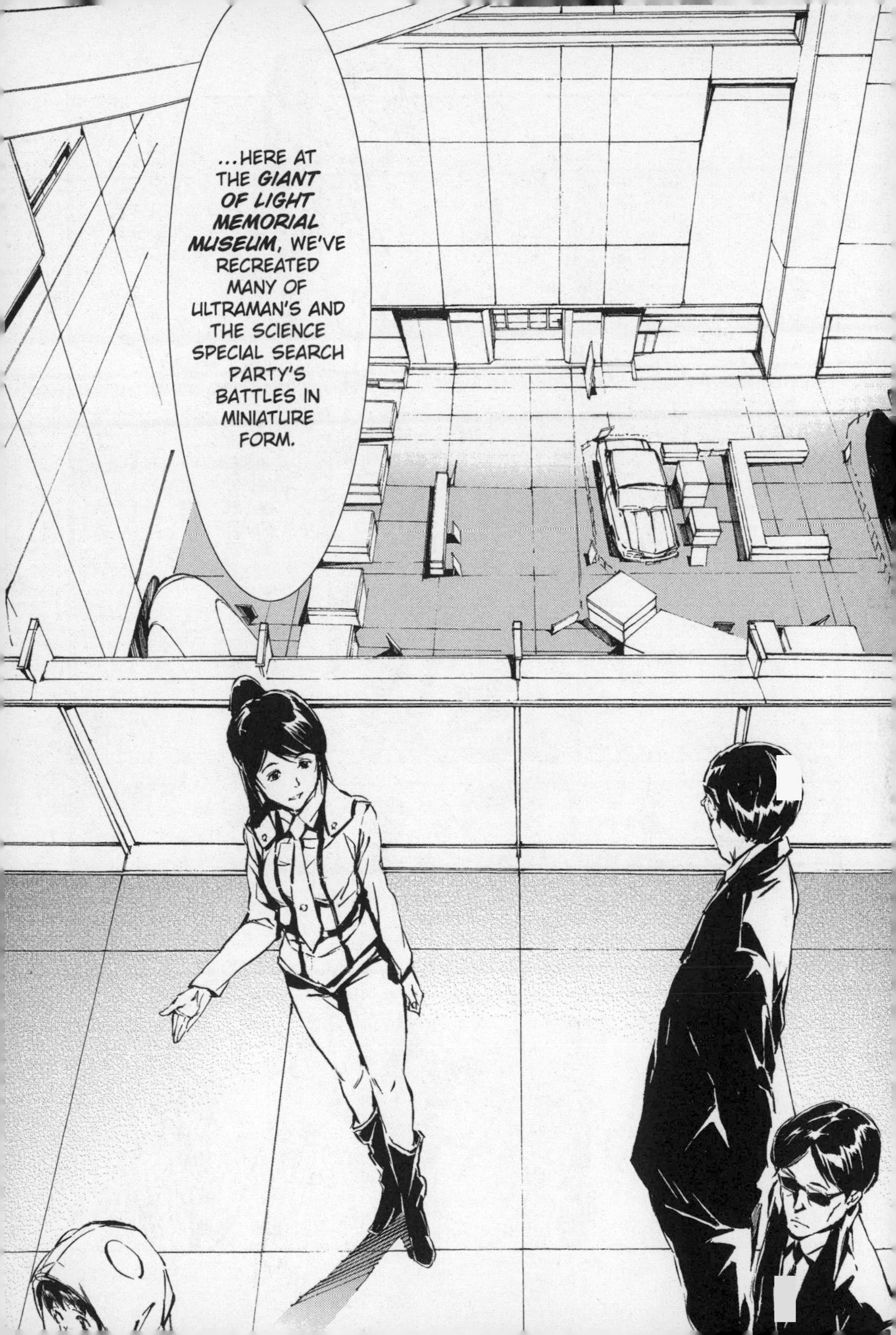
...HERE AT THE GIANT OF LIGHT MEMORIAL MUSEUM, WE'VE RECREATED MANY OF ULTRAMAN'S AND THE SCIENCE SPECIAL SEARCH PARTY'S BATTLES IN MINIATURE FORM.

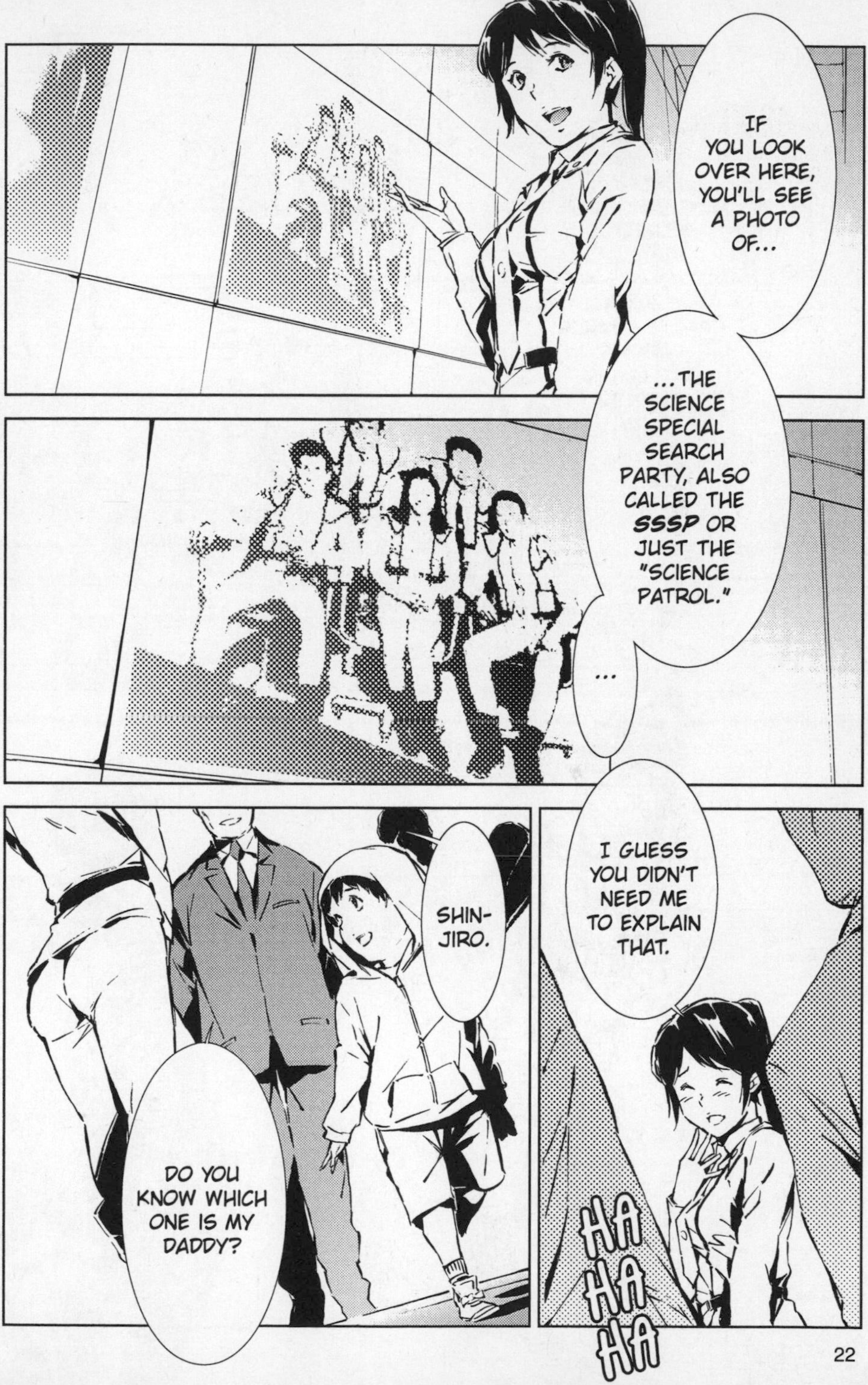
IF YOU LOOK OVER HERE, YOU'LL SEE A PHOTO OF...
...THE SCIENCE SPECIAL SEARCH PARTY, ALSO CALLED THE SSSP OR JUST THE "SCIENCE PATROL."
...
I GUESS YOU DIDN'T NEED ME TO EXPLAIN THAT.
HA HA HA
SHIN-JIRO.
DO YOU KNOW WHICH ONE IS MY DADDY?

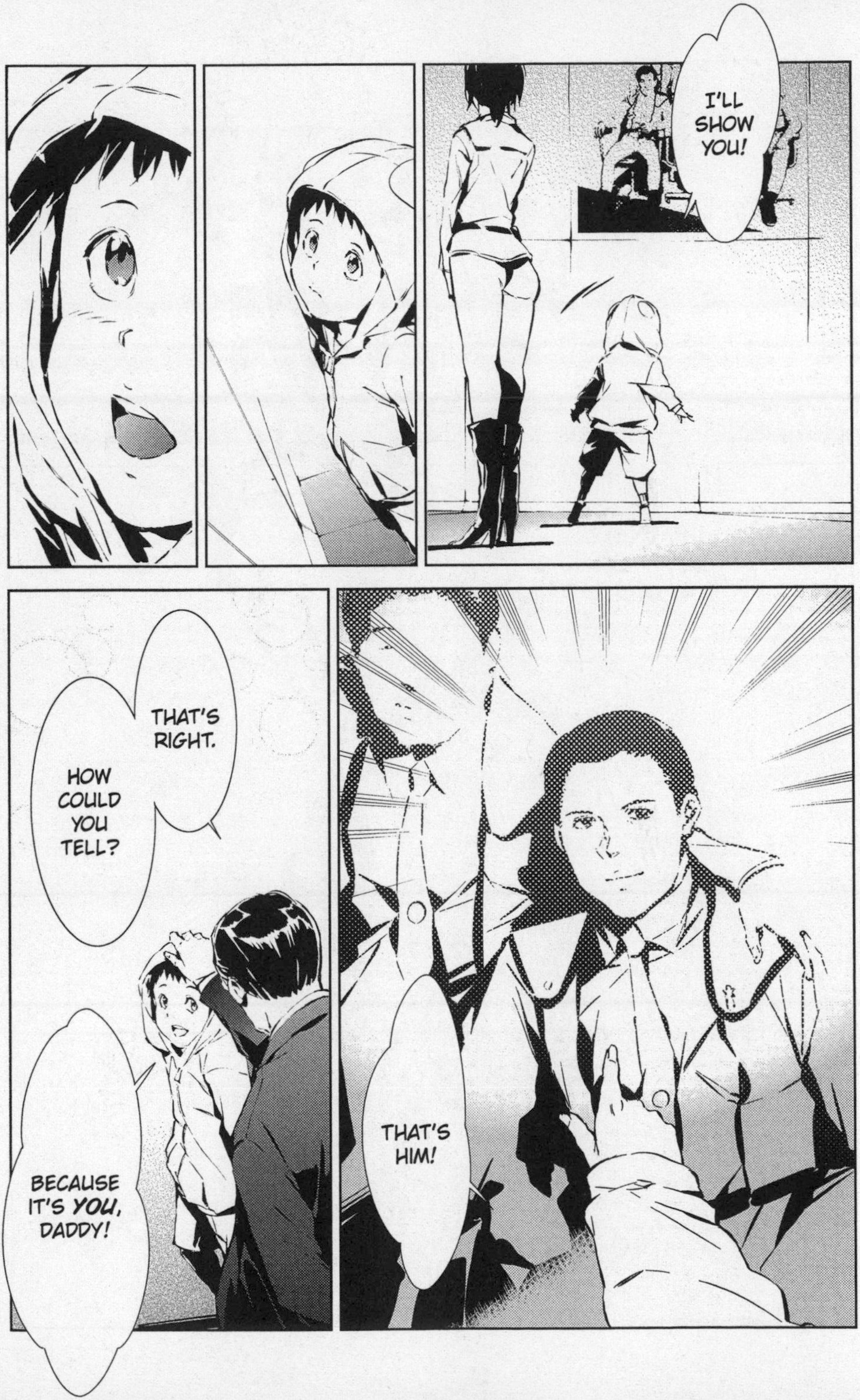
I'LL SHOW YOU!
THAT'S HIM!
THAT'S RIGHT.
HOW COULD YOU TELL?
BECAUSE IT'S *YOU*, DADDY!

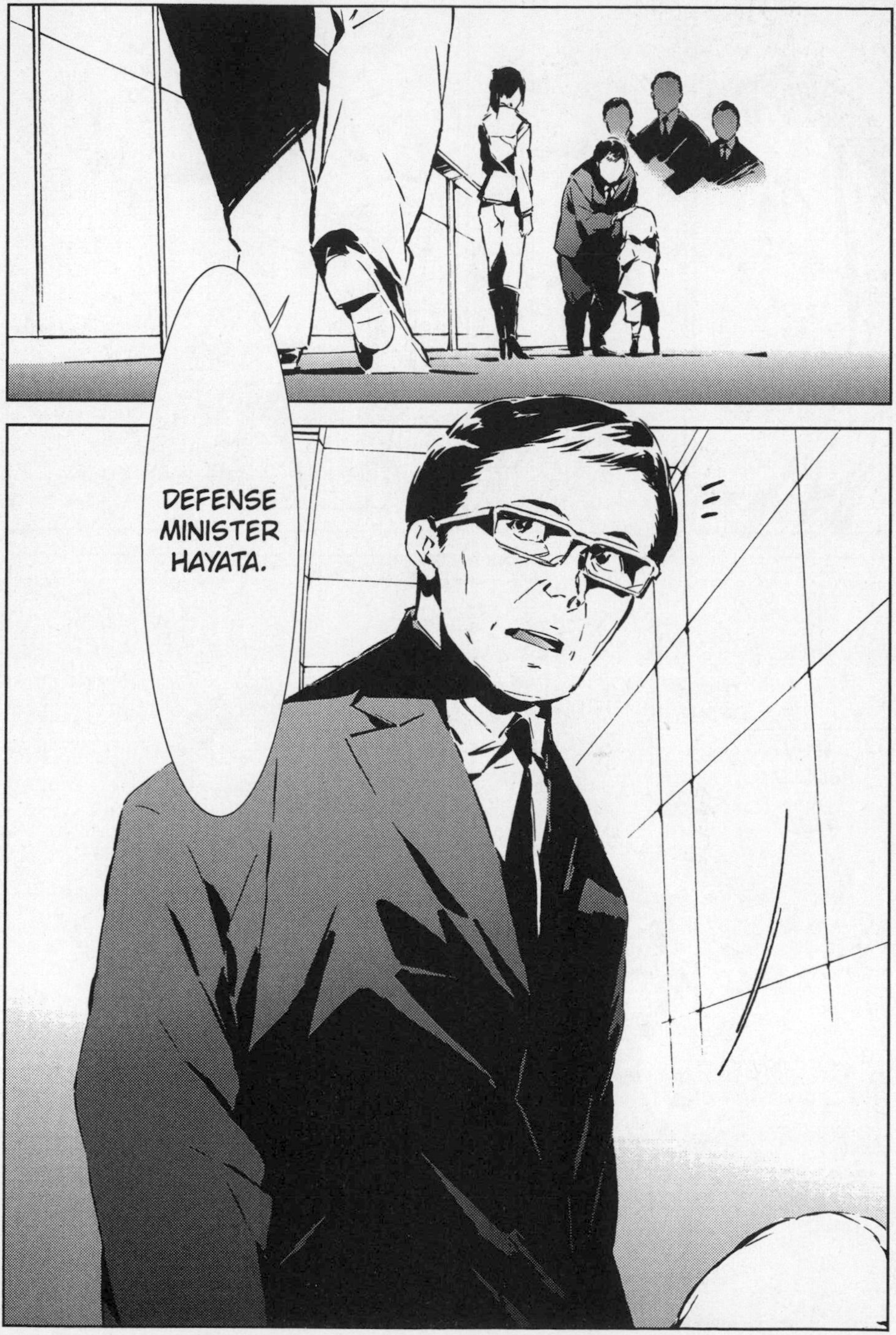
DEFENSE MINISTER HAYATA.

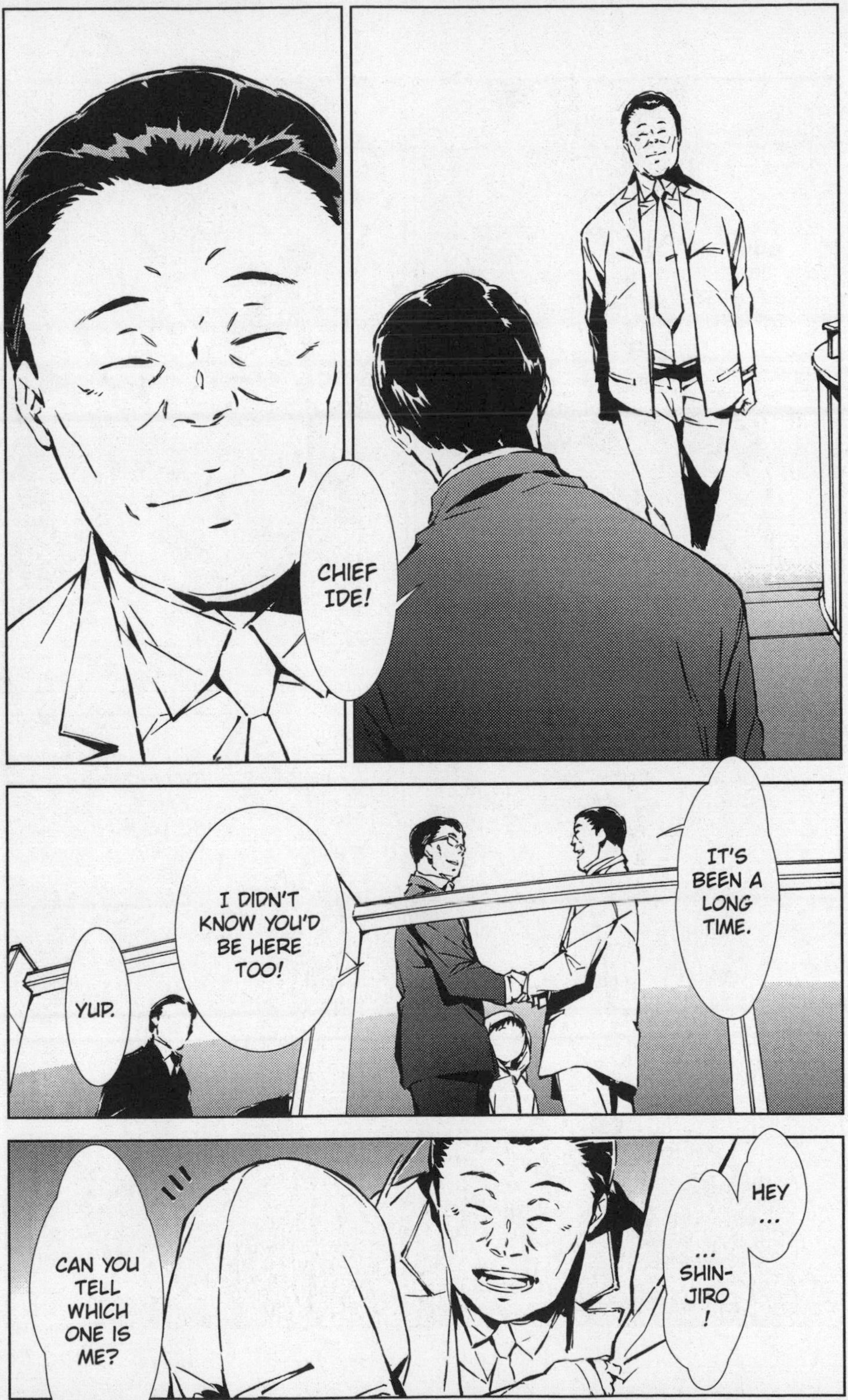
CHIEF IDE!
IT'S BEEN A LONG TIME.
I DIDN'T KNOW YOU'D BE HERE TOO!
YUP.
HEY ...
... SHIN-JIRO!
CAN YOU TELL WHICH ONE IS ME?

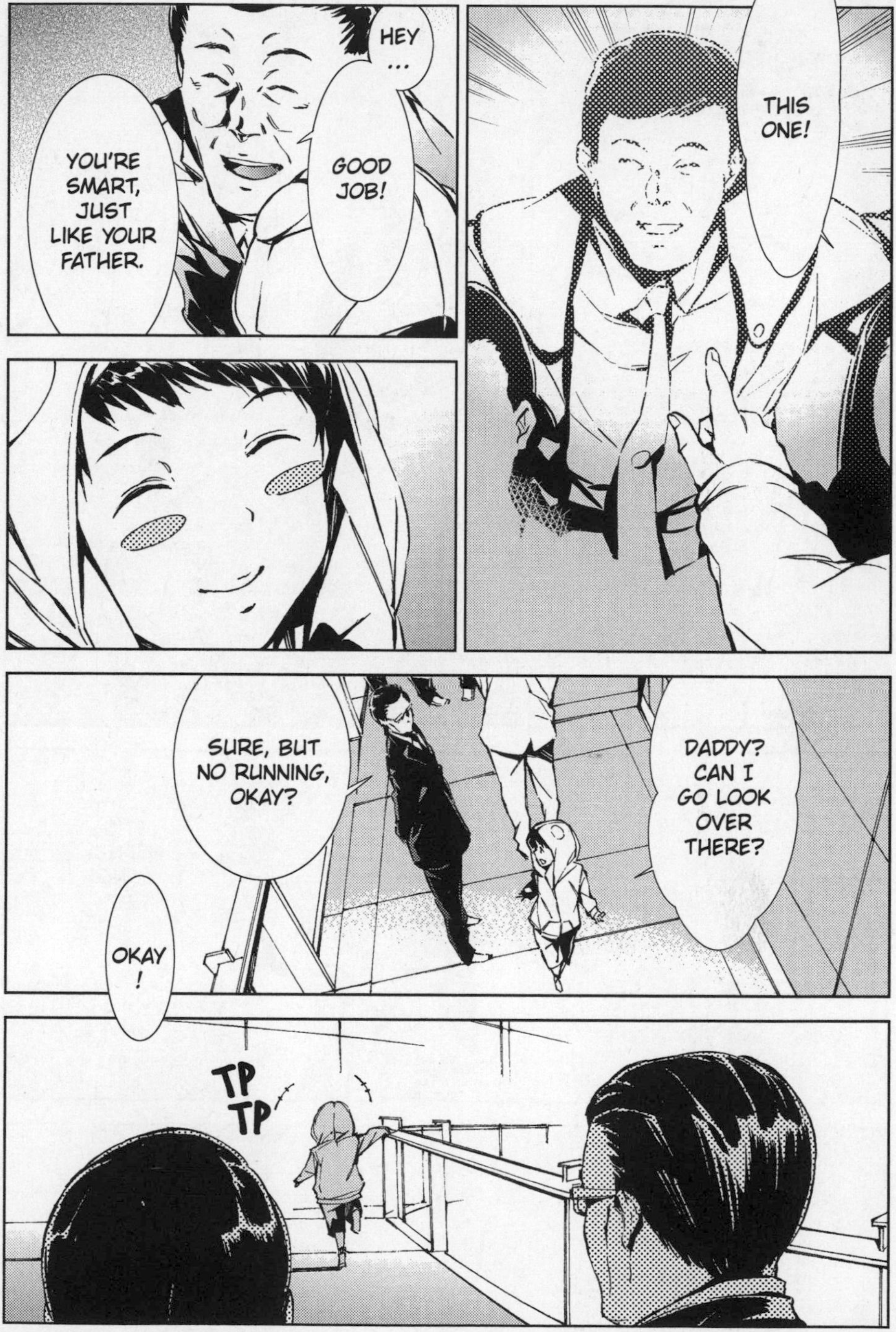
THIS ONE!
HEY ...
GOOD JOB!
YOU'RE SMART, JUST LIKE YOUR FATHER.
DADDY? CAN I GO LOOK OVER THERE?
SURE, BUT NO RUNNING, OKAY?
OKAY!
TP TP

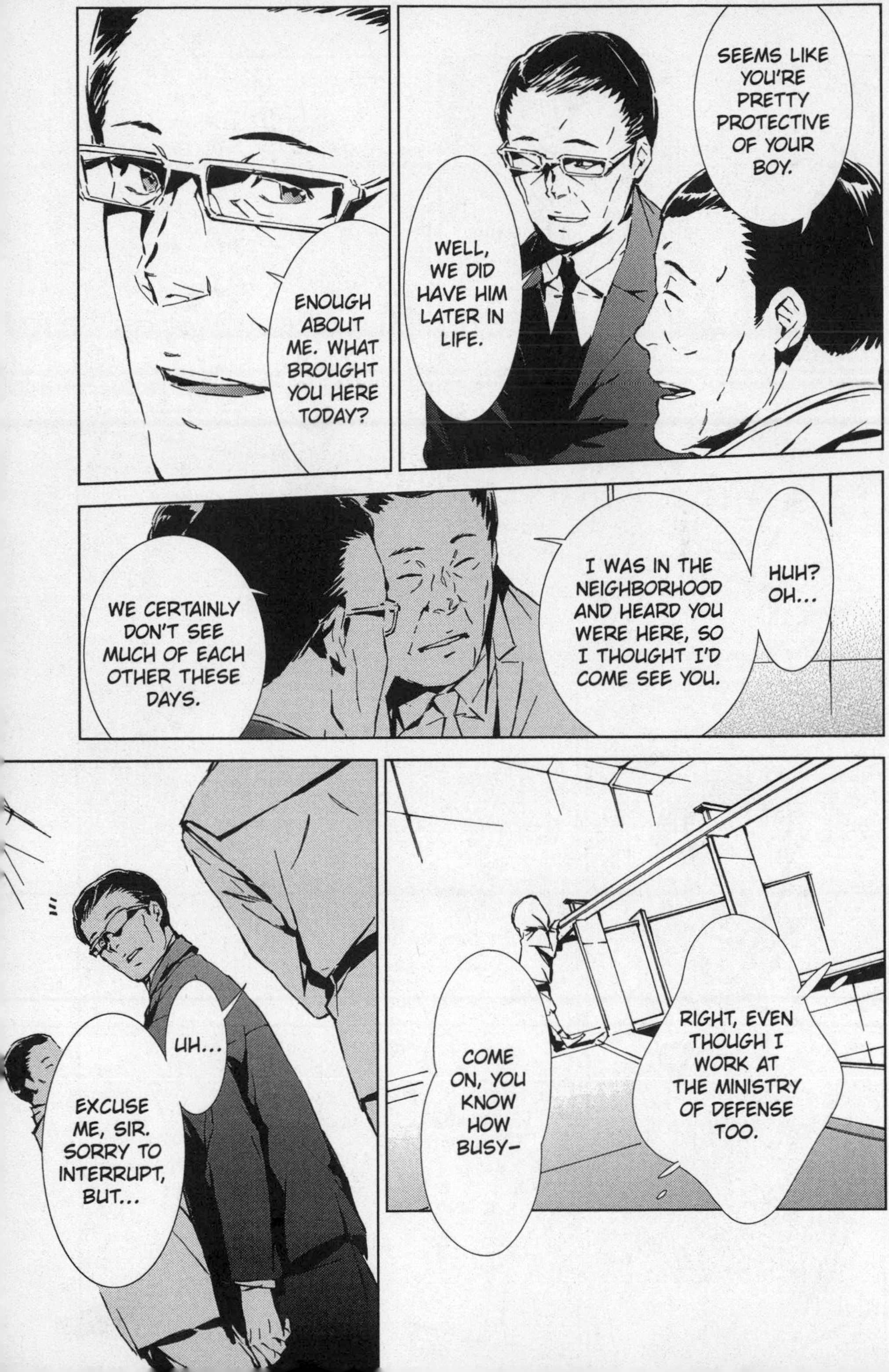
SEEMS LIKE YOU'RE PRETTY PROTECTIVE OF YOUR BOY.
WELL, WE DID HAVE HIM LATER IN LIFE.
ENOUGH ABOUT ME. WHAT BROUGHT YOU HERE TODAY?
HUH? OH...
I WAS IN THE NEIGHBORHOOD AND HEARD YOU WERE HERE, SO I THOUGHT I'D COME SEE YOU.
WE CERTAINLY DON'T SEE MUCH OF EACH OTHER THESE DAYS.
RIGHT, EVEN THOUGH I WORK AT THE MINISTRY OF DEFENSE TOO.
COME ON, YOU KNOW HOW BUSY-
UH...
EXCUSE ME, SIR. SORRY TO INTERRUPT, BUT...

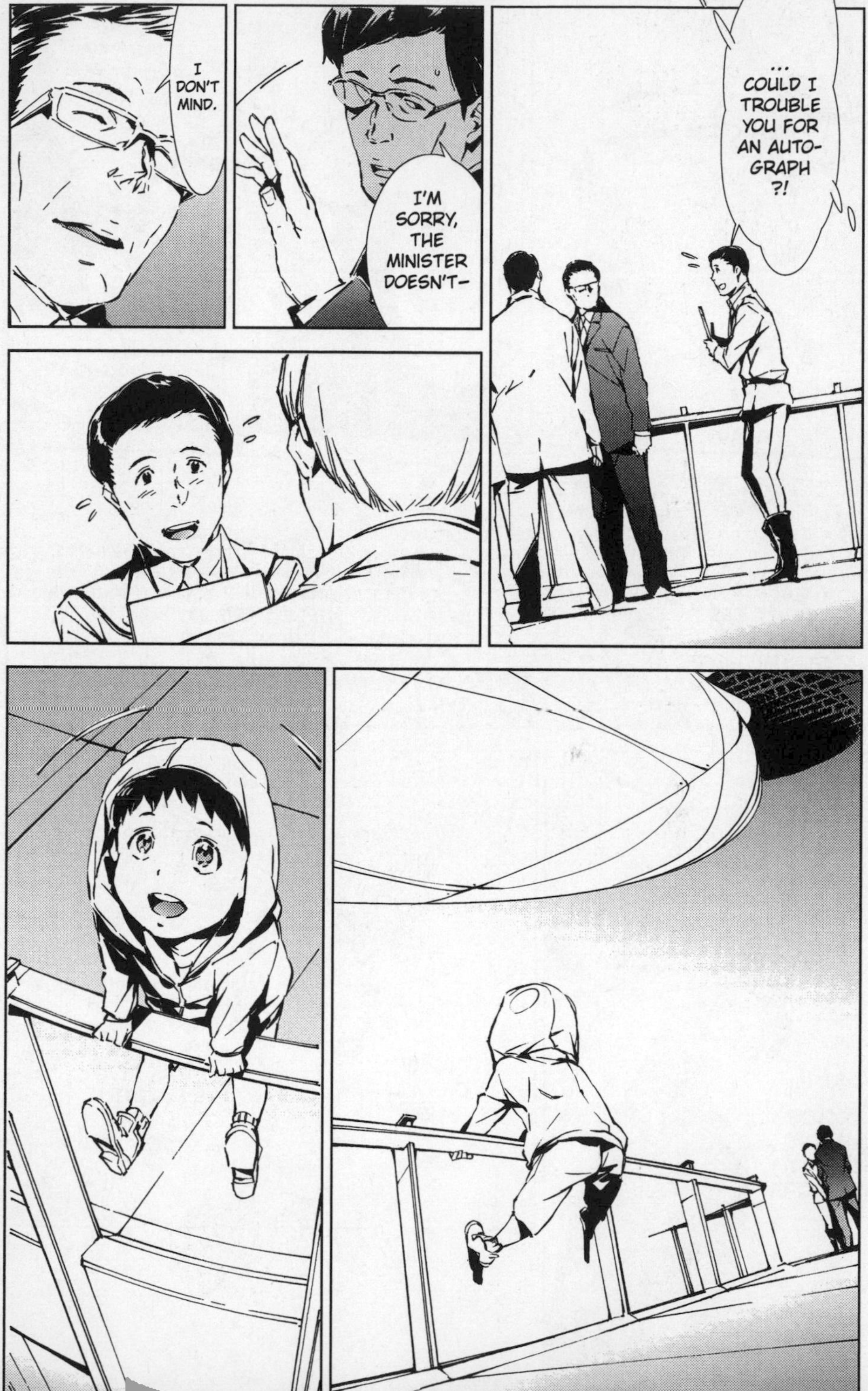
... COULD I TROUBLE YOU FOR AN AUTO-GRAPH ?!
I'M SORRY, THE MINISTER DOESN'T-
I DON'T MIND.

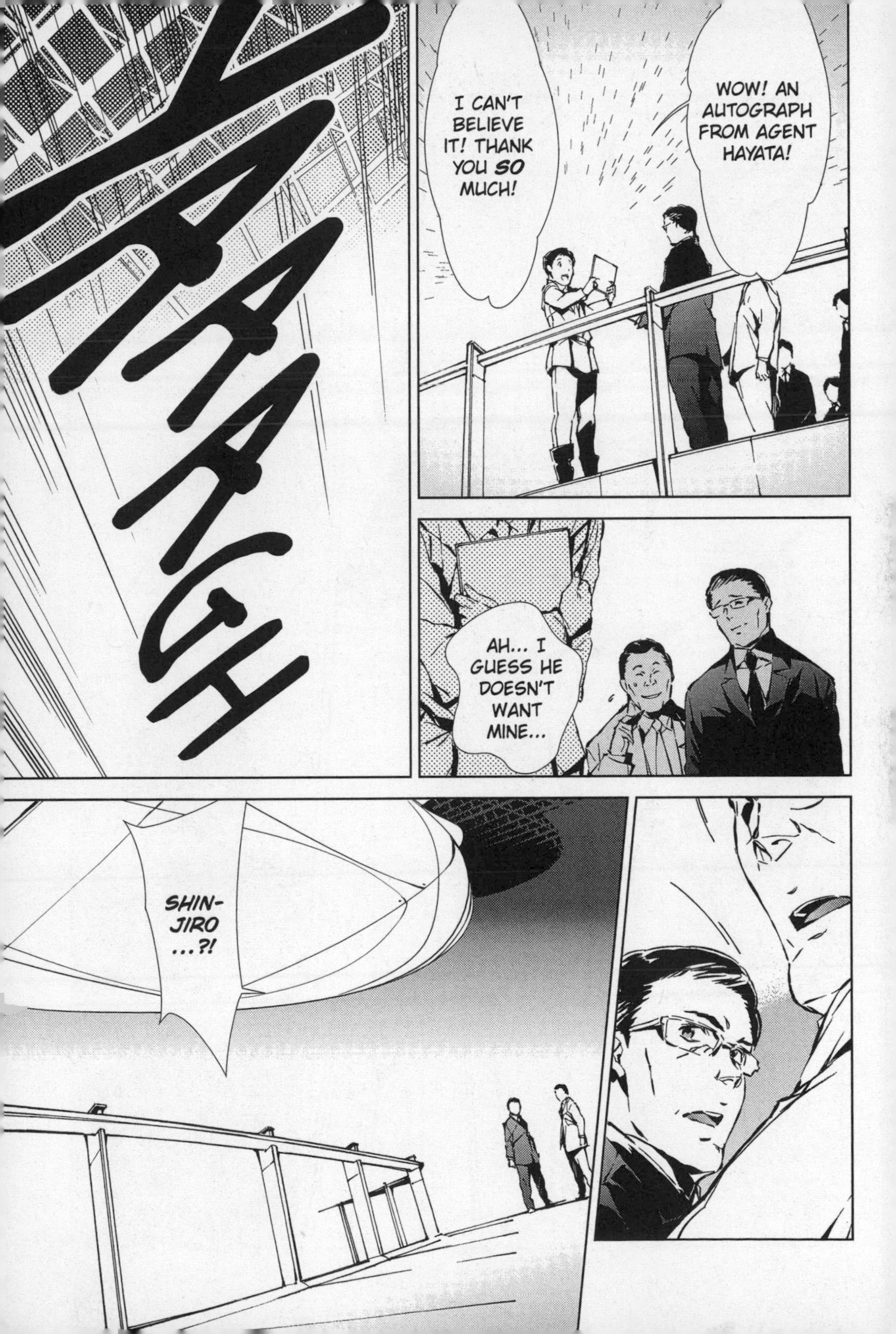
WOW! AN AUTOGRAPH FROM AGENT HAYATA!
I CAN'T BELIEVE IT! THANK YOU SO MUCH!
AH... I GUESS HE DOESN'T WANT MINE...
YAAAGH
SHIN-JIRO ...?!

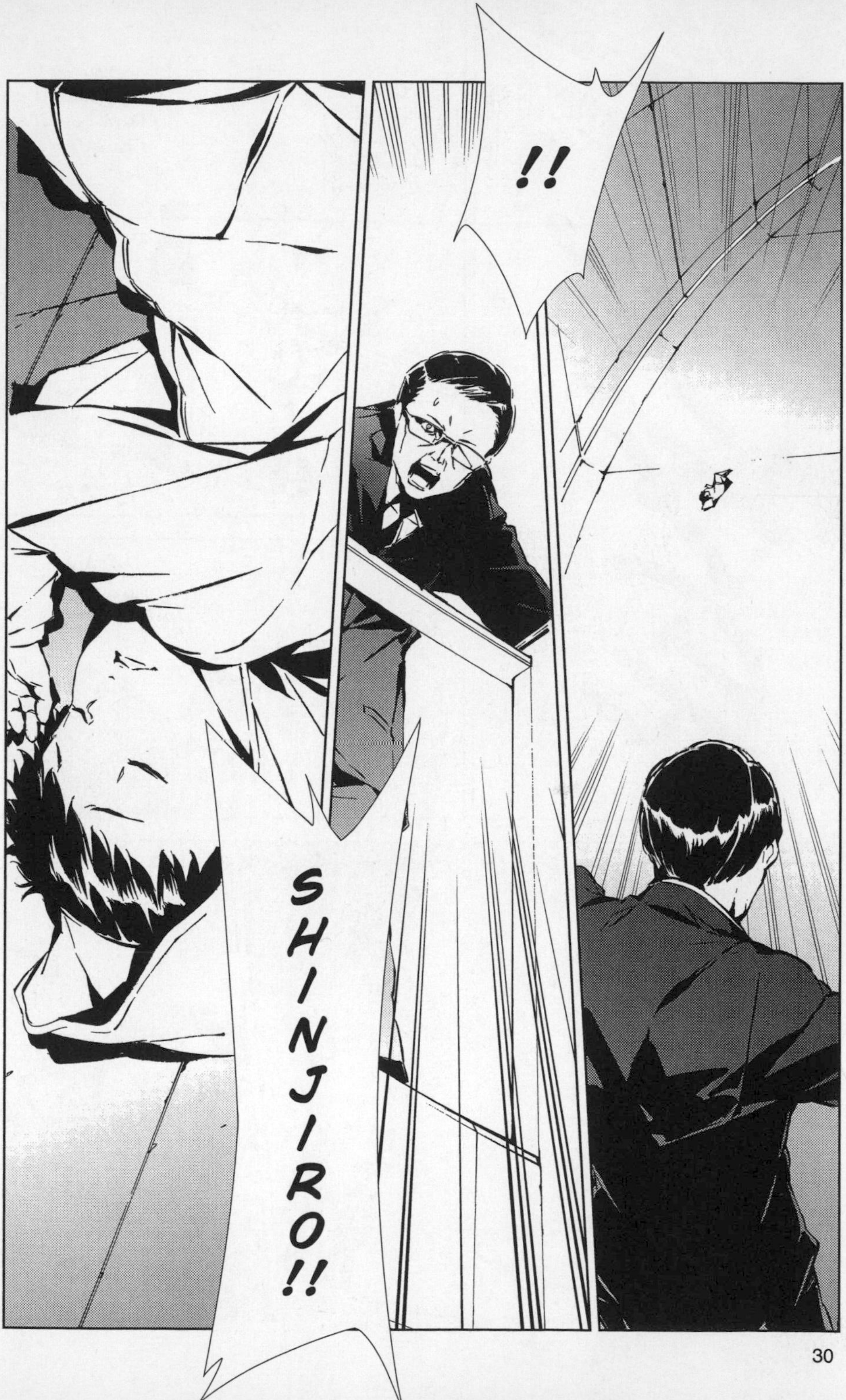
!!
SHINJIRO!!

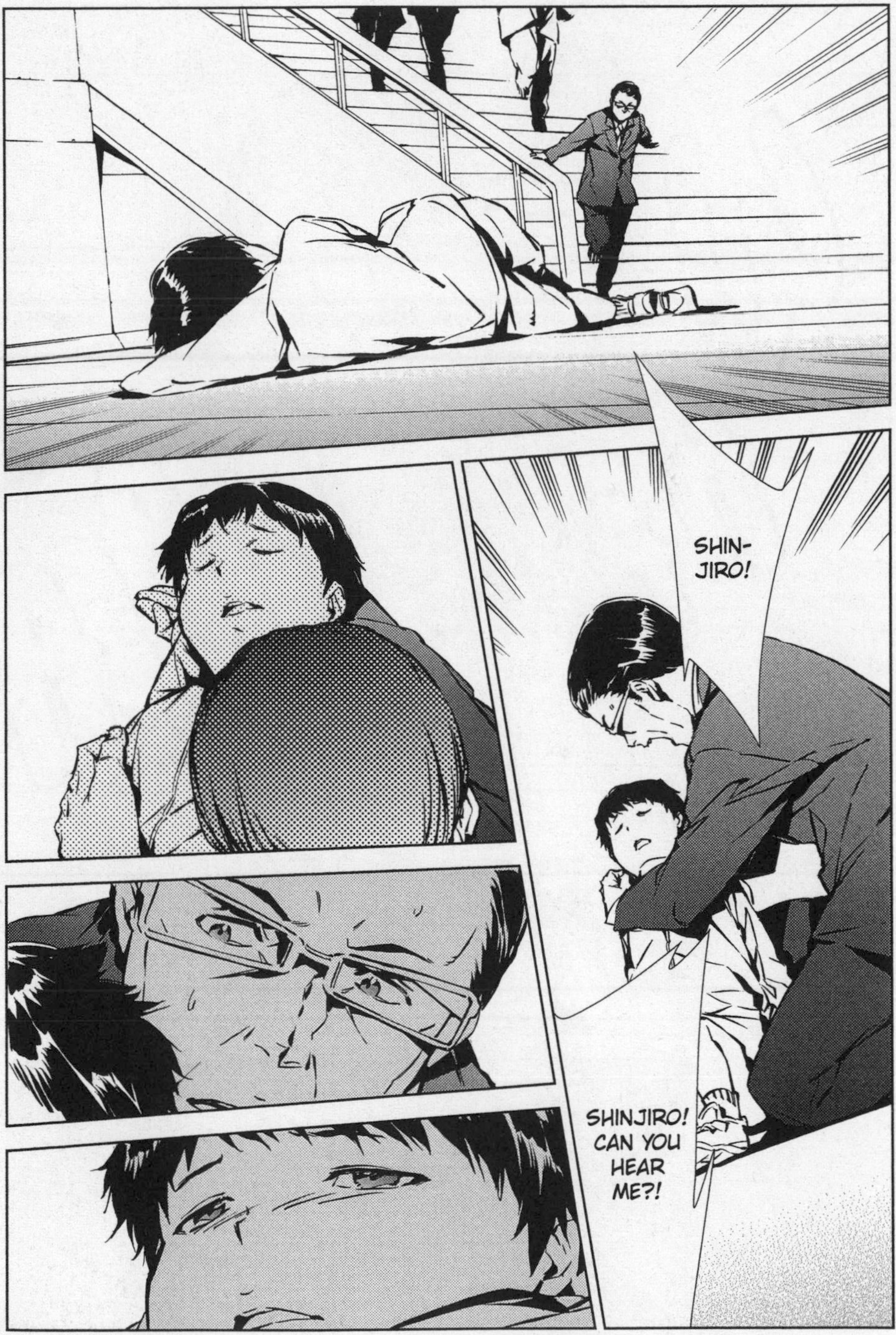
SHIN-
JIRO!
SHINJIRO!
CAN YOU
HEAR
ME?!

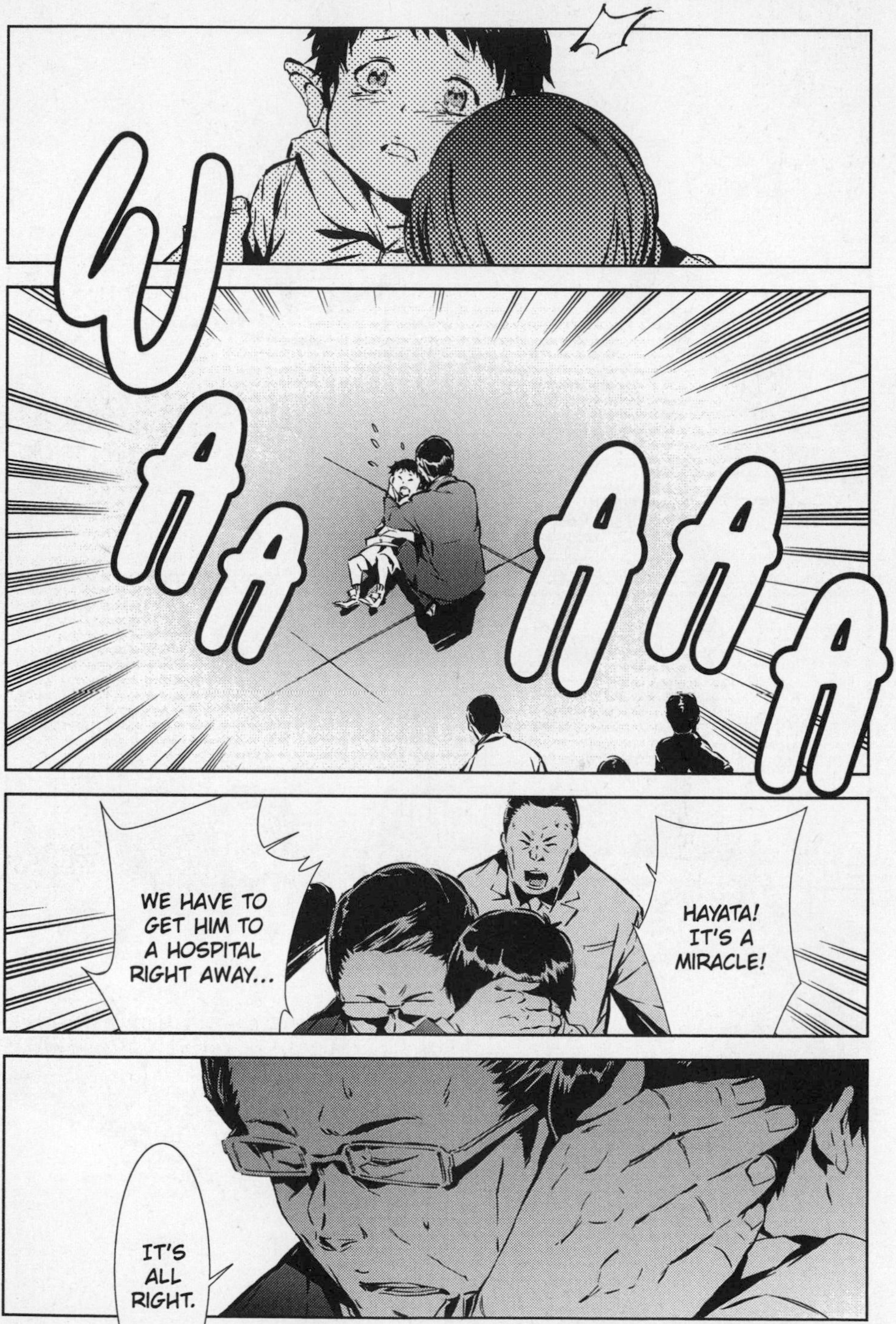
WAAAAAA
HAYATA! IT'S A MIRACLE!
WE HAVE TO GET HIM TO A HOSPITAL RIGHT AWAY...
IT'S ALL RIGHT.

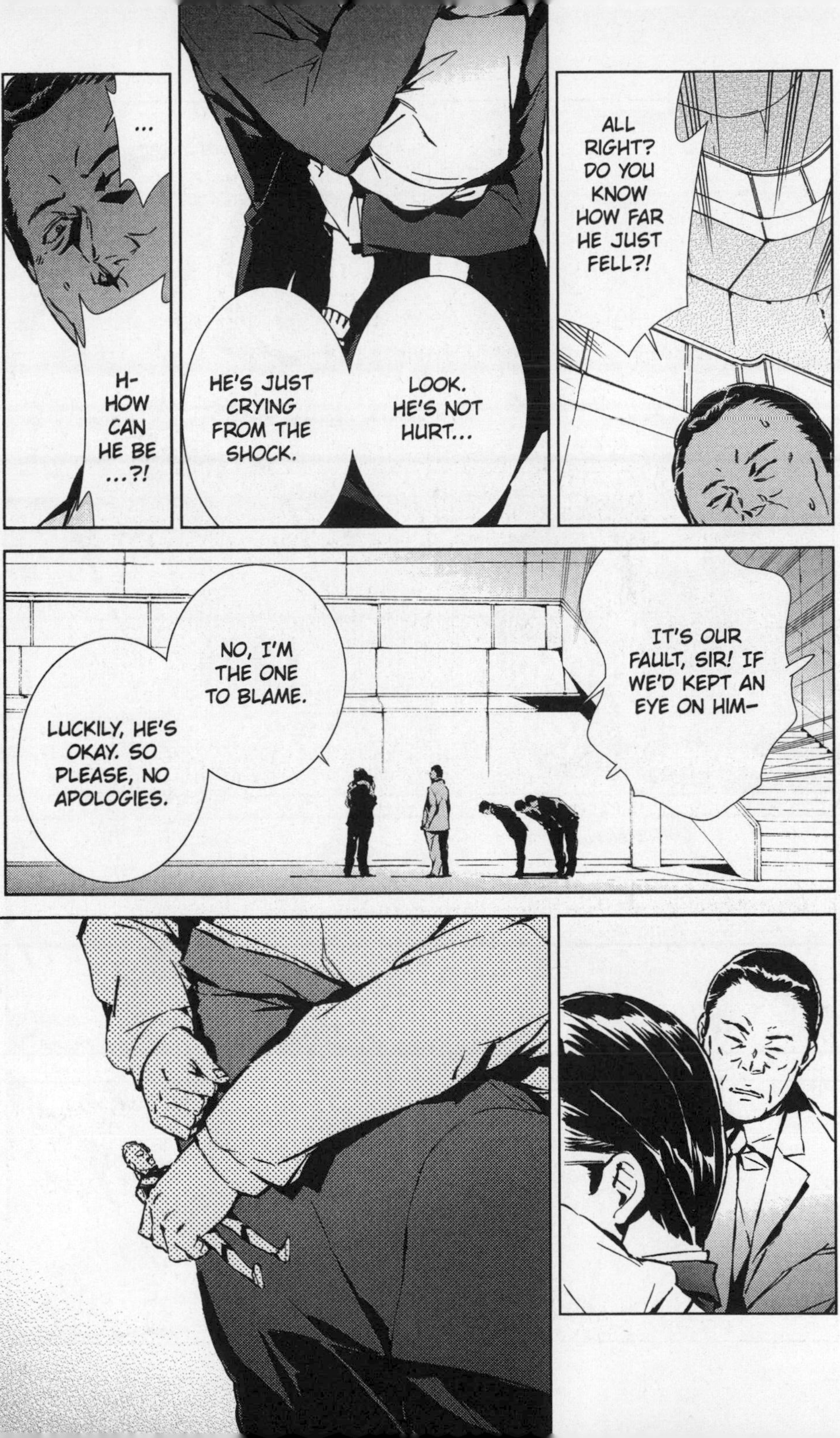
ALL RIGHT? DO YOU KNOW HOW FAR HE JUST FELL?!
LOOK. HE'S NOT HURT...
HE'S JUST CRYING FROM THE SHOCK.
...
H-HOW CAN HE BE ...?!
IT'S OUR FAULT, SIR! IF WE'D KEPT AN EYE ON HIM-
NO, I'M THE ONE TO BLAME.
LUCKILY, HE'S OKAY. SO PLEASE, NO APOLOGIES.

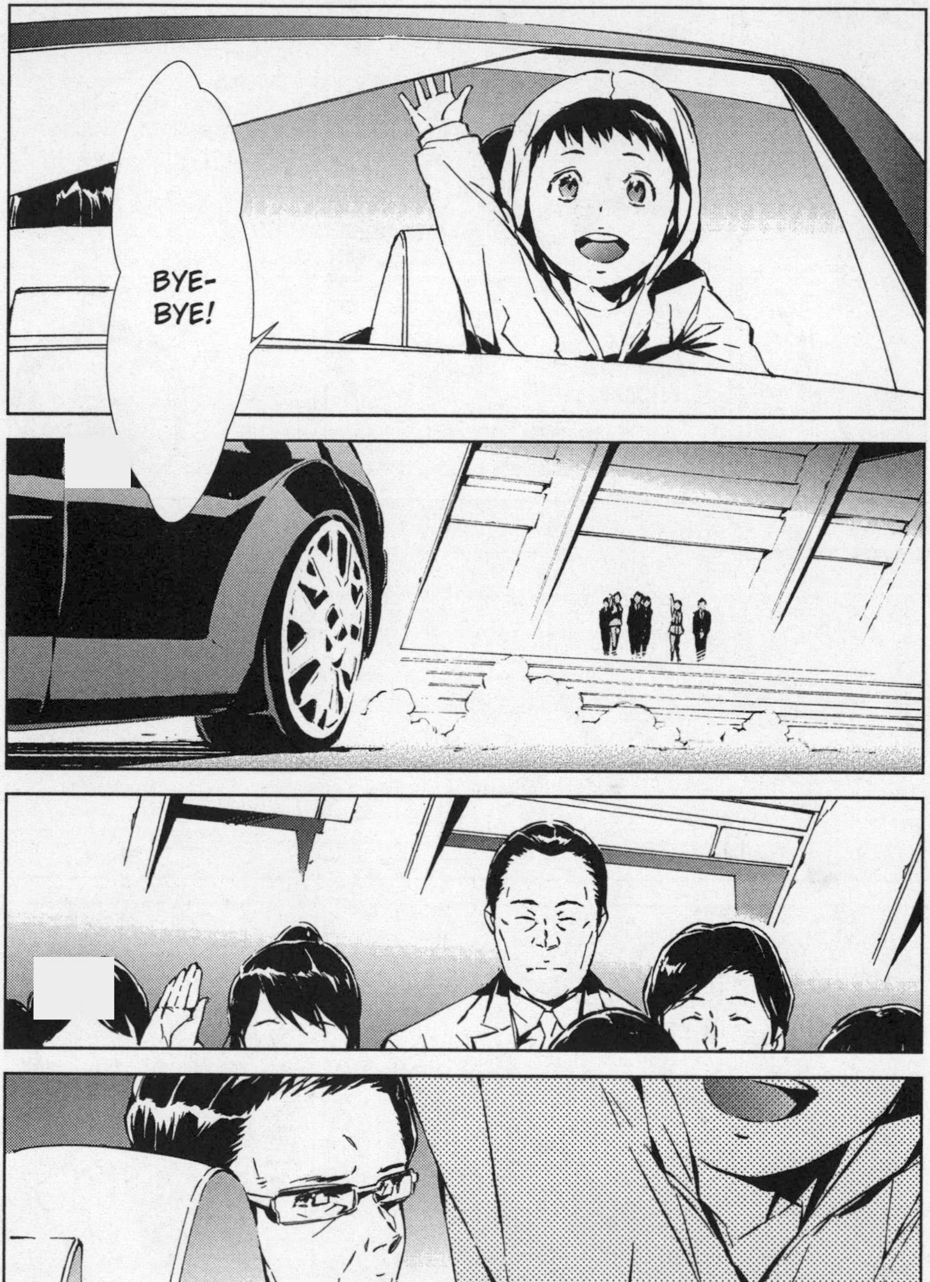
BYE-BYE!

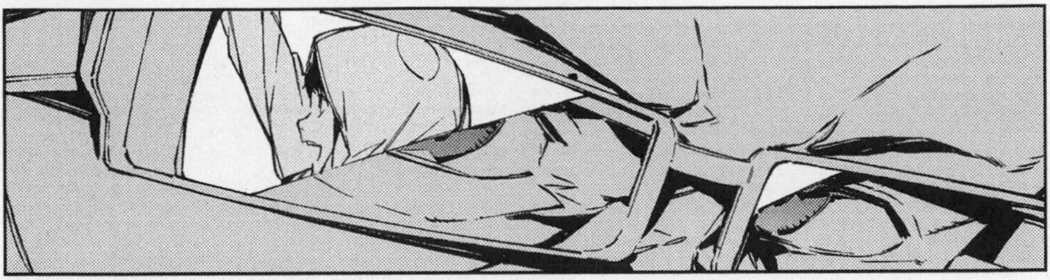

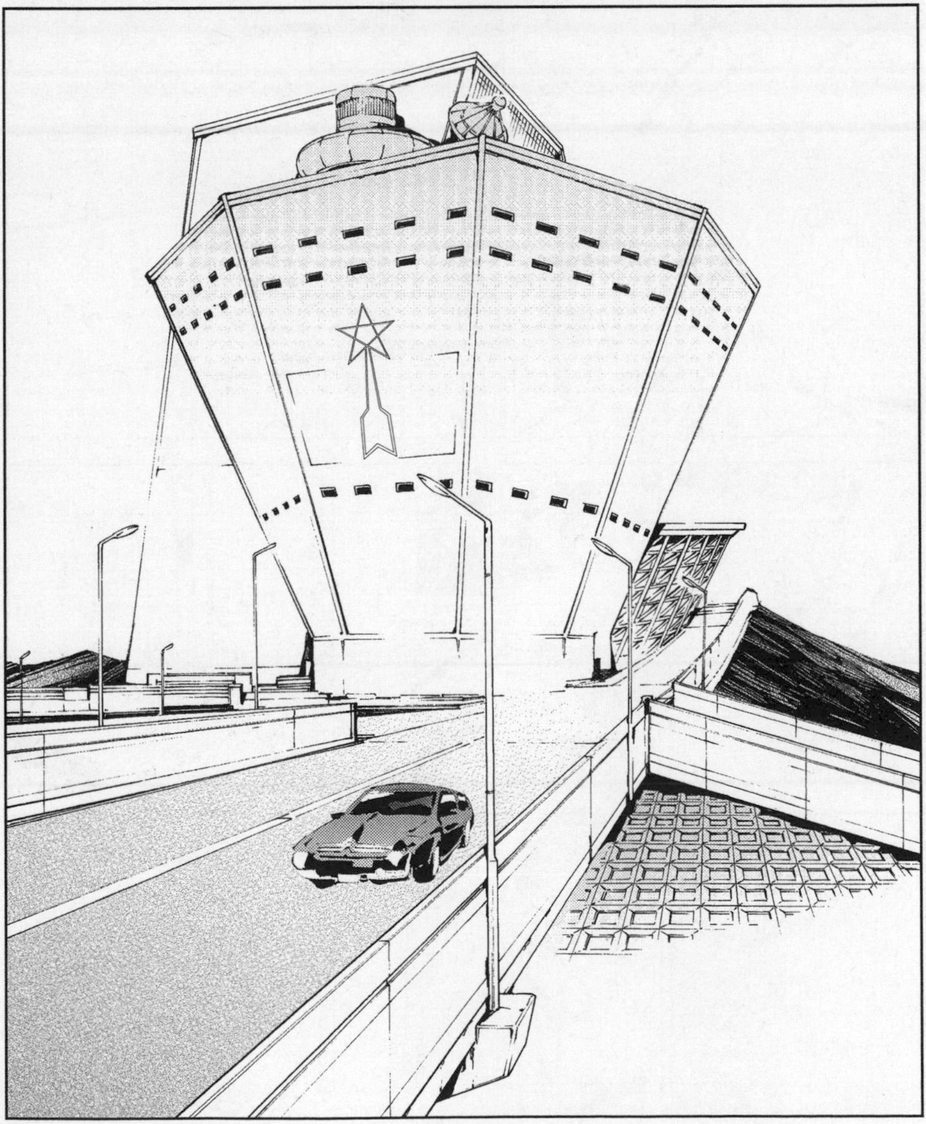

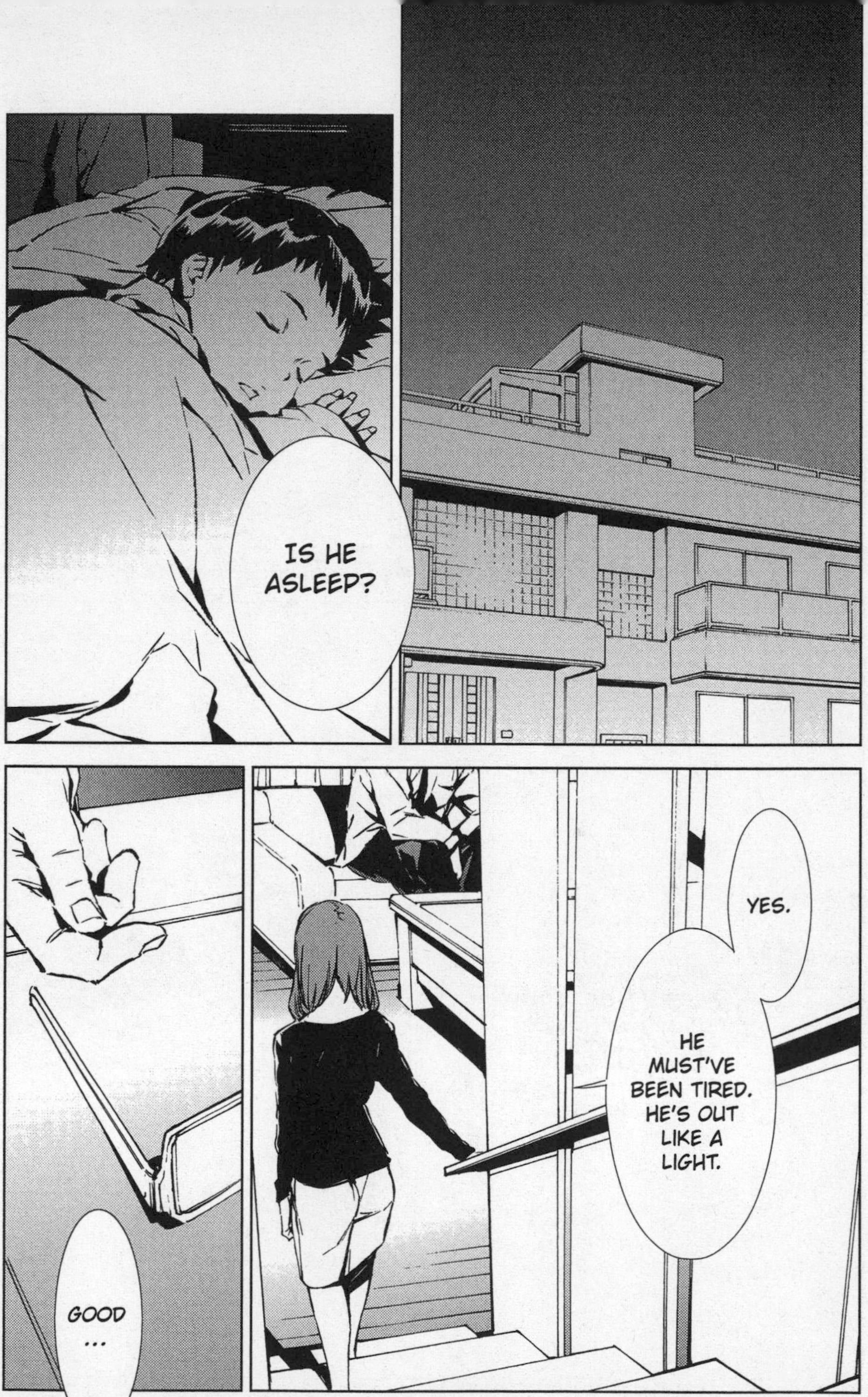
IS HE ASLEEP?
YES.
HE MUST'VE BEEN TIRED. HE'S OUT LIKE A LIGHT.
GOOD ...

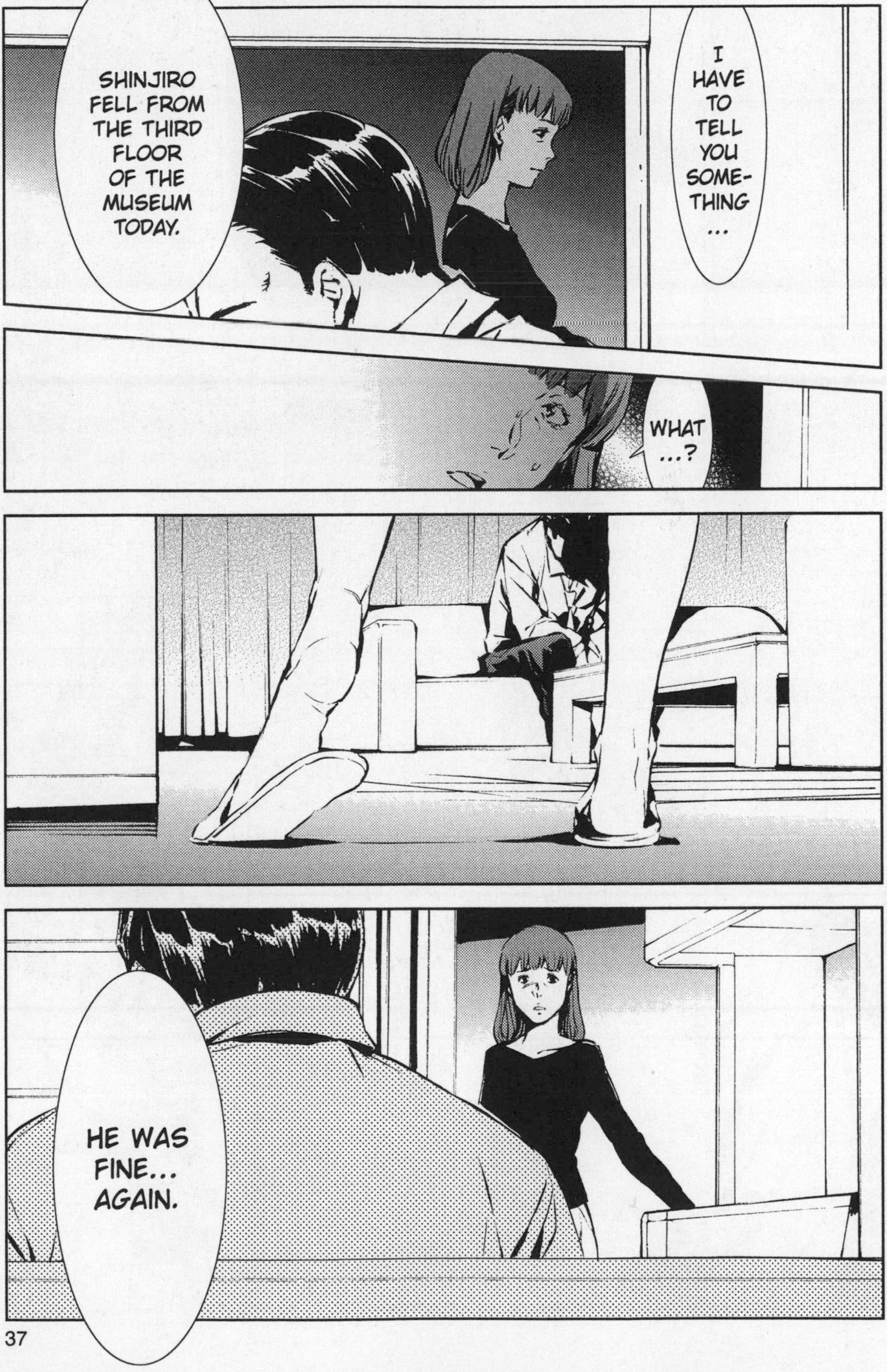
I HAVE TO TELL YOU SOME-THING...
SHINJIRO FELL FROM THE THIRD FLOOR OF THE MUSEUM TODAY.
WHAT...?
HE WAS FINE... AGAIN.

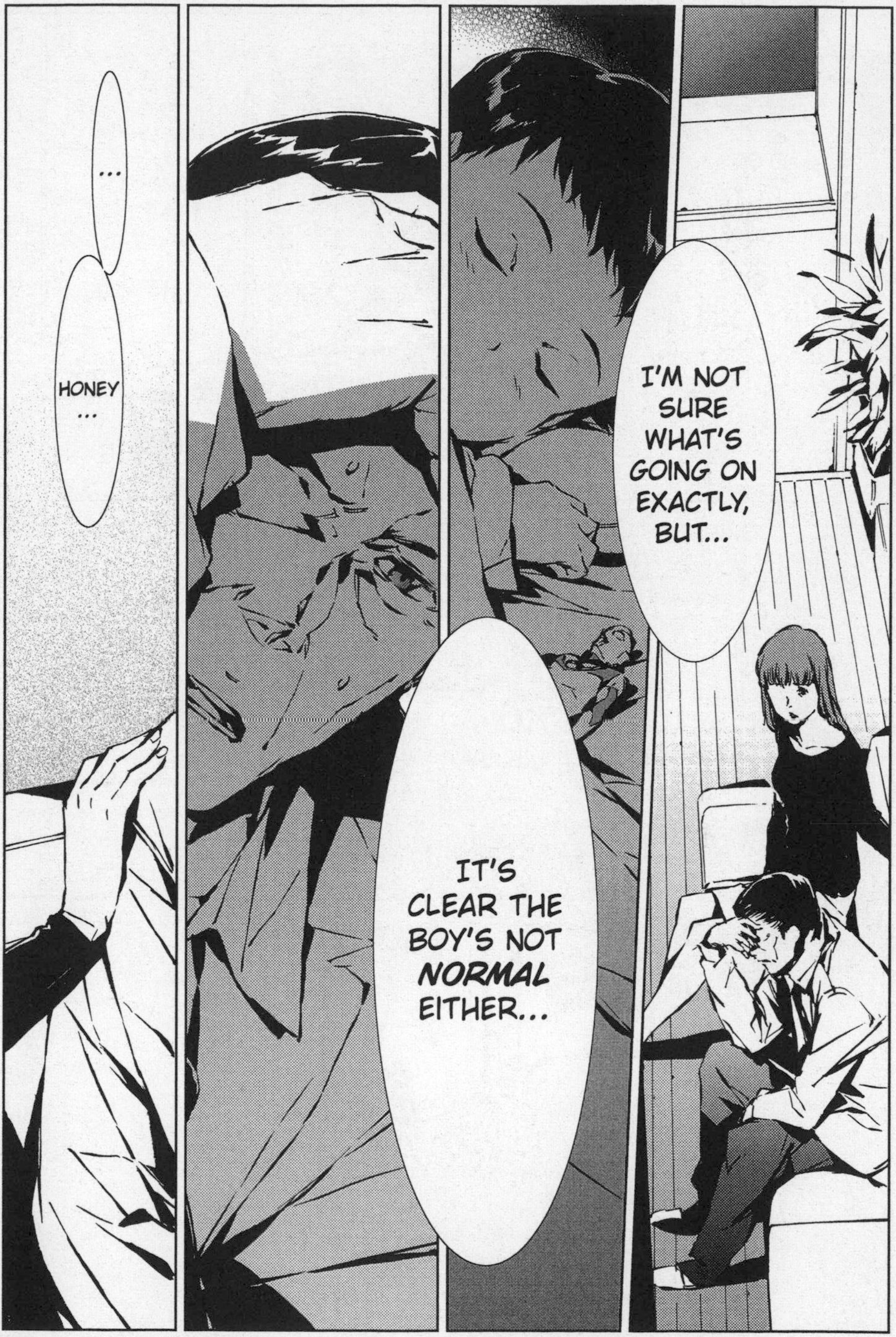
I'M NOT SURE WHAT'S GOING ON EXACTLY, BUT...
IT'S CLEAR THE BOY'S NOT *NORMAL* EITHER...
...
HONEY ...

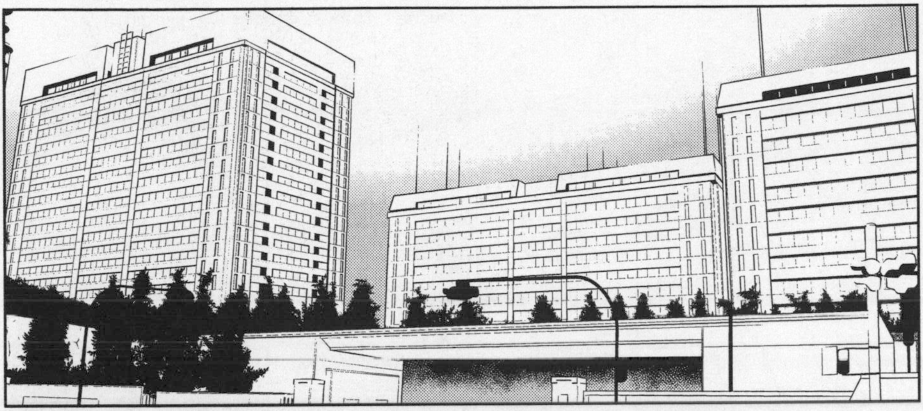

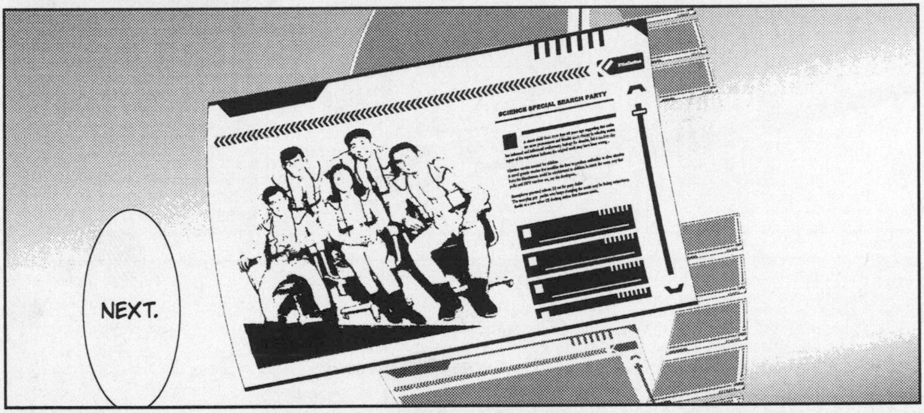
SCIENCE SPECIAL SEARCH PARTY
NEXT.

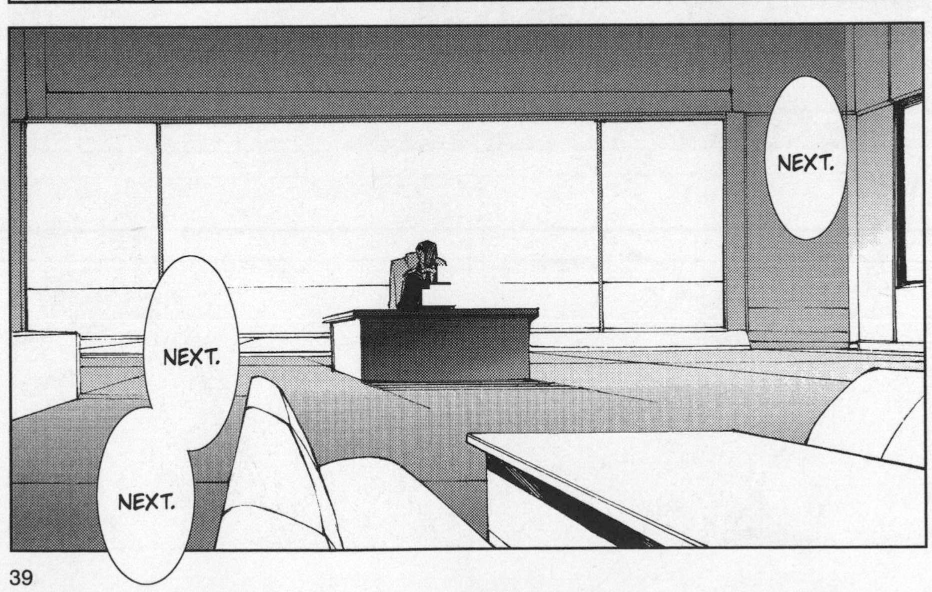
NEXT.
NEXT.
NEXT.

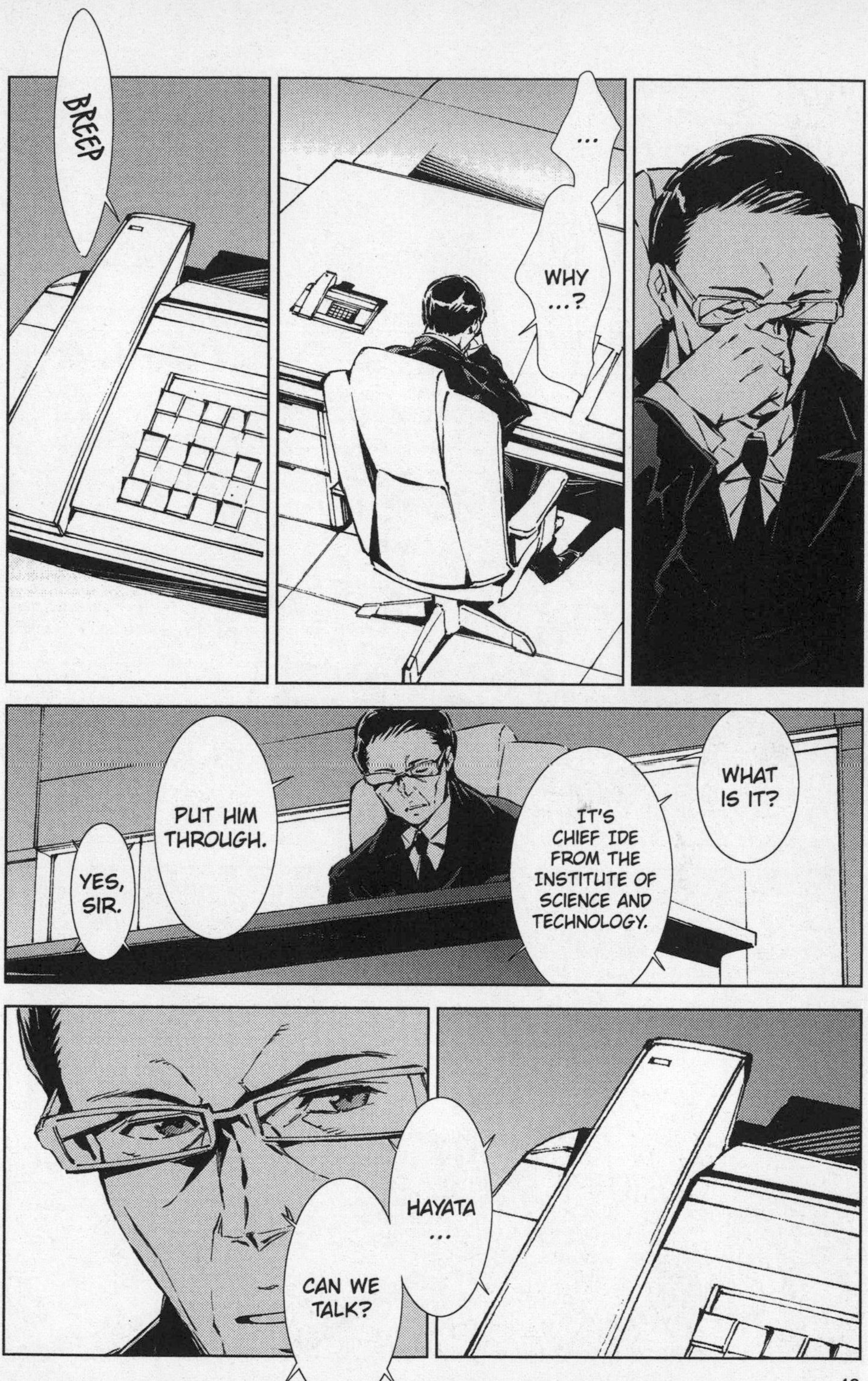
...
WHY ...?
BREEP
WHAT IS IT?
IT'S CHIEF IDE FROM THE INSTITUTE OF SCIENCE AND TECHNOLOGY.
PUT HIM THROUGH.
YES, SIR.
HAYATA ...
CAN WE TALK?

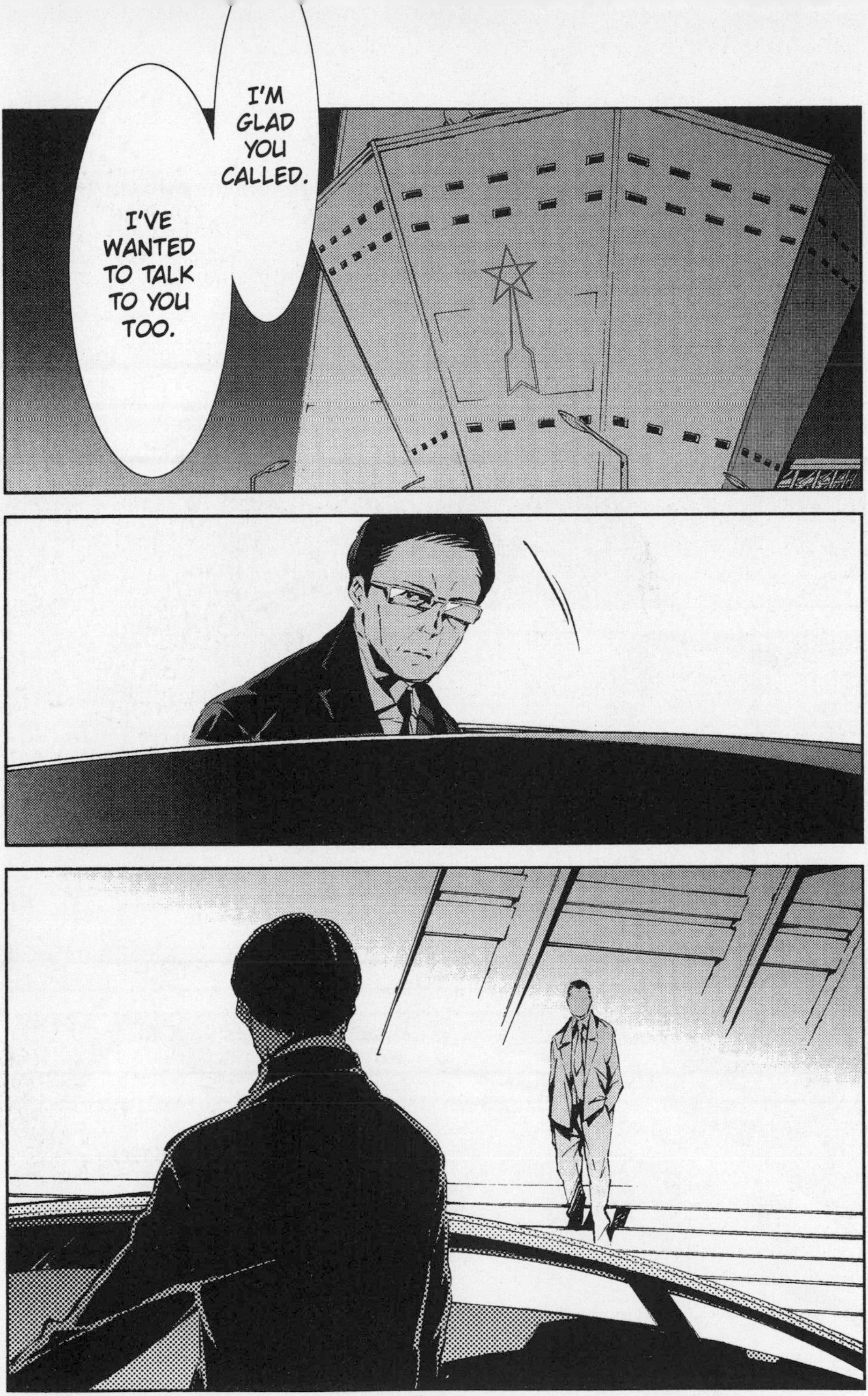
I'M GLAD YOU CALLED.
I'VE WANTED TO TALK TO YOU TOO.

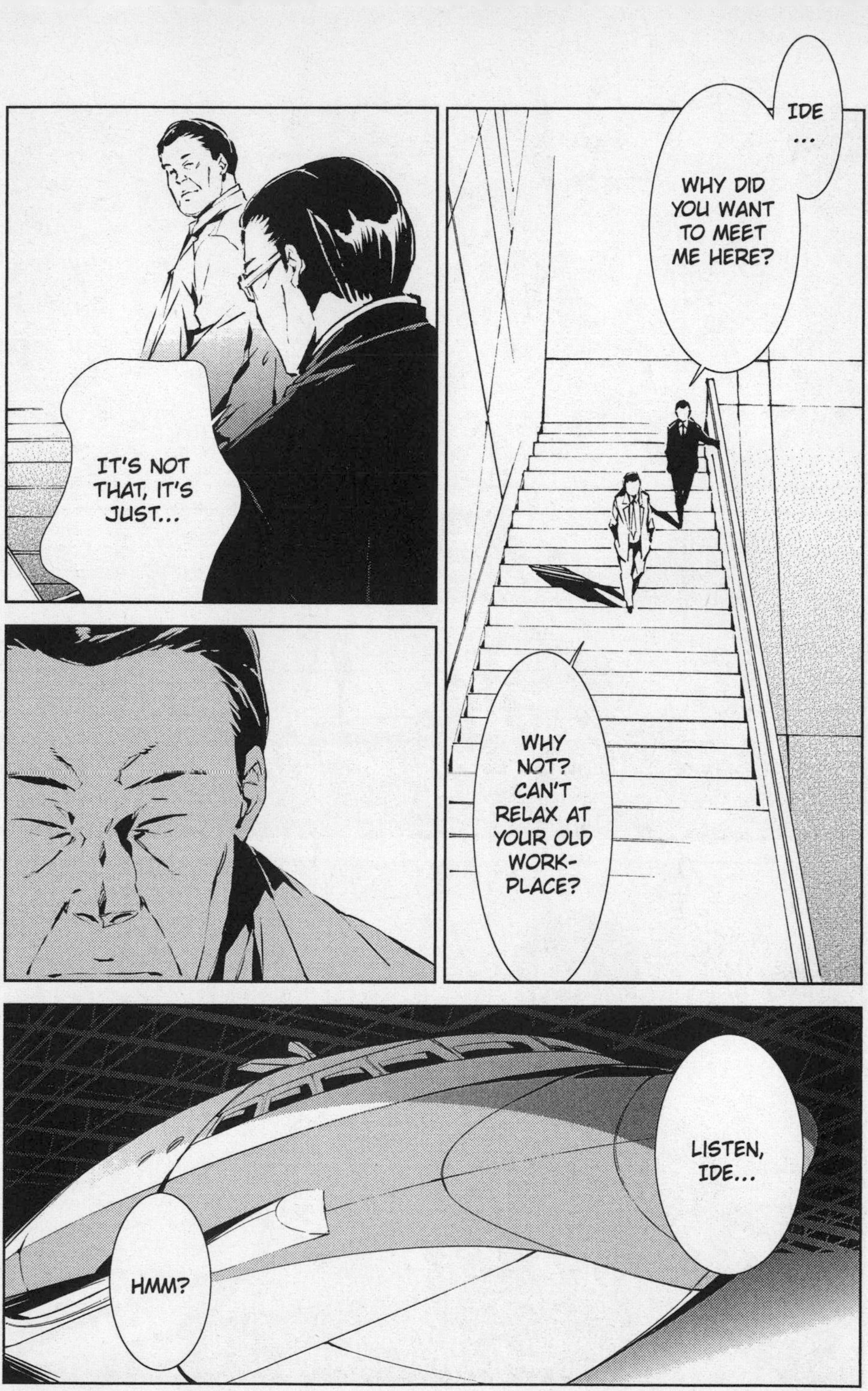
IDE...
WHY DID YOU WANT TO MEET ME HERE?
WHY NOT? CAN'T RELAX AT YOUR OLD WORK-PLACE?
IT'S NOT THAT, IT'S JUST...
LISTEN, IDE...
HMM?

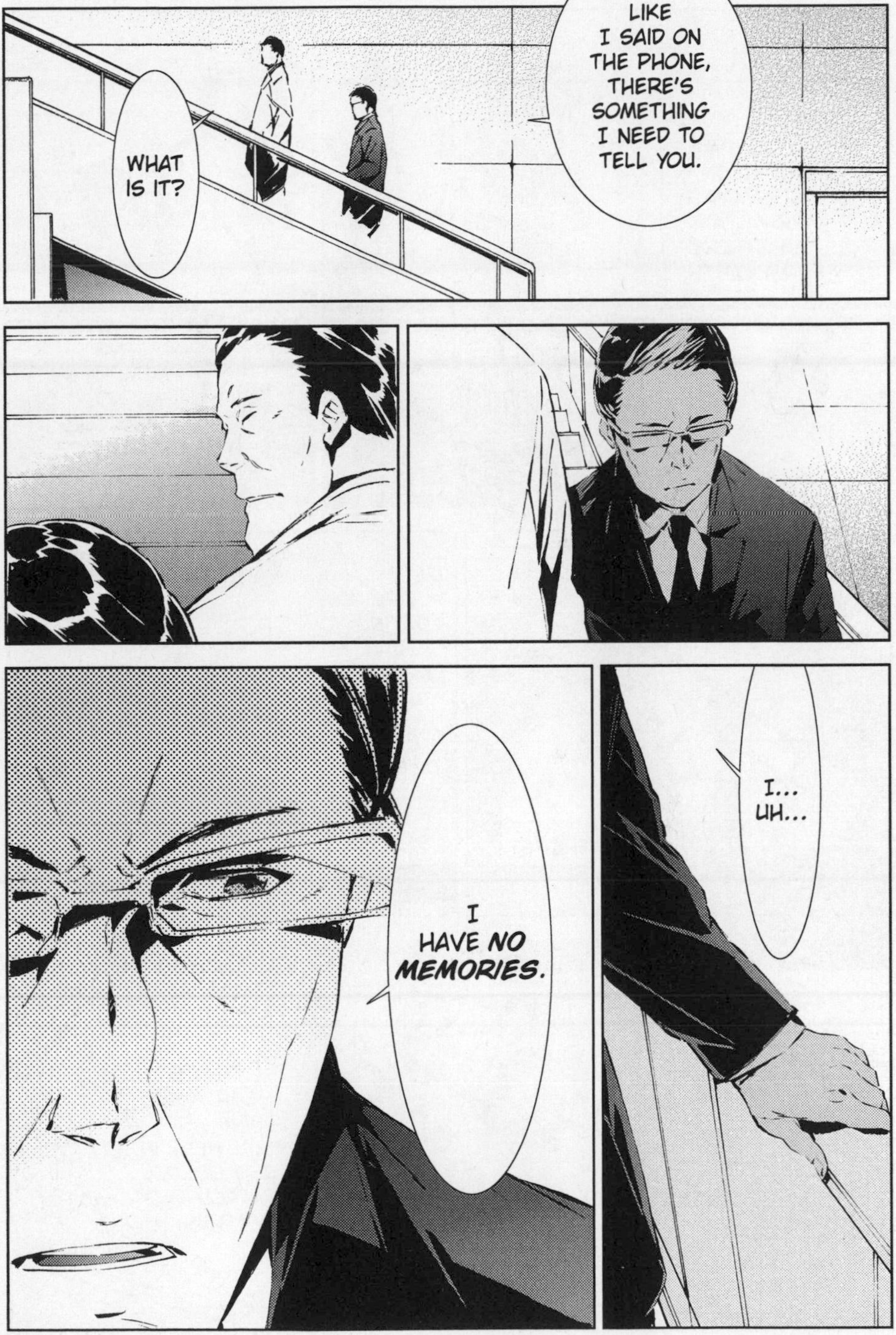
LIKE I SAID ON THE PHONE, THERE'S SOMETHING I NEED TO TELL YOU.
WHAT IS IT?
I... UH...
I HAVE *NO MEMORIES*.

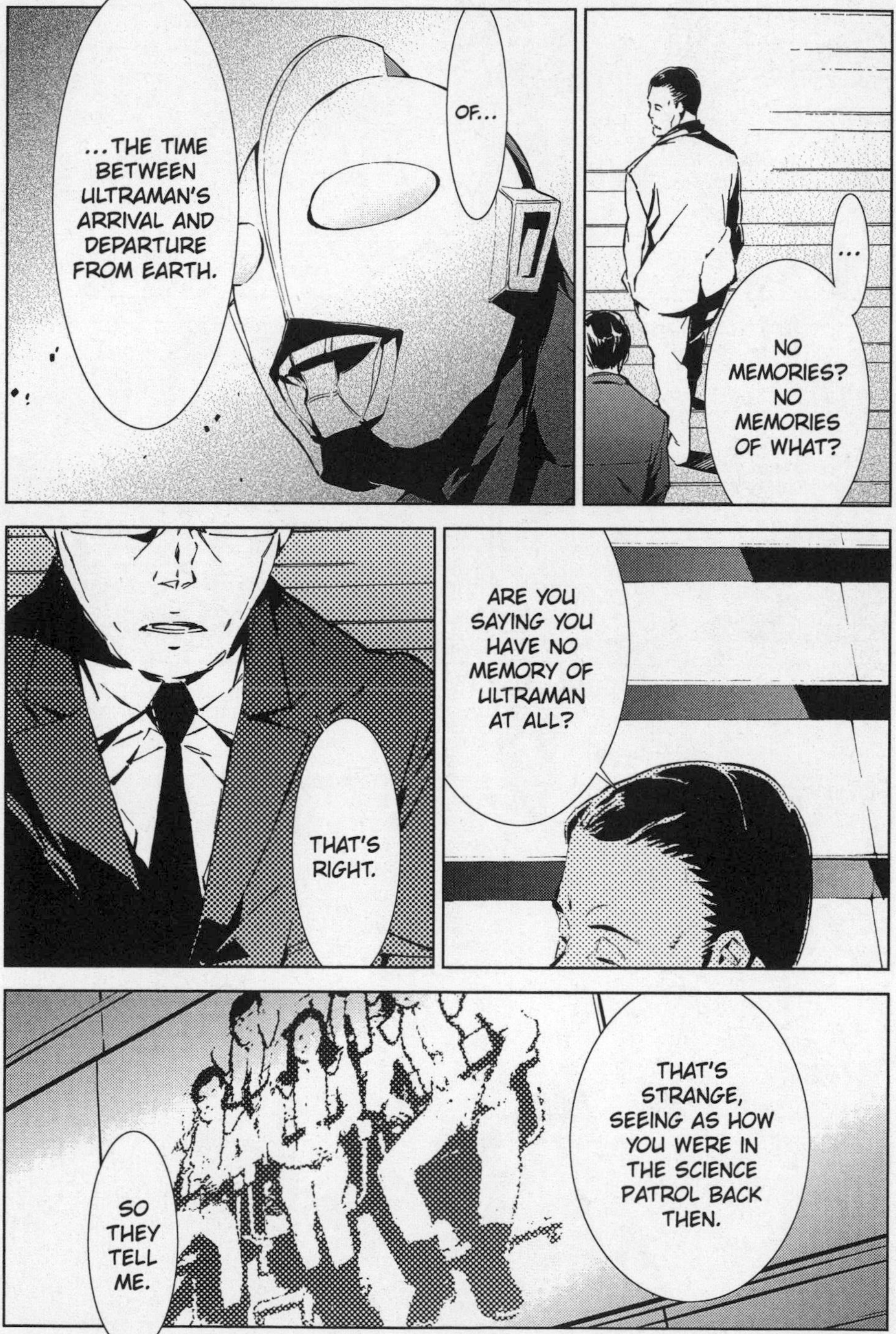
...
NO MEMORIES? NO MEMORIES OF WHAT?
OF...
...THE TIME BETWEEN ULTRAMAN'S ARRIVAL AND DEPARTURE FROM EARTH.
ARE YOU SAYING YOU HAVE NO MEMORY OF ULTRAMAN AT ALL?
THAT'S RIGHT.
THAT'S STRANGE, SEEING AS HOW YOU WERE IN THE SCIENCE PATROL BACK THEN.
SO THEY TELL ME.

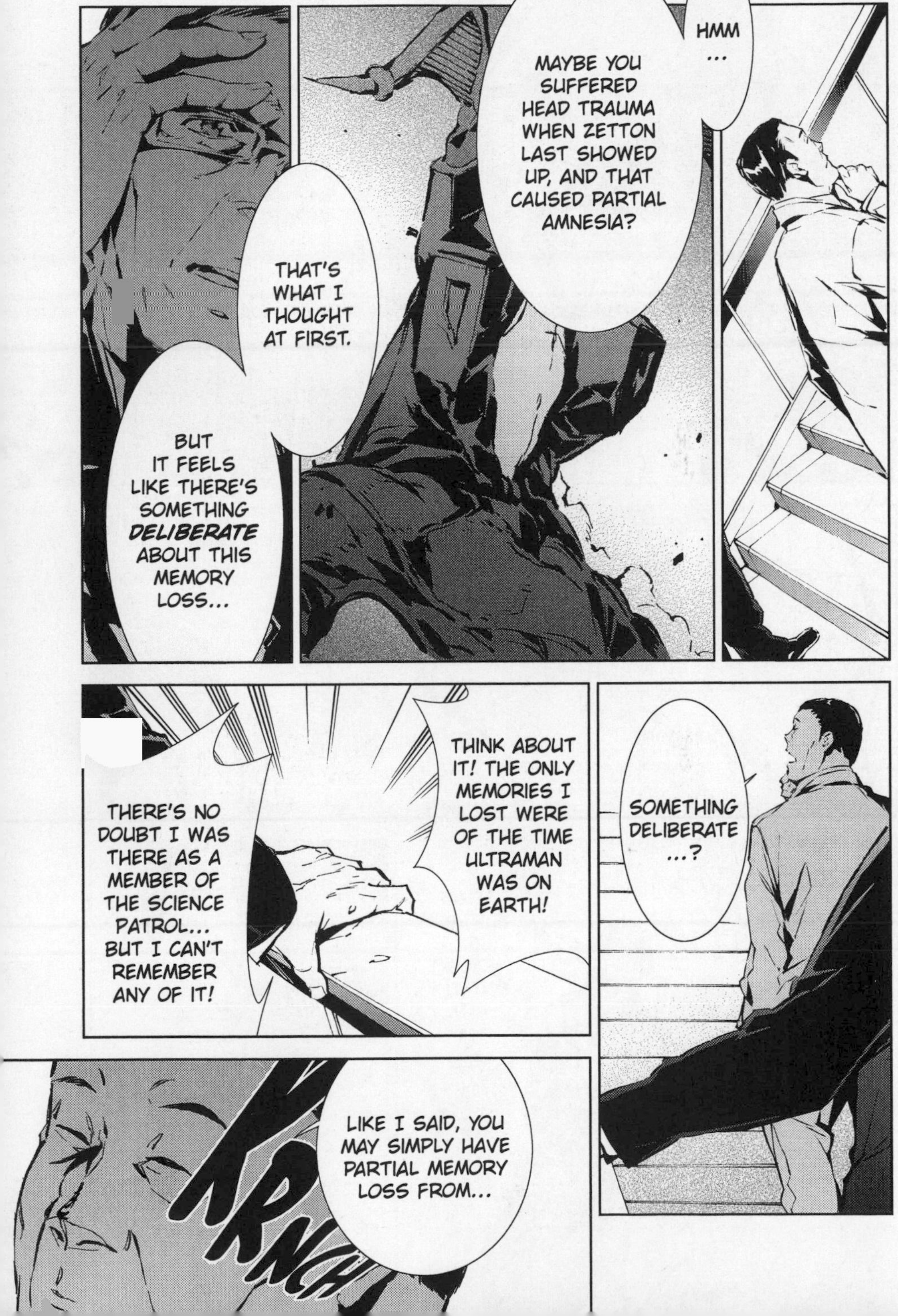
HMM ...
MAYBE YOU SUFFERED HEAD TRAUMA WHEN ZETTON LAST SHOWED UP, AND THAT CAUSED PARTIAL AMNESIA?
THAT'S WHAT I THOUGHT AT FIRST.
BUT IT FEELS LIKE THERE'S SOMETHING DELIBERATE ABOUT THIS MEMORY LOSS...
SOMETHING DELIBERATE ...?
THINK ABOUT IT! THE ONLY MEMORIES I LOST WERE OF THE TIME ULTRAMAN WAS ON EARTH!
THERE'S NO DOUBT I WAS THERE AS A MEMBER OF THE SCIENCE PATROL... BUT I CAN'T REMEMBER ANY OF IT!
LIKE I SAID, YOU MAY SIMPLY HAVE PARTIAL MEMORY LOSS FROM...
KRNCH

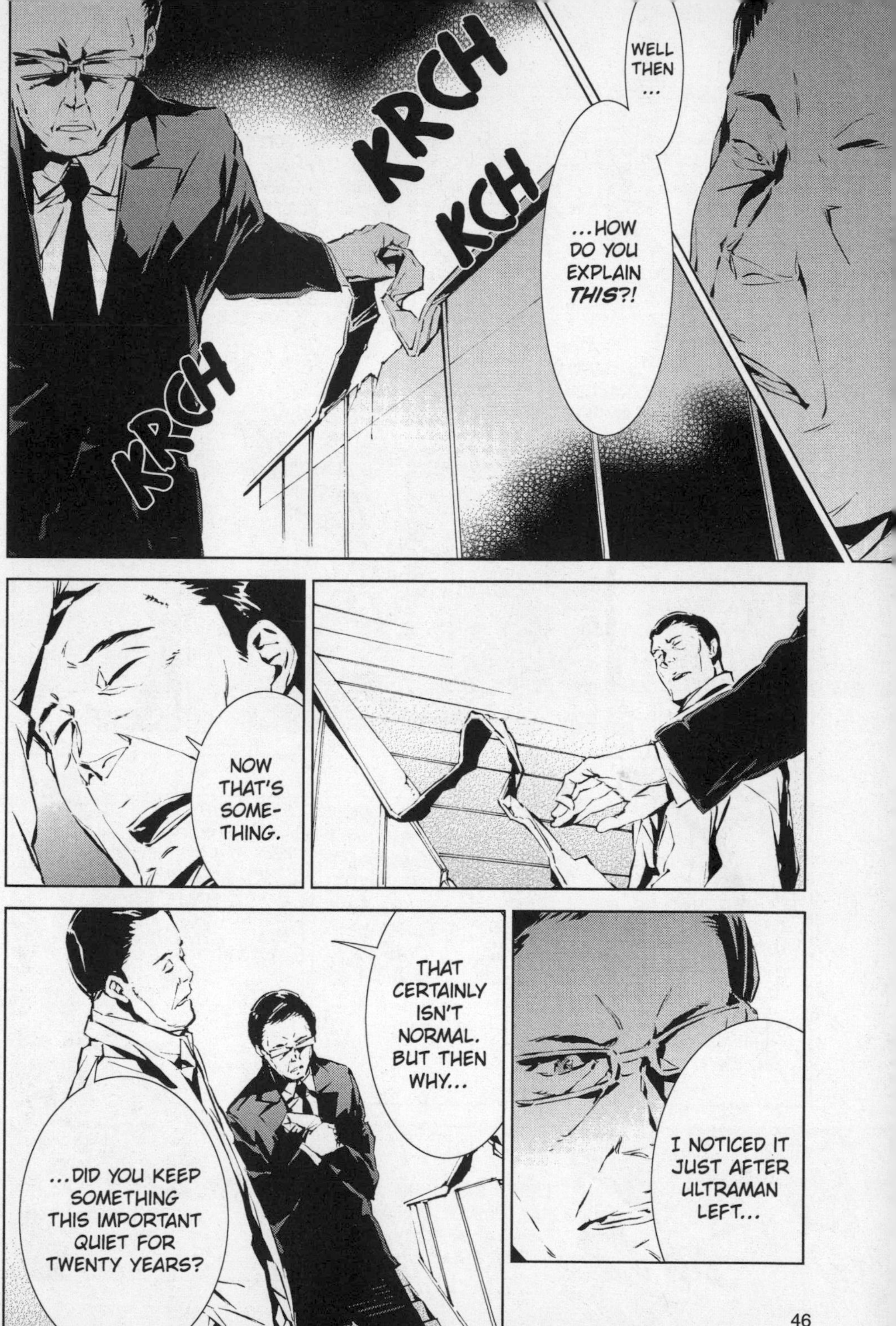
WELL THEN ...
...HOW DO YOU EXPLAIN *THIS*?!
KRCH KCH
KRCH
NOW THAT'S SOME-THING.
I NOTICED IT JUST AFTER ULTRAMAN LEFT...
THAT CERTAINLY ISN'T NORMAL. BUT THEN WHY...
...DID YOU KEEP SOMETHING THIS IMPORTANT QUIET FOR TWENTY YEARS?

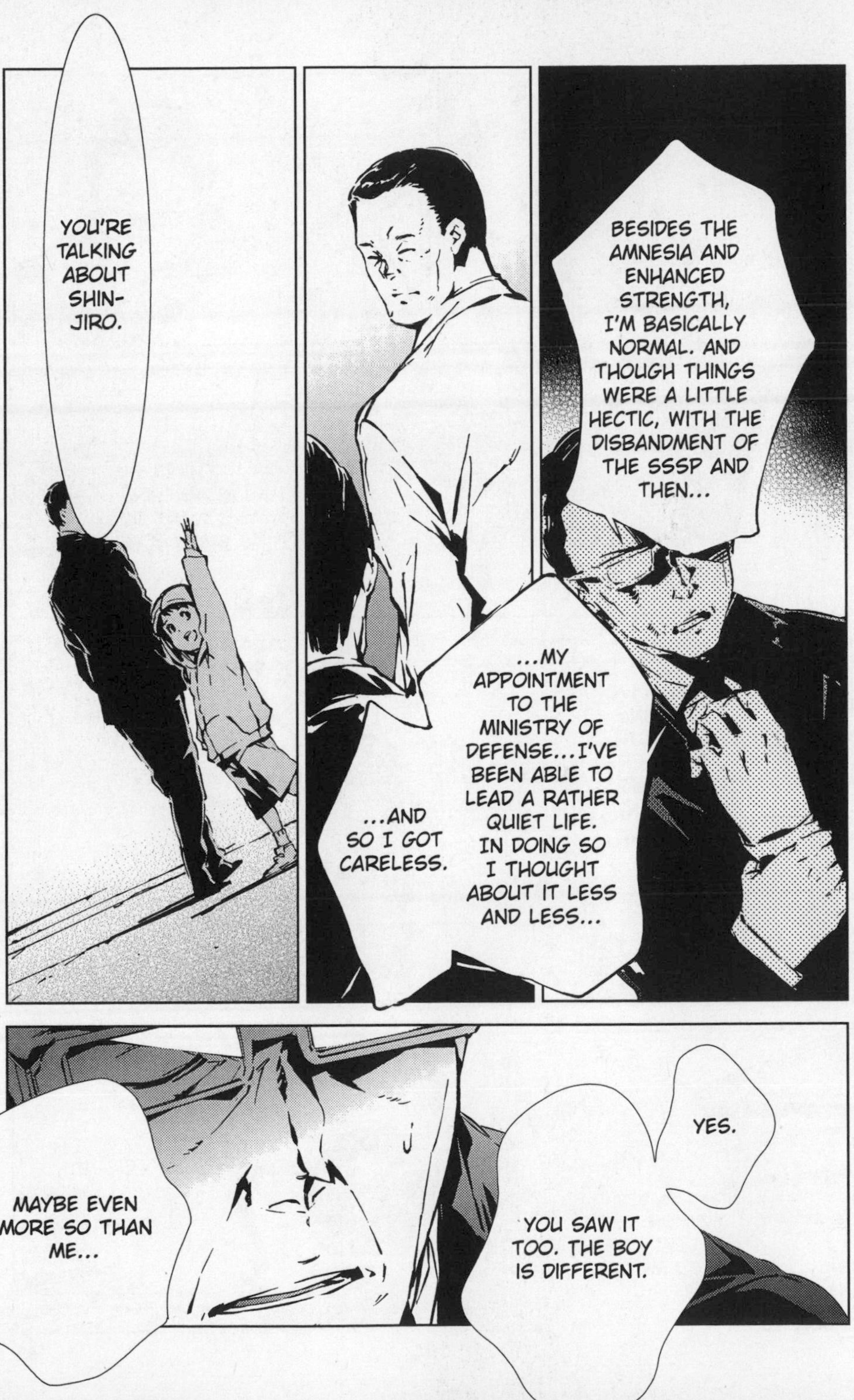
BESIDES THE AMNESIA AND ENHANCED STRENGTH, I'M BASICALLY NORMAL. AND THOUGH THINGS WERE A LITTLE HECTIC, WITH THE DISBANDMENT OF THE SSSP AND THEN...
...MY APPOINTMENT TO THE MINISTRY OF DEFENSE...I'VE BEEN ABLE TO LEAD A RATHER QUIET LIFE. IN DOING SO I THOUGHT ABOUT IT LESS AND LESS...
...AND SO I GOT CARELESS.
YOU'RE TALKING ABOUT SHIN-JIRO.
YES.
YOU SAW IT TOO. THE BOY IS DIFFERENT.
MAYBE EVEN MORE SO THAN ME...

THERE'S SOMETHING I WANT TO SHOW YOU.

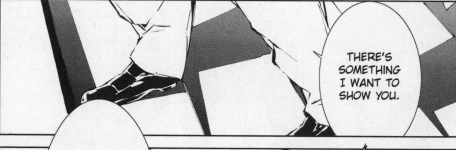

IT MAY HAVE SOMETHING TO DO WITH WHAT'S HAPPENING TO YOU AND SHINJIRO.

C'MON. LET'S HEAD OVER TO MY LAB.

!

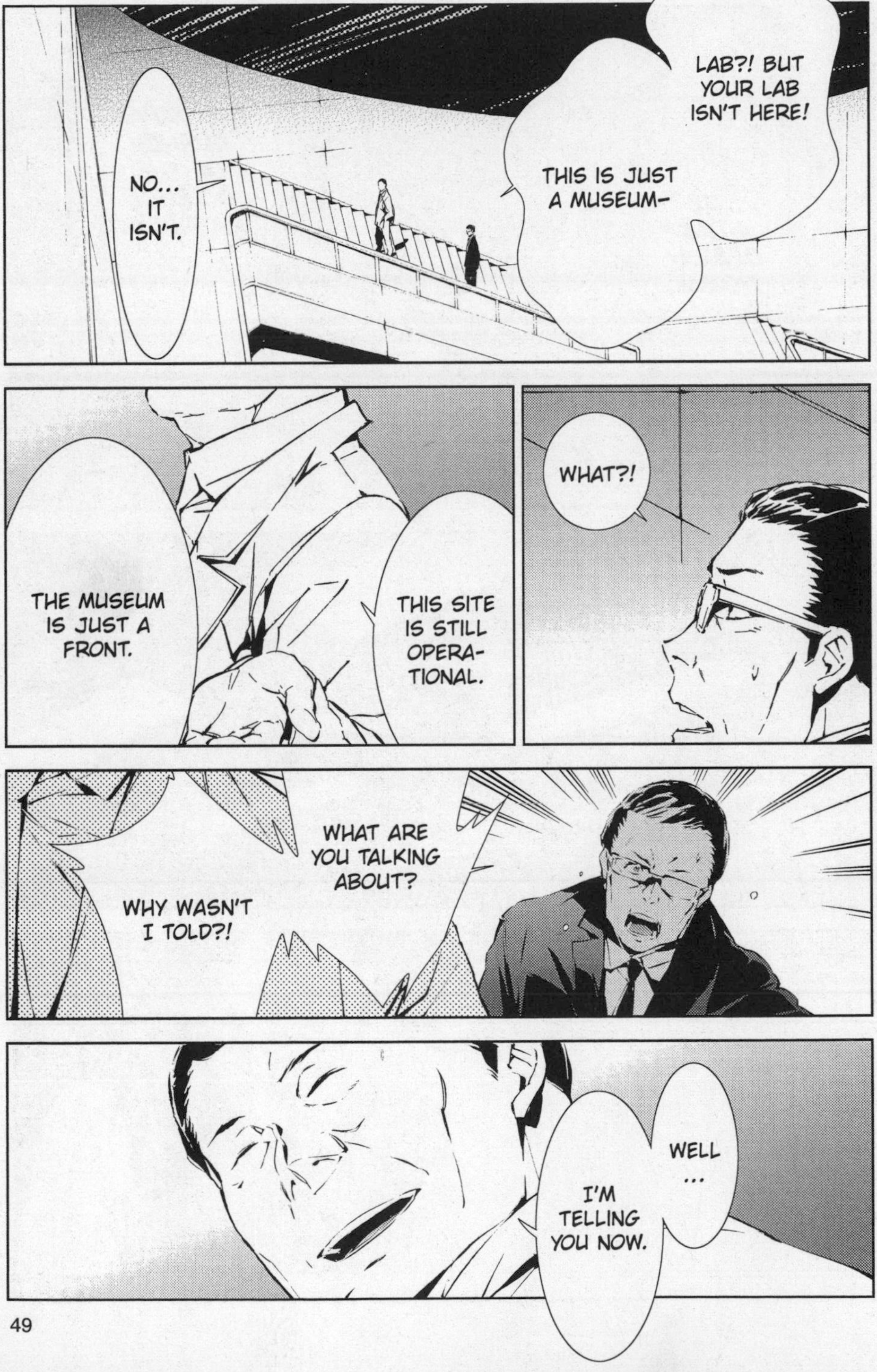
LAB?! BUT YOUR LAB ISN'T HERE!
THIS IS JUST A MUSEUM-
NO... IT ISN'T.
WHAT?!
THIS SITE IS STILL OPERA-TIONAL.
THE MUSEUM IS JUST A FRONT.
WHAT ARE YOU TALKING ABOUT?
WHY WASN'T I TOLD?!
WELL ...
I'M TELLING YOU NOW.

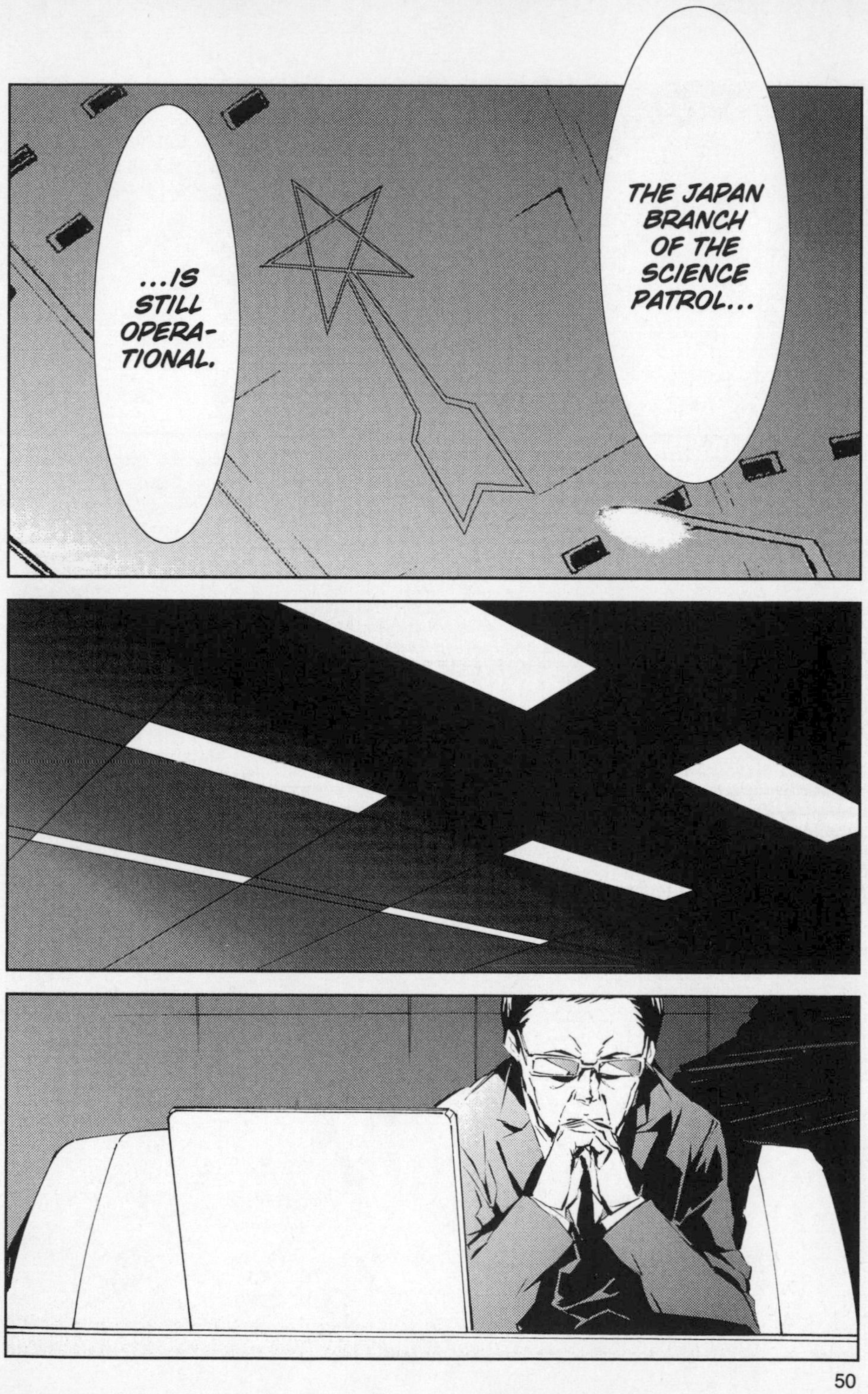
THE JAPAN BRANCH OF THE SCIENCE PATROL...
...IS STILL OPERA-TIONAL.

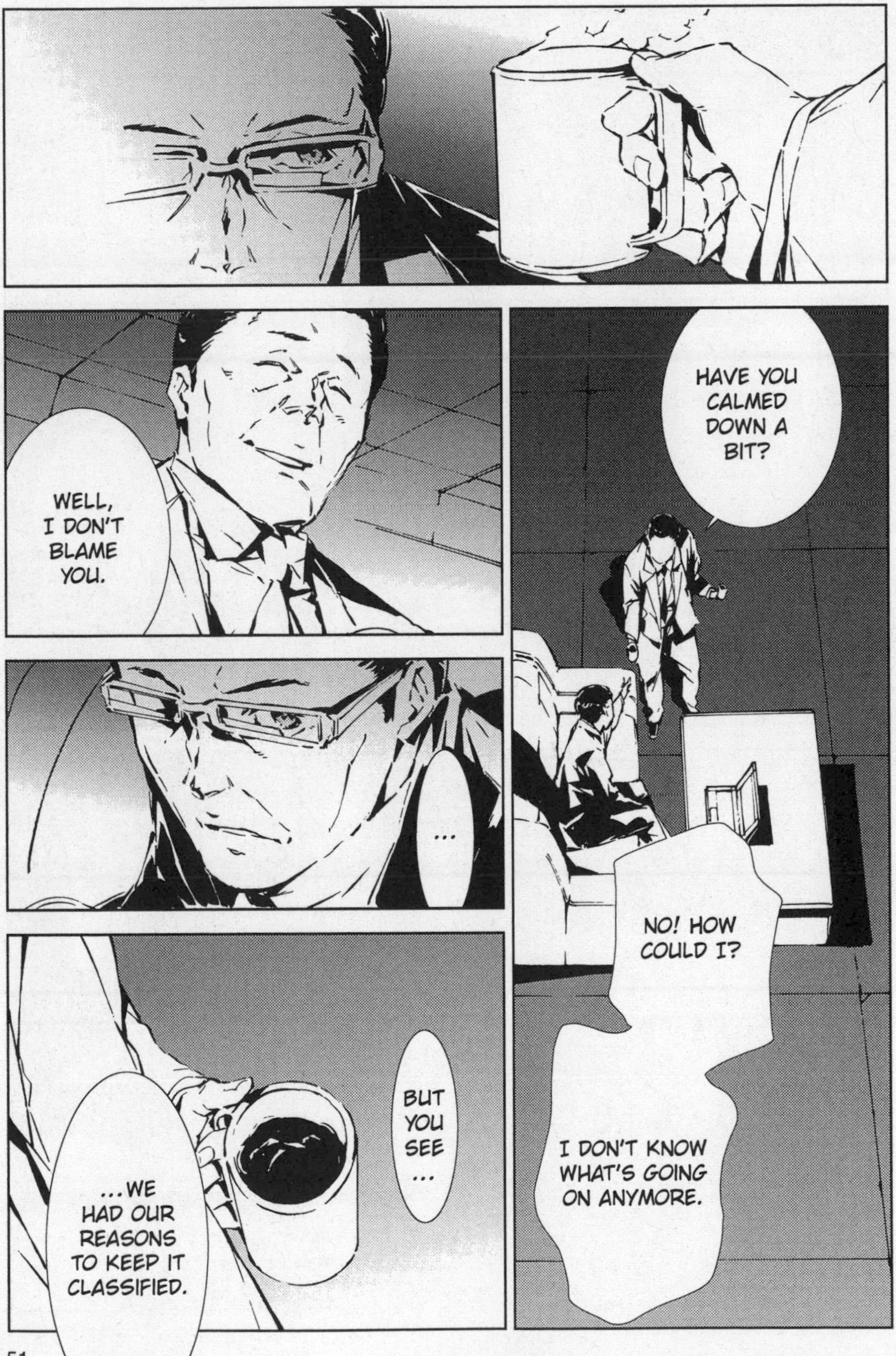
HAVE YOU CALMED DOWN A BIT?
NO! HOW COULD I?
I DON'T KNOW WHAT'S GOING ON ANYMORE.
WELL, I DON'T BLAME YOU.
...
BUT YOU SEE...
...WE HAD OUR REASONS TO KEEP IT CLASSIFIED.

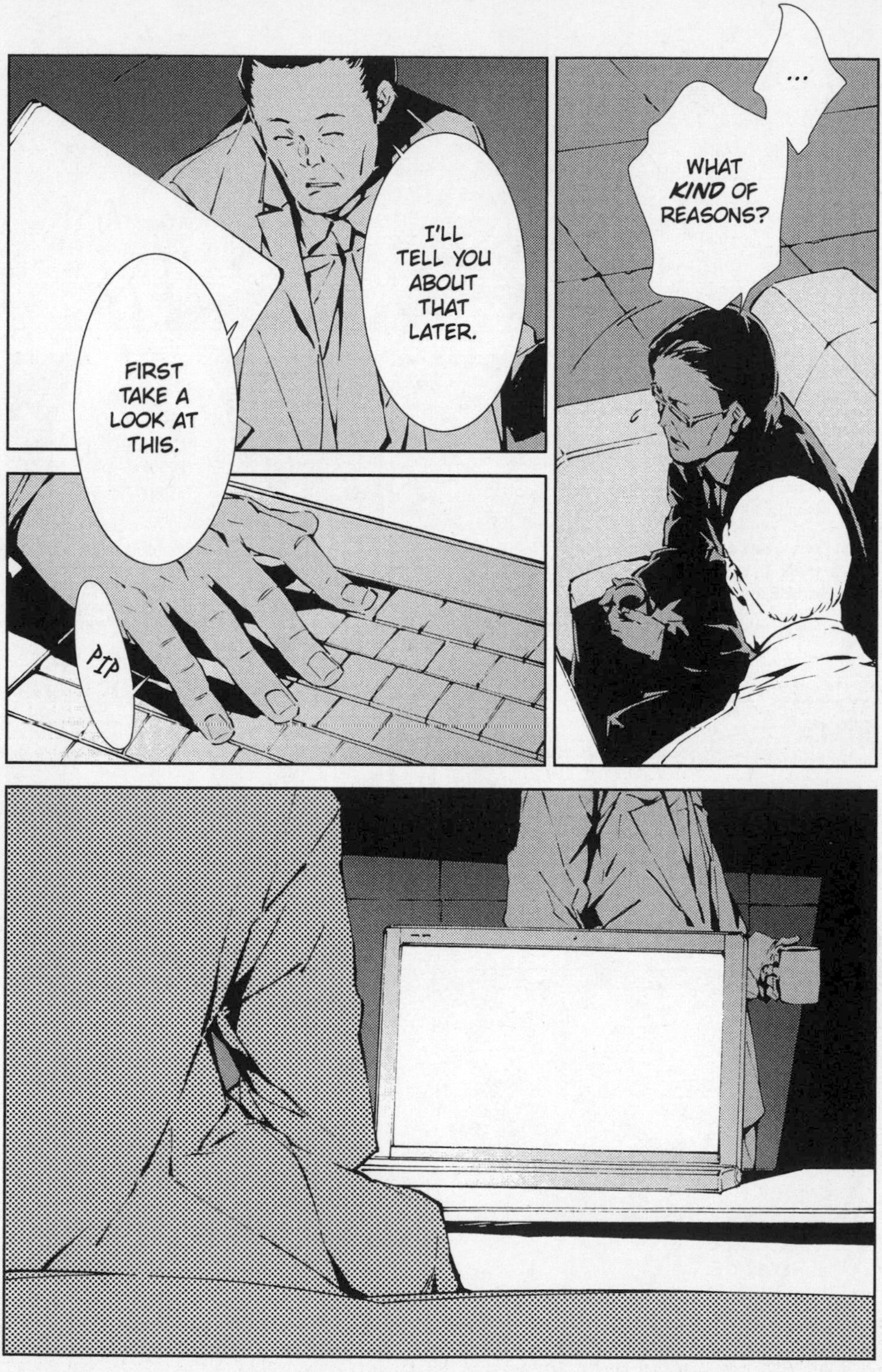
...
WHAT KIND OF REASONS?
I'LL TELL YOU ABOUT THAT LATER.
FIRST TAKE A LOOK AT THIS.
PIP

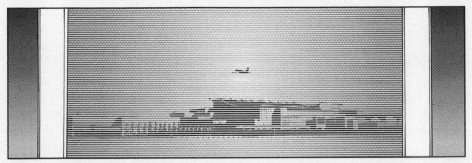

THIS IS THAT AIRPLANE CRASH FROM SIX MONTHS AGO.

I REMEMBER THE FOOTAGE WAS FILMED BY A CIVILIAN. IT WAS ALL OVER THE NEWS.

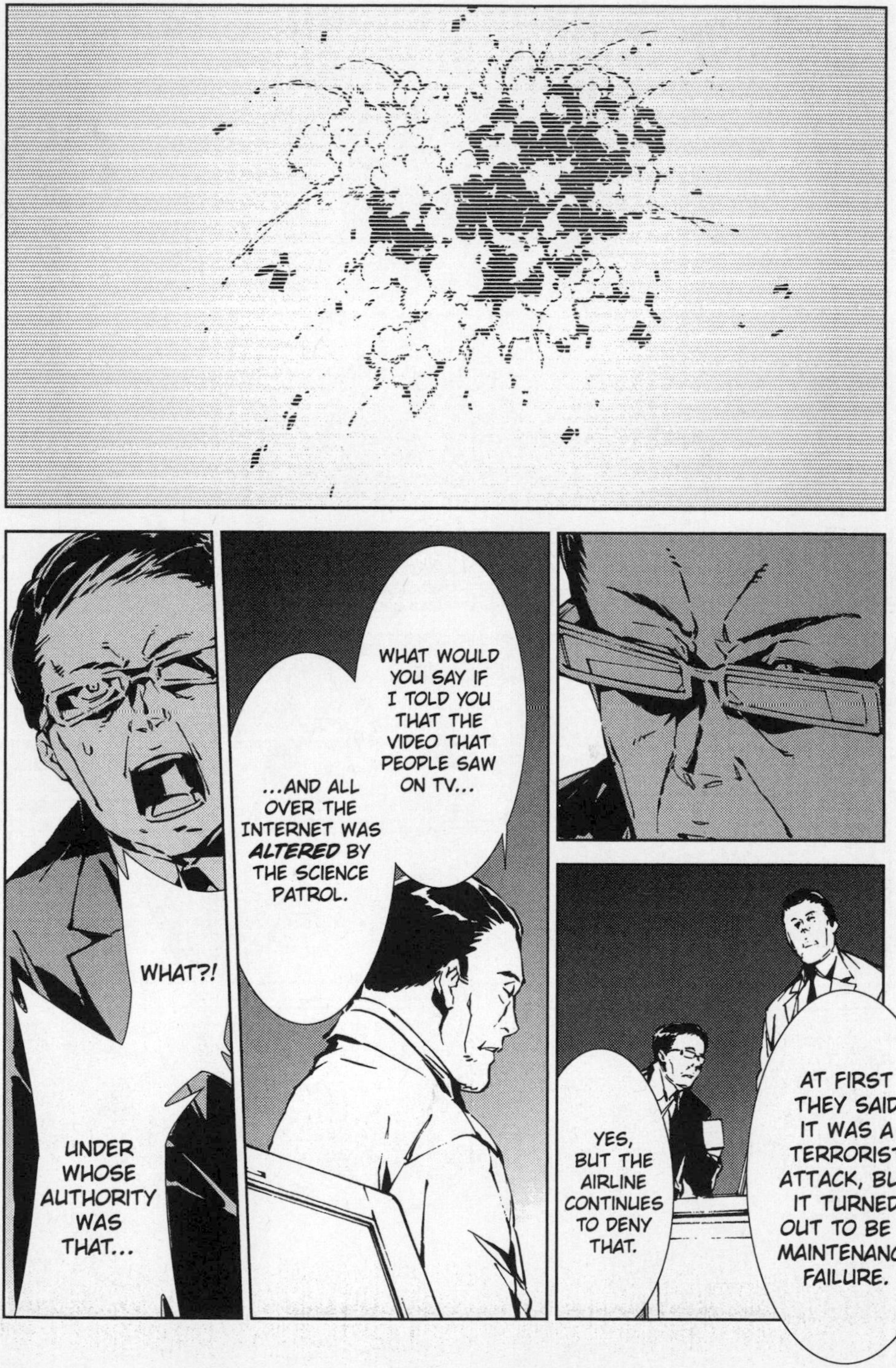
AT FIRST THEY SAID IT WAS A TERRORIST ATTACK, BUT IT TURNED OUT TO BE A MAINTENANCE FAILURE.
YES, BUT THE AIRLINE CONTINUES TO DENY THAT.
WHAT WOULD YOU SAY IF I TOLD YOU THAT THE VIDEO THAT PEOPLE SAW ON TV...
...AND ALL OVER THE INTERNET WAS *ALTERED* BY THE SCIENCE PATROL.
WHAT?!
UNDER WHOSE AUTHORITY WAS THAT...

MINE.

WHY WOULD YOU...?

WHAT I'M ABOUT TO SHOW YOU IS THE MASTER FILE...BEFORE ALTERATION.

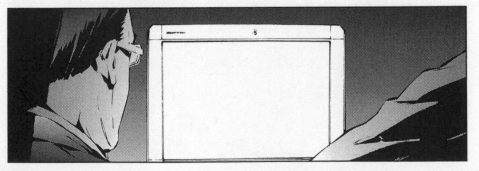

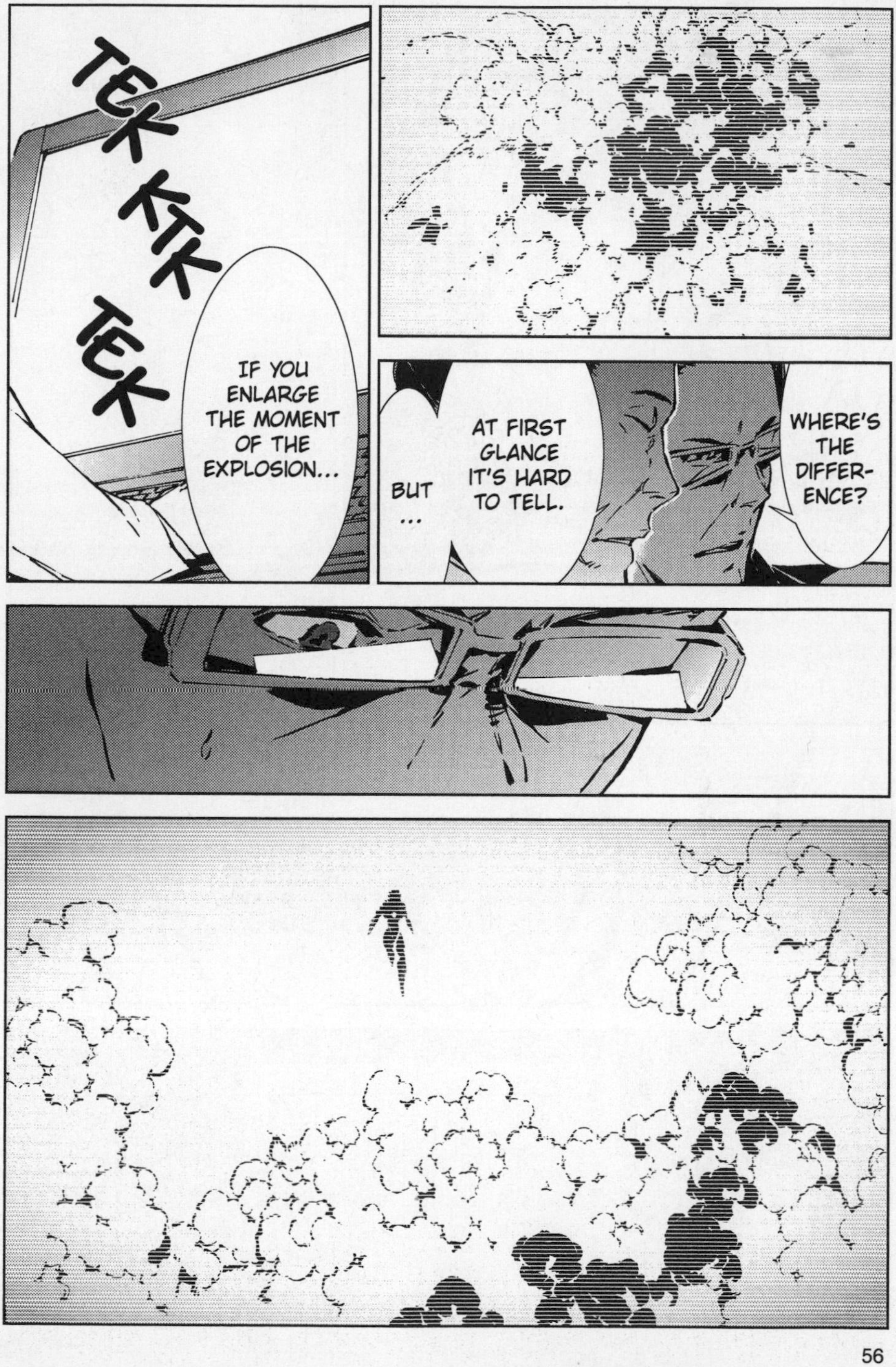
WHERE'S THE DIFFER-ENCE?
AT FIRST GLANCE IT'S HARD TO TELL.
BUT ...
TEK KTK TEK
IF YOU ENLARGE THE MOMENT OF THE EXPLOSION...

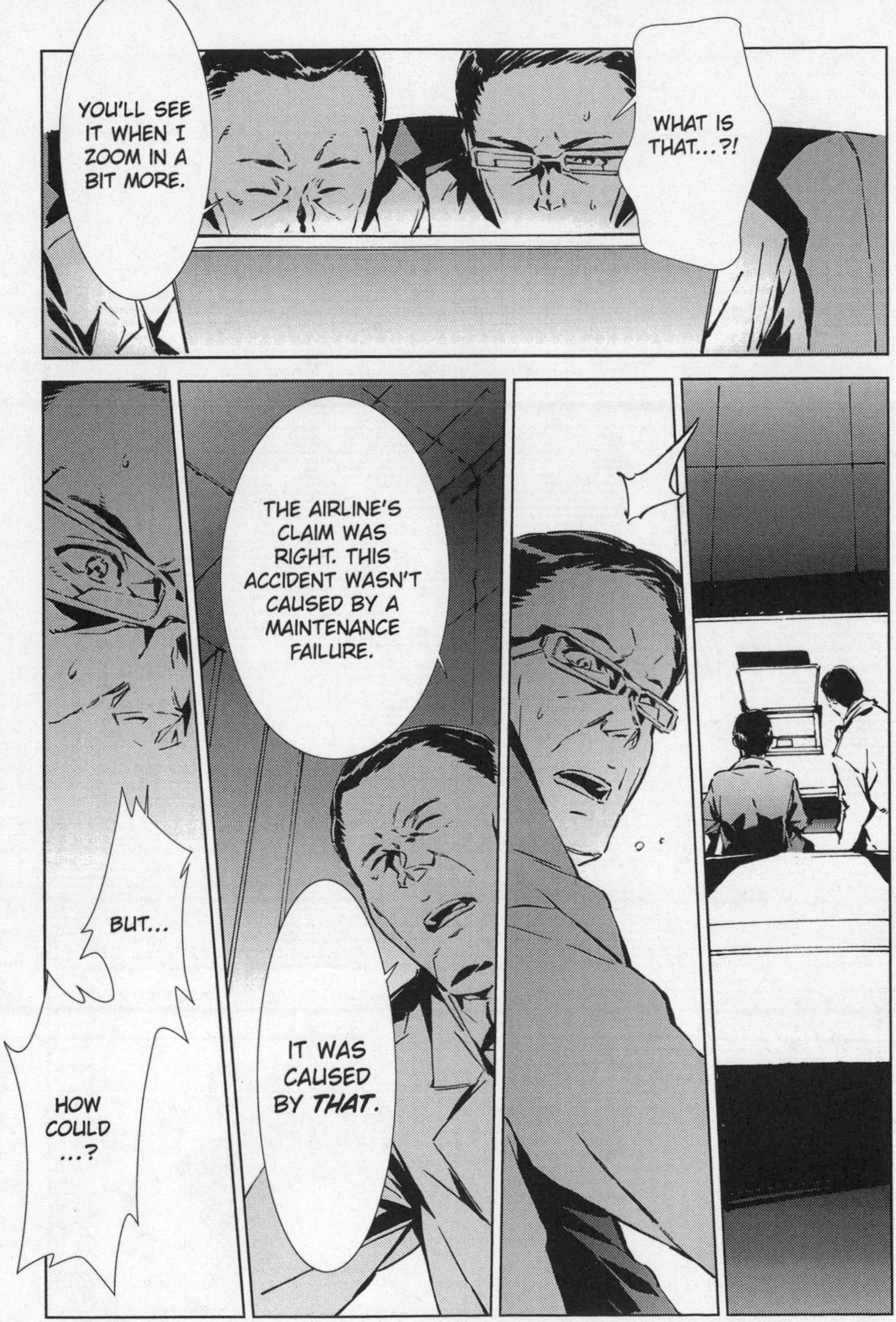
WHAT IS THAT...?!
YOU'LL SEE IT WHEN I ZOOM IN A BIT MORE.
THE AIRLINE'S CLAIM WAS RIGHT. THIS ACCIDENT WASN'T CAUSED BY A MAINTENANCE FAILURE.
IT WAS CAUSED BY *THAT*.
BUT...
HOW COULD ...?

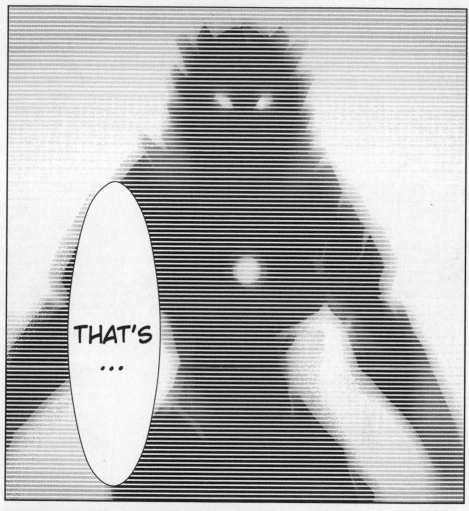

THAT'S
...

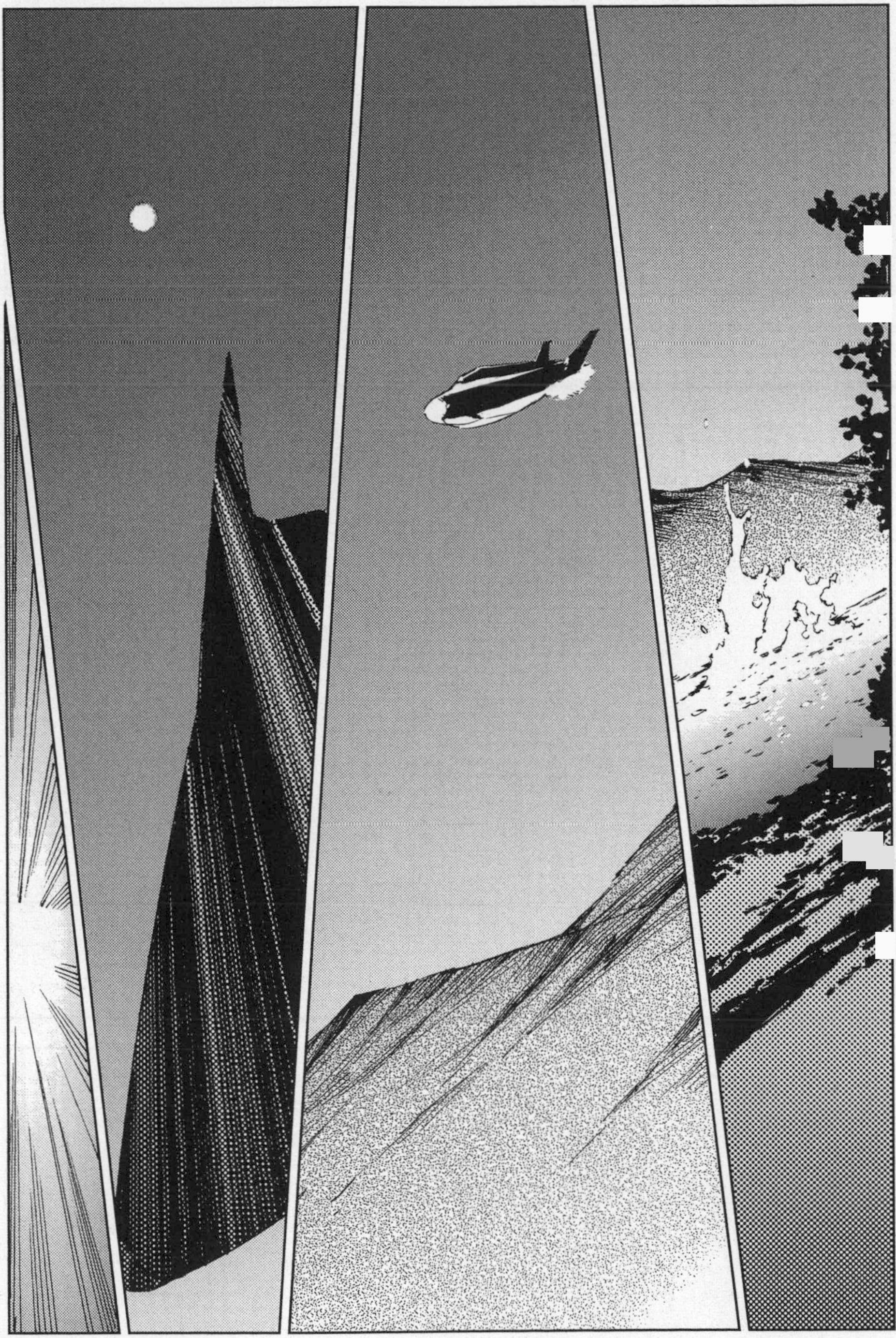

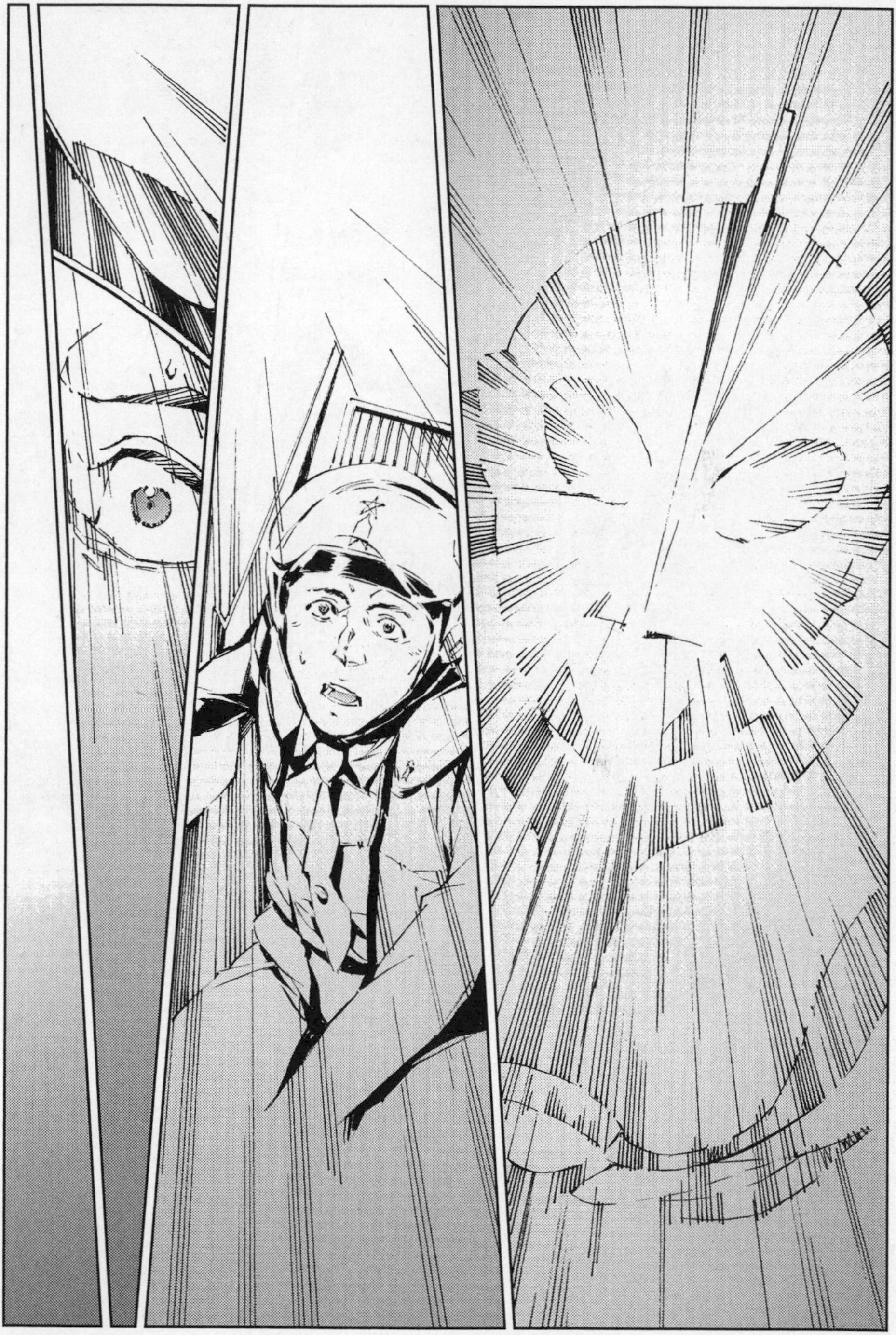

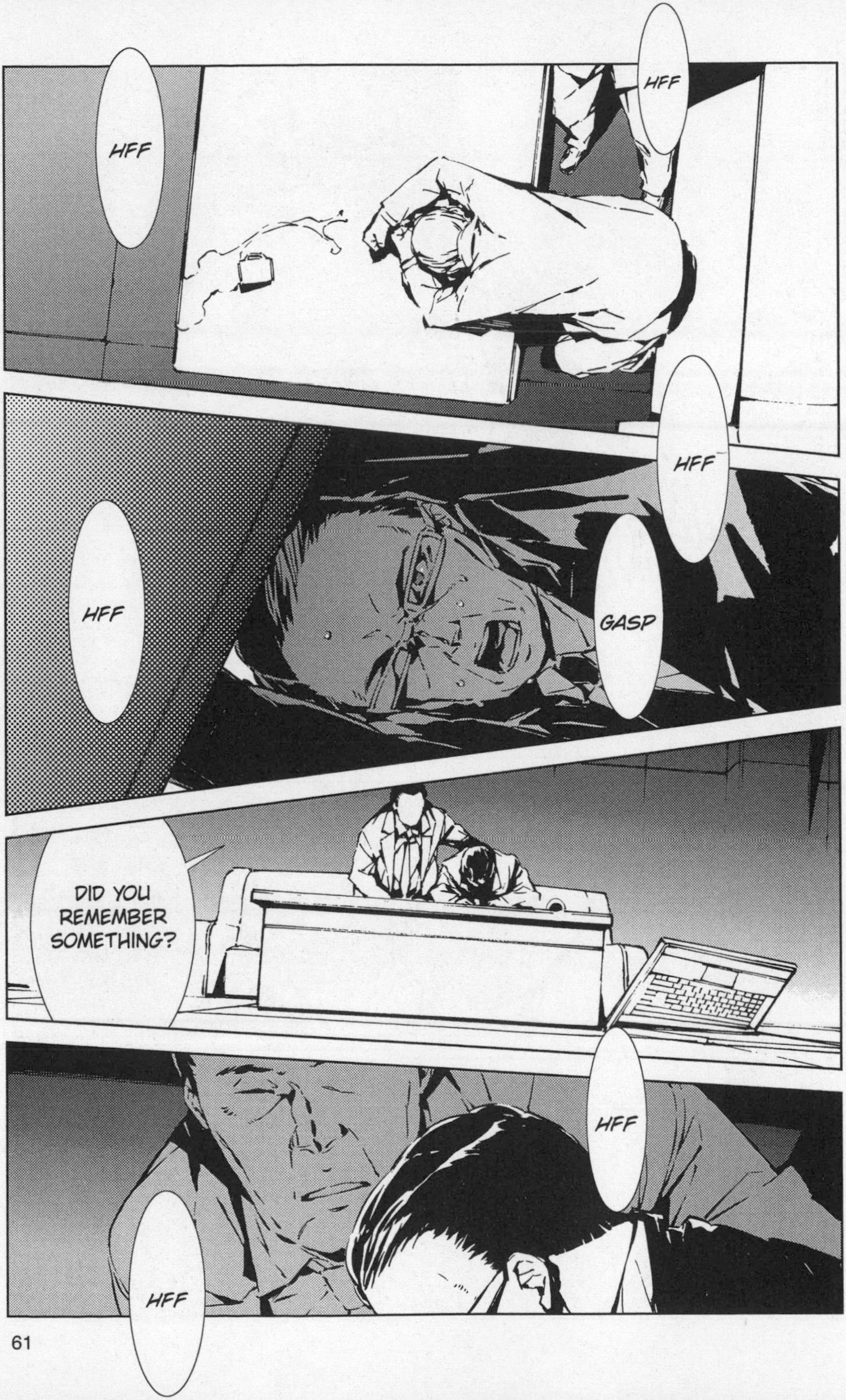
HFF
HFF
HFF
GASP
HFF
DID YOU REMEMBER SOMETHING?
HFF
HFF

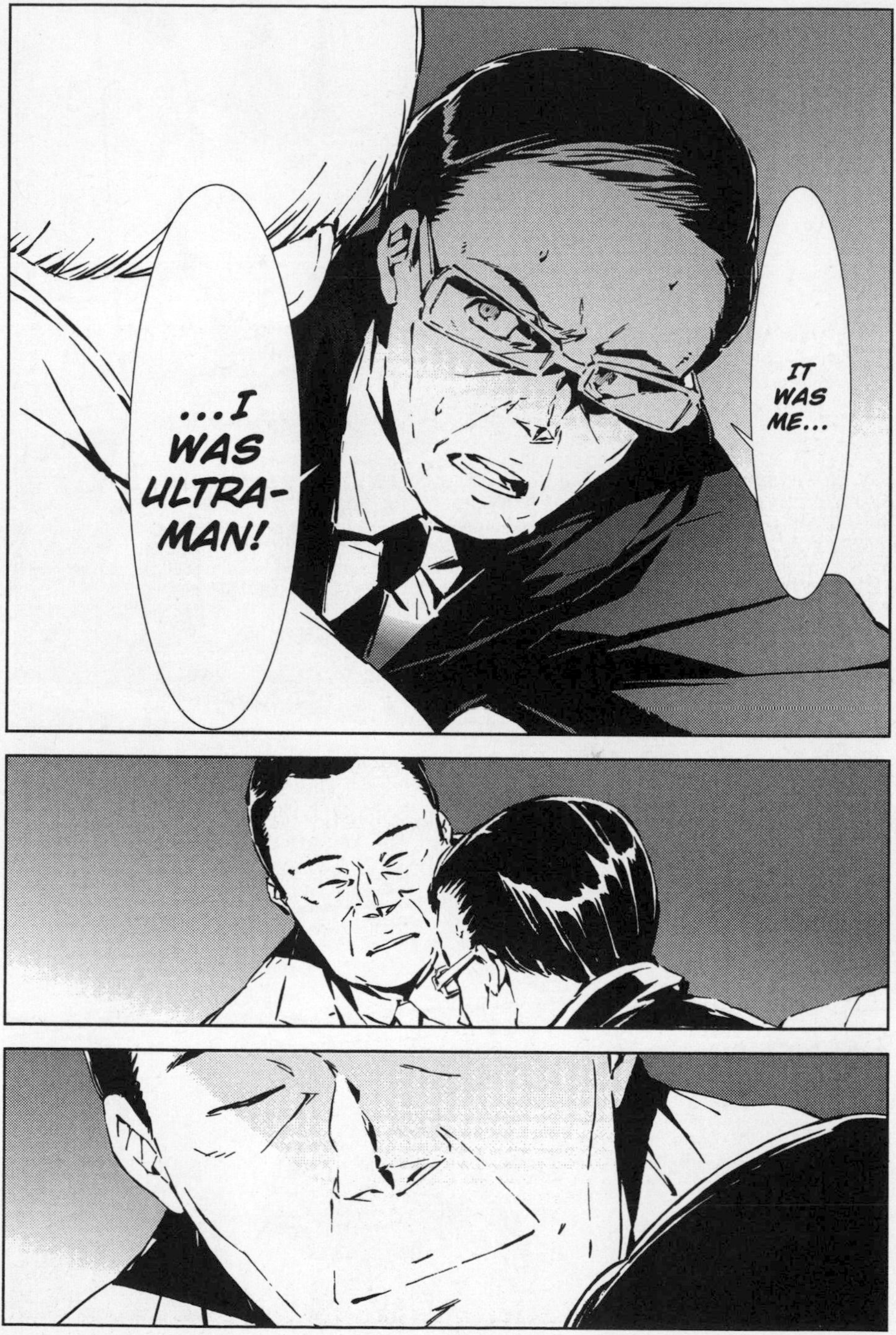
IT WAS ME...
...I WAS ULTRA-MAN!

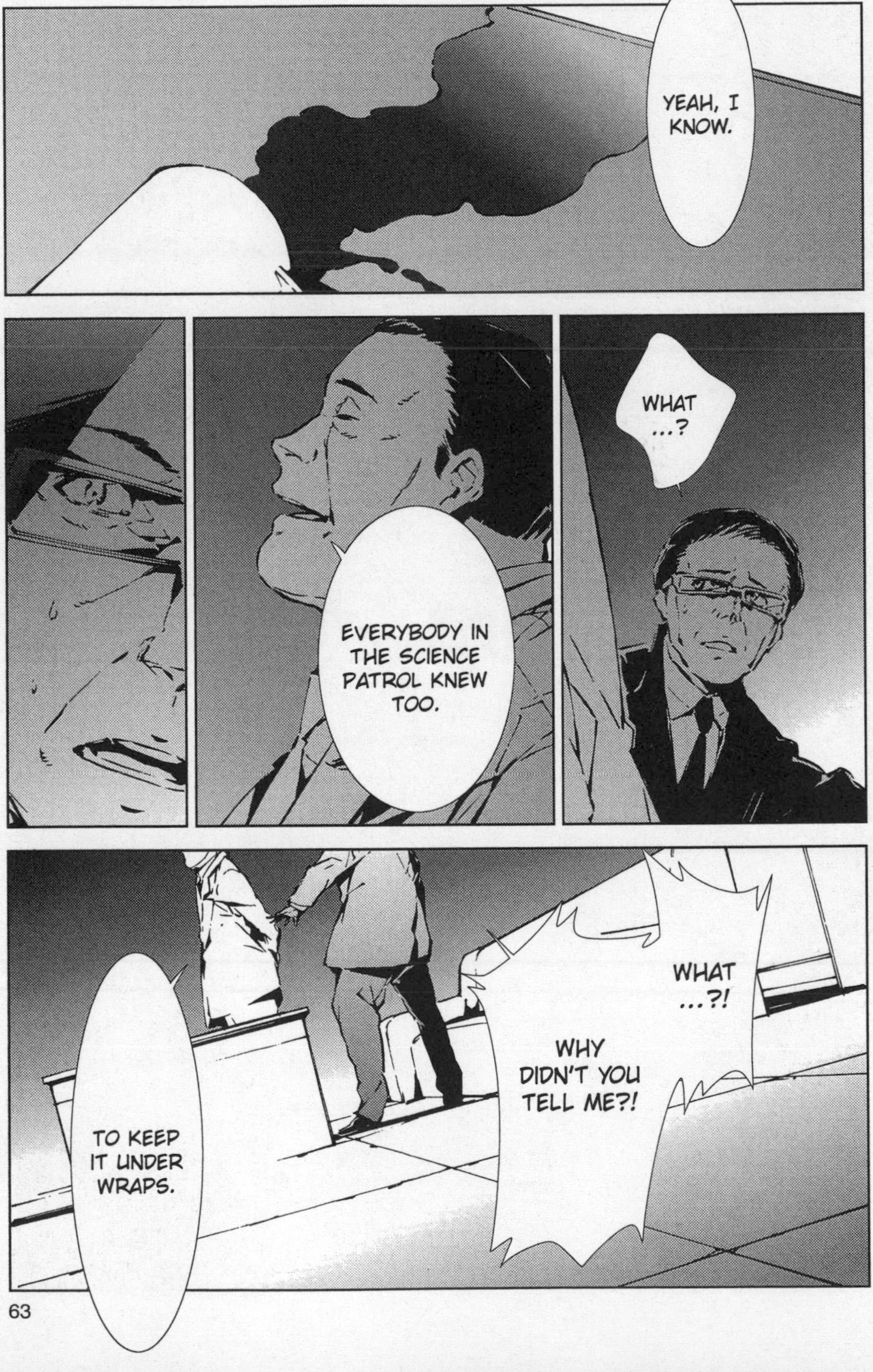
YEAH, I KNOW.
WHAT ...?
EVERYBODY IN THE SCIENCE PATROL KNEW TOO.
WHAT ...?!
WHY DIDN'T YOU TELL ME?!
TO KEEP IT UNDER WRAPS.

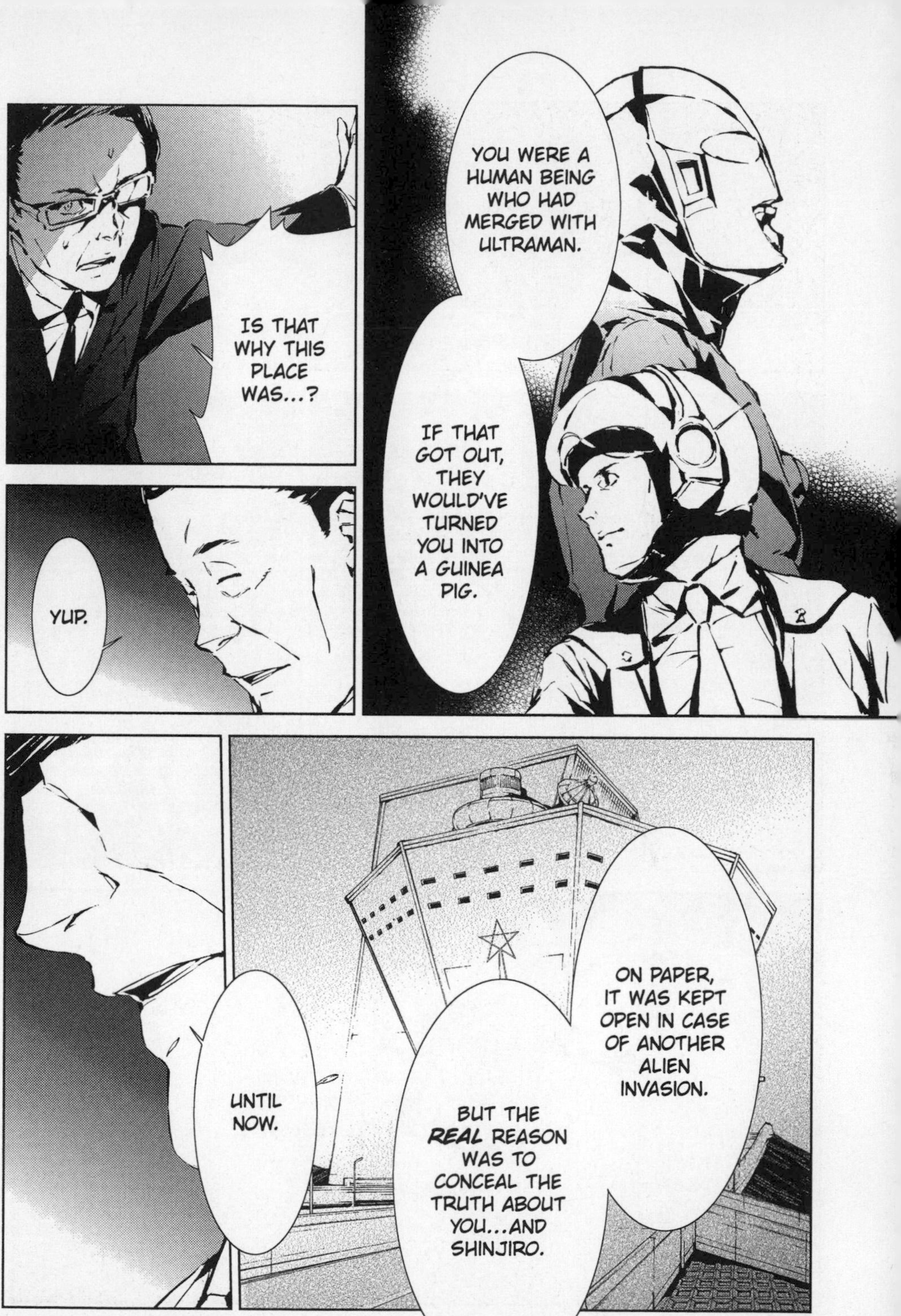
YOU WERE A HUMAN BEING WHO HAD MERGED WITH ULTRAMAN.
IF THAT GOT OUT, THEY WOULD'VE TURNED YOU INTO A GUINEA PIG.
IS THAT WHY THIS PLACE WAS...?
YUP.
ON PAPER, IT WAS KEPT OPEN IN CASE OF ANOTHER ALIEN INVASION.
BUT THE ***REAL*** REASON WAS TO CONCEAL THE TRUTH ABOUT YOU...AND SHINJIRO.
UNTIL NOW.

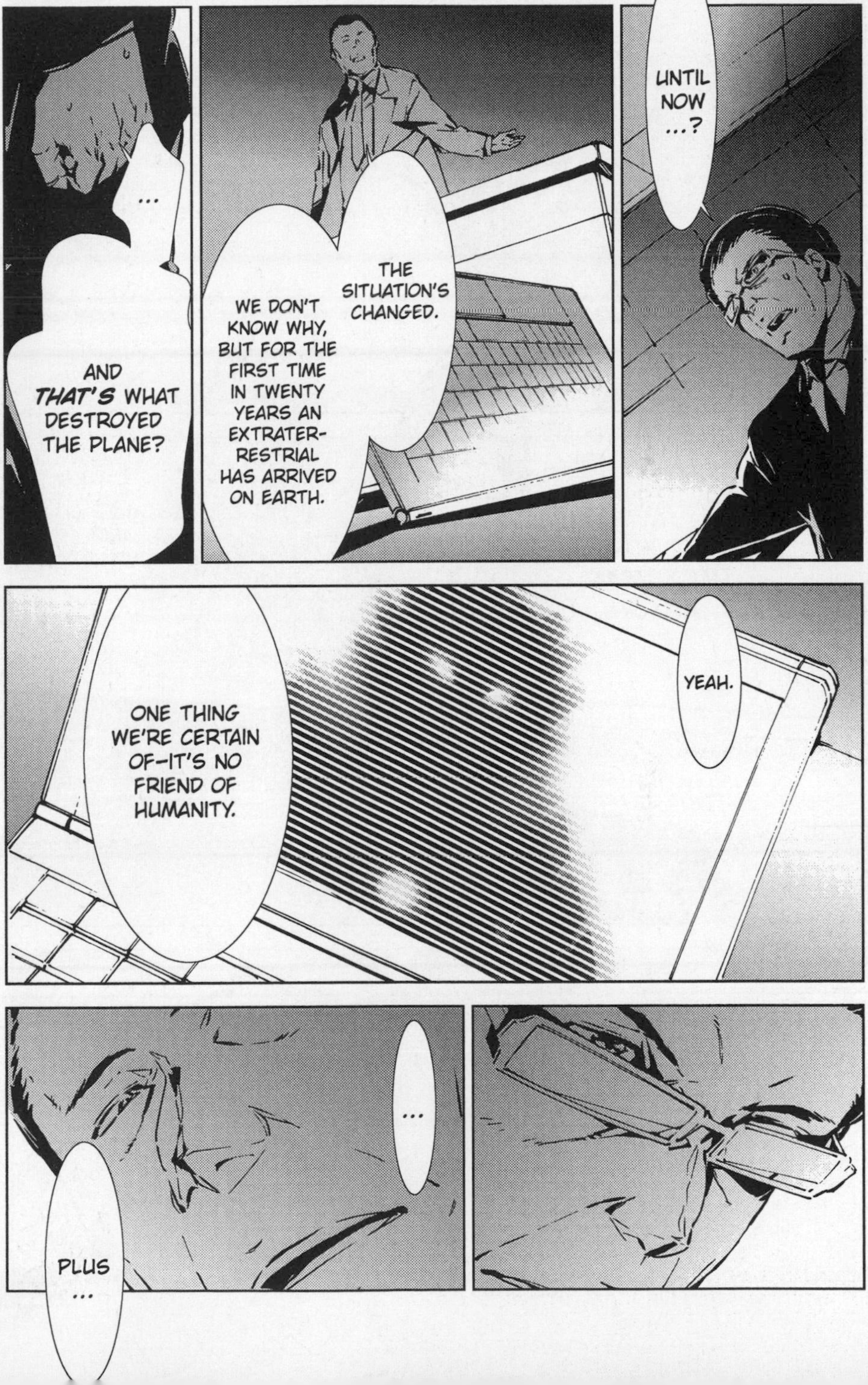
UNTIL NOW ...?
THE SITUATION'S CHANGED.
WE DON'T KNOW WHY, BUT FOR THE FIRST TIME IN TWENTY YEARS AN EXTRATER-RESTRIAL HAS ARRIVED ON EARTH.
...
AND *THAT'S* WHAT DESTROYED THE PLANE?
YEAH.
ONE THING WE'RE CERTAIN OF—IT'S NO FRIEND OF HUMANITY.
...
PLUS ...

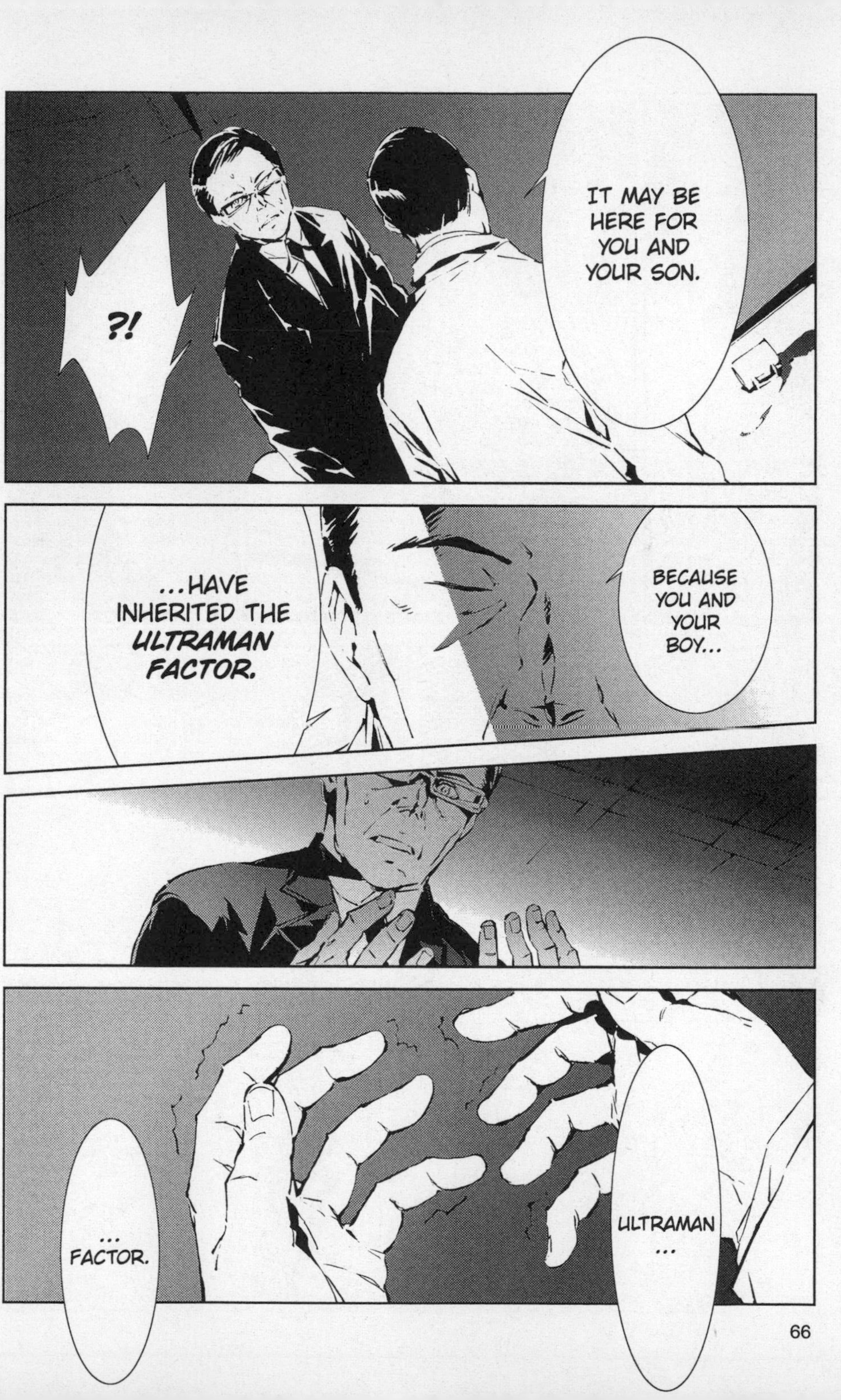
IT MAY BE HERE FOR YOU AND YOUR SON.
?!
BECAUSE YOU AND YOUR BOY...
...HAVE INHERITED THE *ULTRAMAN FACTOR.*
ULTRAMAN ...
... FACTOR.

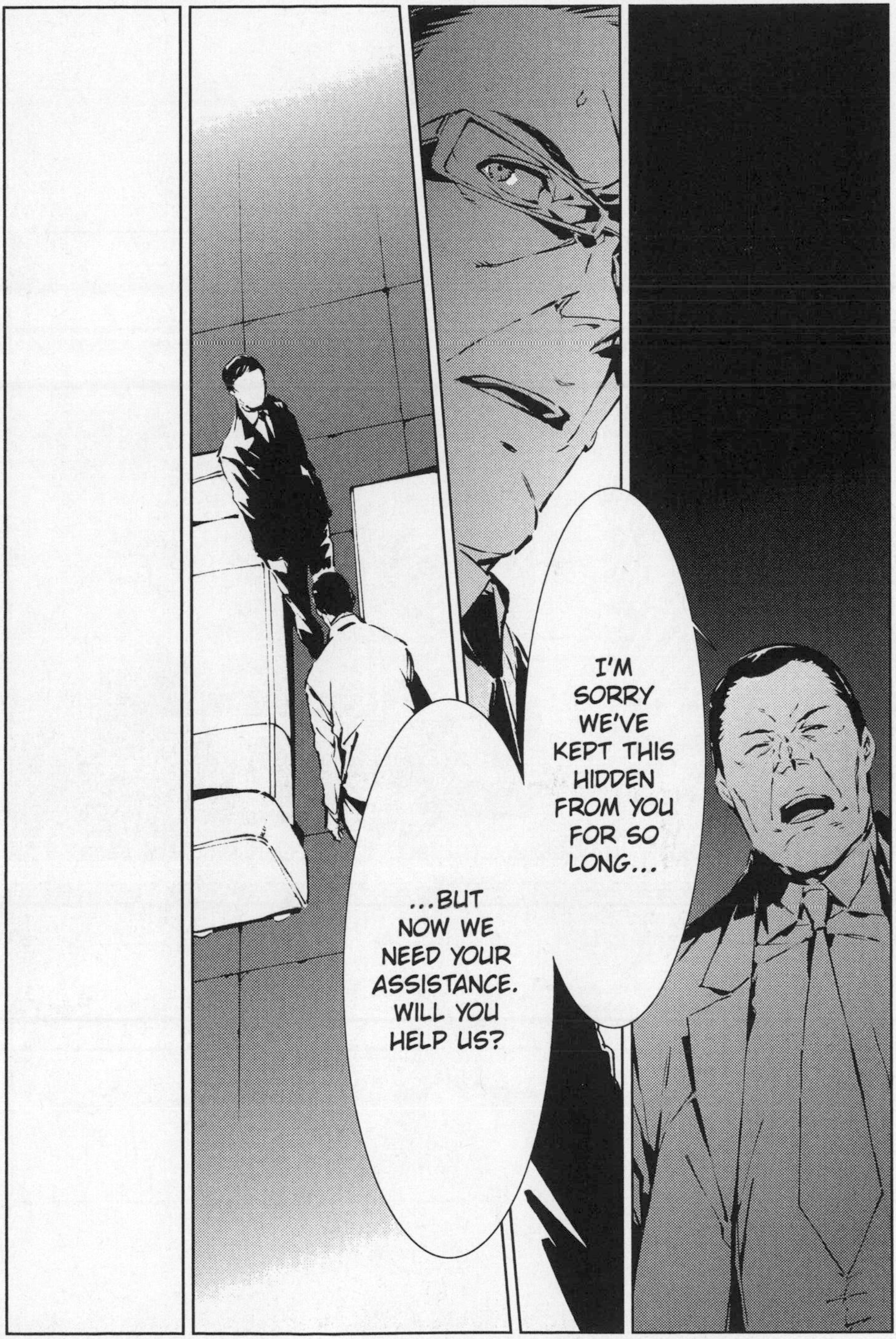

I'M SORRY WE'VE KEPT THIS HIDDEN FROM YOU FOR SO LONG...
...BUT NOW WE NEED YOUR ASSISTANCE. WILL YOU HELP US?

TWELVE YEARS LATER

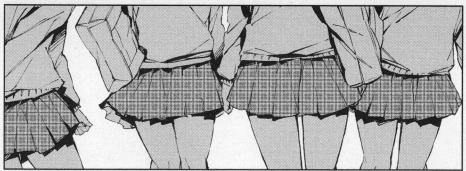

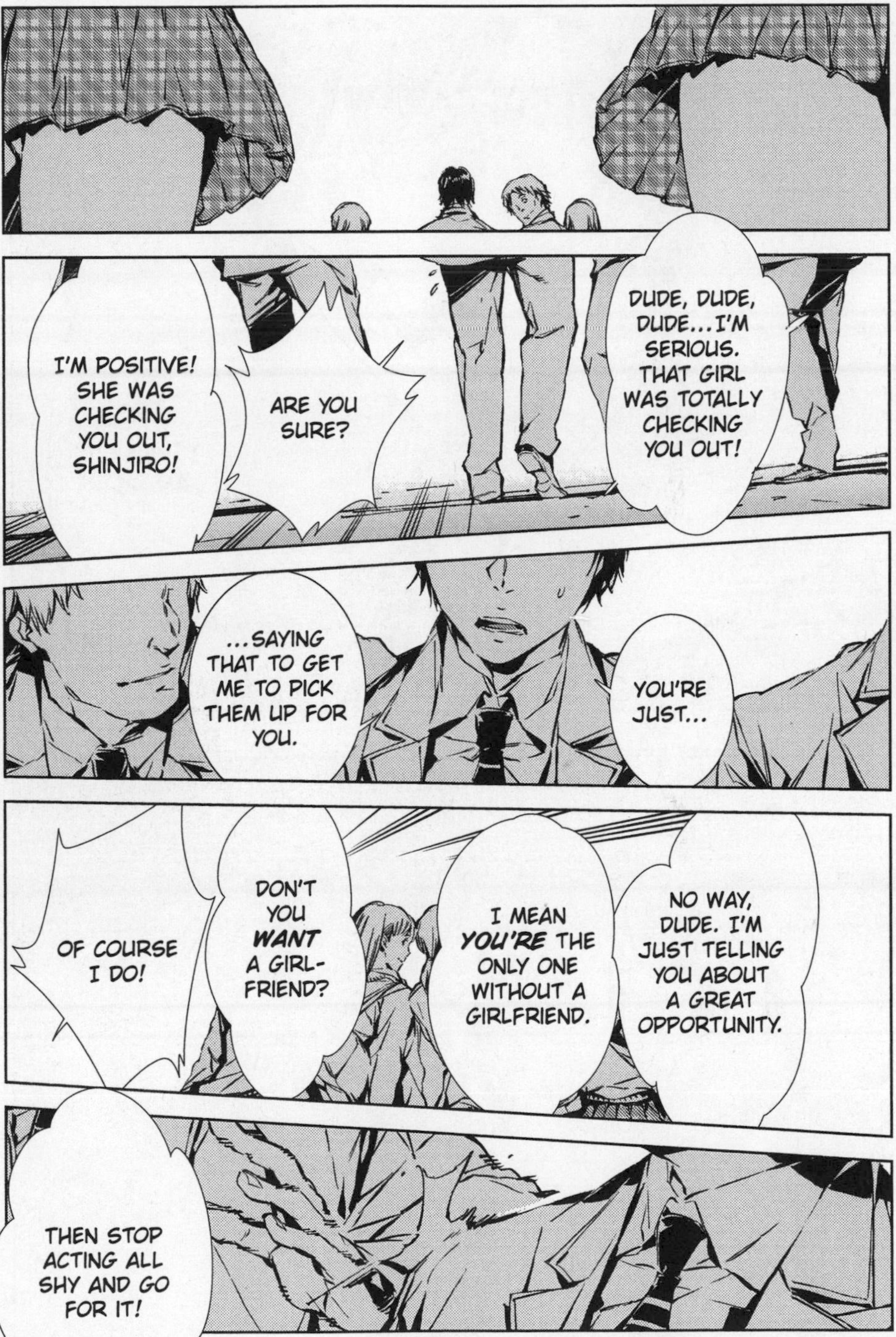
DUDE, DUDE, DUDE...I'M SERIOUS. THAT GIRL WAS TOTALLY CHECKING YOU OUT!
ARE YOU SURE?
I'M POSITIVE! SHE WAS CHECKING YOU OUT, SHINJIRO!
YOU'RE JUST...
...SAYING THAT TO GET ME TO PICK THEM UP FOR YOU.
NO WAY, DUDE. I'M JUST TELLING YOU ABOUT A GREAT OPPORTUNITY.
I MEAN *YOU'RE* THE ONLY ONE WITHOUT A GIRLFRIEND.
DON'T YOU *WANT* A GIRL-FRIEND?
OF COURSE I DO!
THEN STOP ACTING ALL SHY AND GO FOR IT!

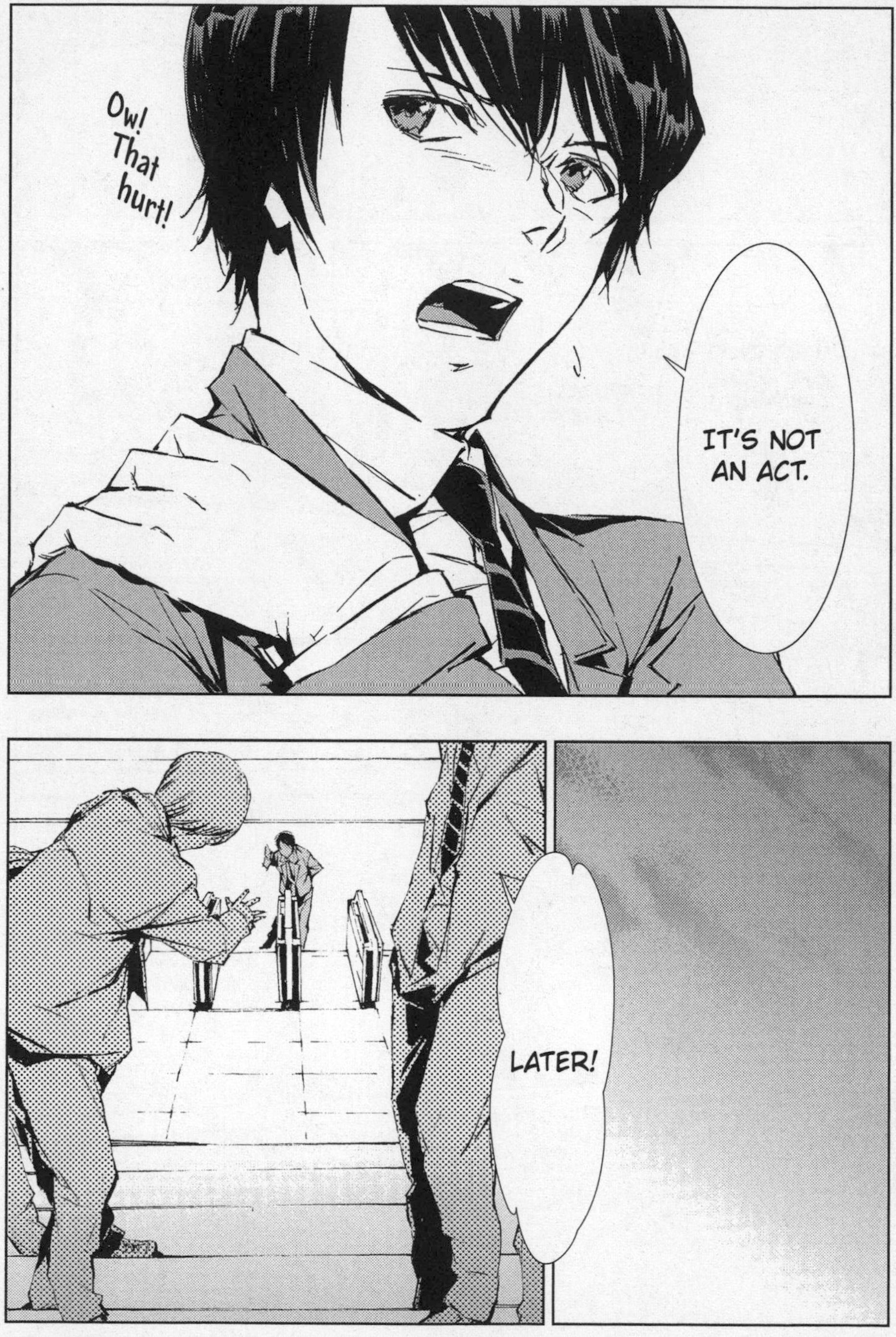
Ow! That hurt!
IT'S NOT AN ACT.
LATER!

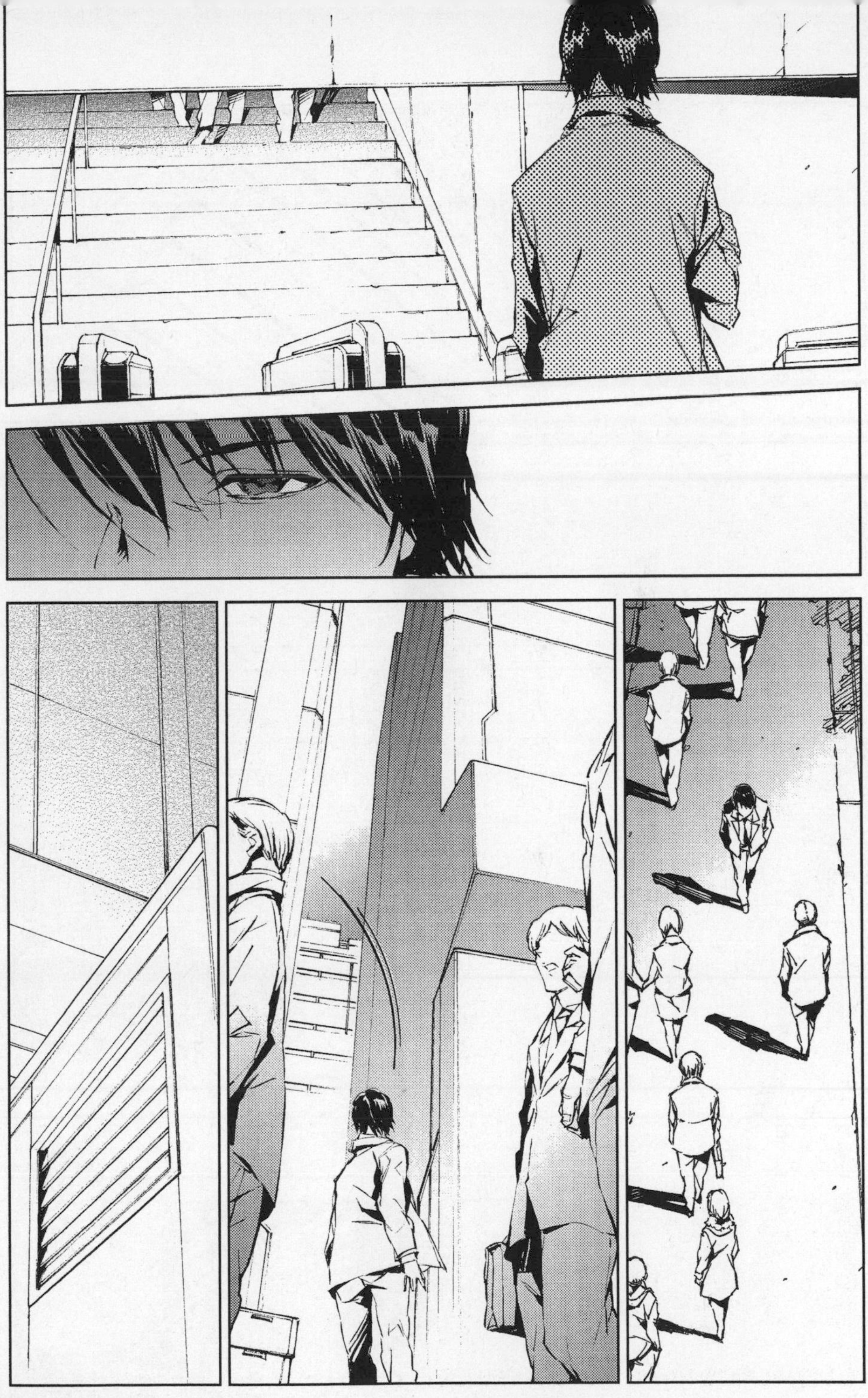

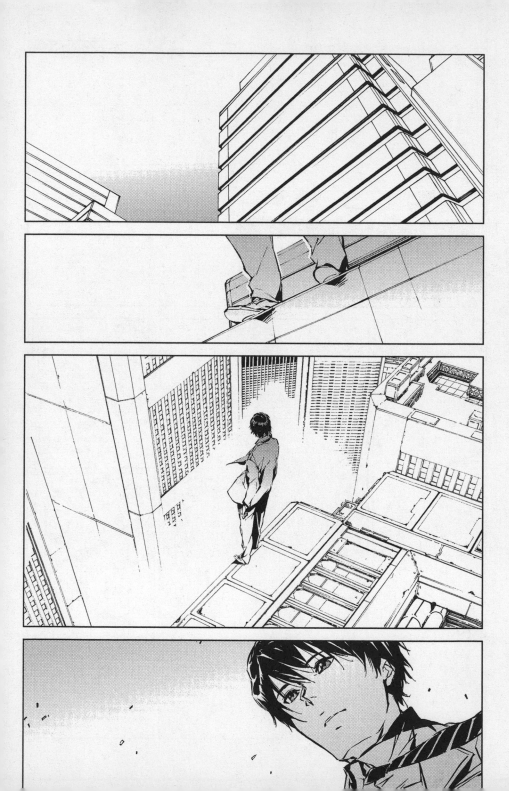

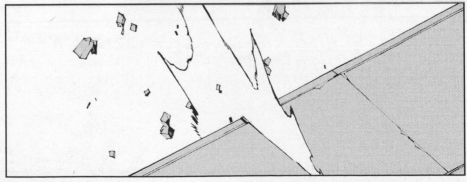

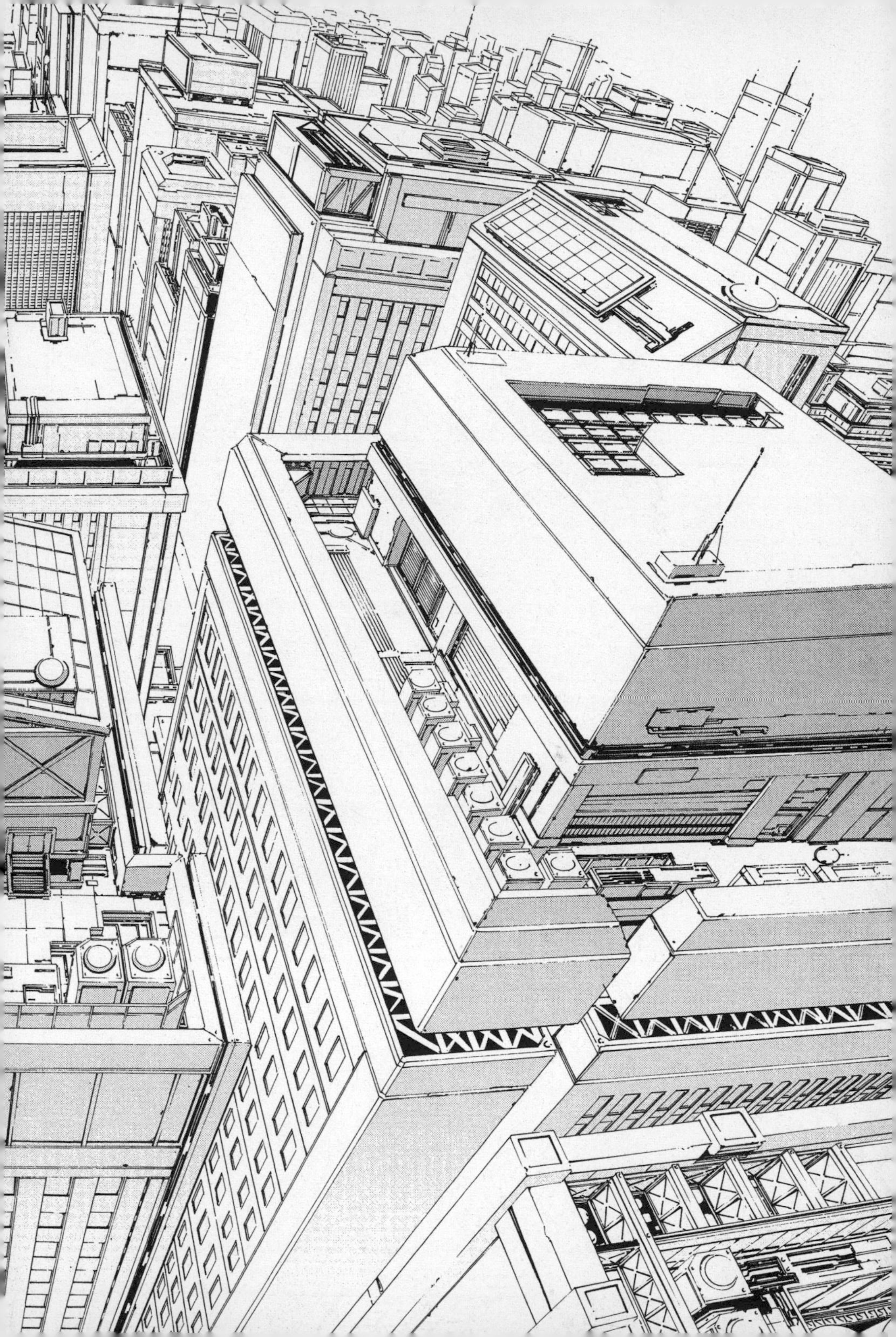

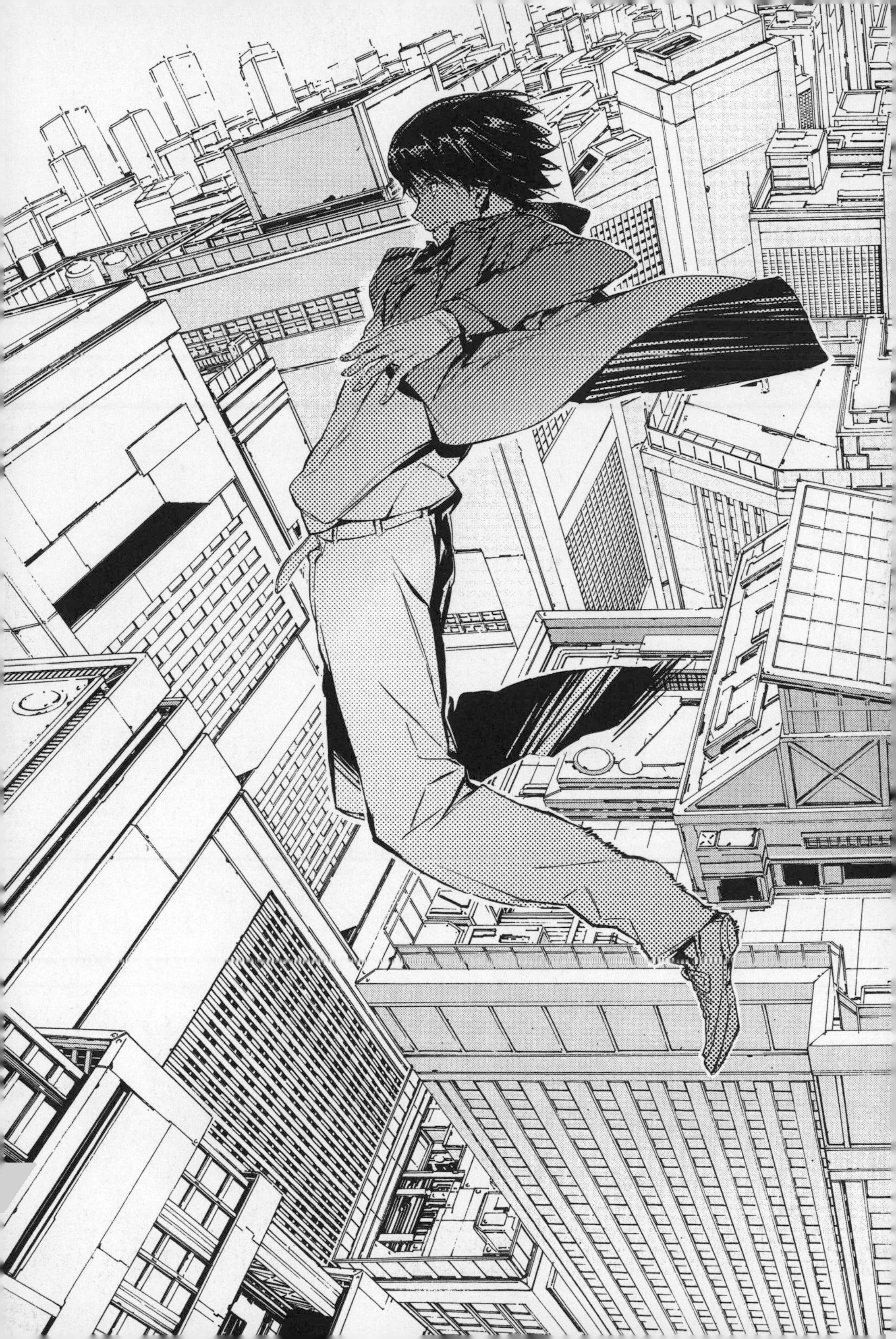

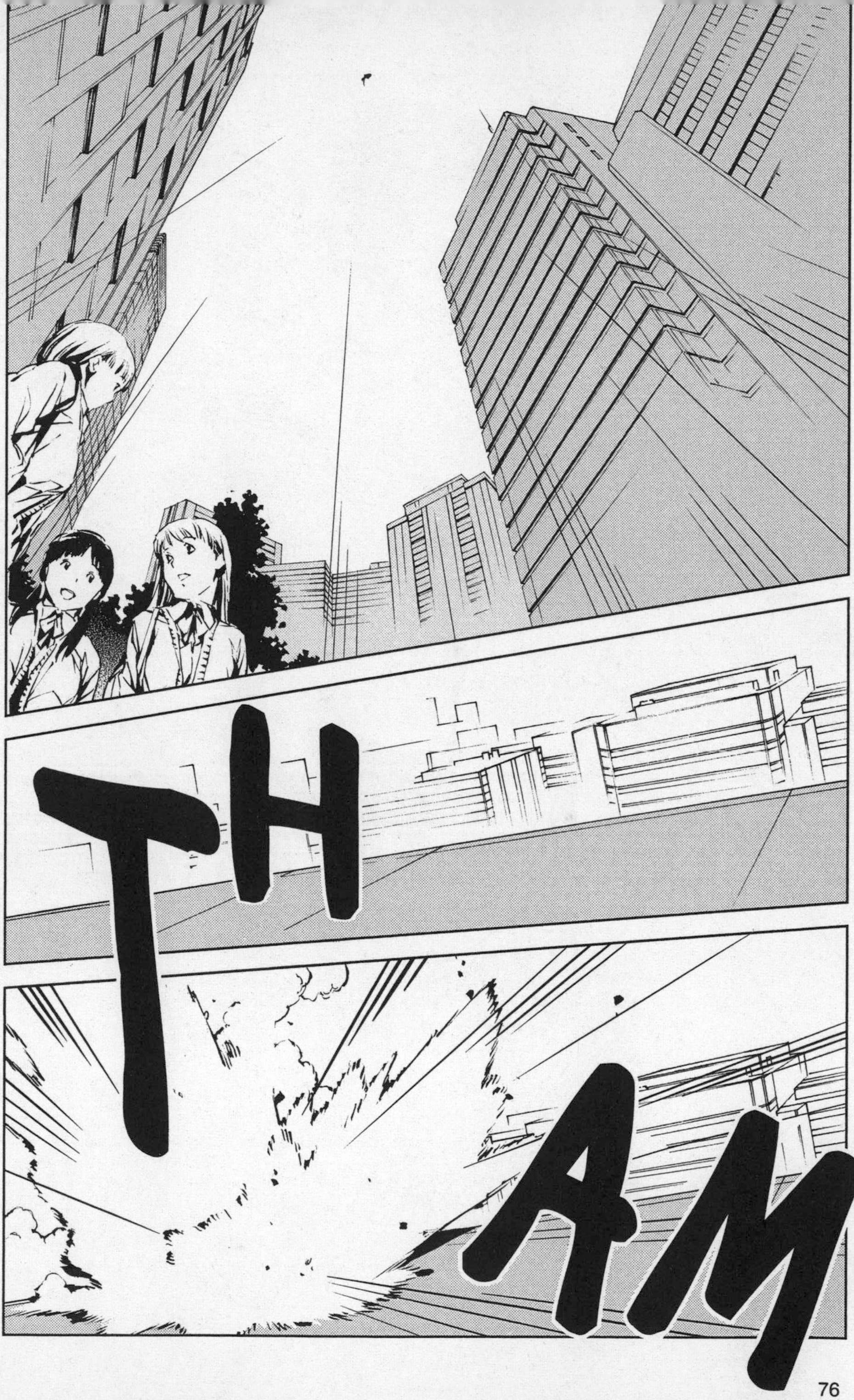
THAM

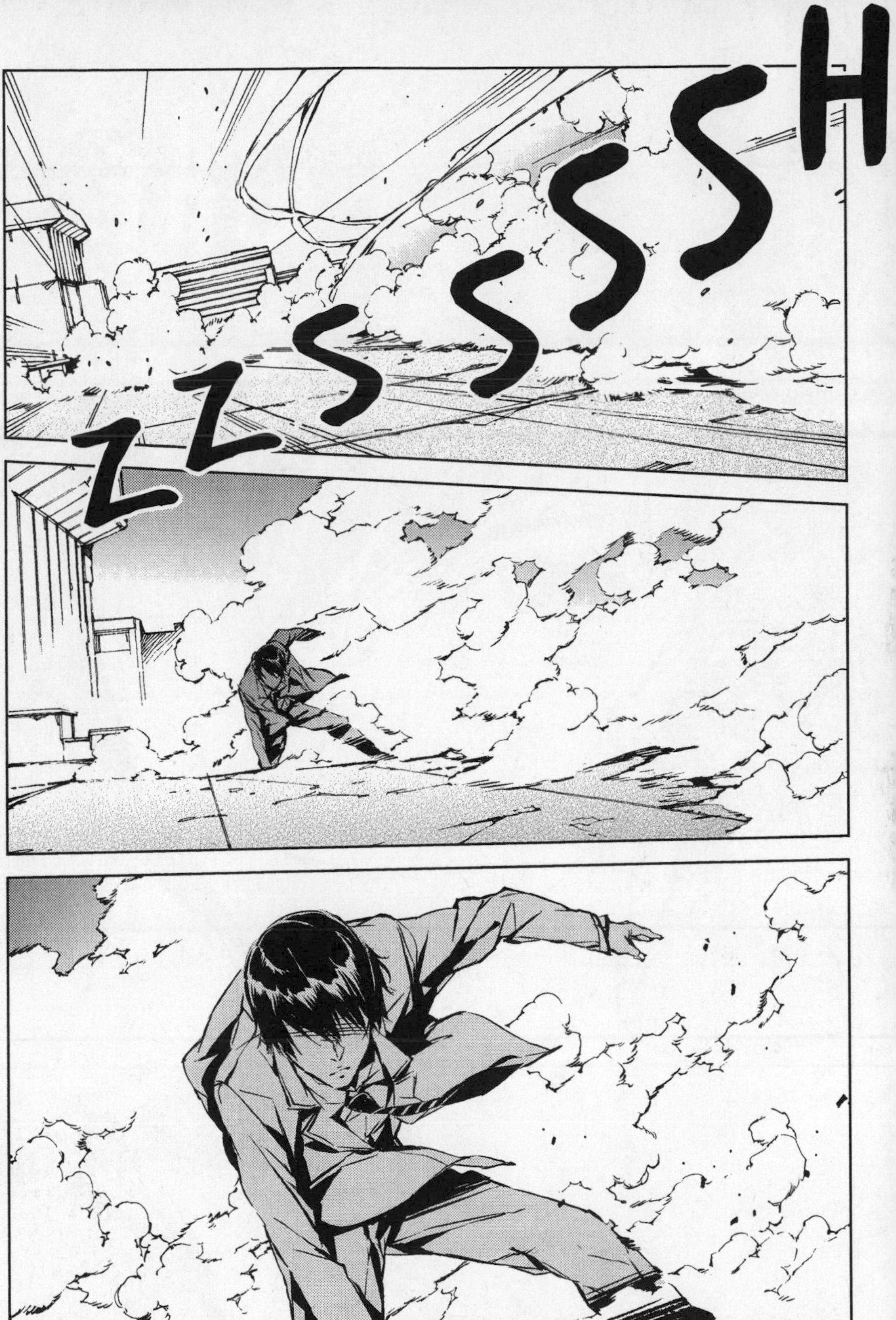
ZZSSSSSH

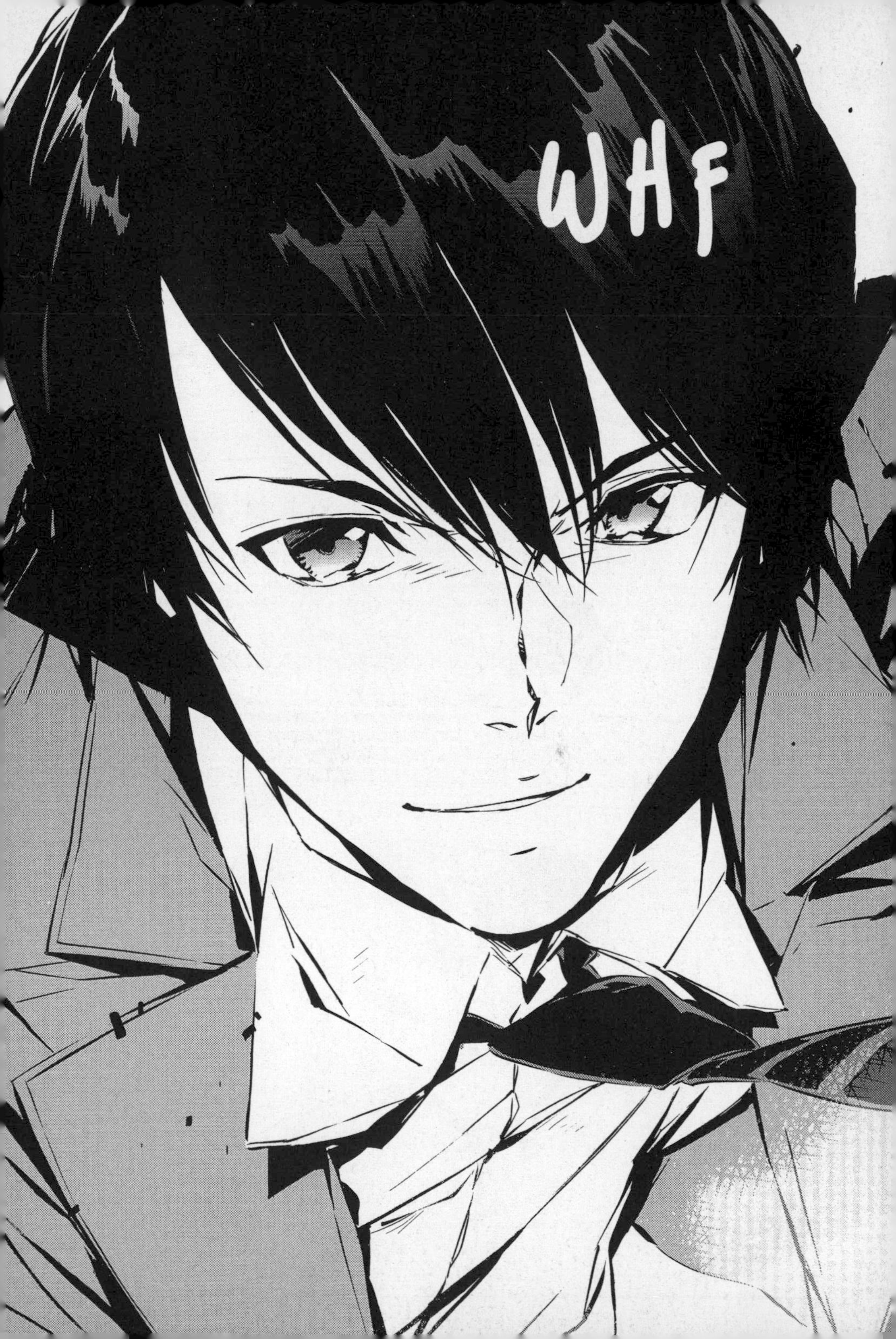
WHF

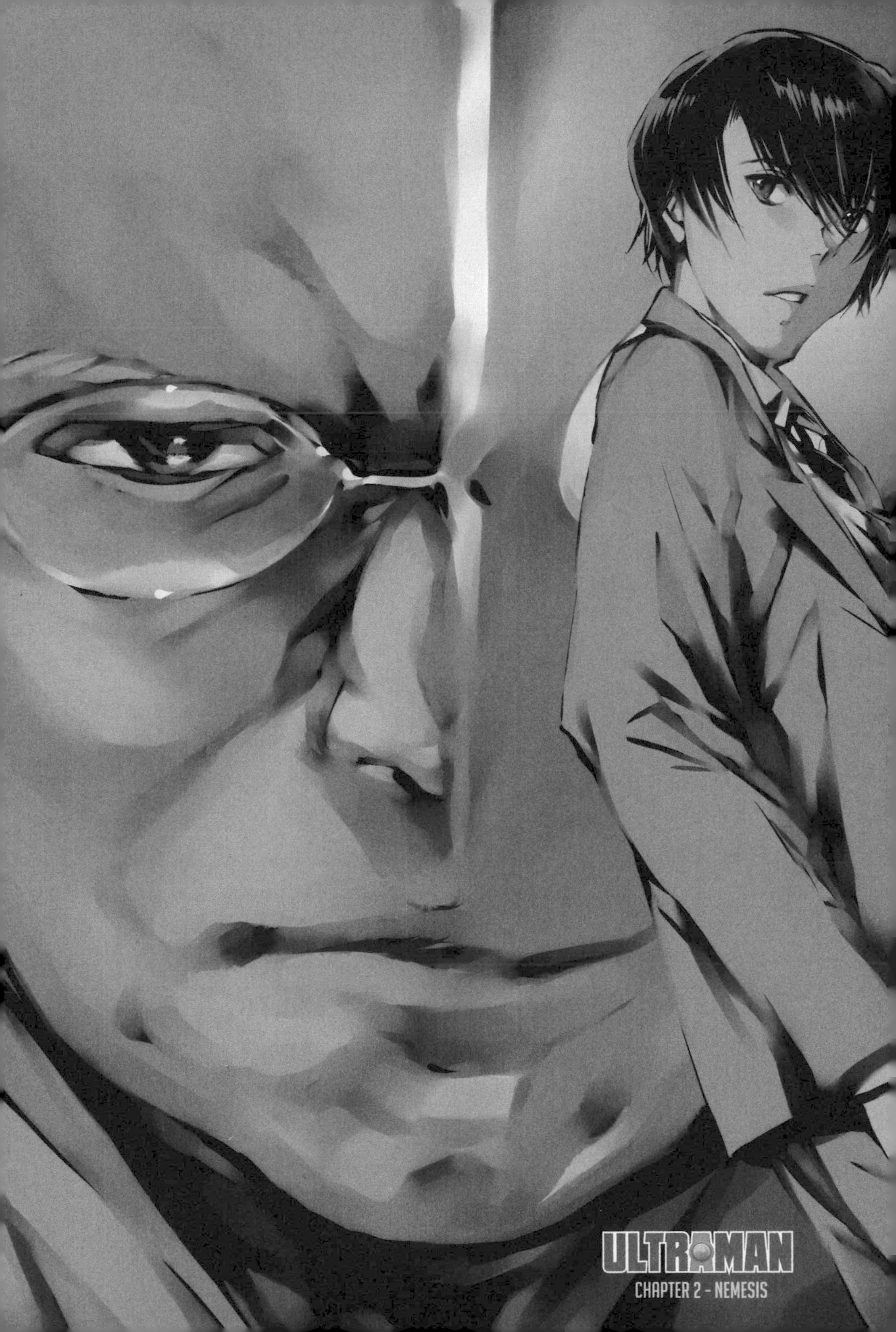
ULTRAMAN
CHAPTER 2 - NEMESIS

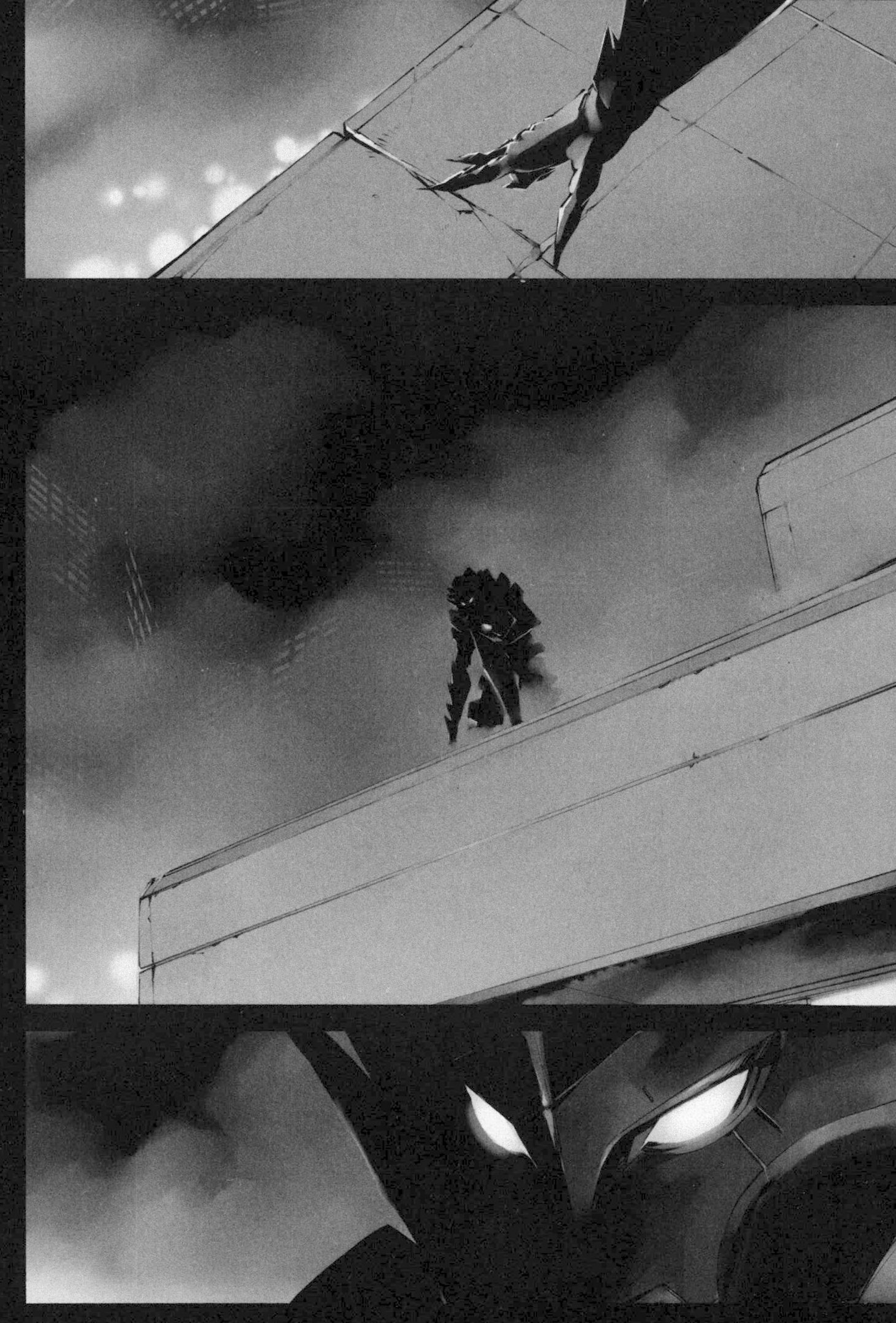

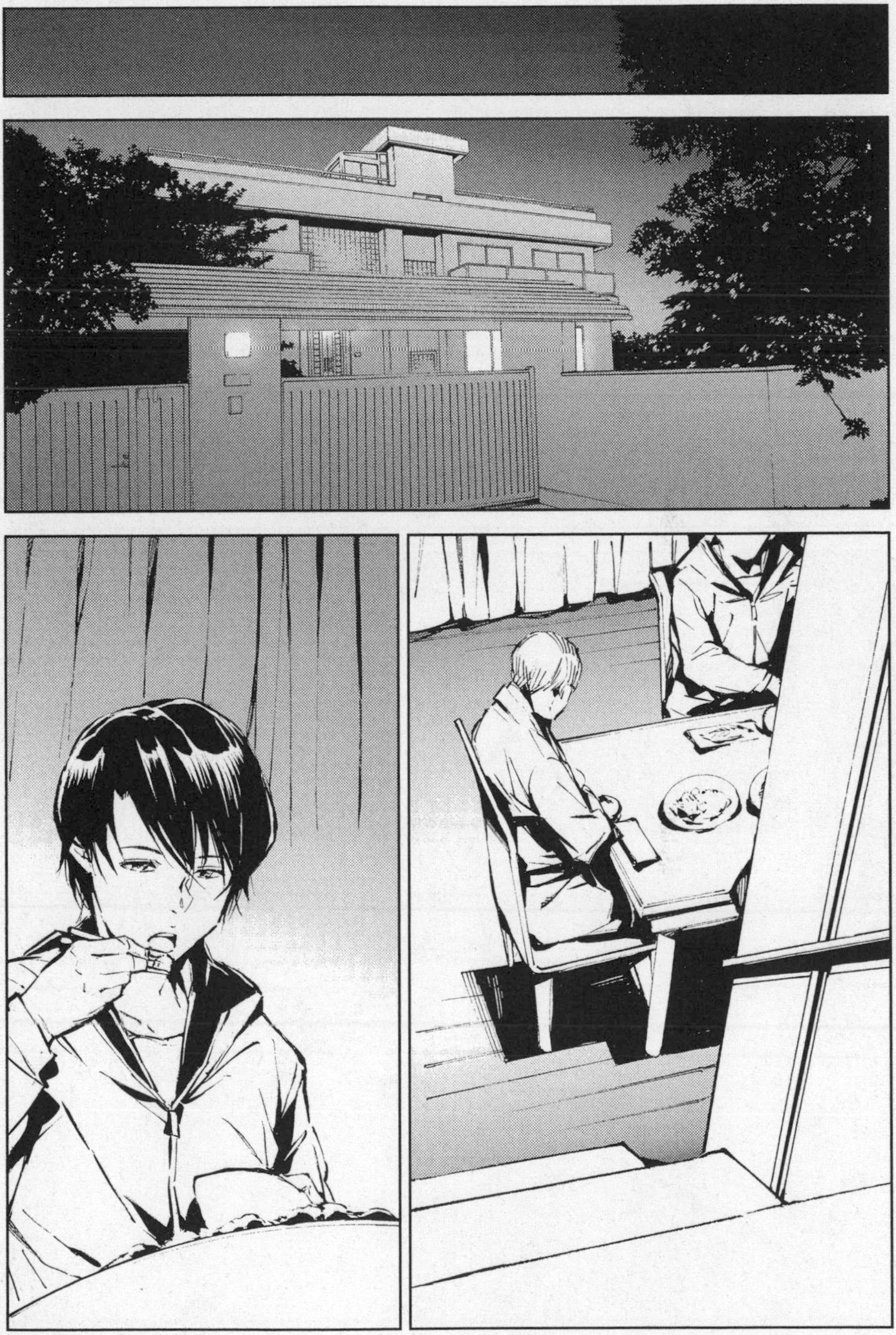

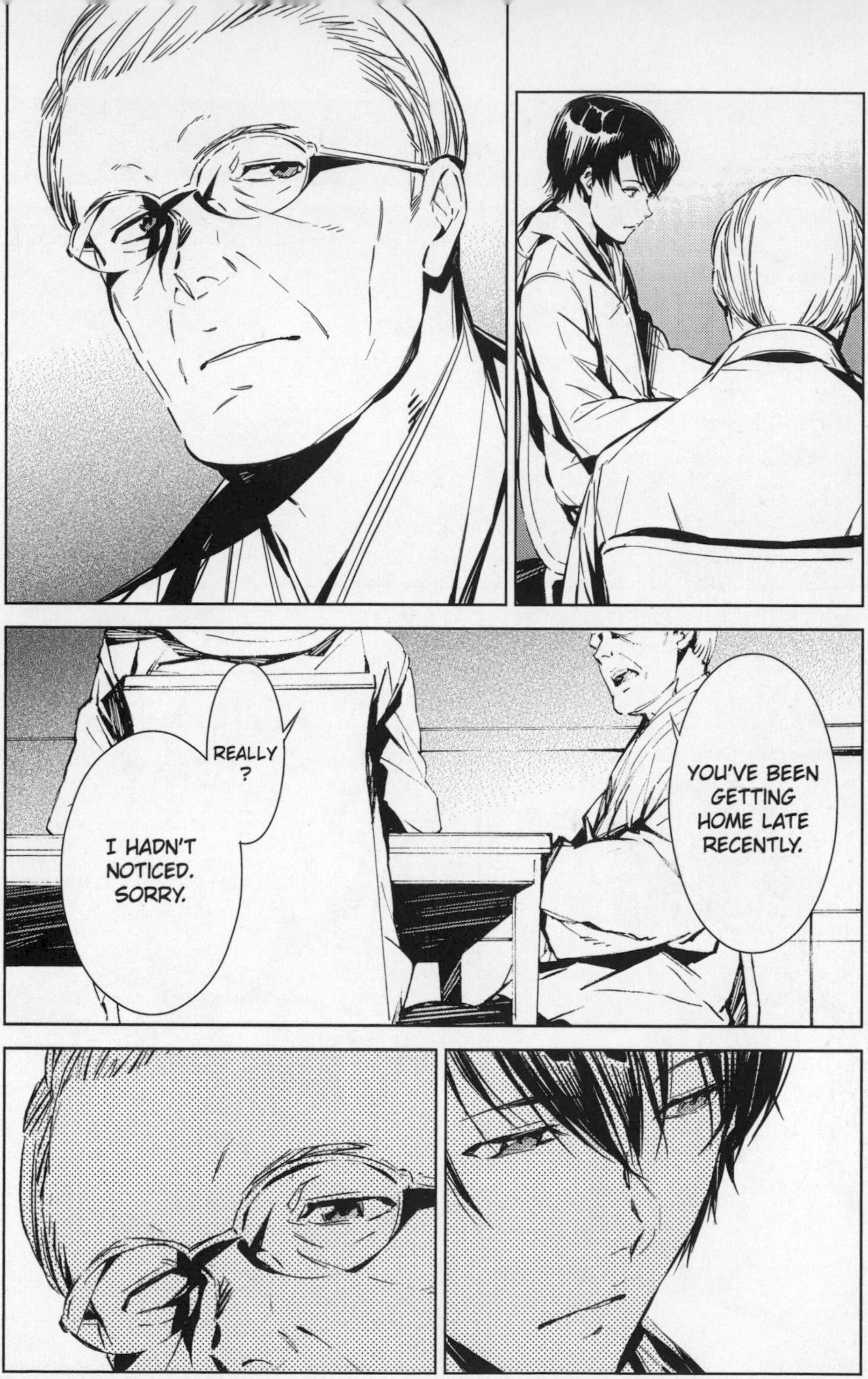
YOU'VE BEEN GETTING HOME LATE RECENTLY.
REALLY ?
I HADN'T NOTICED. SORRY.

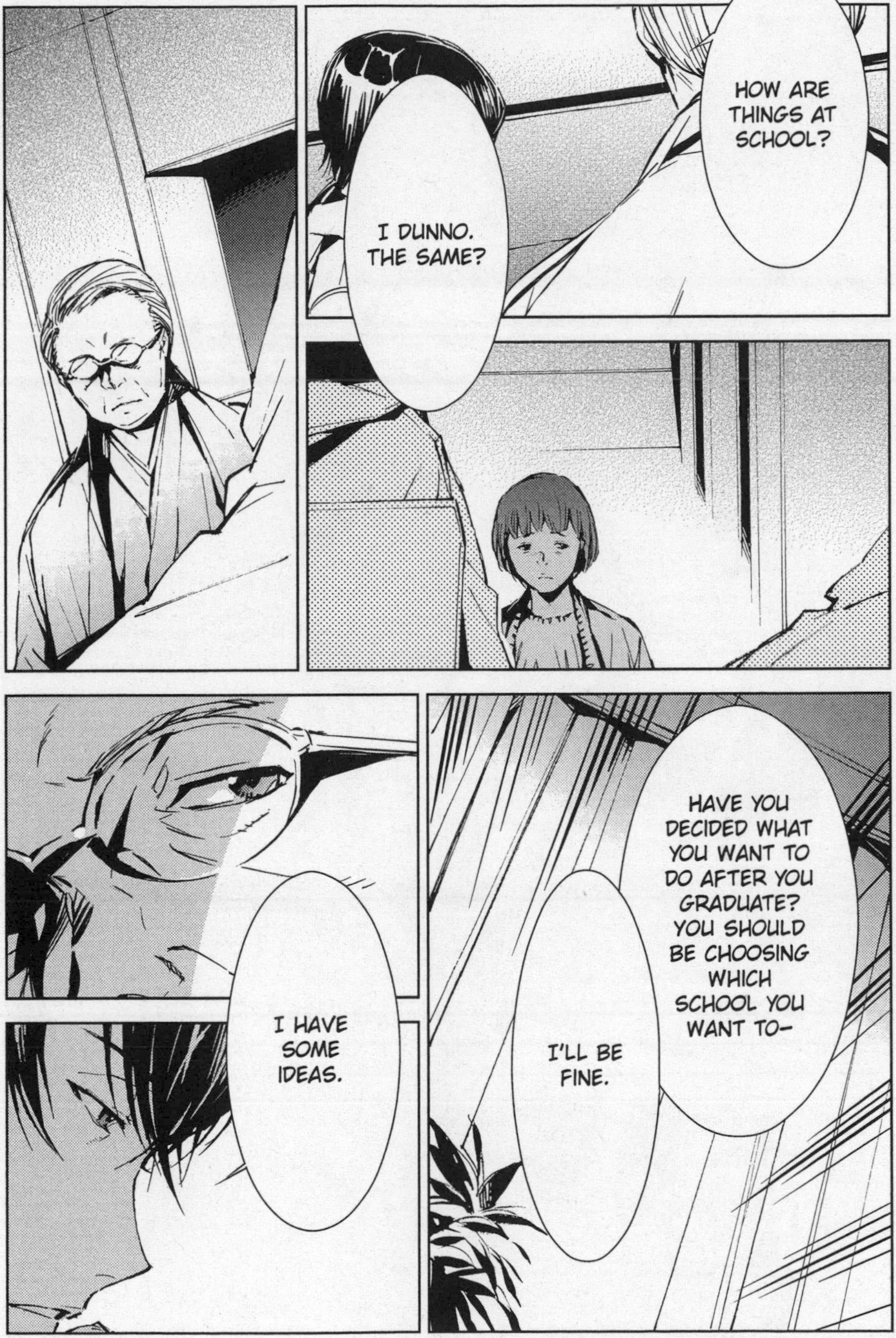
HOW ARE THINGS AT SCHOOL?
I DUNNO. THE SAME?
HAVE YOU DECIDED WHAT YOU WANT TO DO AFTER YOU GRADUATE? YOU SHOULD BE CHOOSING WHICH SCHOOL YOU WANT TO–
I'LL BE FINE.
I HAVE SOME IDEAS.

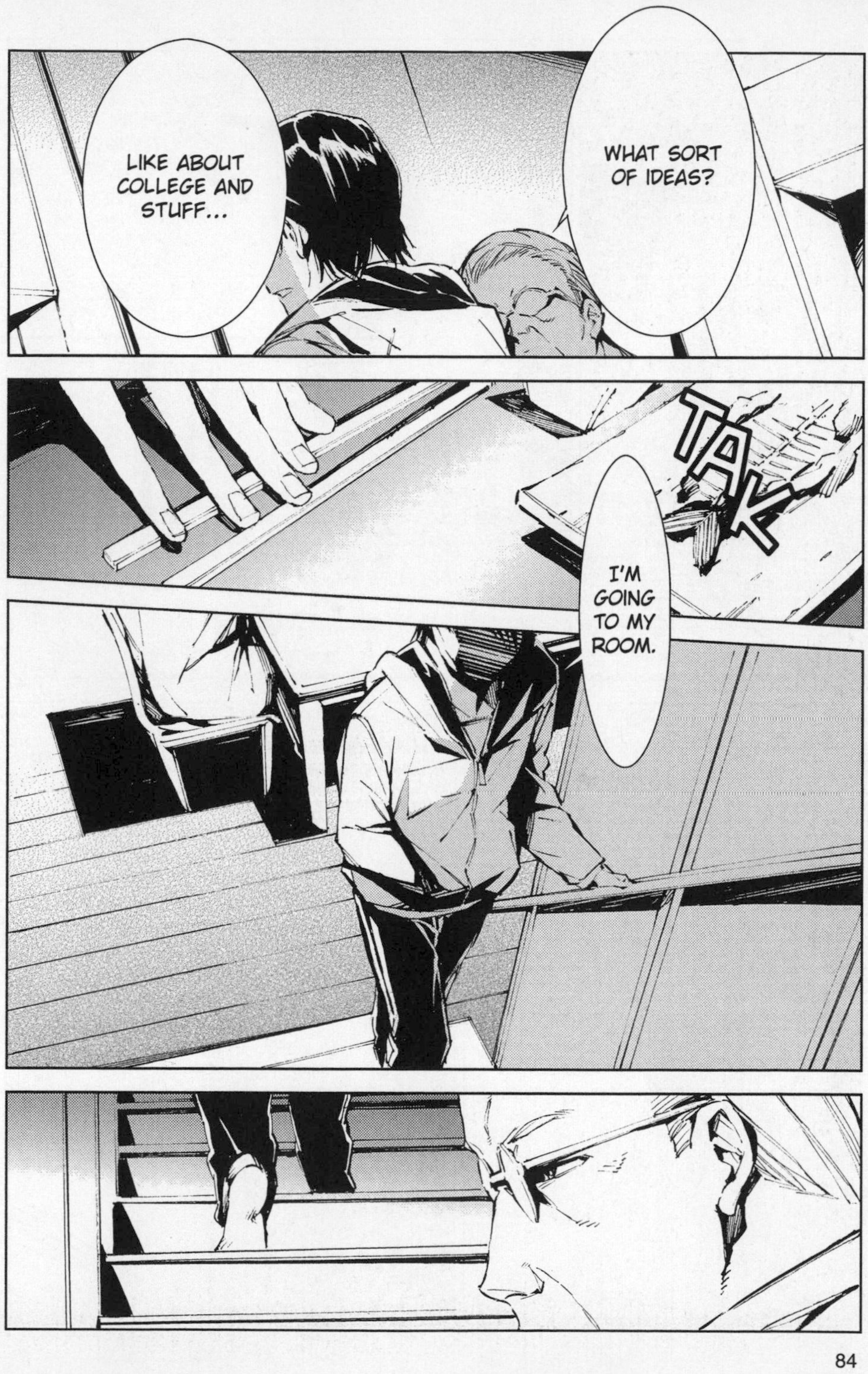
WHAT SORT OF IDEAS?
LIKE ABOUT COLLEGE AND STUFF...
TAK
I'M GOING TO MY ROOM.

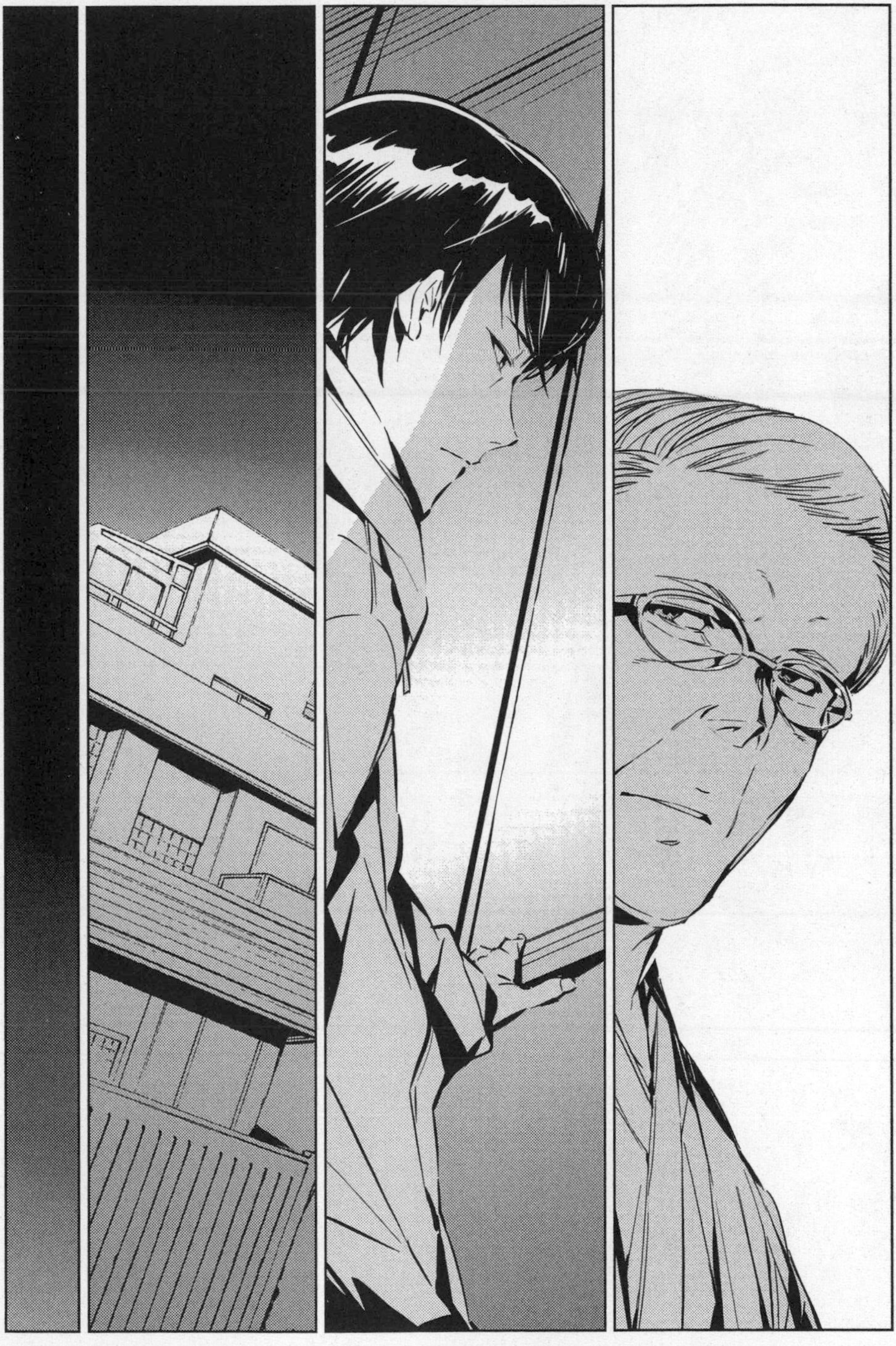

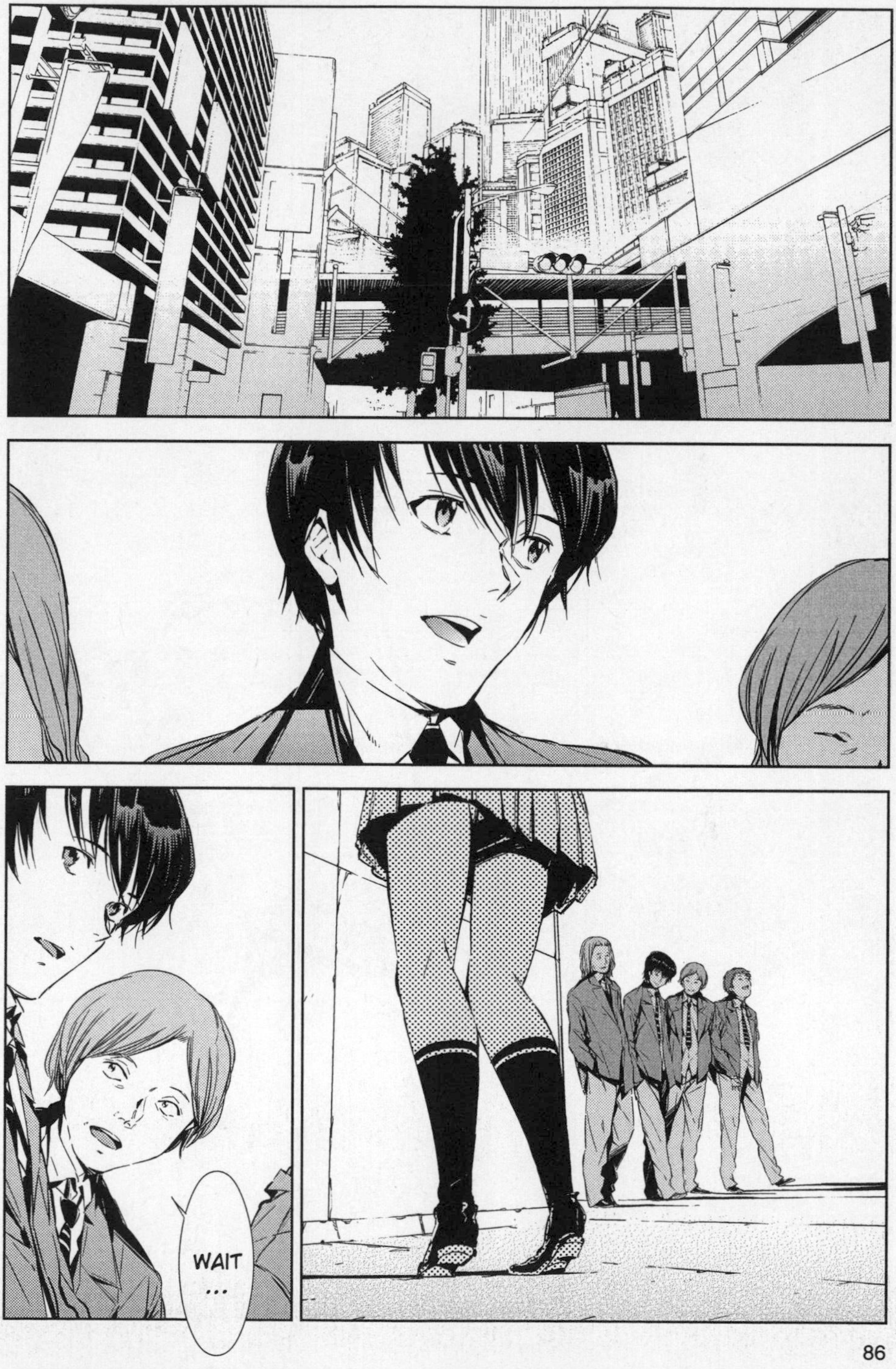
WAIT ...

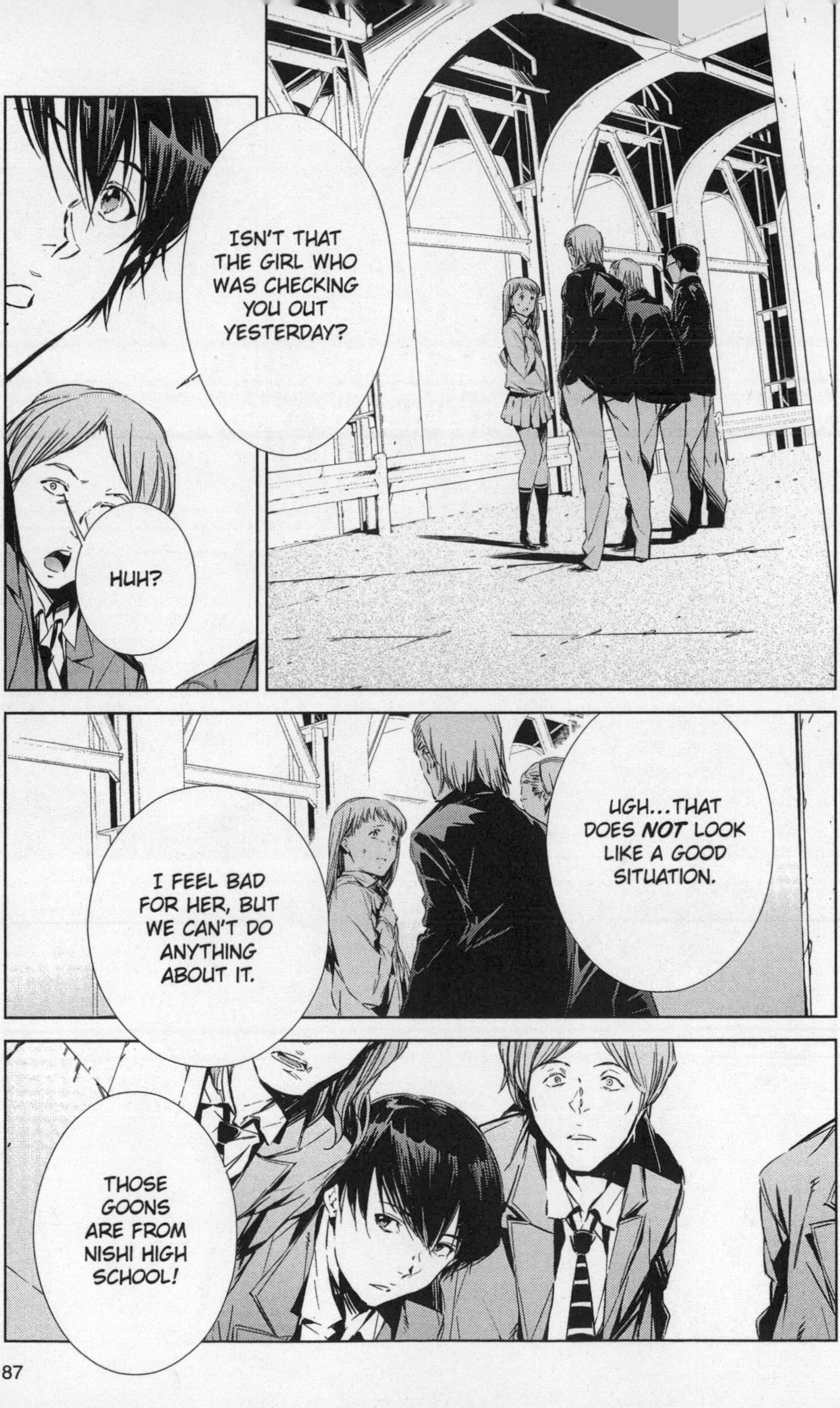
ISN'T THAT THE GIRL WHO WAS CHECKING YOU OUT YESTERDAY?
HUH?
UGH...THAT DOES *NOT* LOOK LIKE A GOOD SITUATION.
I FEEL BAD FOR HER, BUT WE CAN'T DO ANYTHING ABOUT IT.
THOSE GOONS ARE FROM NISHI HIGH SCHOOL!

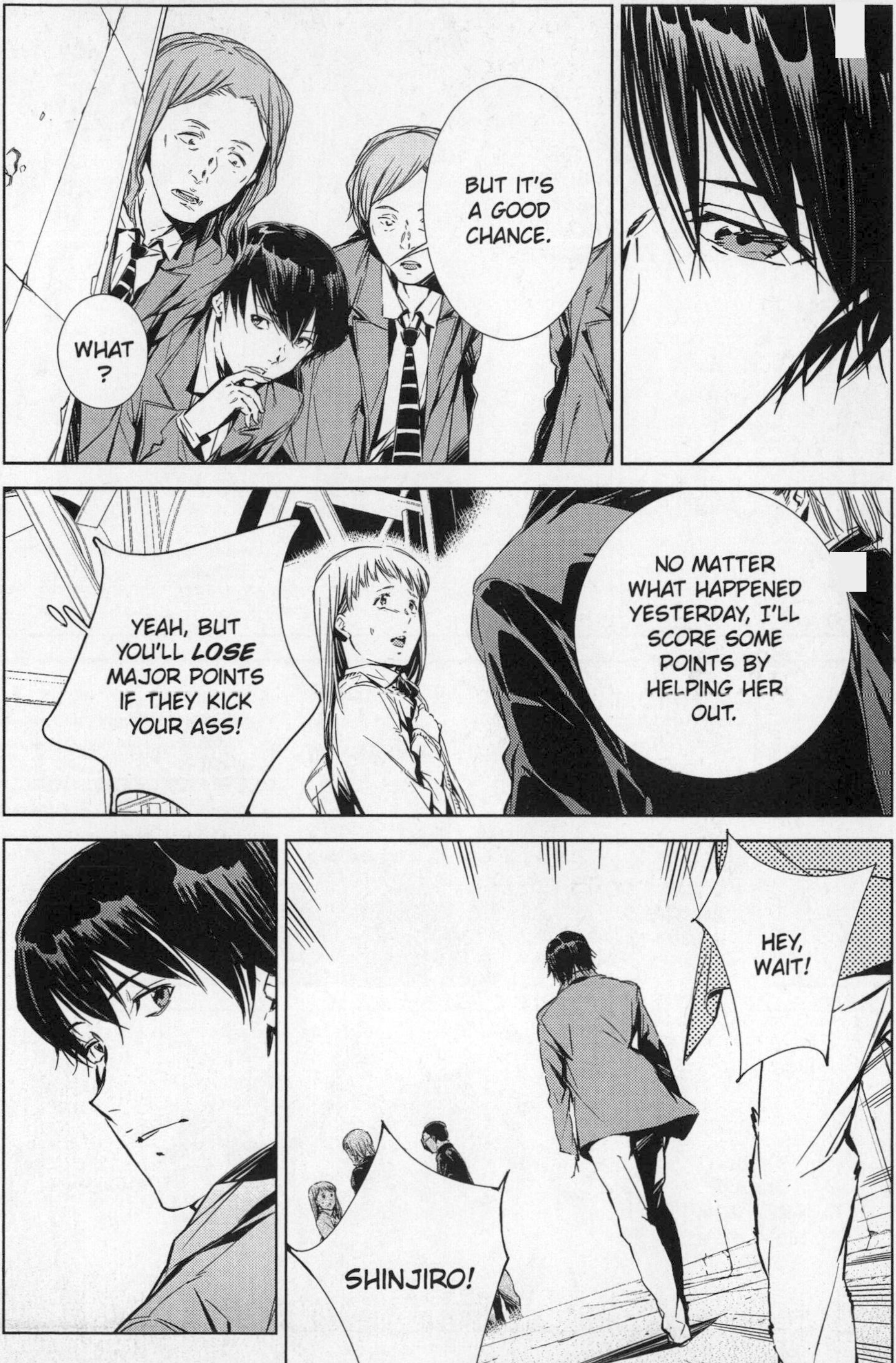
BUT IT'S A GOOD CHANCE.
WHAT ?
NO MATTER WHAT HAPPENED YESTERDAY, I'LL SCORE SOME POINTS BY HELPING HER OUT.
YEAH, BUT YOU'LL ***LOSE*** MAJOR POINTS IF THEY KICK YOUR ASS!
HEY, WAIT!
SHINJIRO!

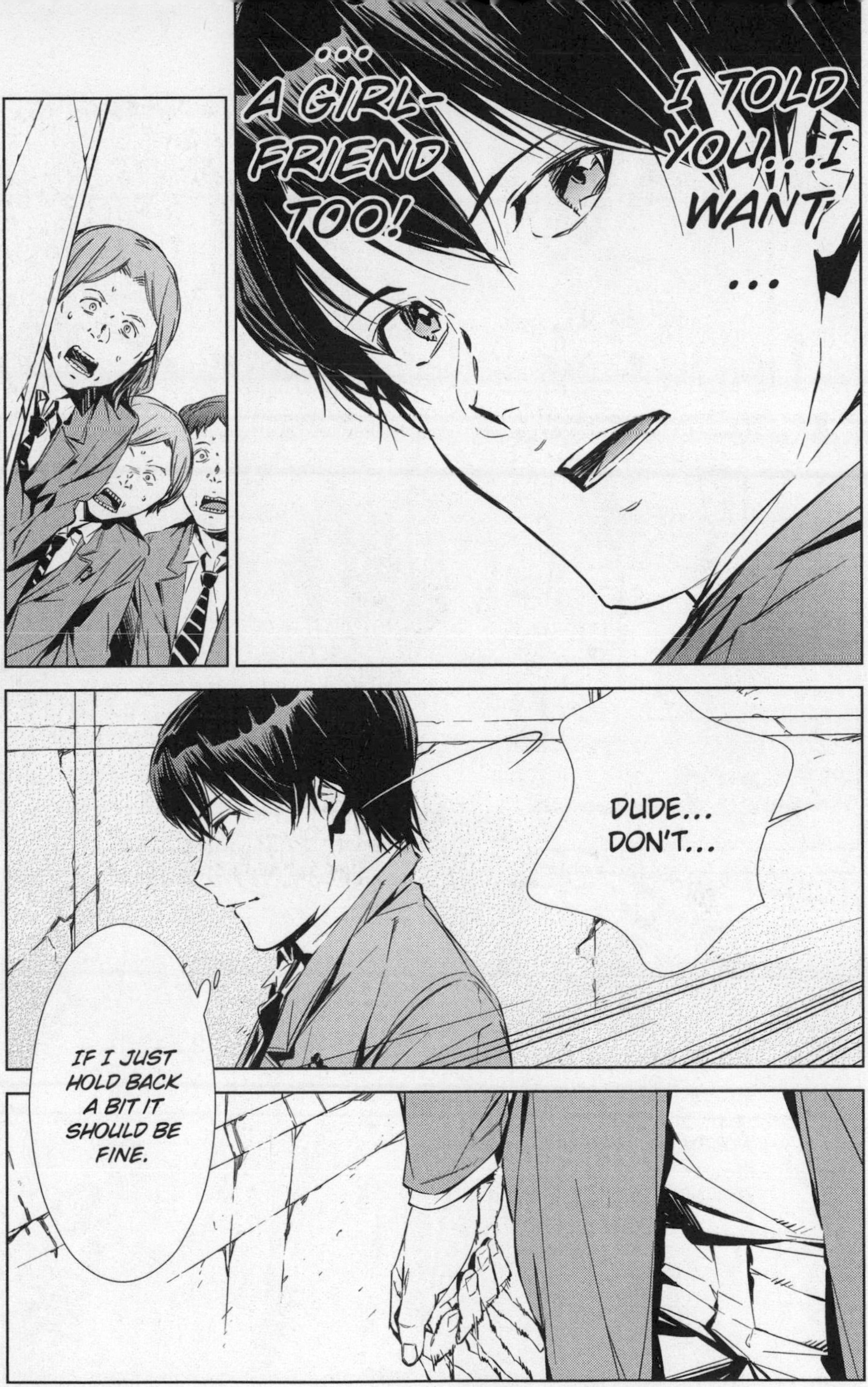
I TOLD YOU...I WANT ...
...A GIRL-FRIEND TOO!
DUDE... DON'T...
IF I JUST HOLD BACK A BIT IT SHOULD BE FINE.

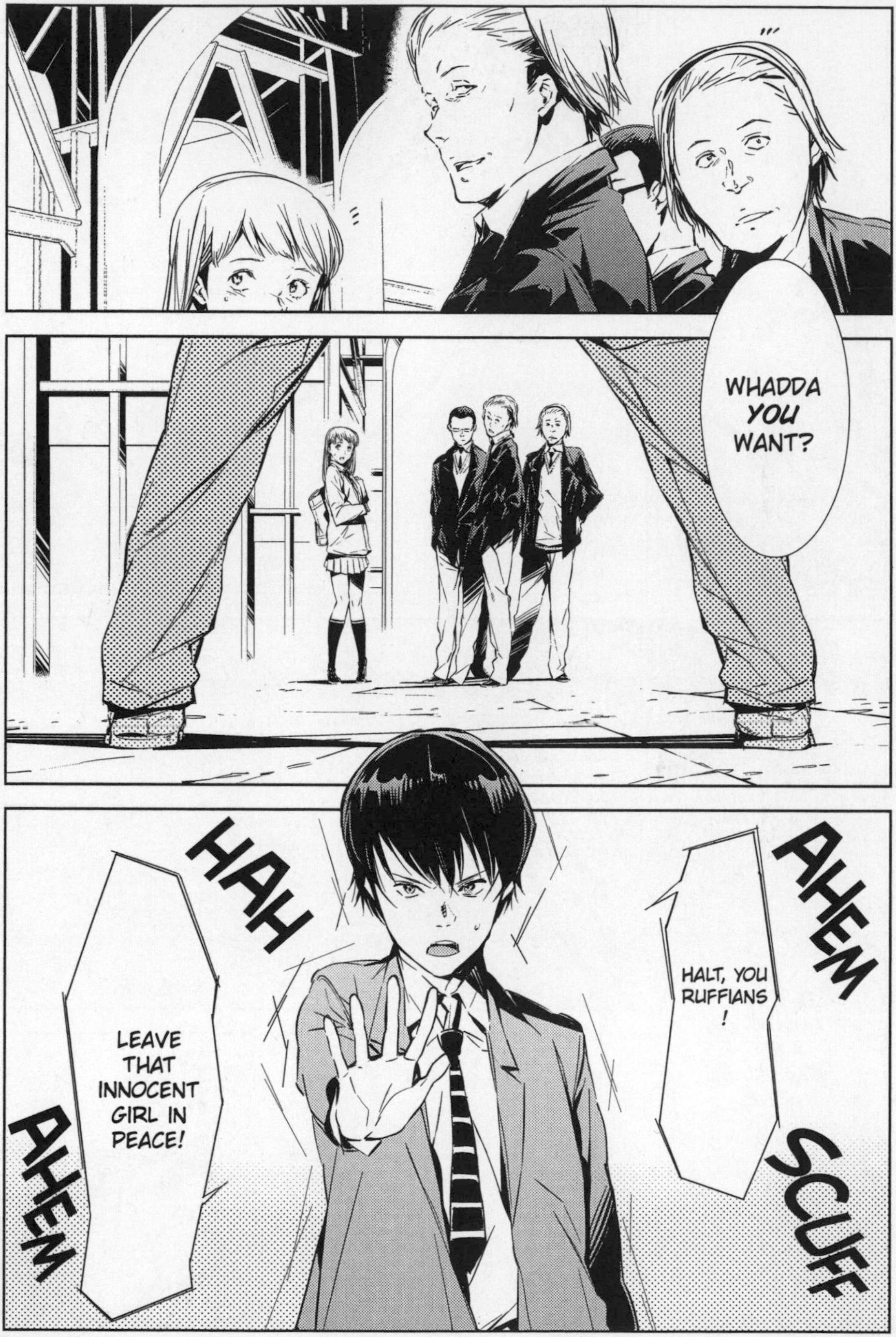
WHADDA YOU WANT?
AHEM
HALT, YOU RUFFIANS!
SCUFF
HAH
LEAVE THAT INNOCENT GIRL IN PEACE!
AHEM

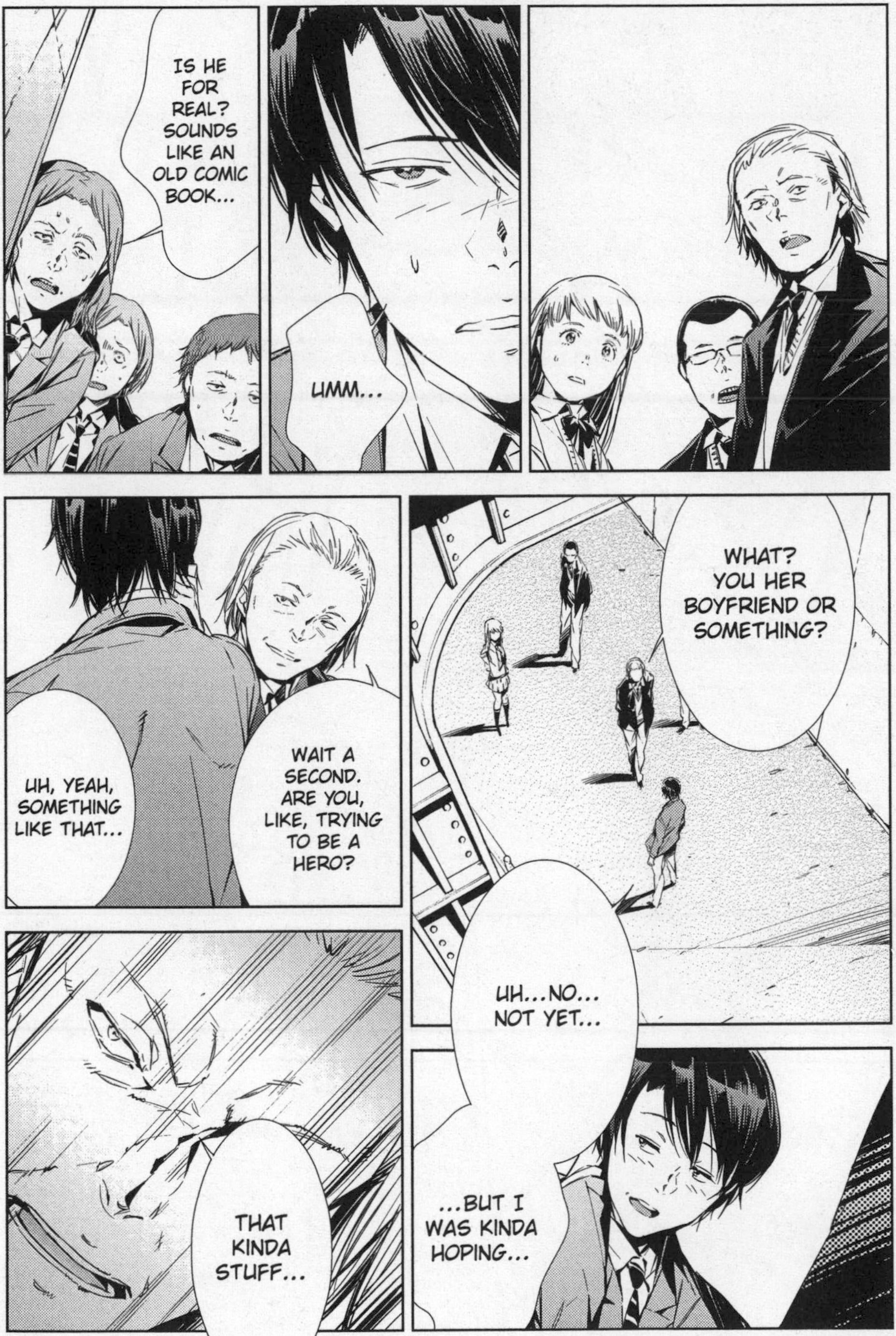
UMM...
IS HE FOR REAL? SOUNDS LIKE AN OLD COMIC BOOK...
WHAT? YOU HER BOYFRIEND OR SOMETHING?
UH...NO... NOT YET...
...BUT I WAS KINDA HOPING...
WAIT A SECOND. ARE YOU, LIKE, TRYING TO BE A HERO?
UH, YEAH, SOMETHING LIKE THAT...
THAT KINDA STUFF...

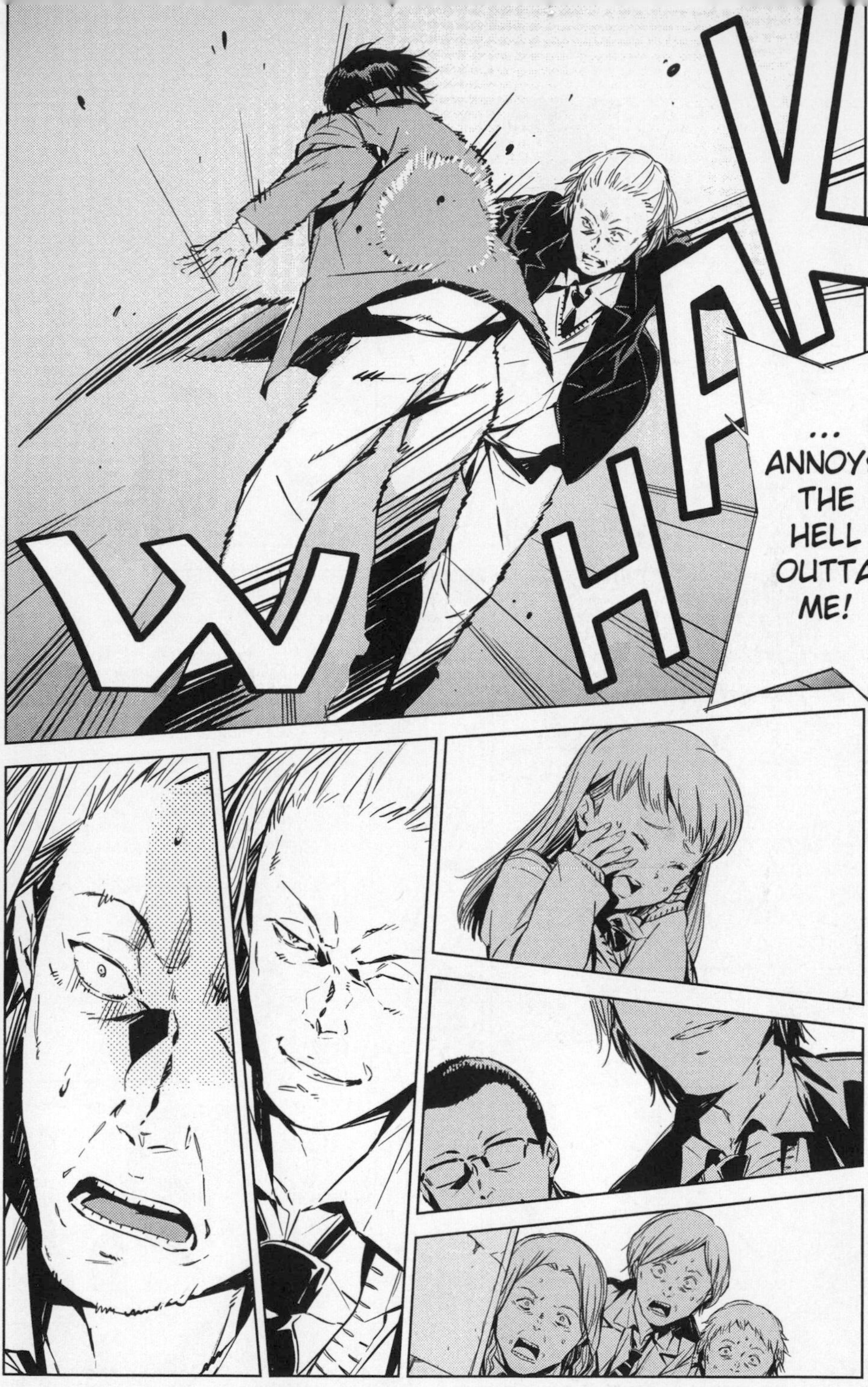
WHAK
... ANNOYS THE HELL OUTTA ME!

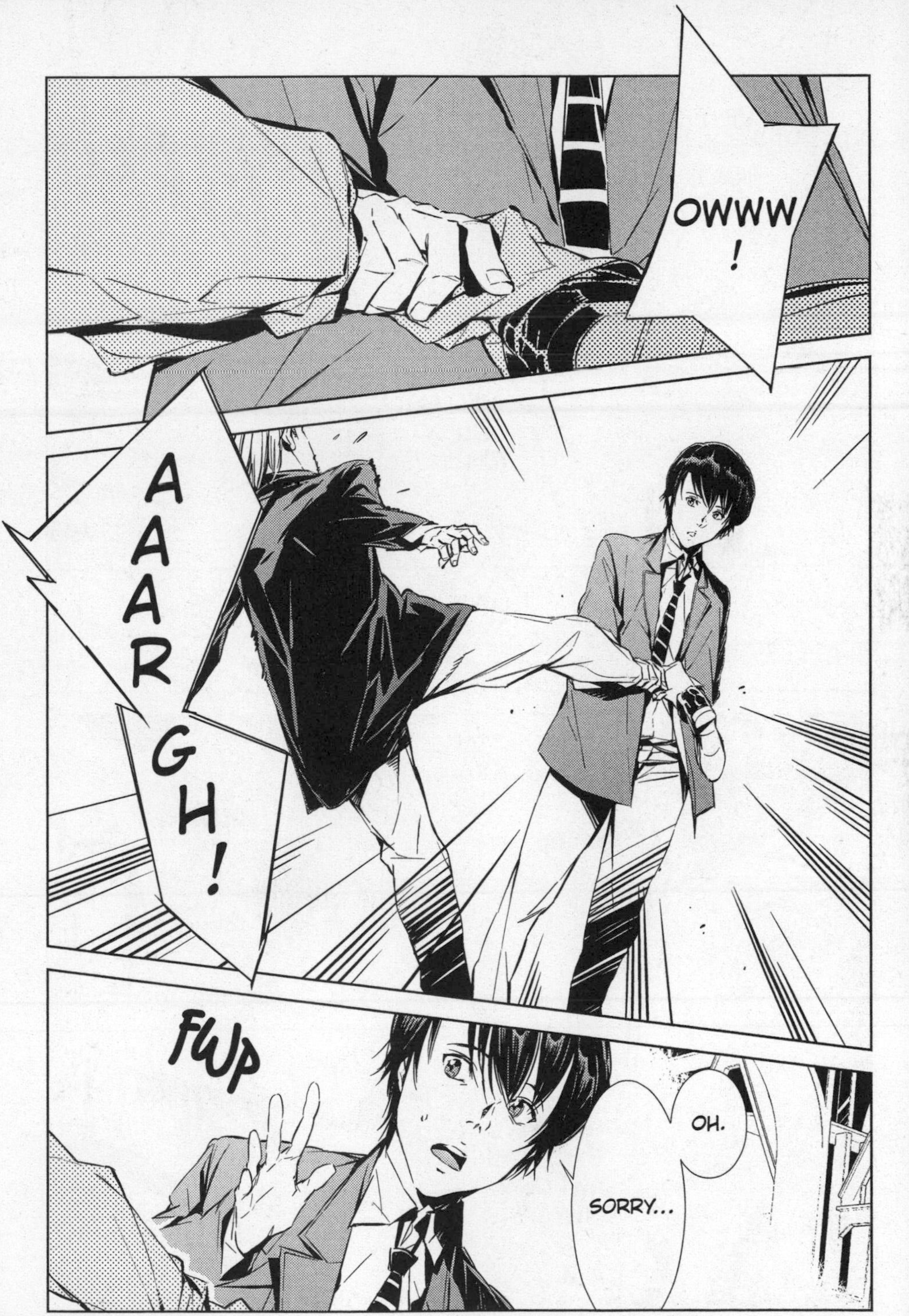
OWWW!
AAARGH!
FWP
OH.
SORRY...

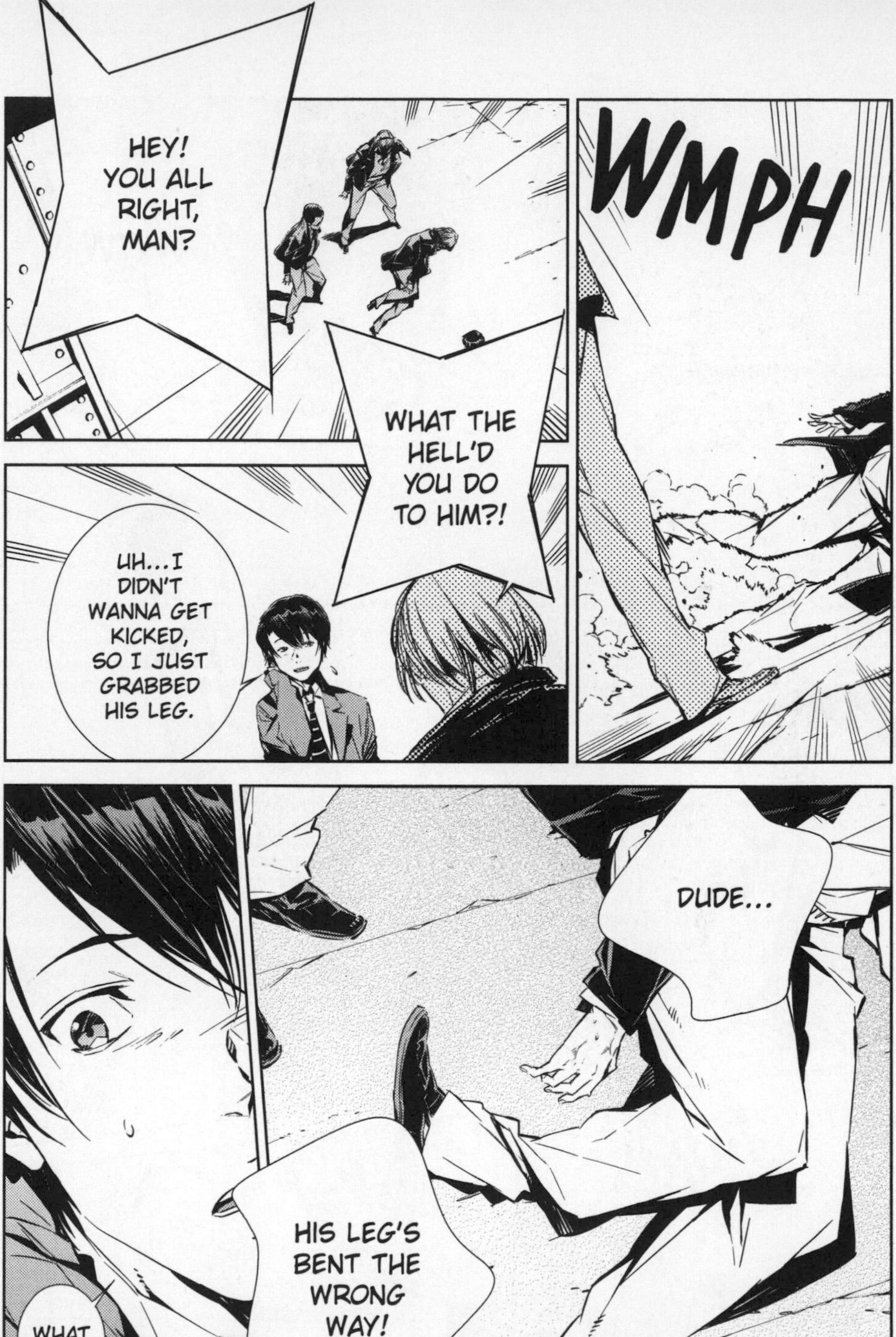
WMPH
HEY! YOU ALL RIGHT, MAN?
WHAT THE HELL'D YOU DO TO HIM?!
UH...I DIDN'T WANNA GET KICKED, SO I JUST GRABBED HIS LEG.
DUDE...
HIS LEG'S BENT THE WRONG WAY!
WHAT?

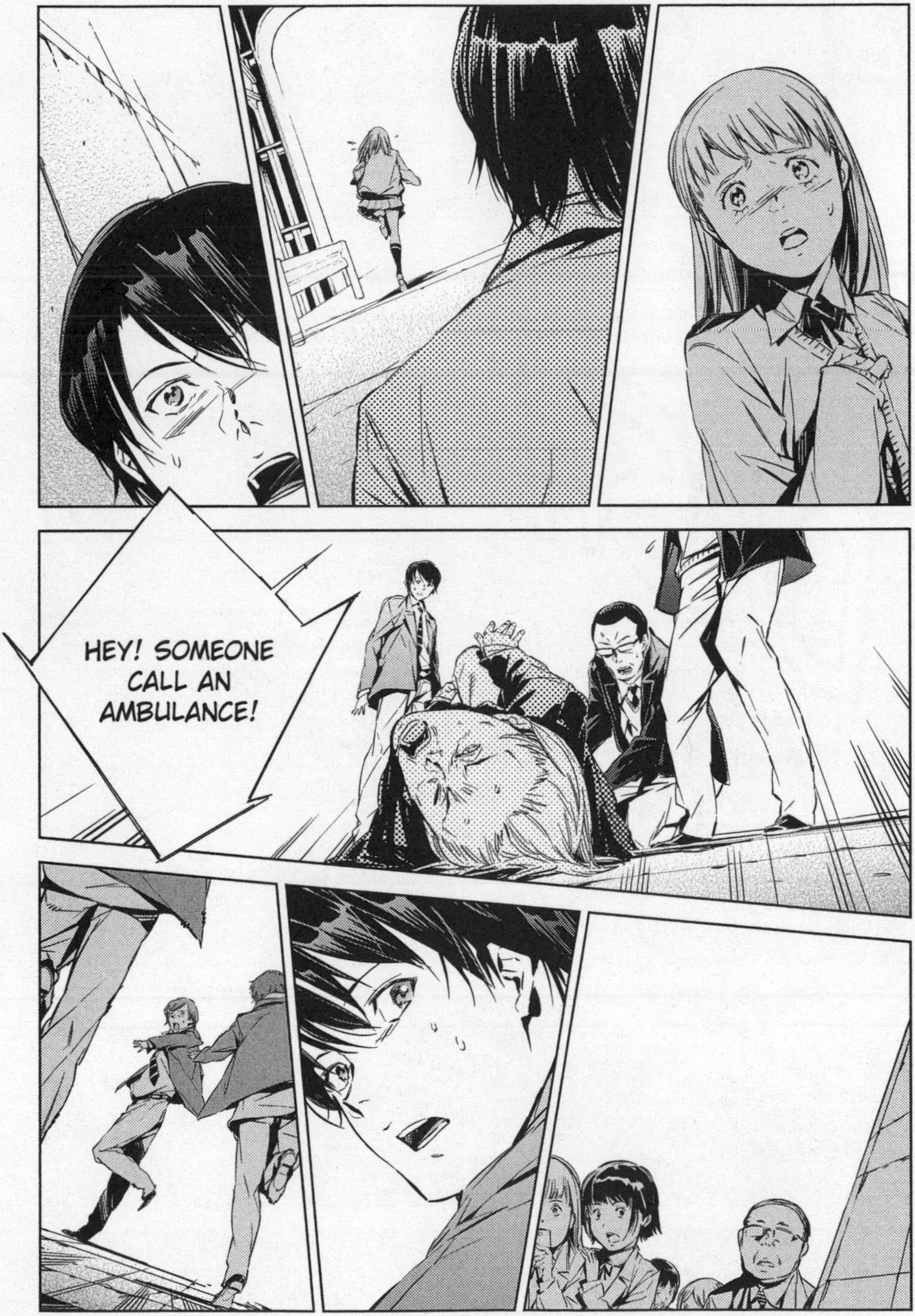
HEY! SOMEONE CALL AN AMBULANCE!

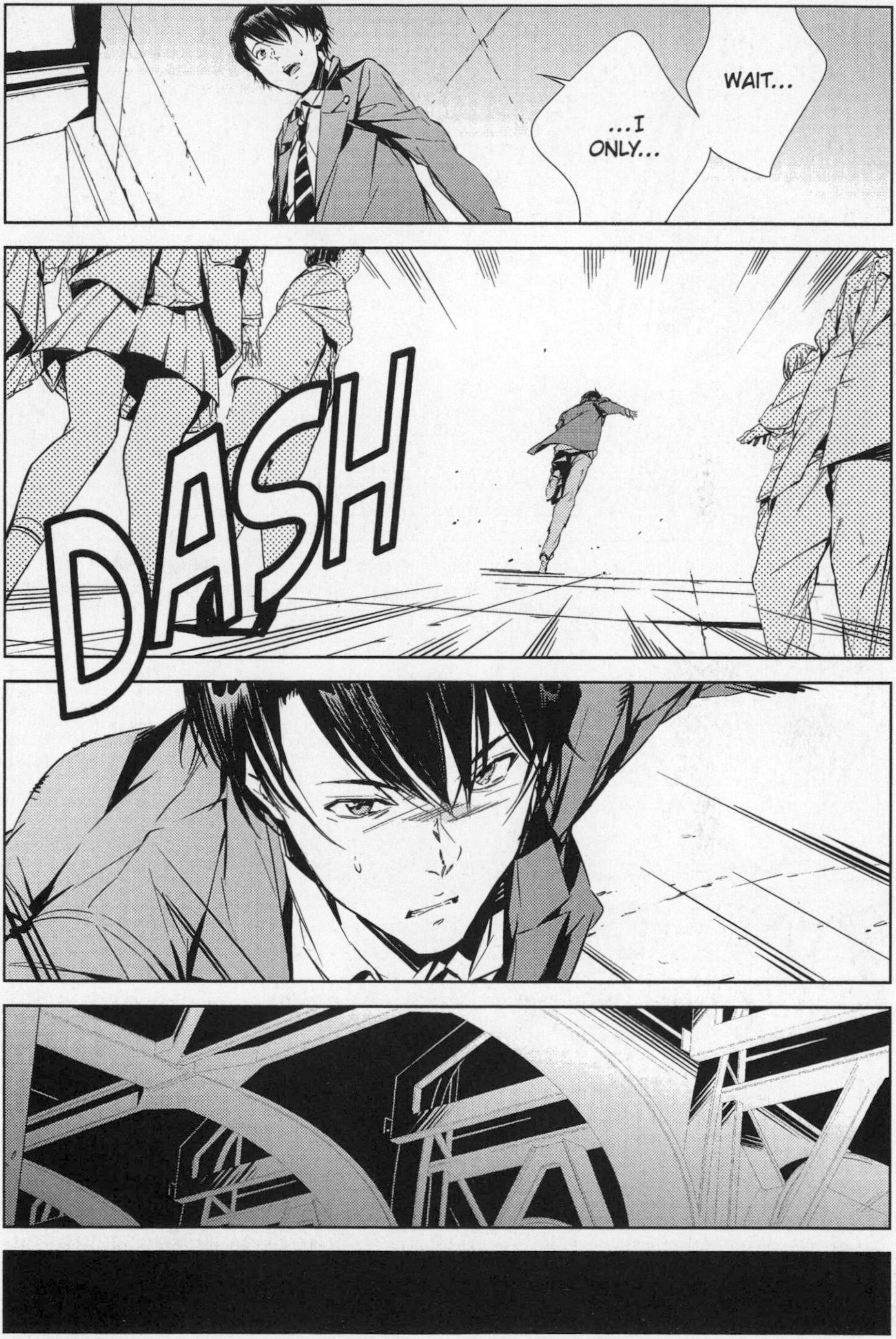
WAIT...
...I ONLY...
DASH

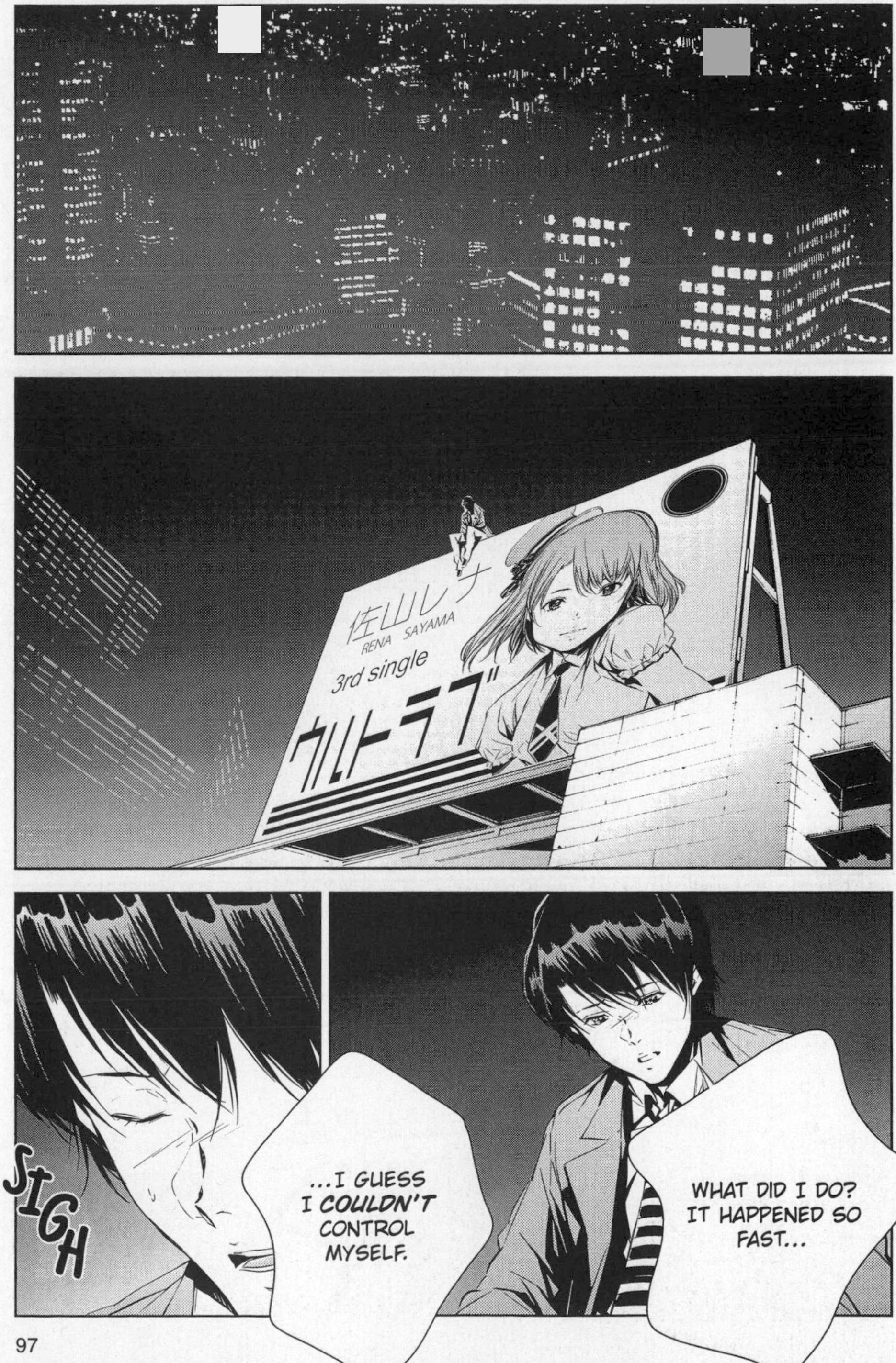
佐山レナ
RENA SAYAMA
3rd single
ウルトラブ
WHAT DID I DO? IT HAPPENED SO FAST...
...I GUESS I COULDN'T CONTROL MYSELF.
SIGH

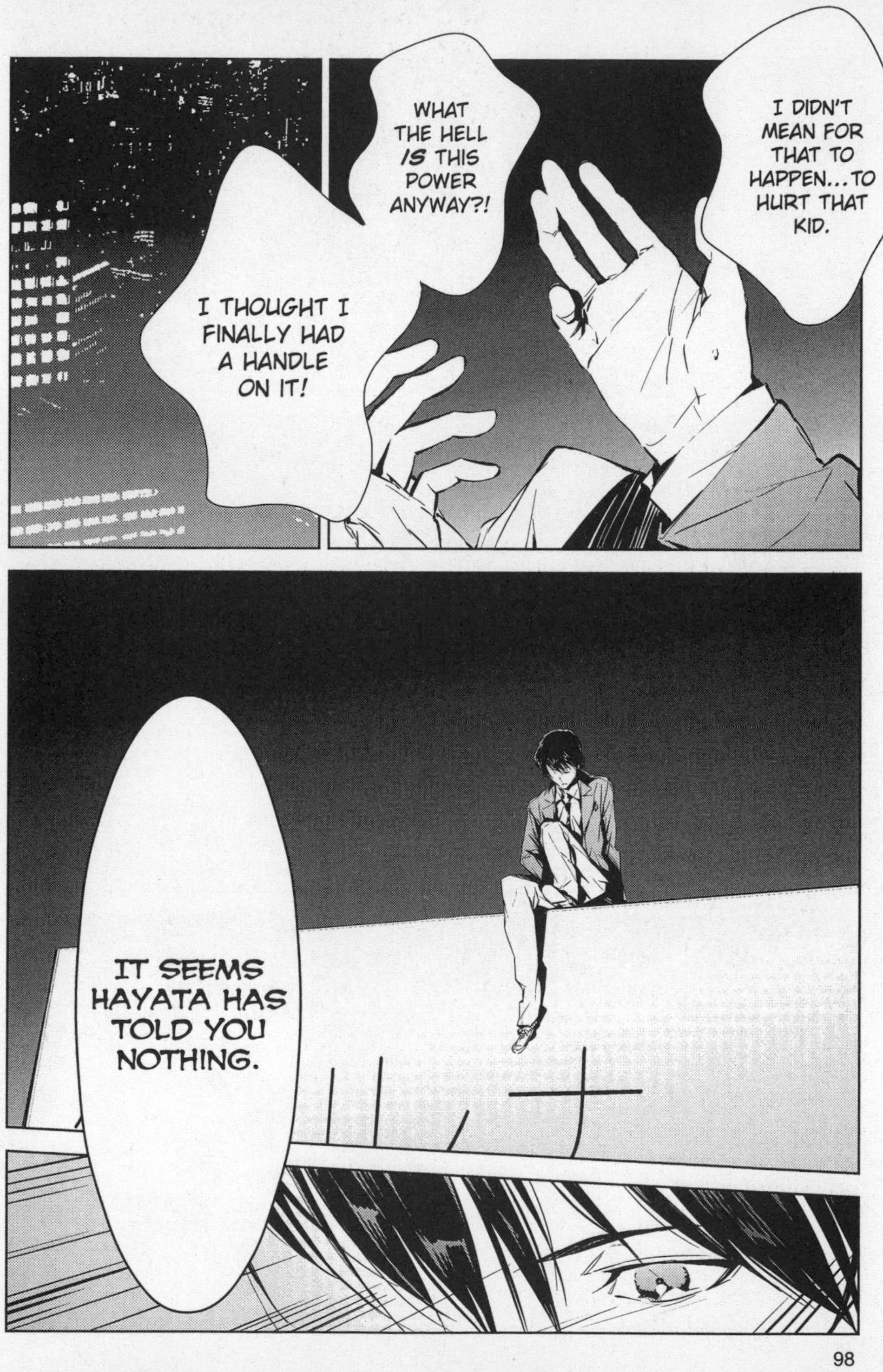
I DIDN'T MEAN FOR THAT TO HAPPEN...TO HURT THAT KID.
WHAT THE HELL *IS* THIS POWER ANYWAY?!
I THOUGHT I FINALLY HAD A HANDLE ON IT!
IT SEEMS HAYATA HAS TOLD YOU NOTHING.

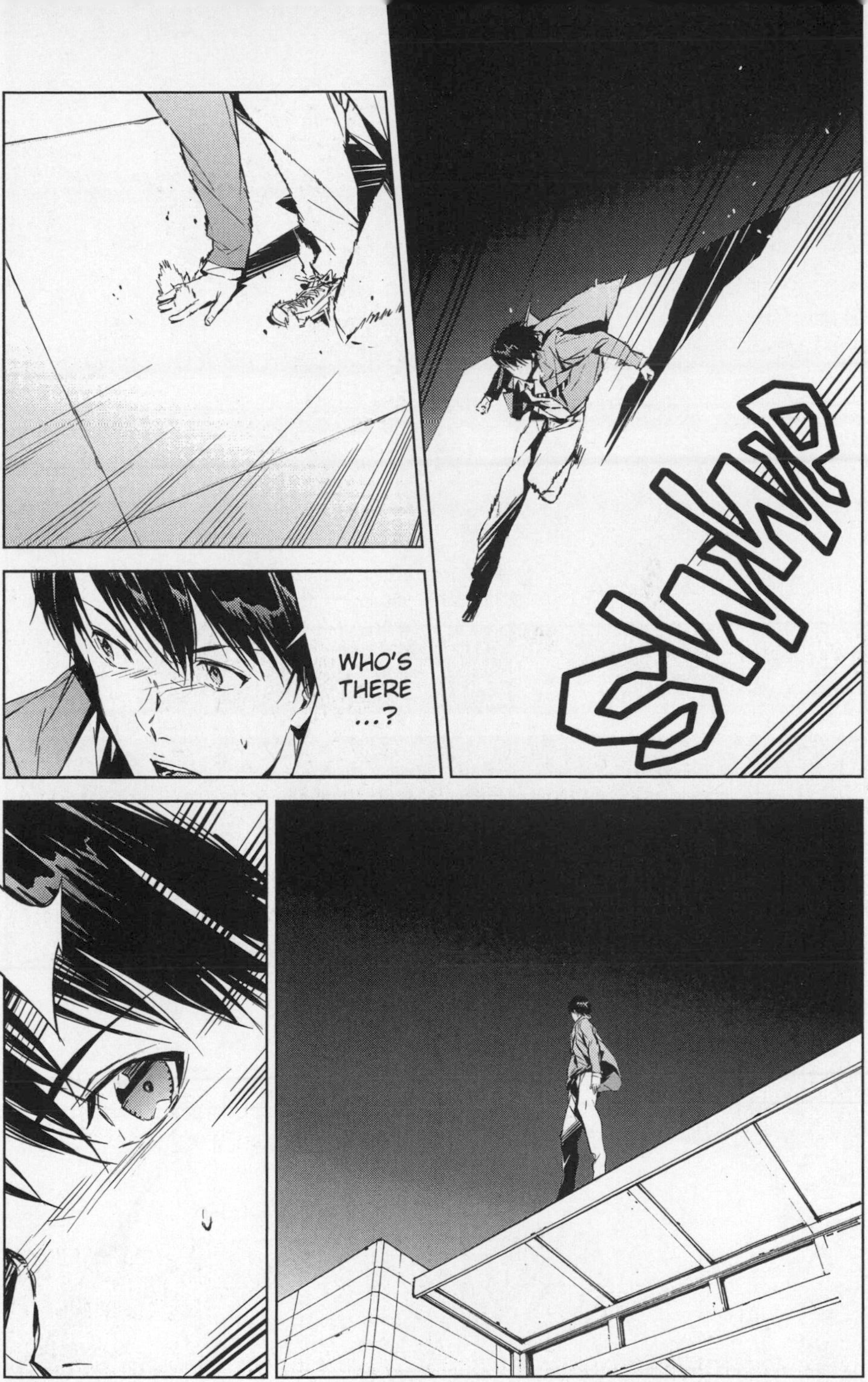
WHO'S THERE ...?

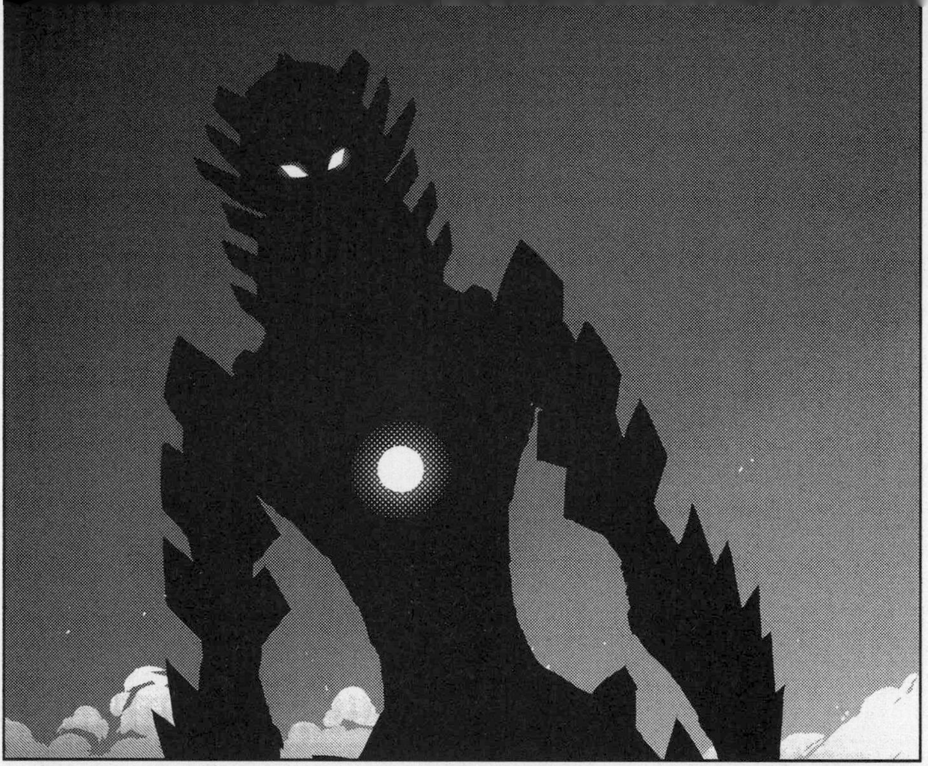
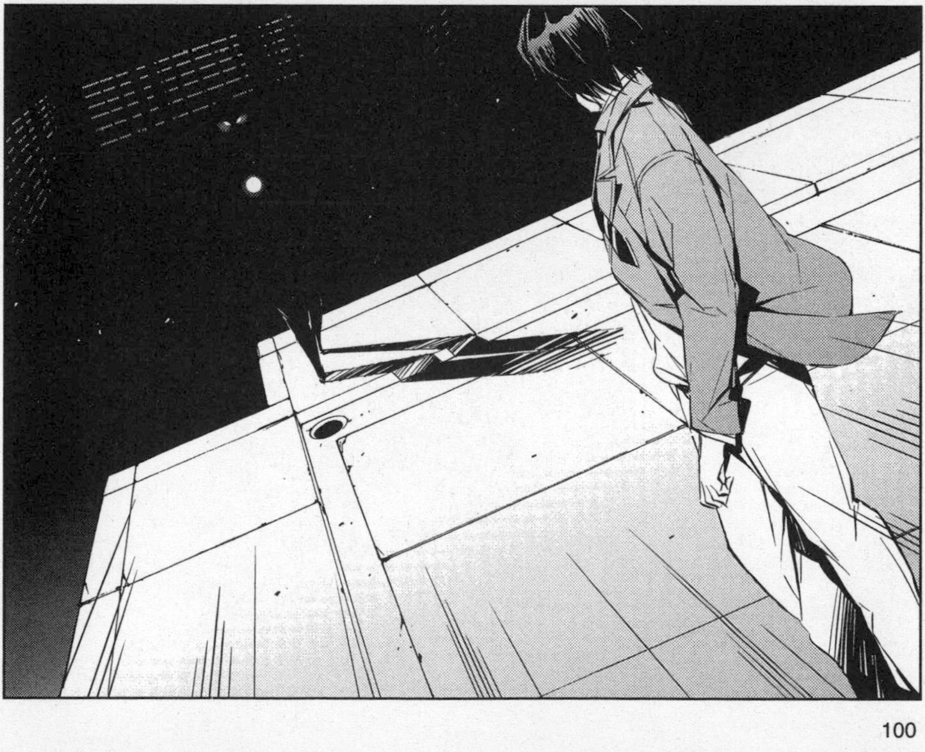

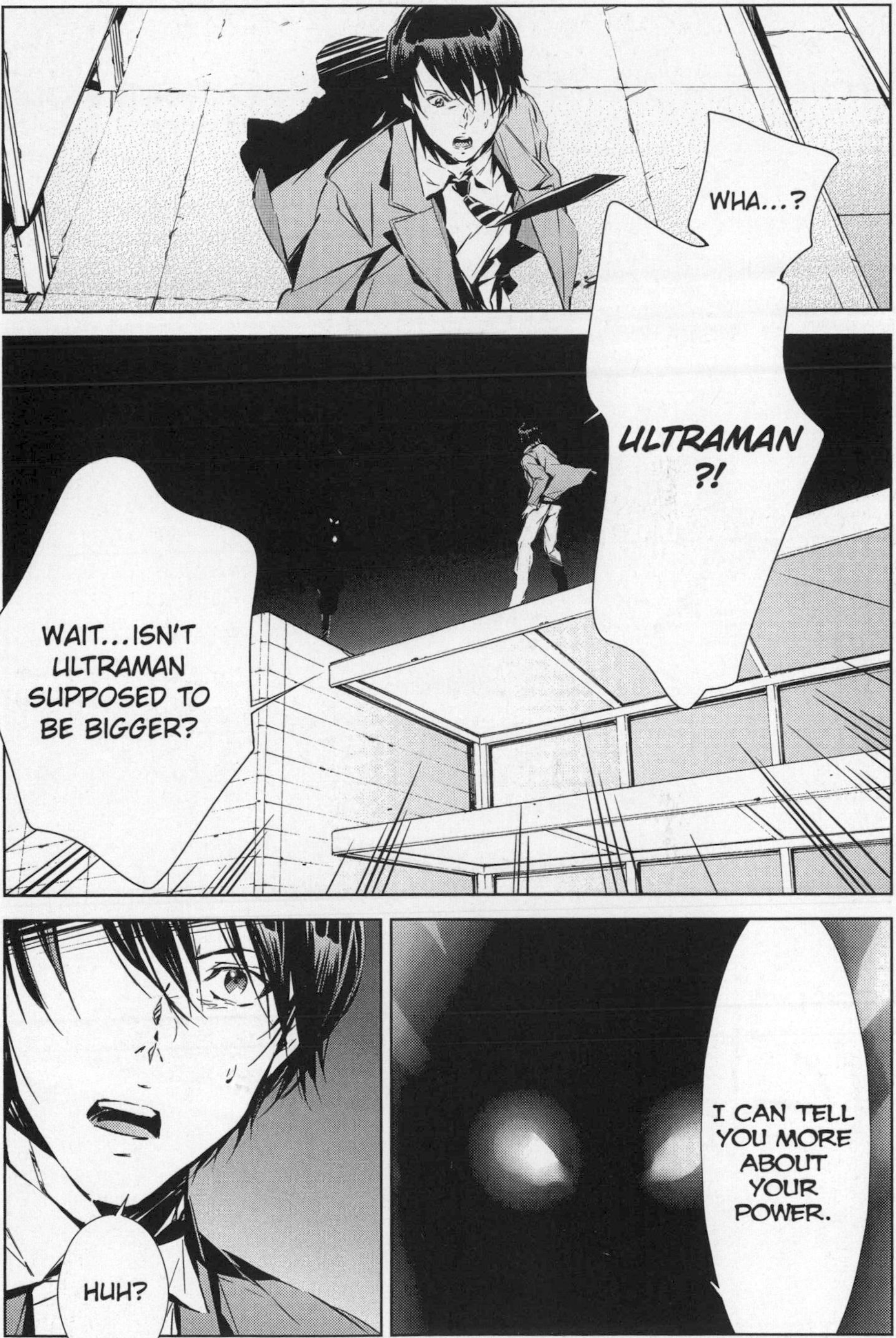
WHA...?
ULTRAMAN ?!
WAIT...ISN'T ULTRAMAN SUPPOSED TO BE BIGGER?
I CAN TELL YOU MORE ABOUT YOUR POWER.
HUH?

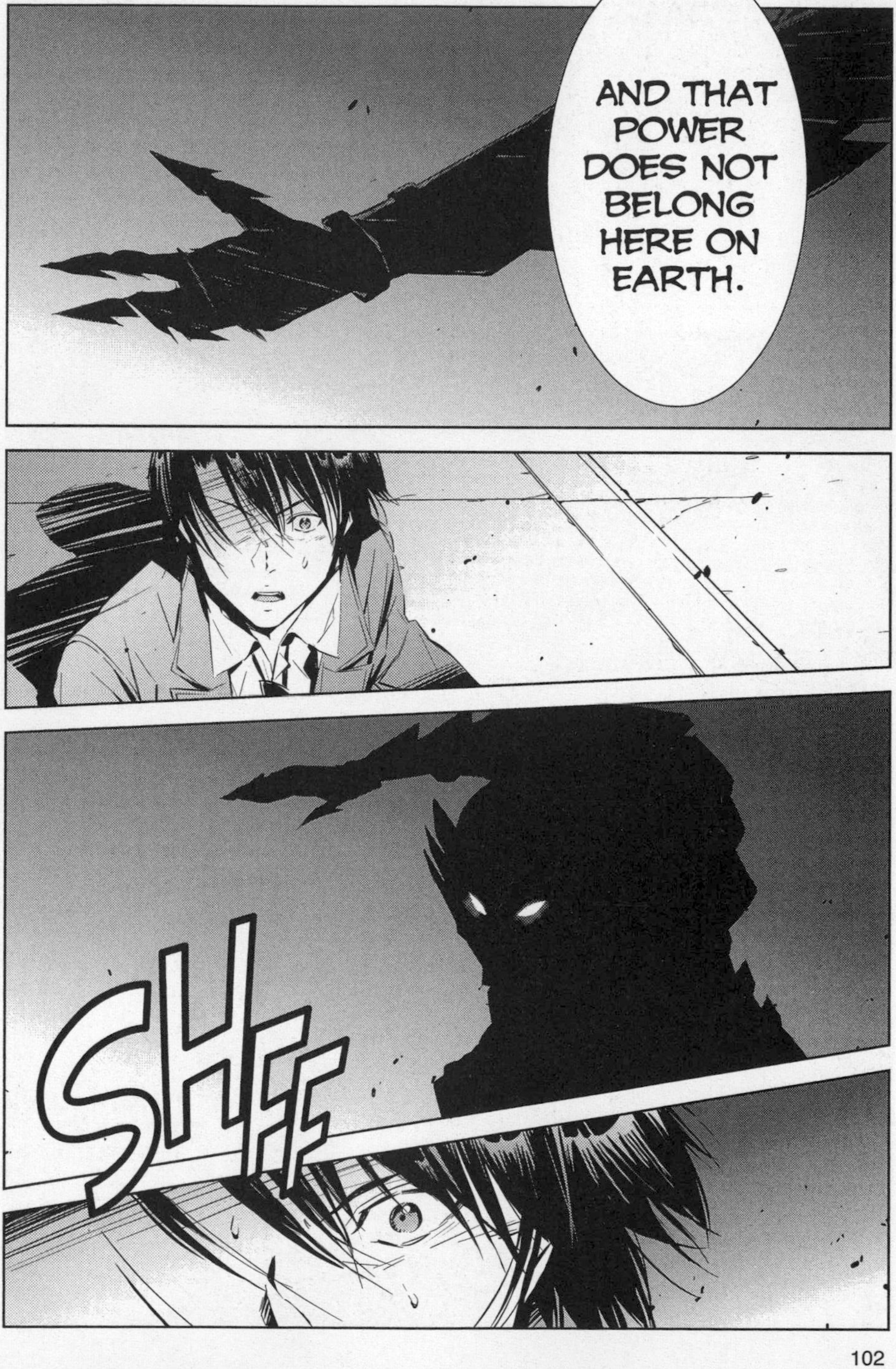
AND THAT POWER DOES NOT BELONG HERE ON EARTH.
SHFF

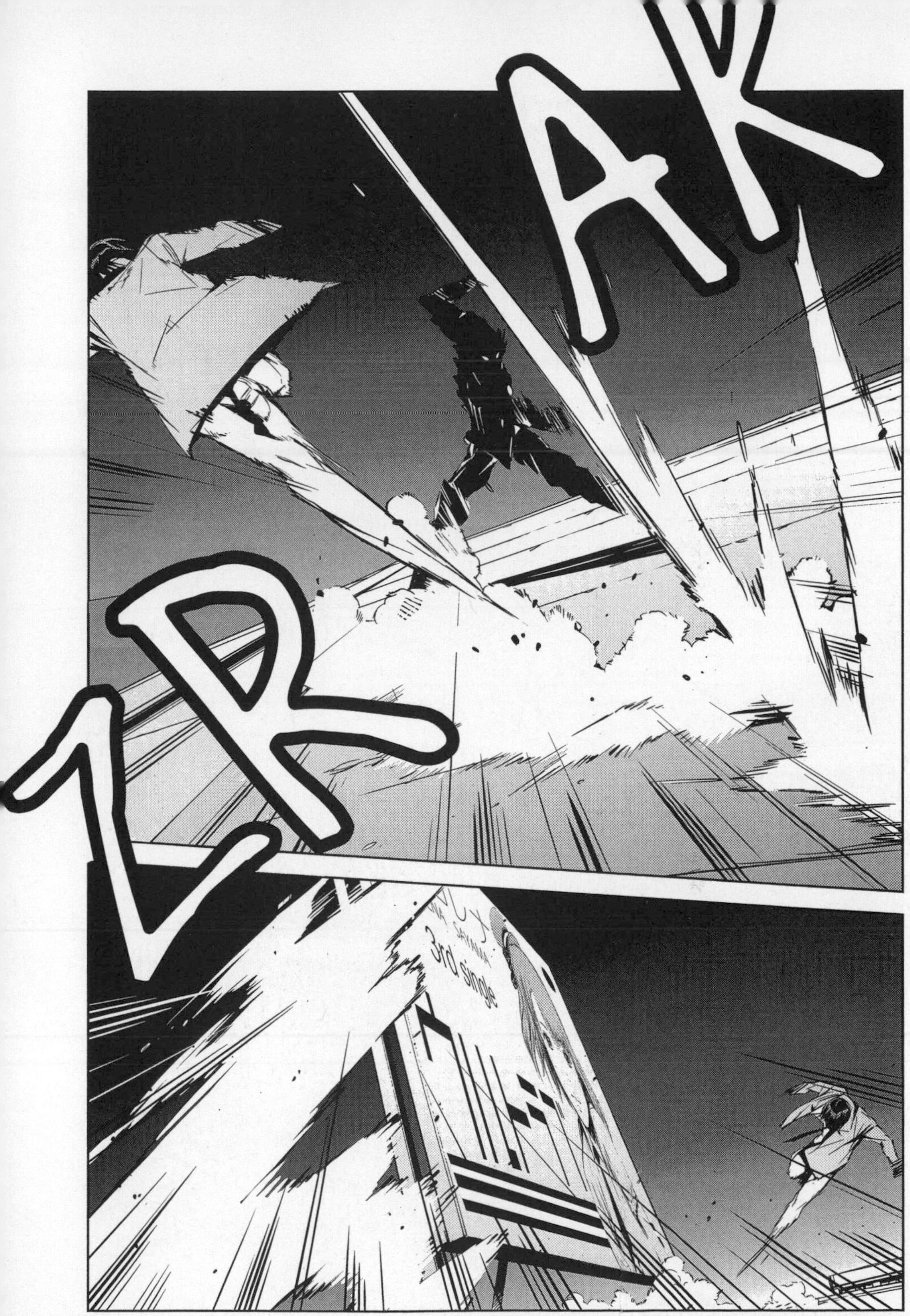
ZRAK
SAYAMA
3rd. single

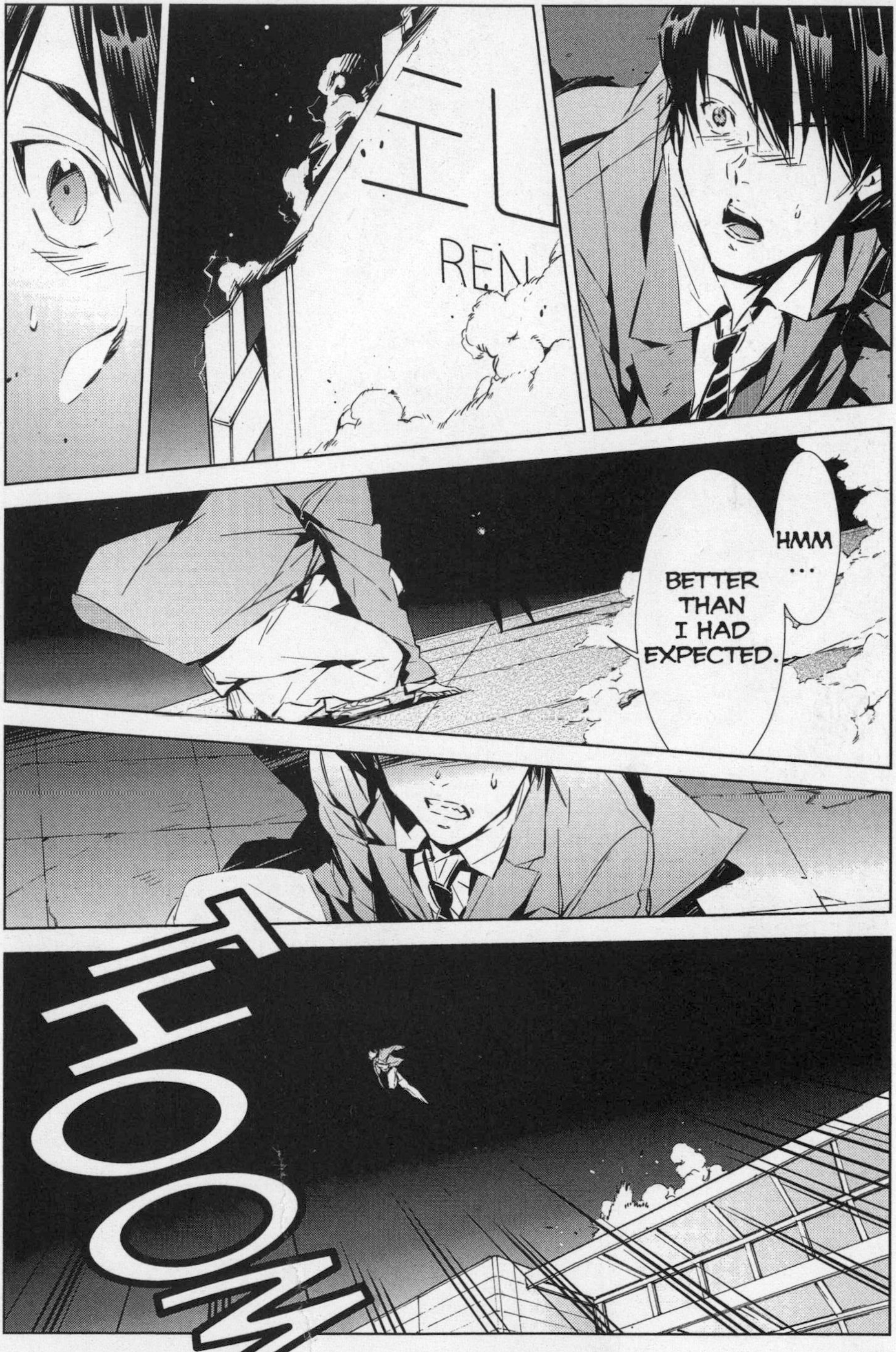
REN
HMM... BETTER THAN I HAD EXPECTED.
THOOM

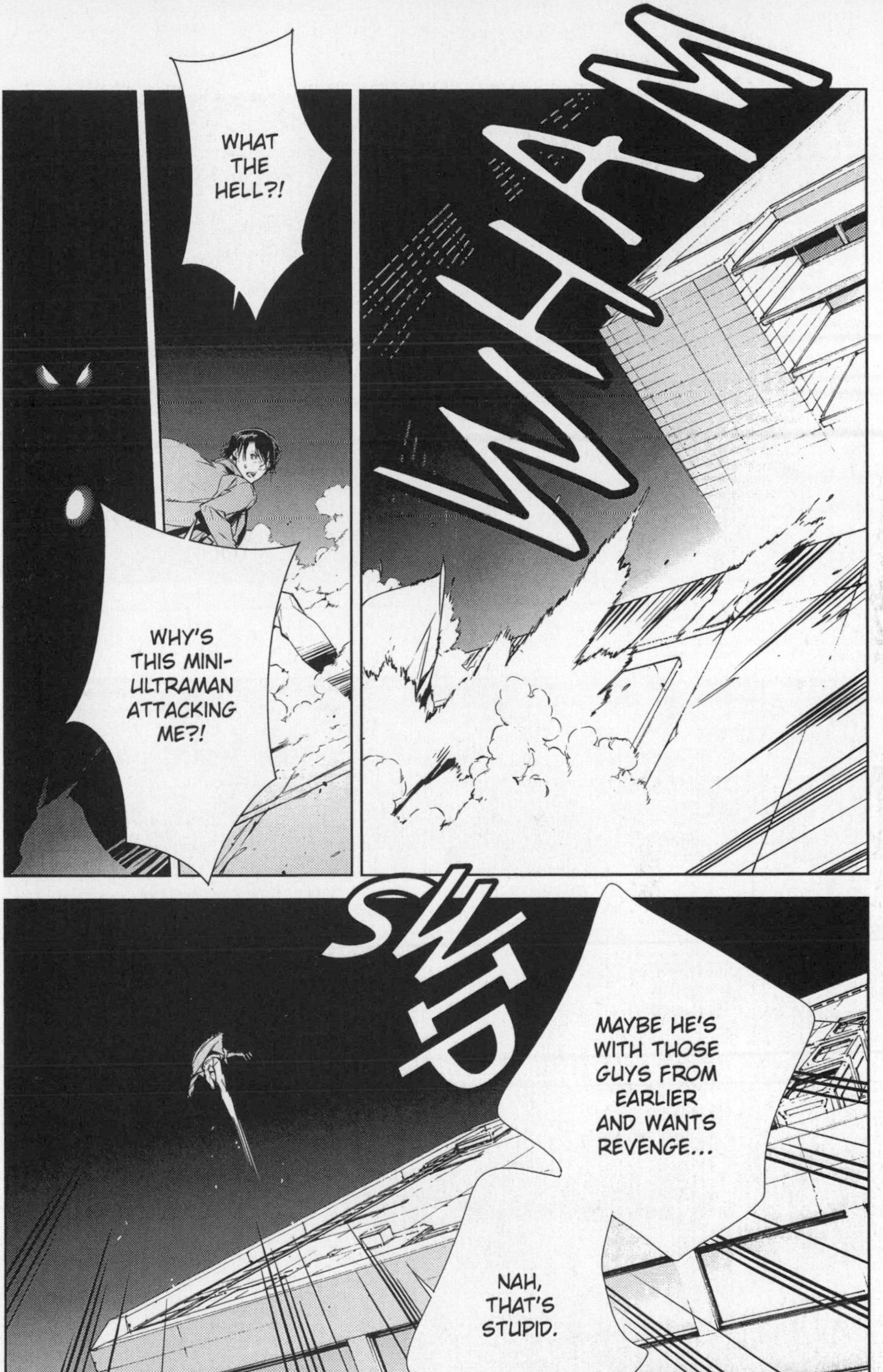
WHAM
WHAT THE HELL?!
WHY'S THIS MINI-ULTRAMAN ATTACKING ME?!
SWIP
MAYBE HE'S WITH THOSE GUYS FROM EARLIER AND WANTS REVENGE...
NAH, THAT'S STUPID.

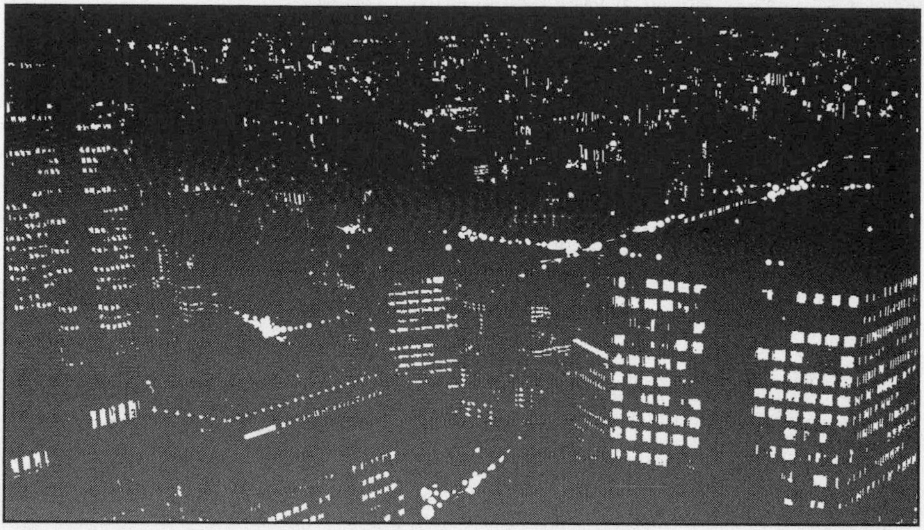
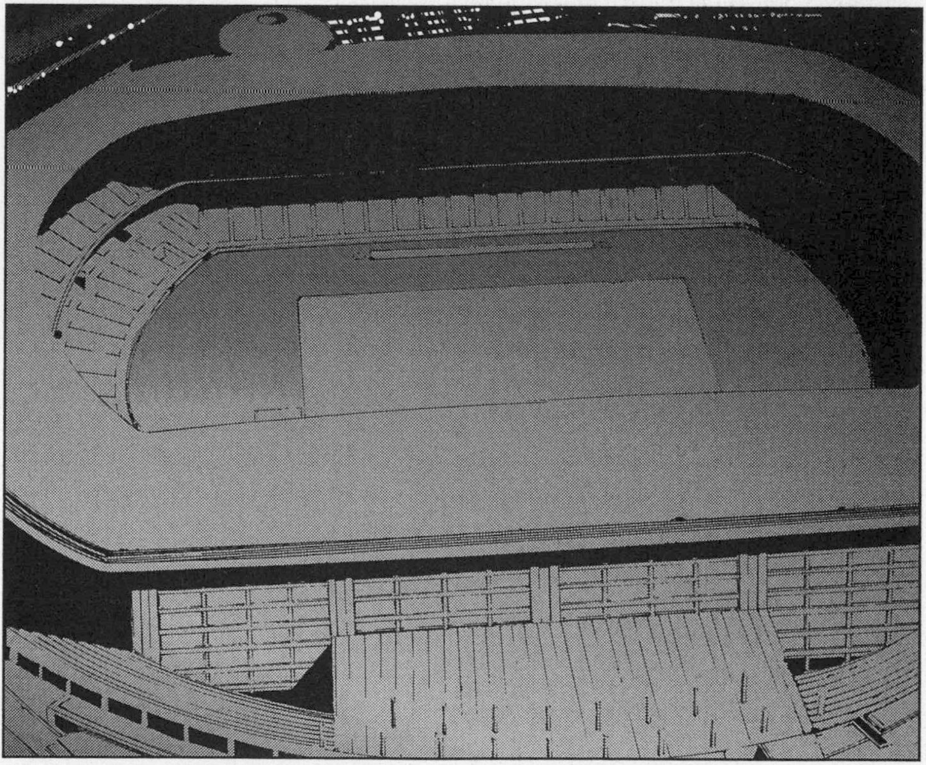

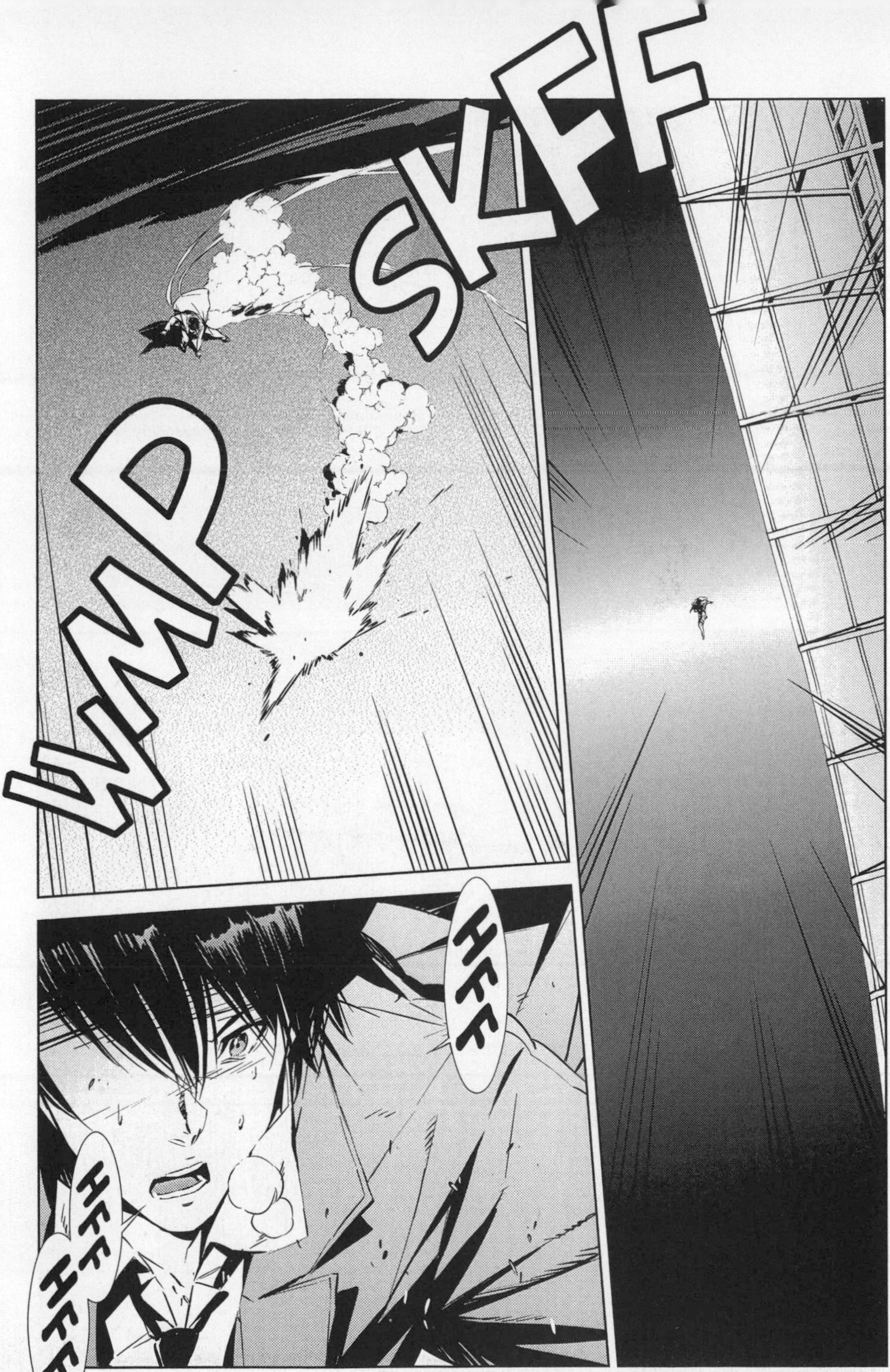
SKFF
WMP
HFF
HFF
HFF HFF

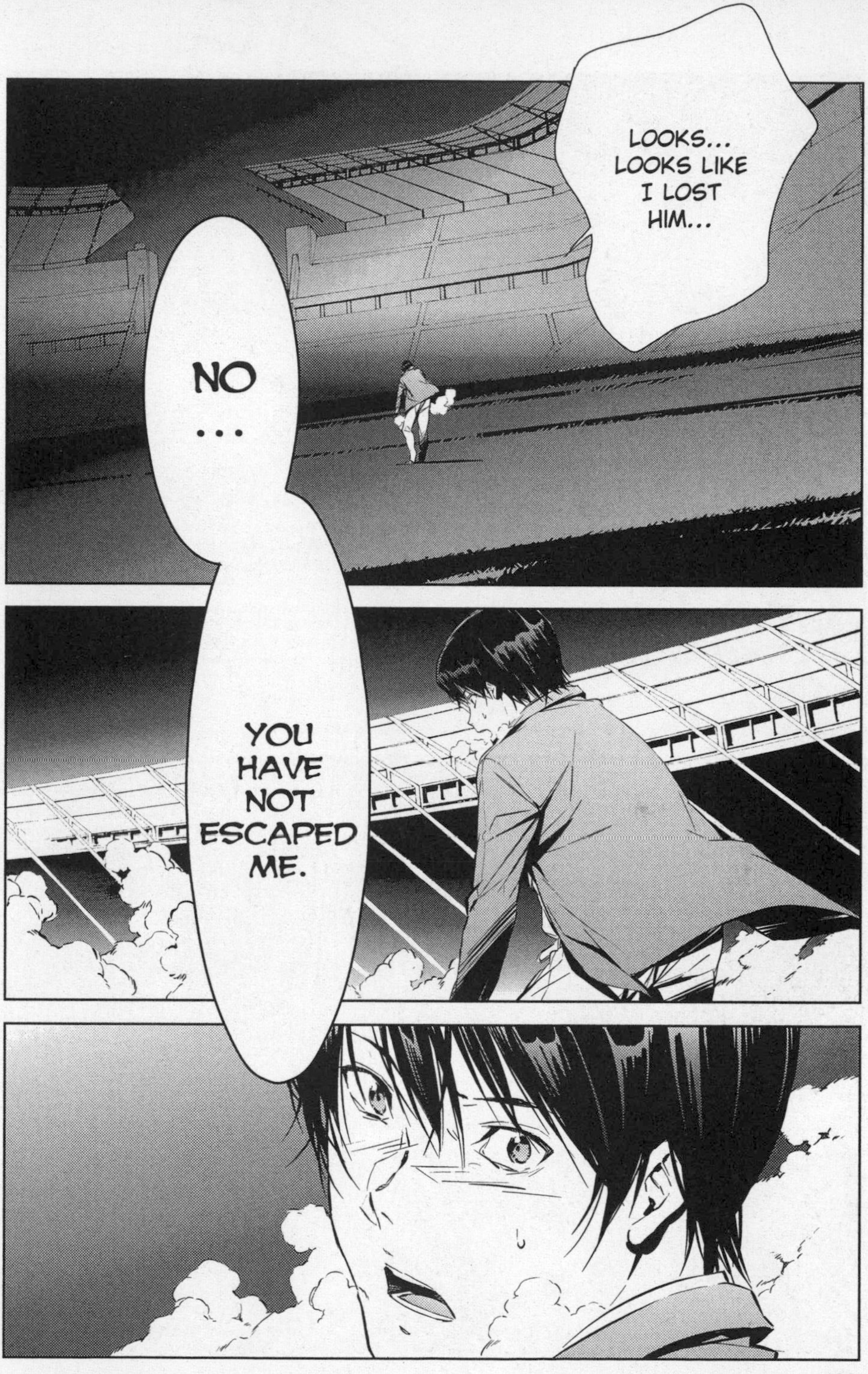
LOOKS... LOOKS LIKE I LOST HIM...
NO ... YOU HAVE NOT ESCAPED ME.

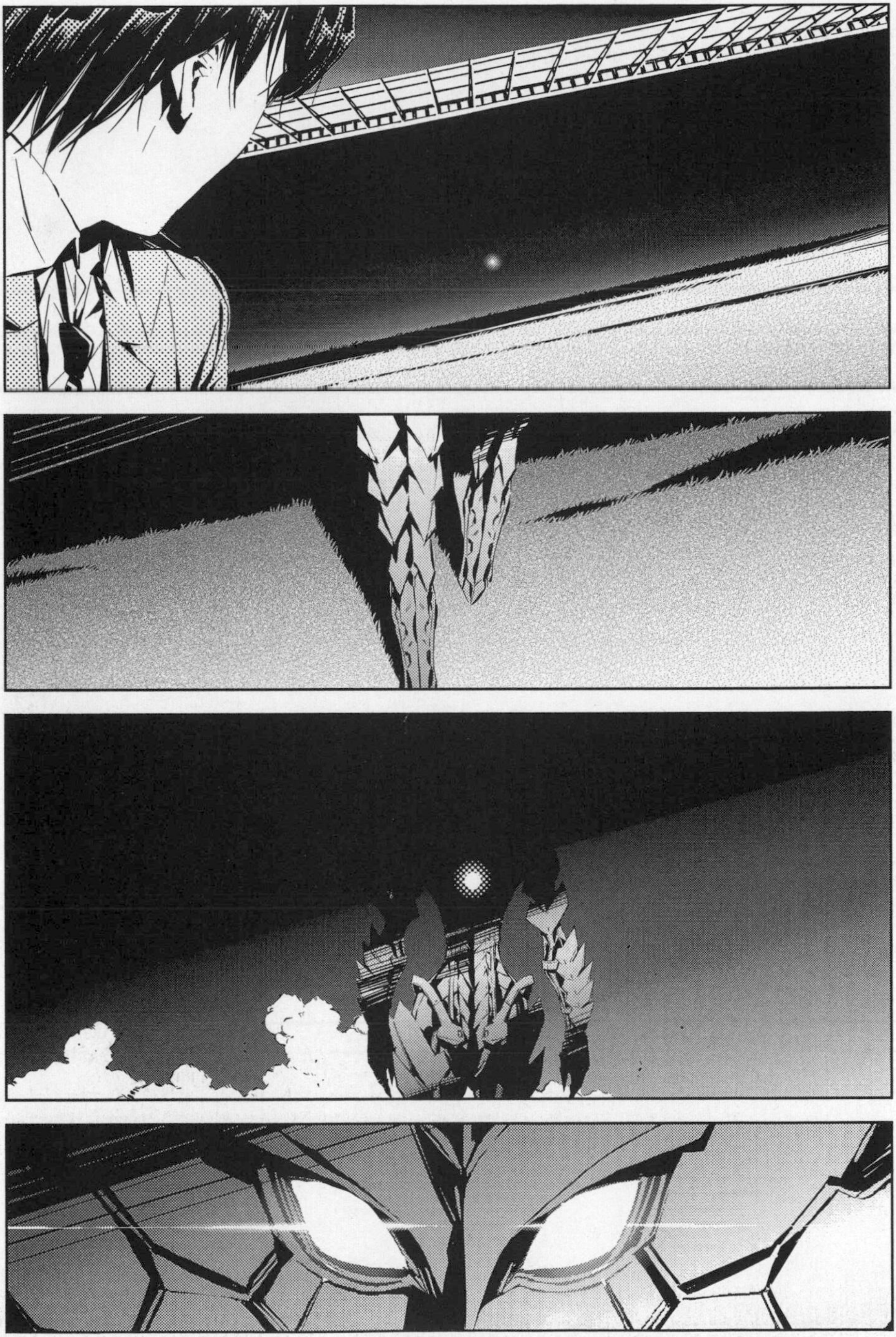

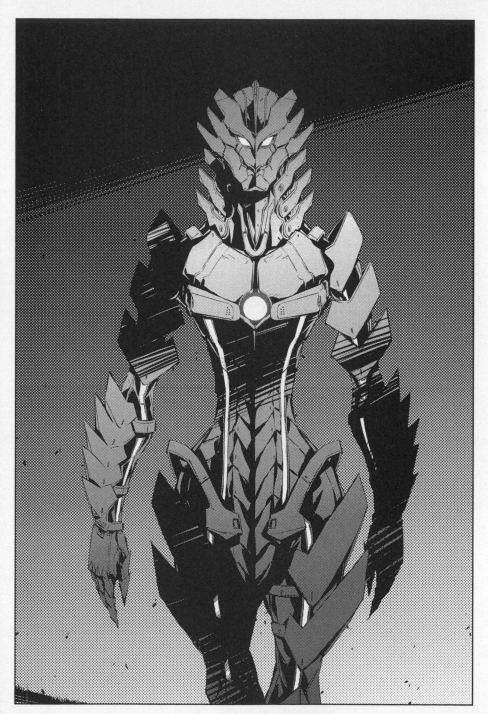

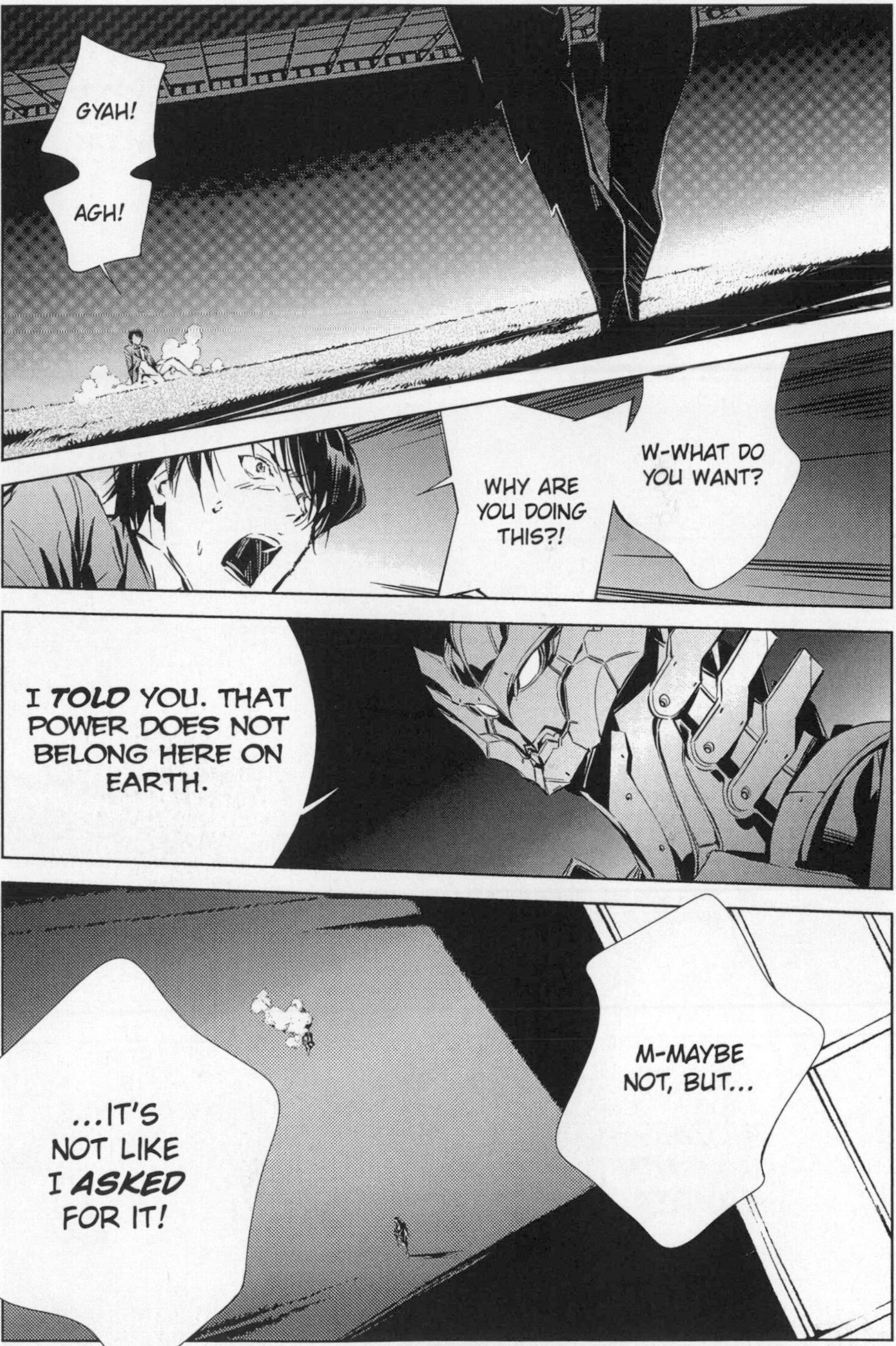
GYAH!
AGH!
W-WHAT DO YOU WANT?
WHY ARE YOU DOING THIS?!
I *TOLD* YOU. THAT POWER DOES NOT BELONG HERE ON EARTH.
M-MAYBE NOT, BUT...
...IT'S NOT LIKE I *ASKED* FOR IT!

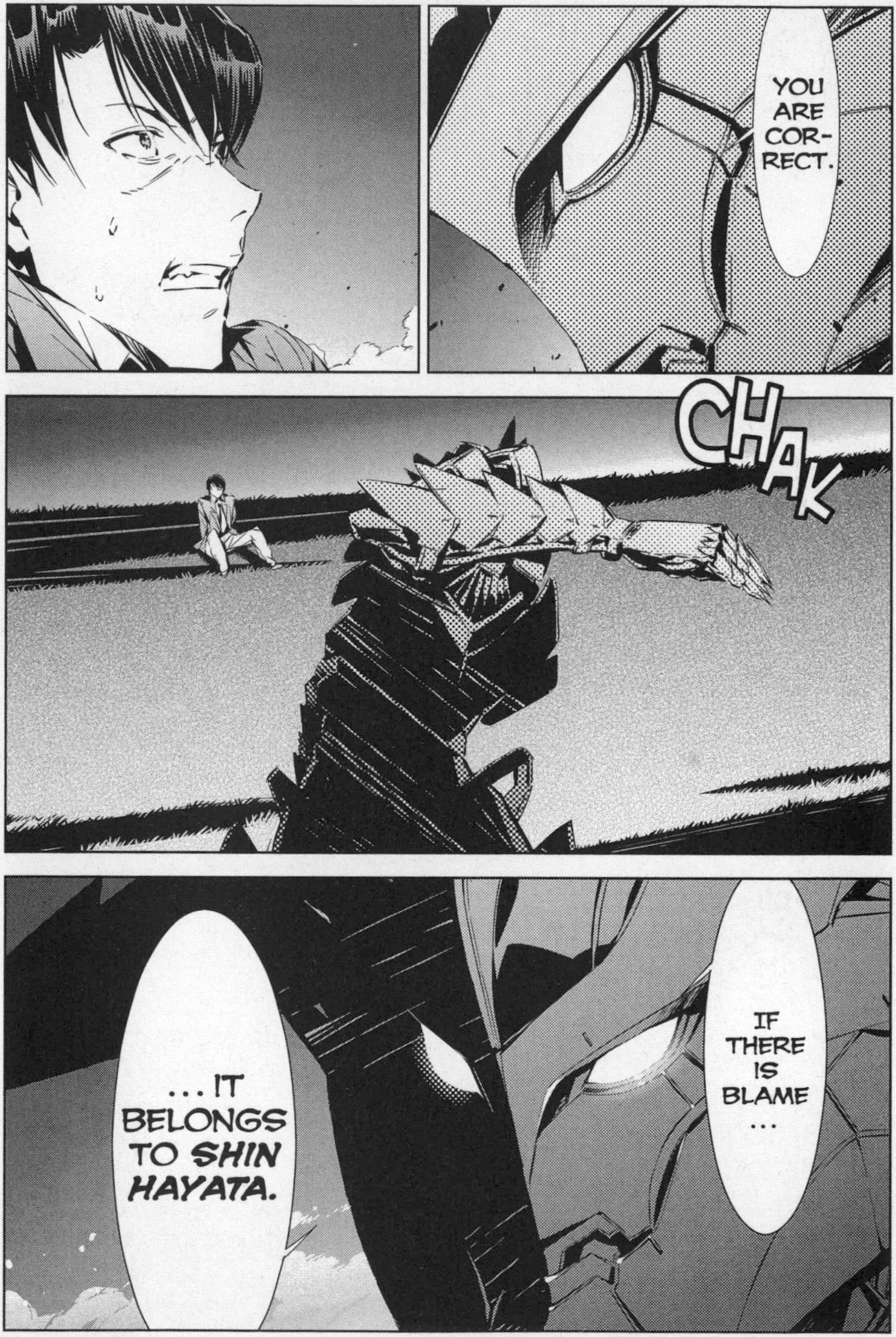
YOU ARE COR-RECT.
CHAK
IF THERE IS BLAME ...
... IT BELONGS TO SHIN HAYATA.

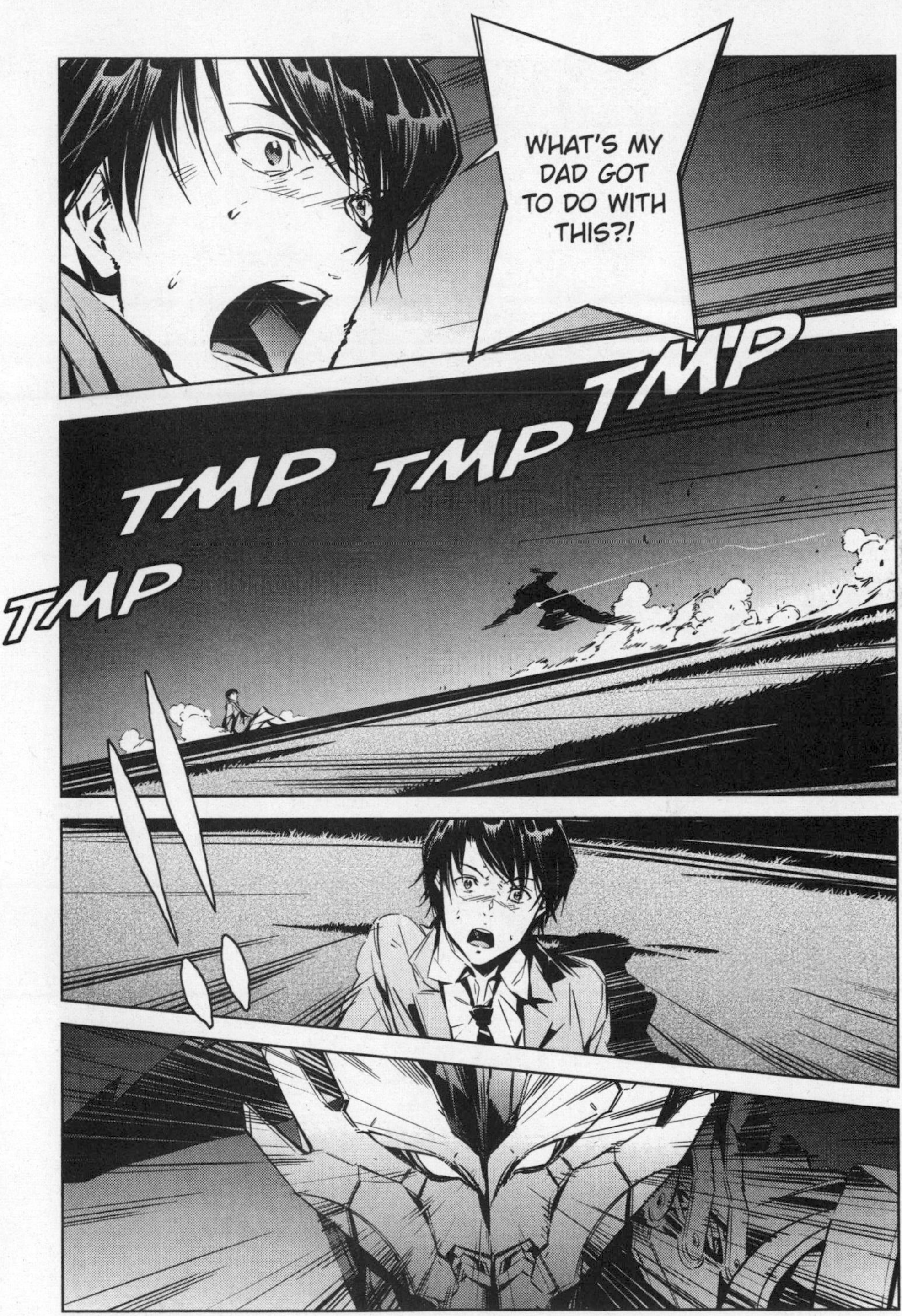
WHAT'S MY DAD GOT TO DO WITH THIS?!
TMP TMP TMP TMP

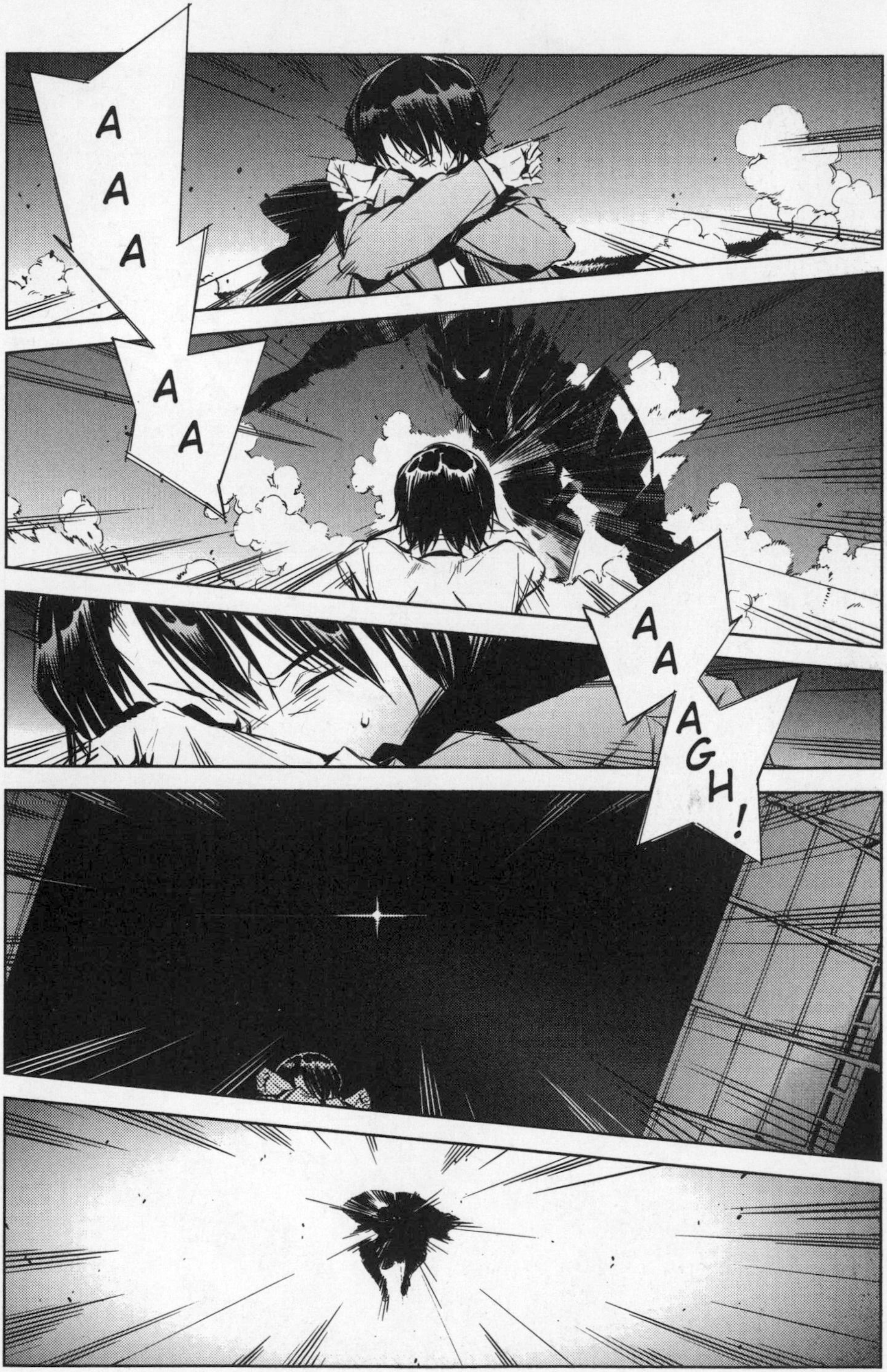
AAAAAA
AAAGH!

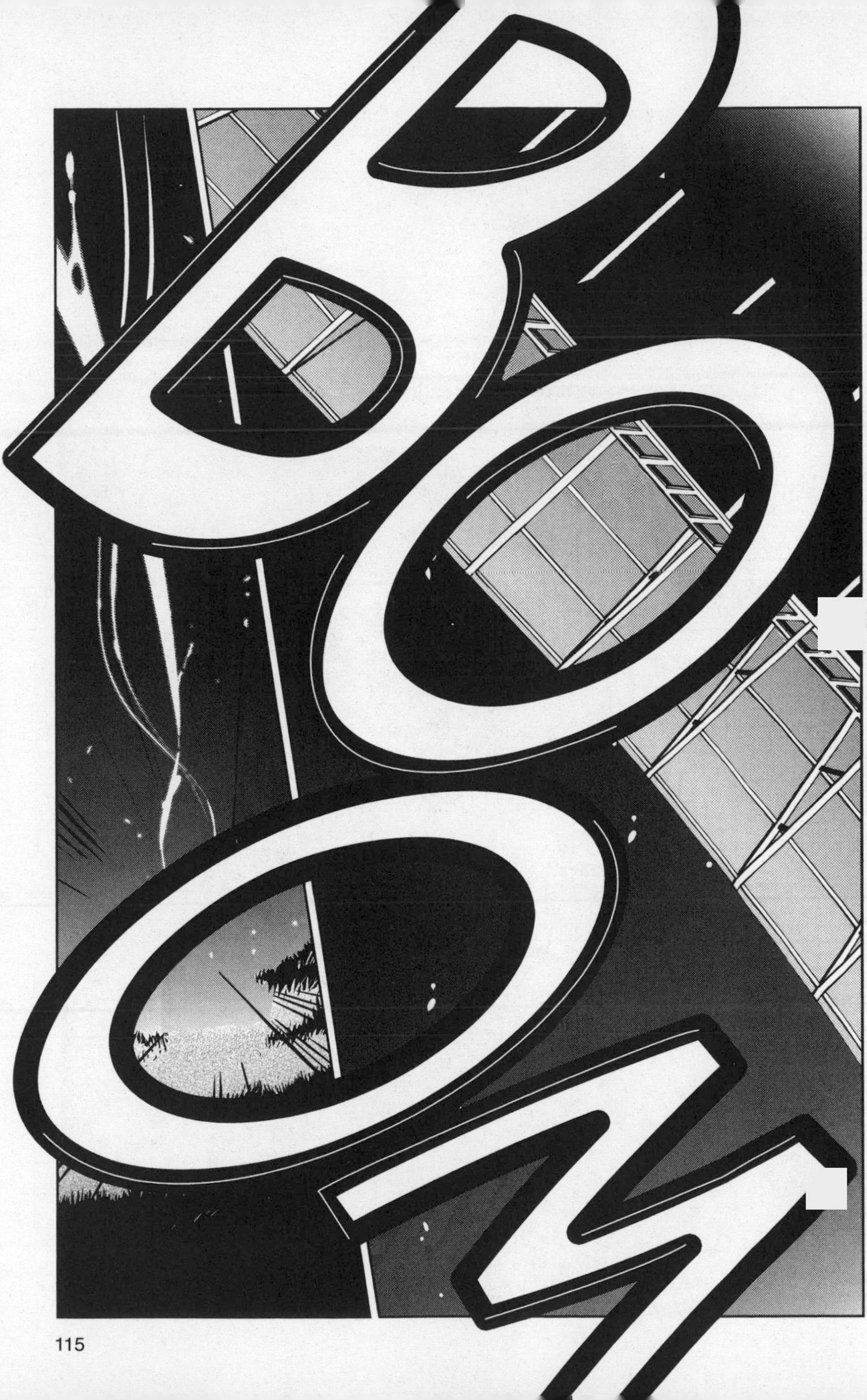
DOOM

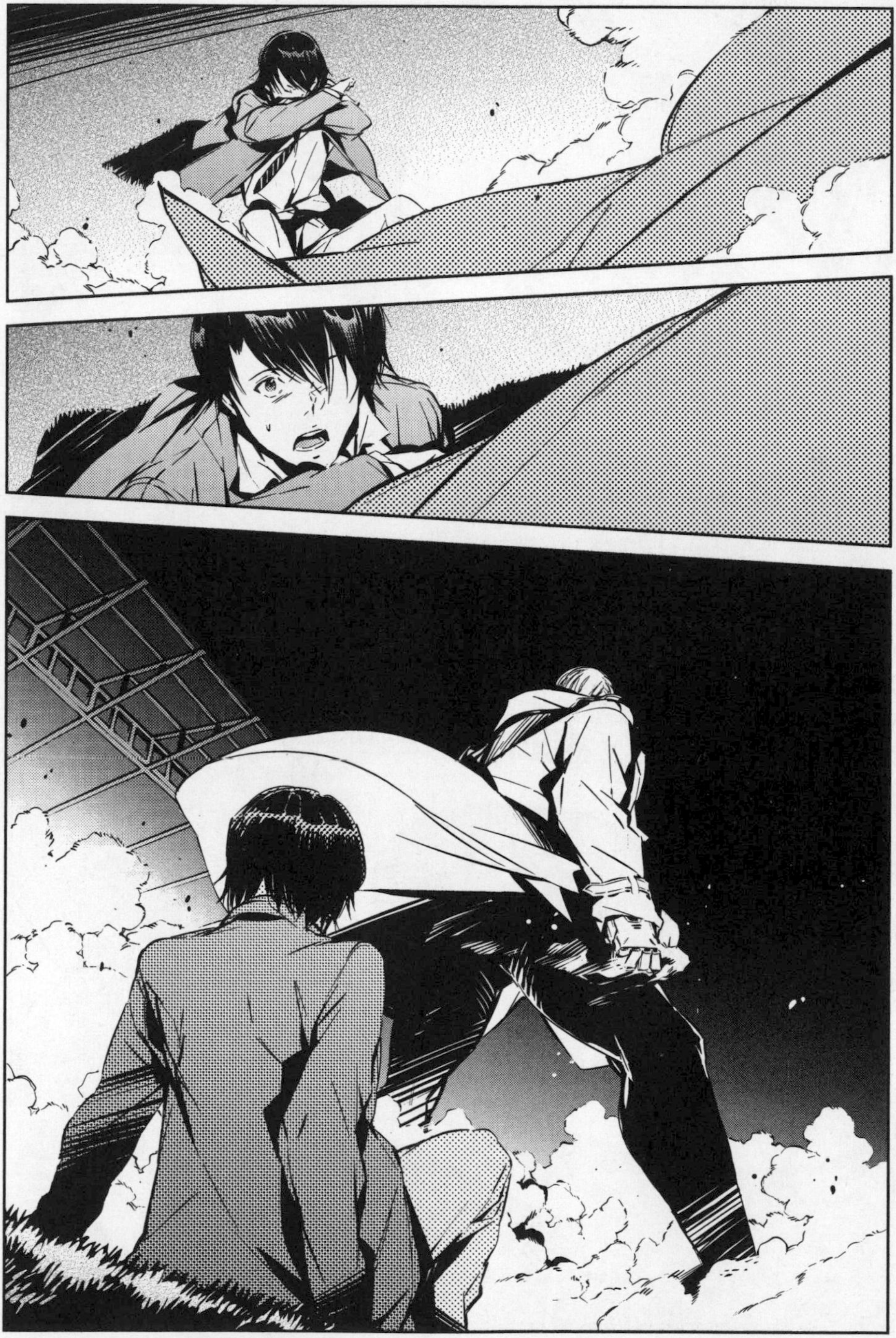

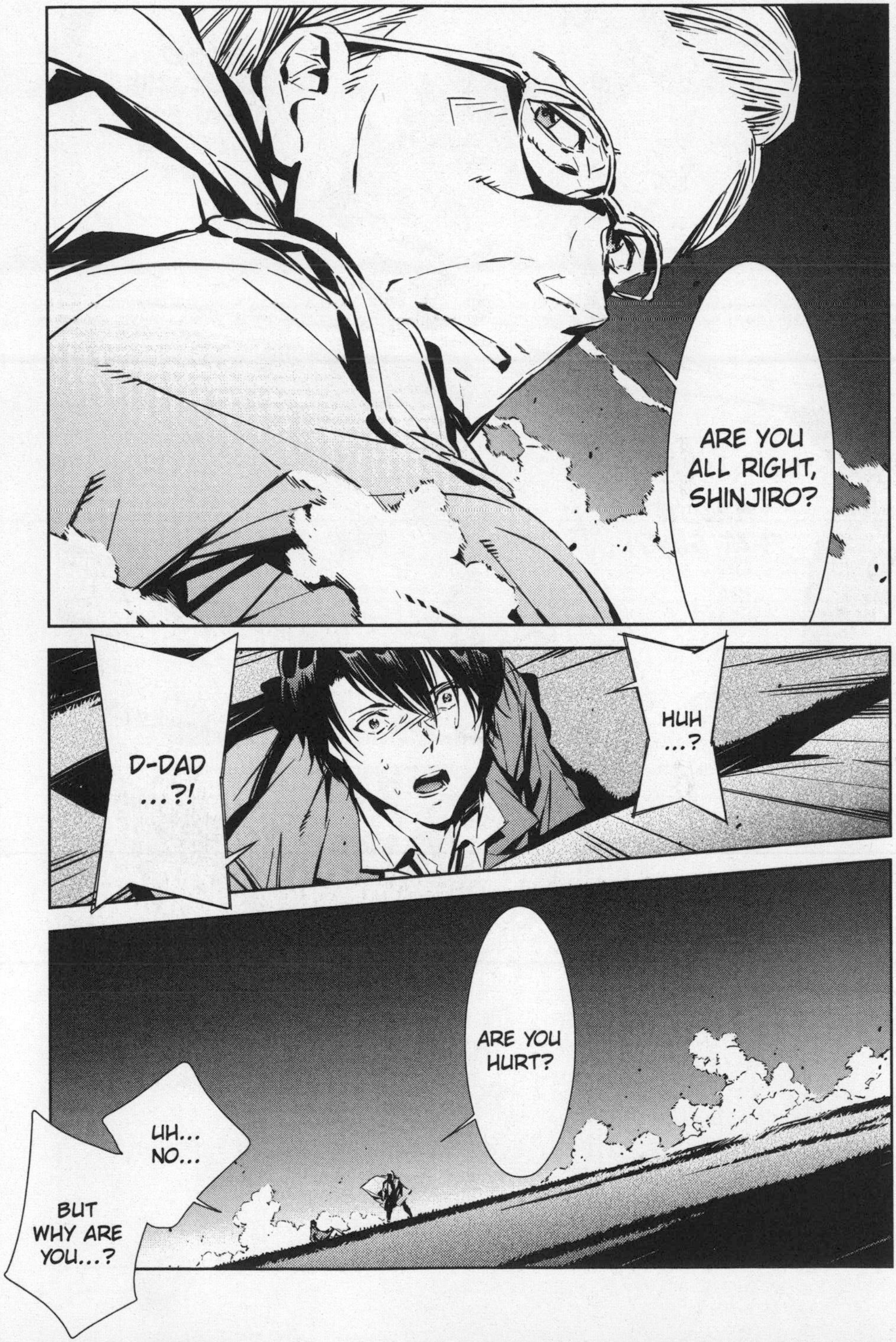
ARE YOU ALL RIGHT, SHINJIRO?
HUH ...?
D-DAD ...?!
ARE YOU HURT?
UH... NO...
BUT WHY ARE YOU...?

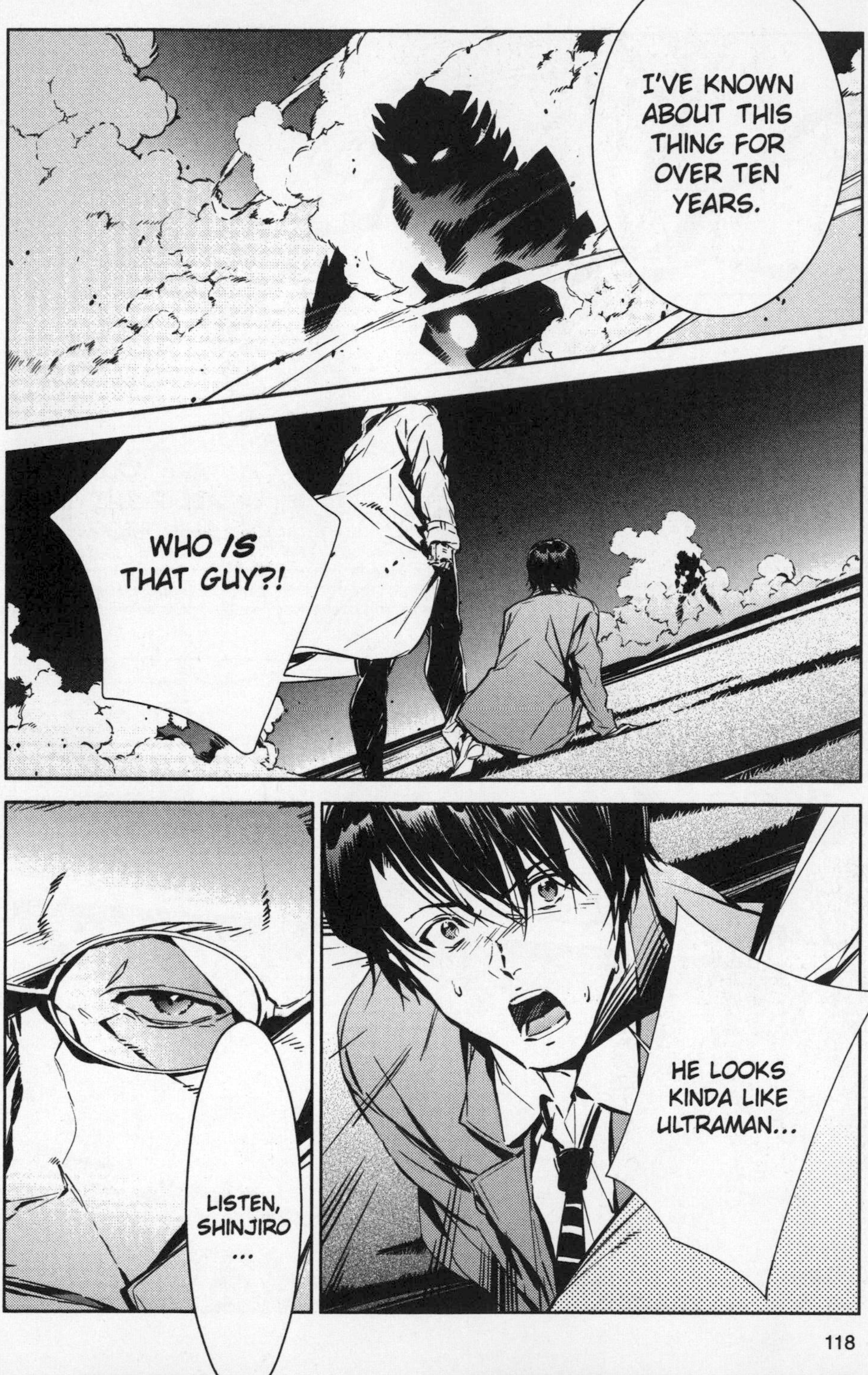
I'VE KNOWN ABOUT THIS THING FOR OVER TEN YEARS.
WHO *IS* THAT GUY?!
HE LOOKS KINDA LIKE ULTRAMAN...
LISTEN, SHINJIRO ...

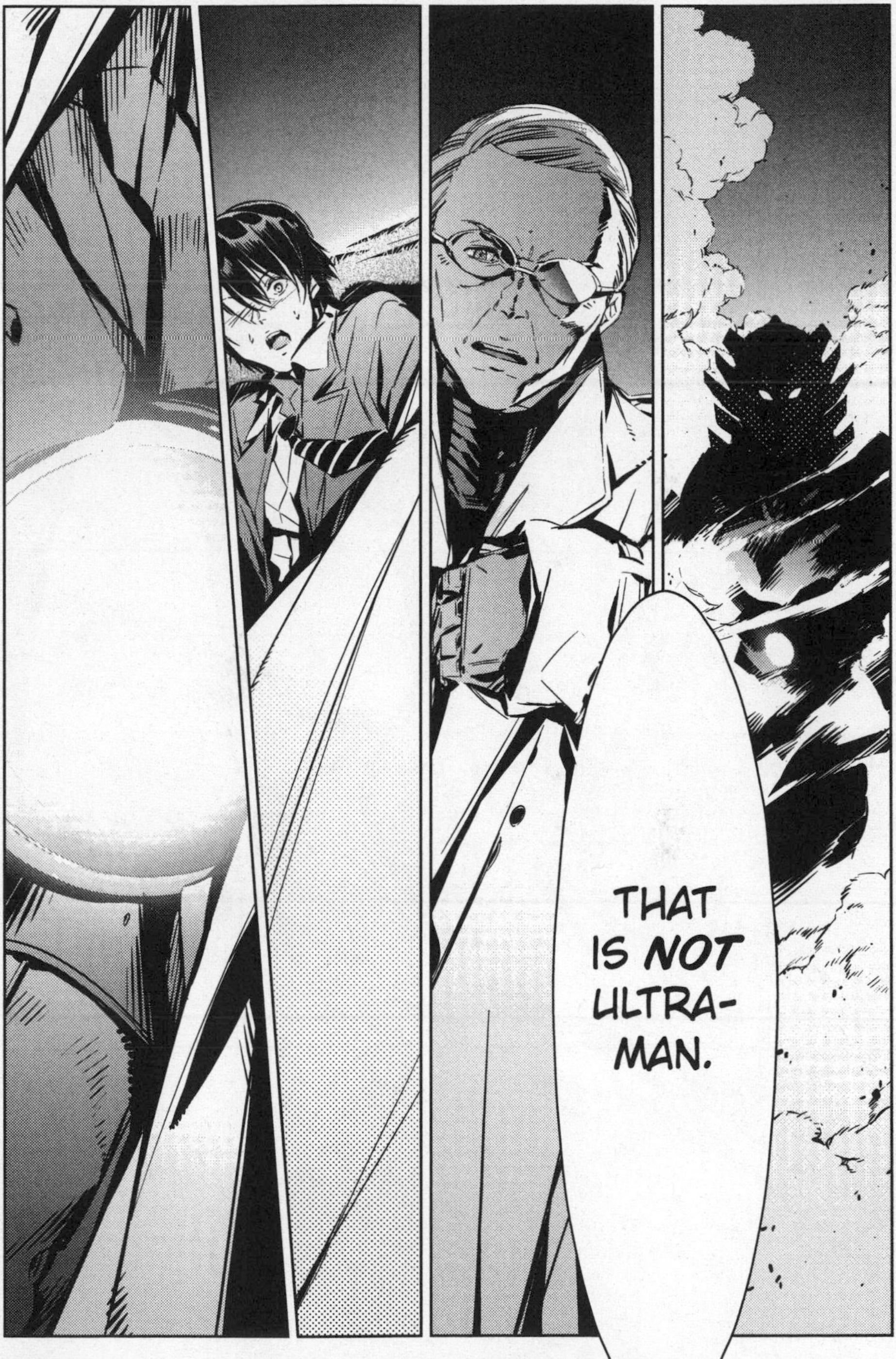
THAT IS NOT ULTRA-MAN.

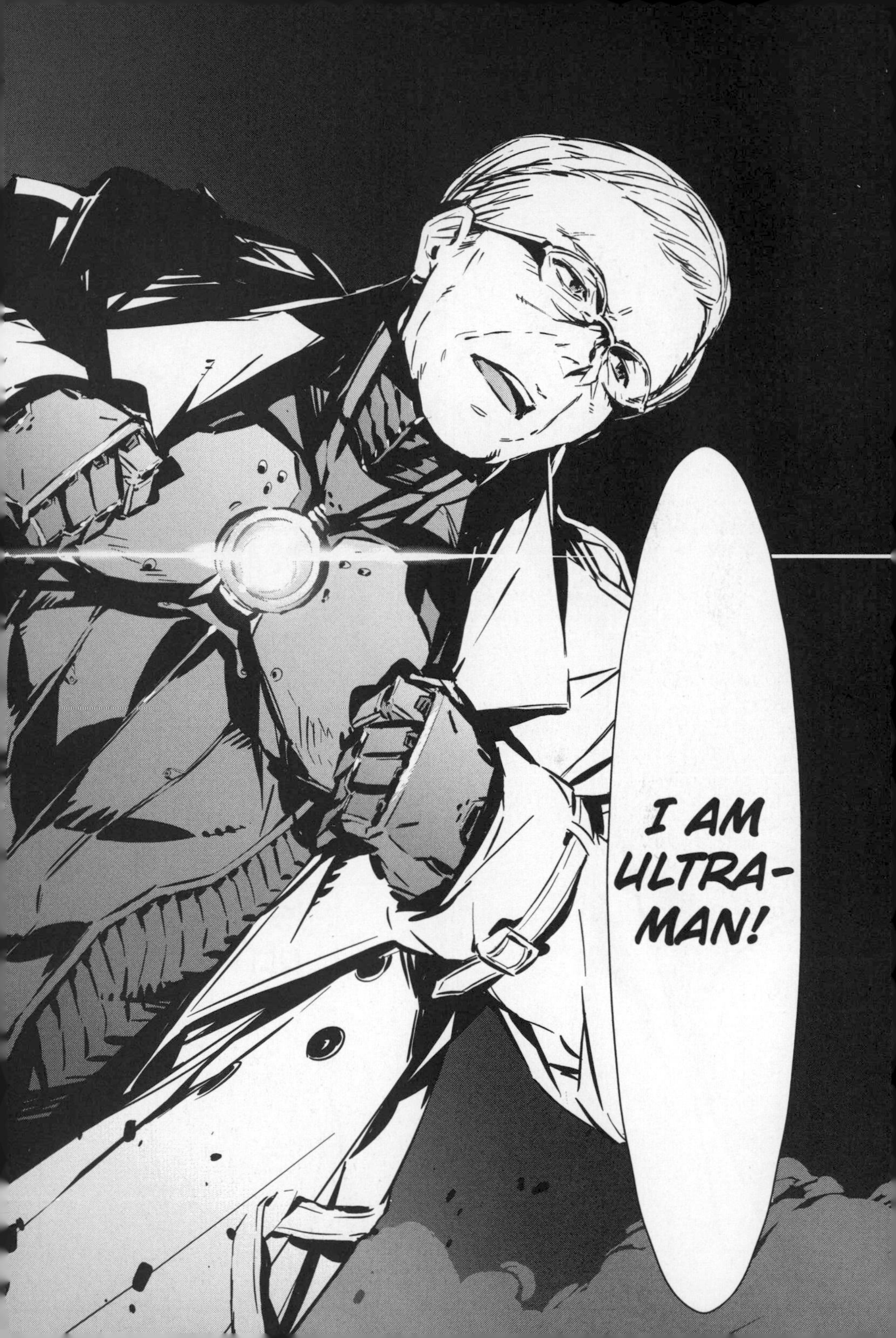
I AM ULTRA-MAN!

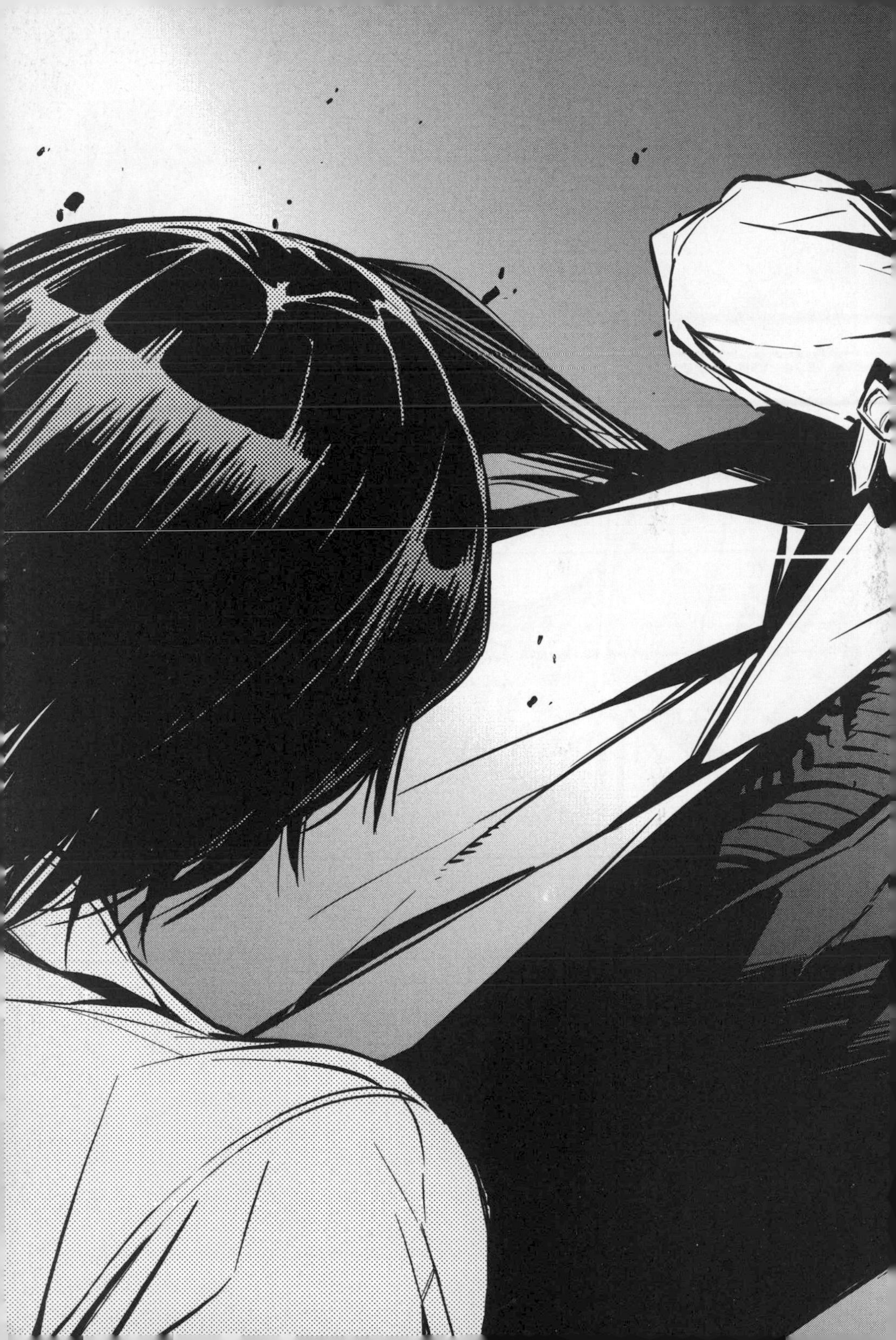

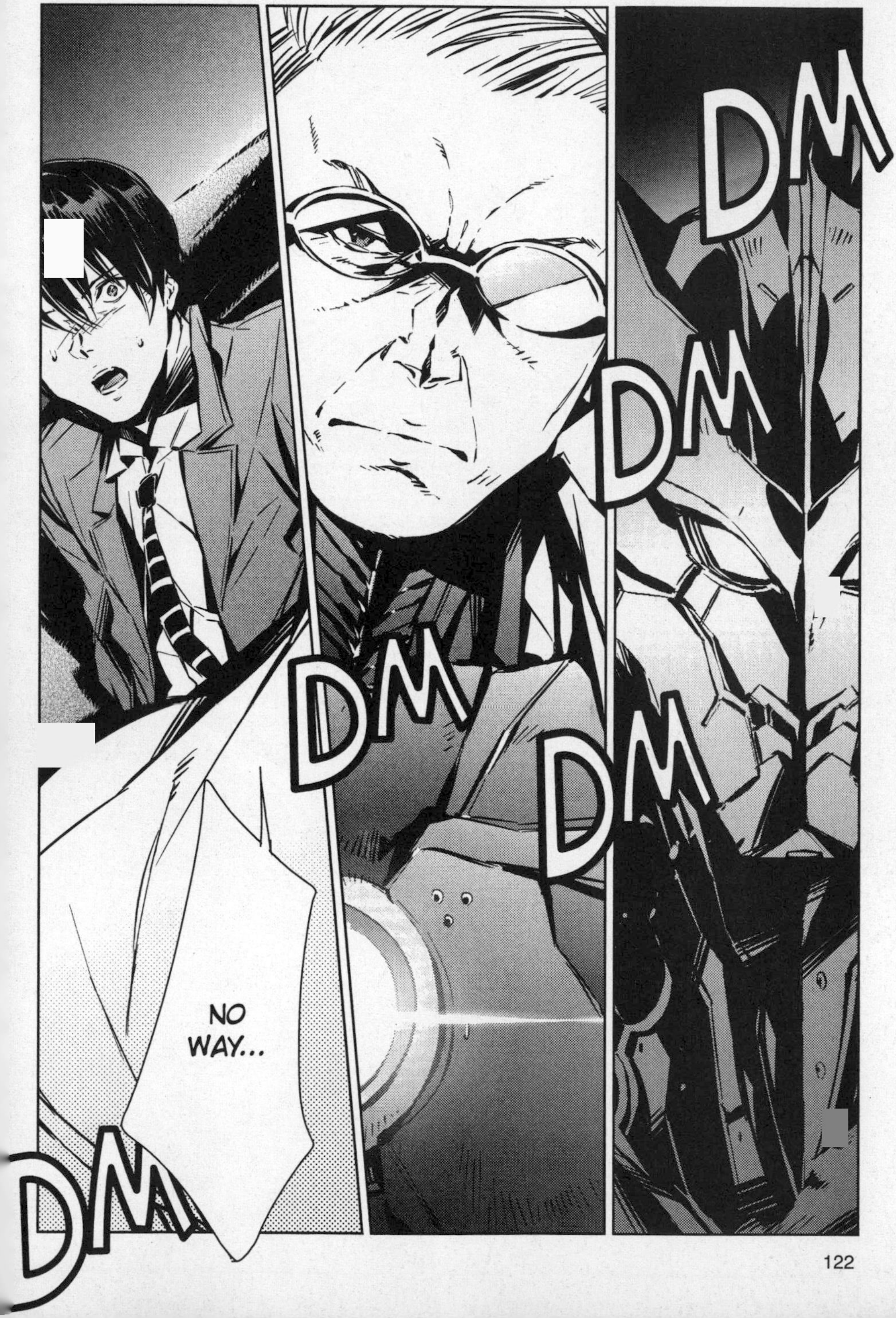
DM
DM
DM
DM
NO WAY...
DM

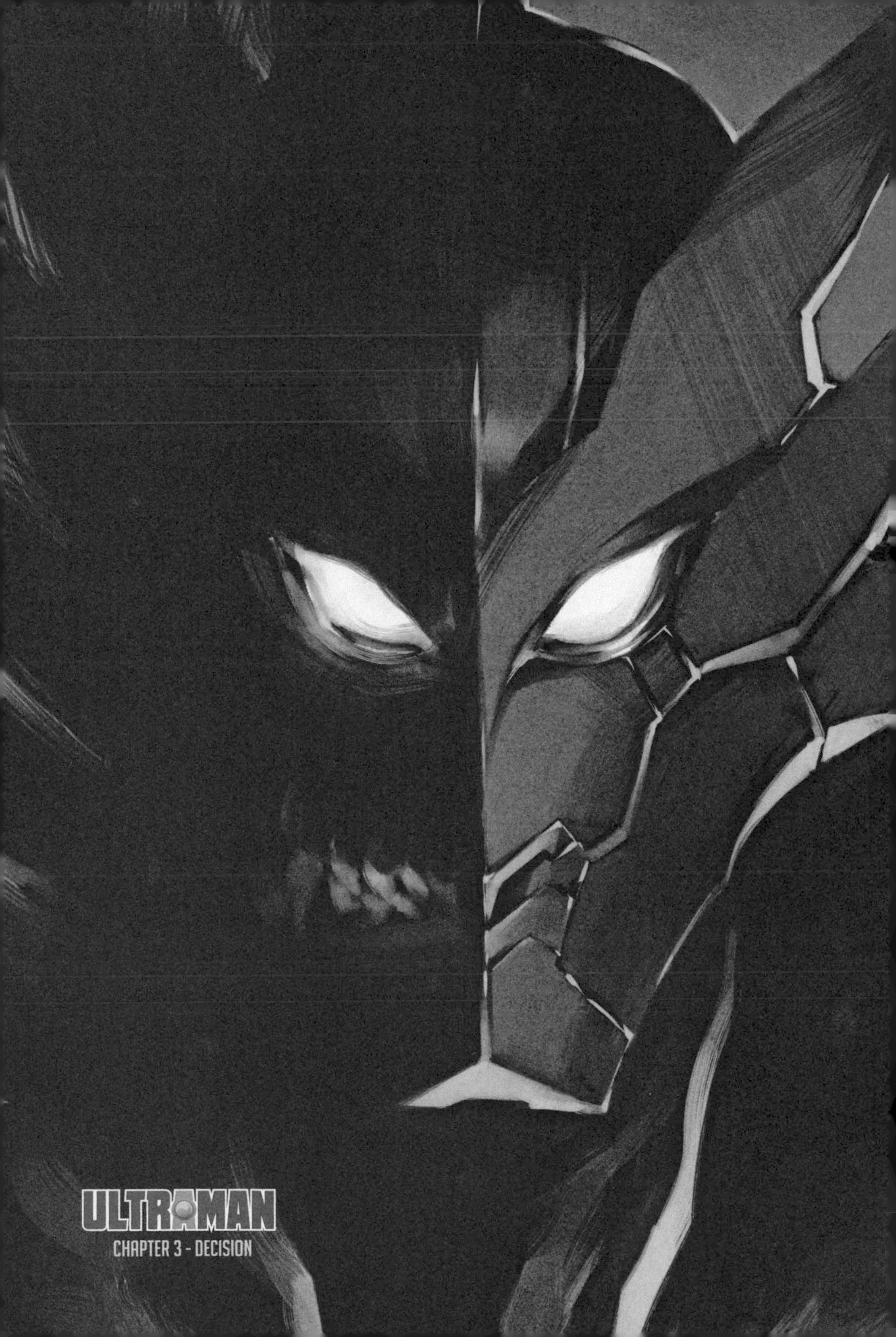
ULTRAMAN
CHAPTER 3 - DECISION

ULTRAMAN

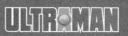

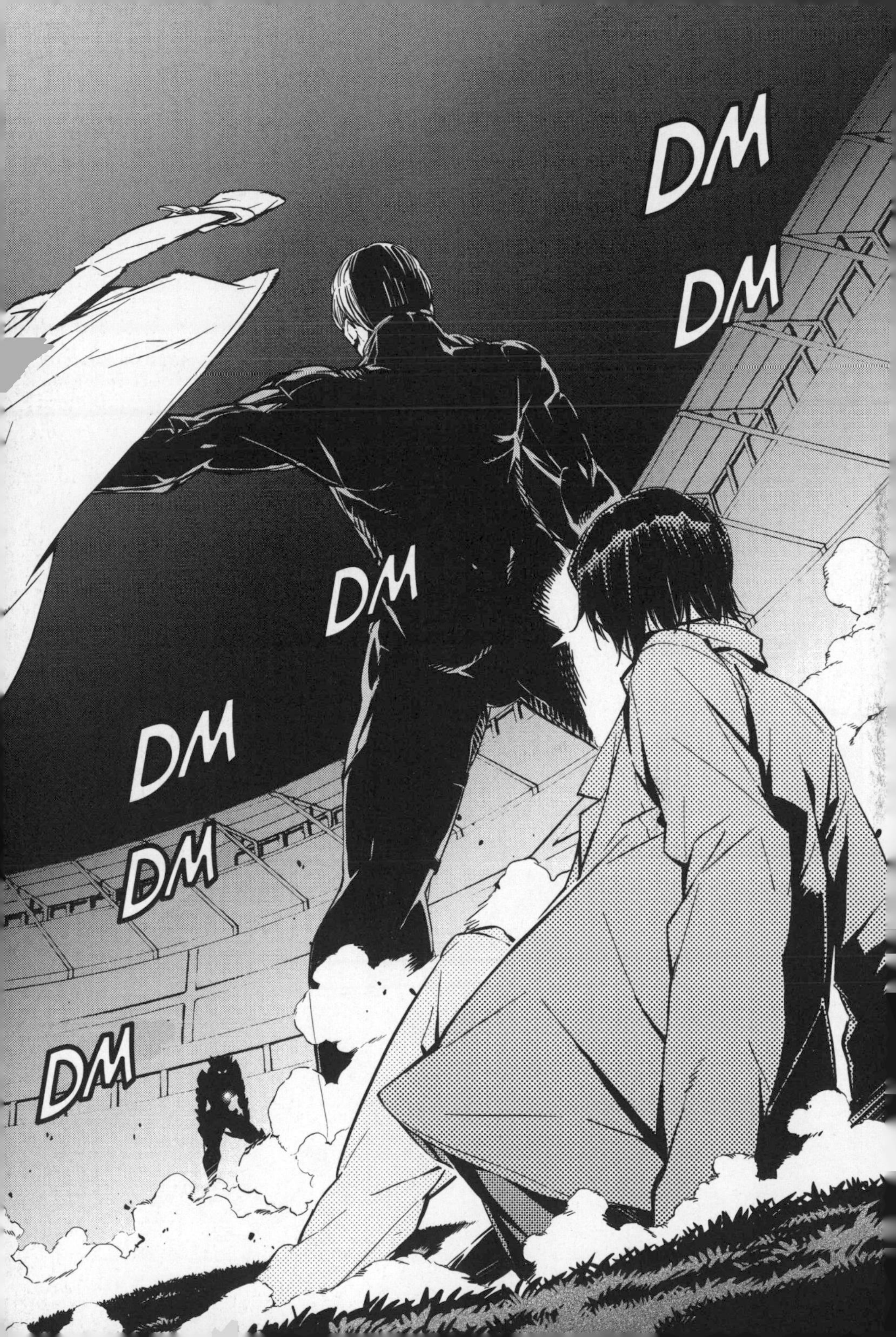
DM
DM
DM
DM
DM
DM

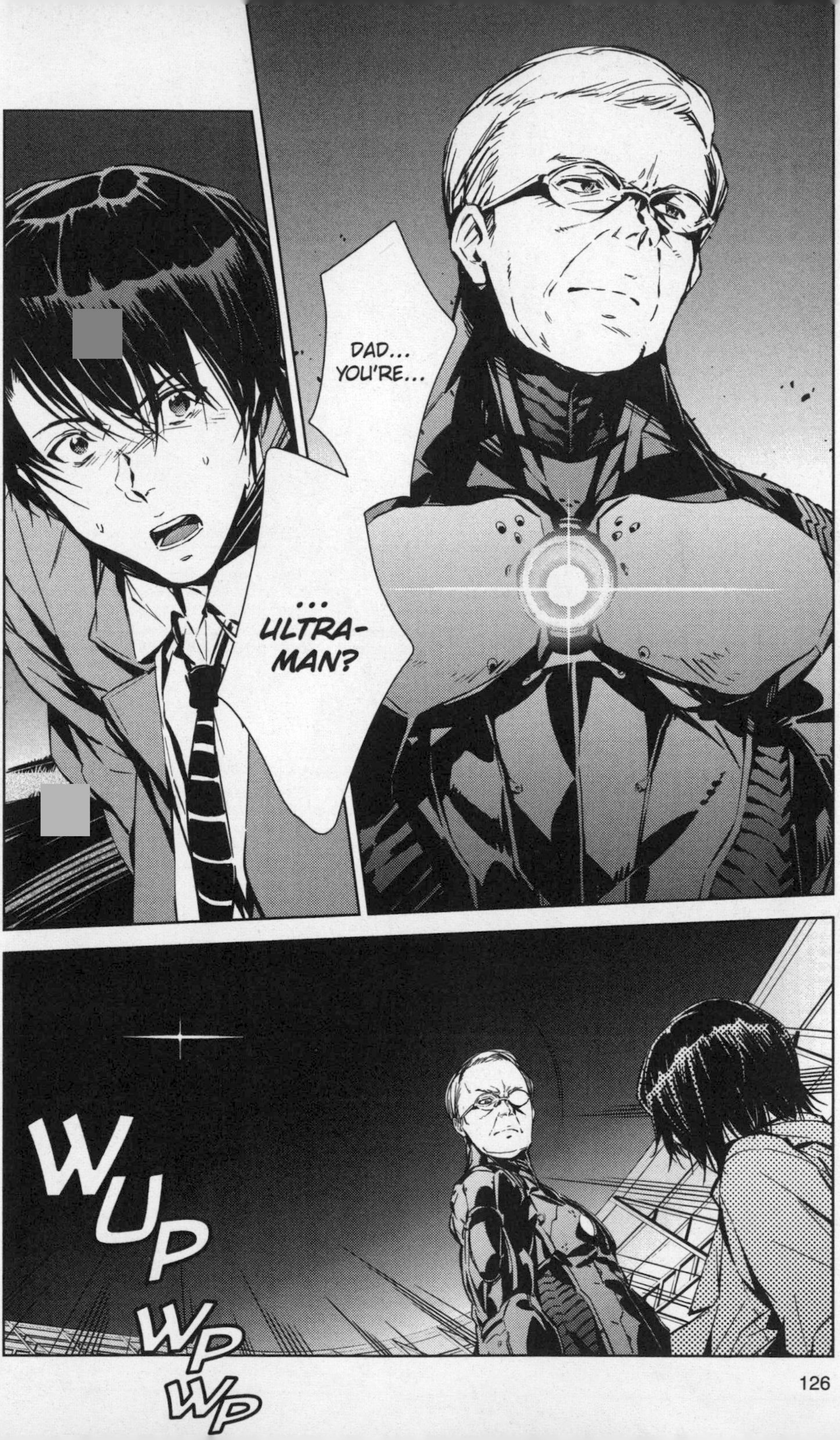
DAD... YOU'RE...
... ULTRA-MAN?
WUP WP WP

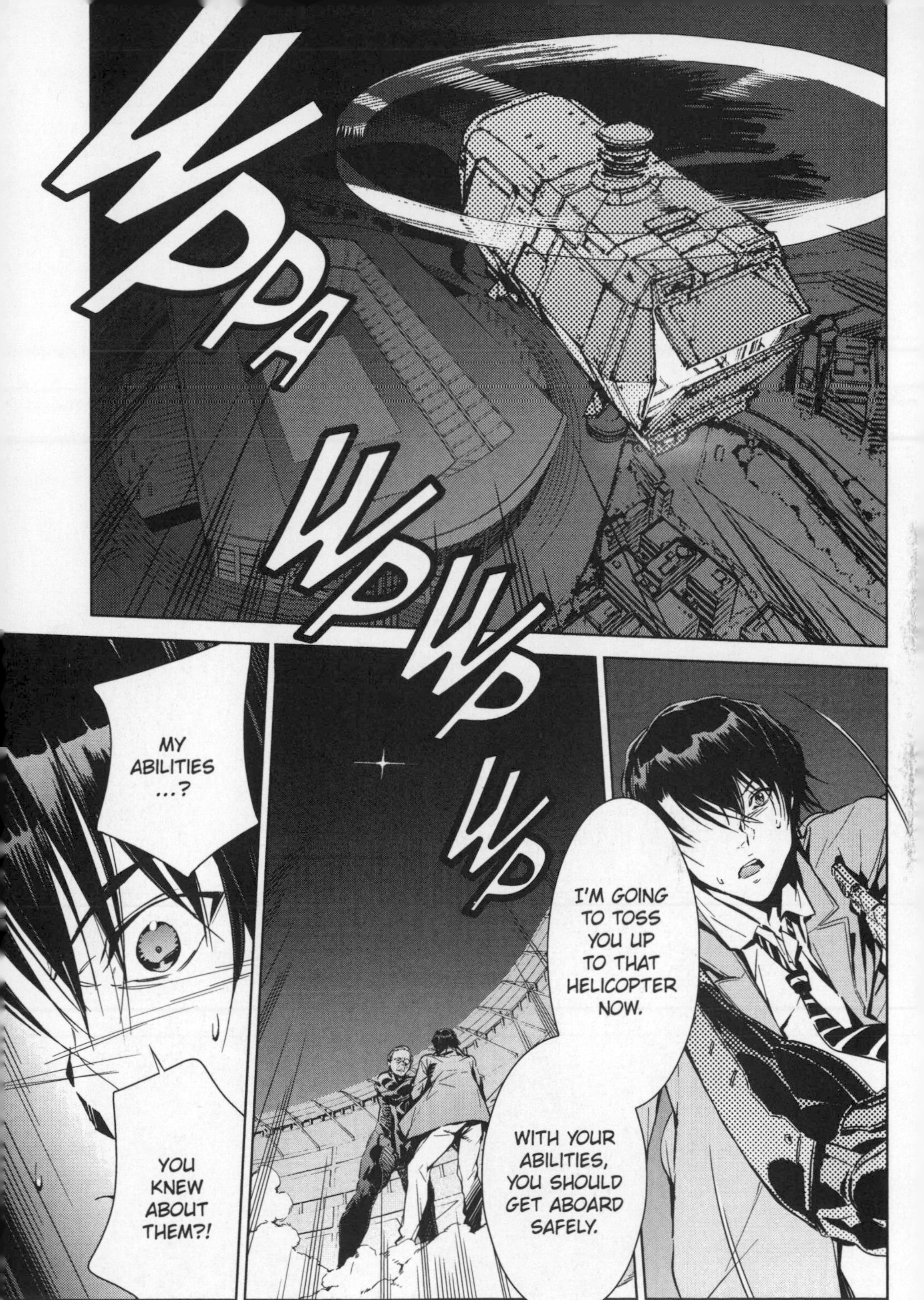
WPPA
WPWPWP
I'M GOING TO TOSS YOU UP TO THAT HELICOPTER NOW.
WITH YOUR ABILITIES, YOU SHOULD GET ABOARD SAFELY.
WP
MY ABILITIES ...?
YOU KNEW ABOUT THEM?!

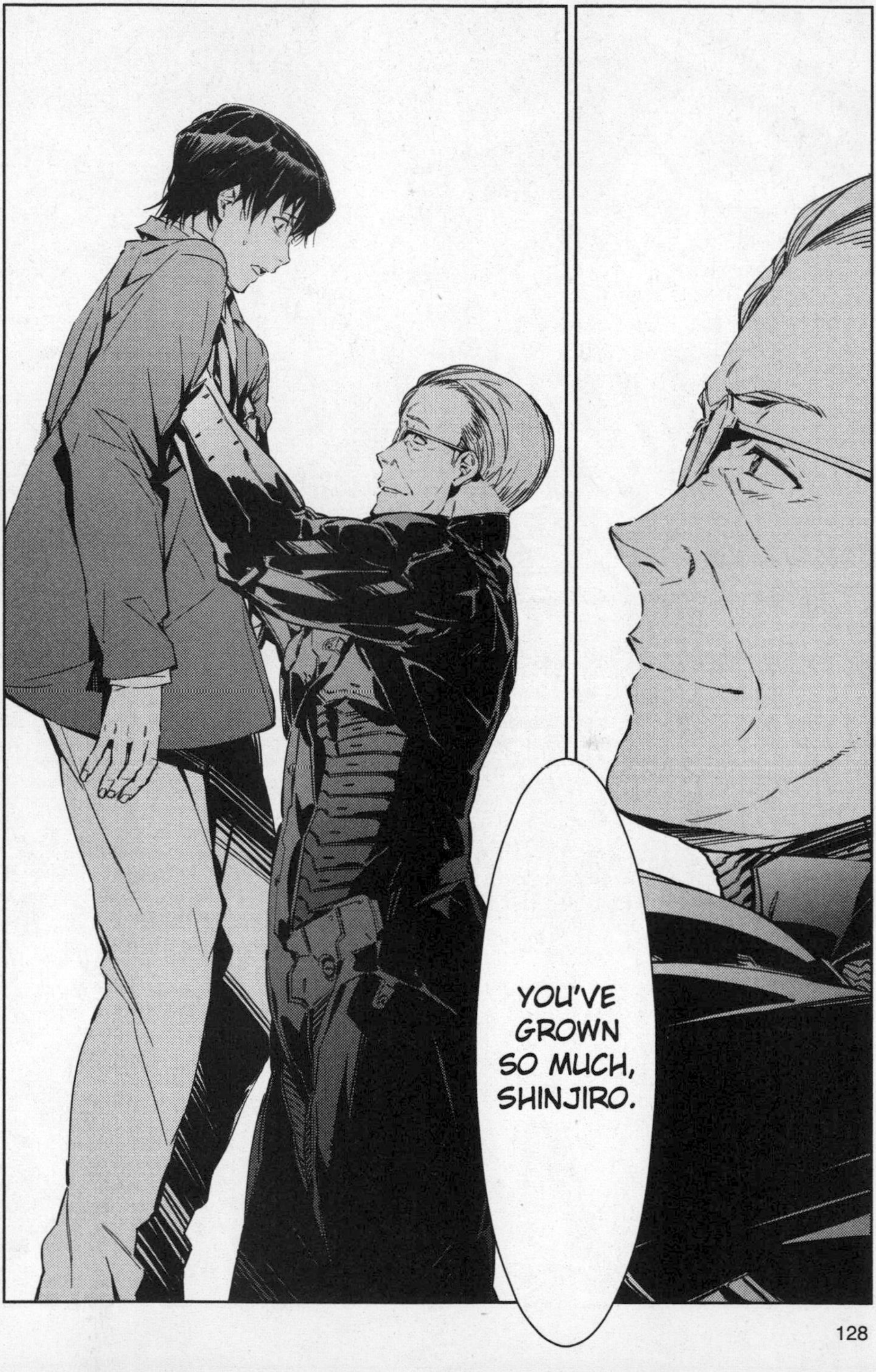
YOU'VE GROWN SO MUCH, SHINJIRO.

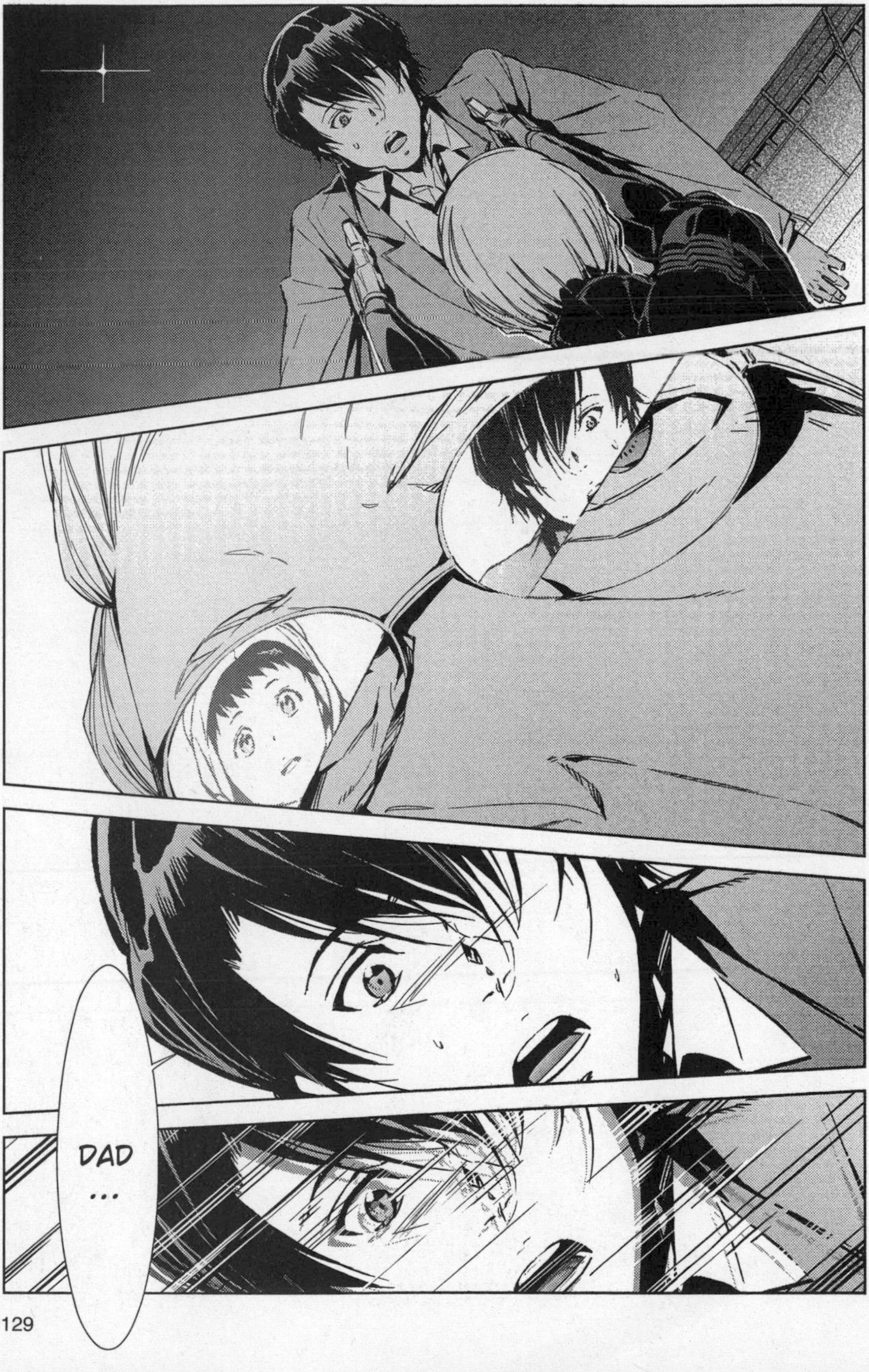
DAD
...

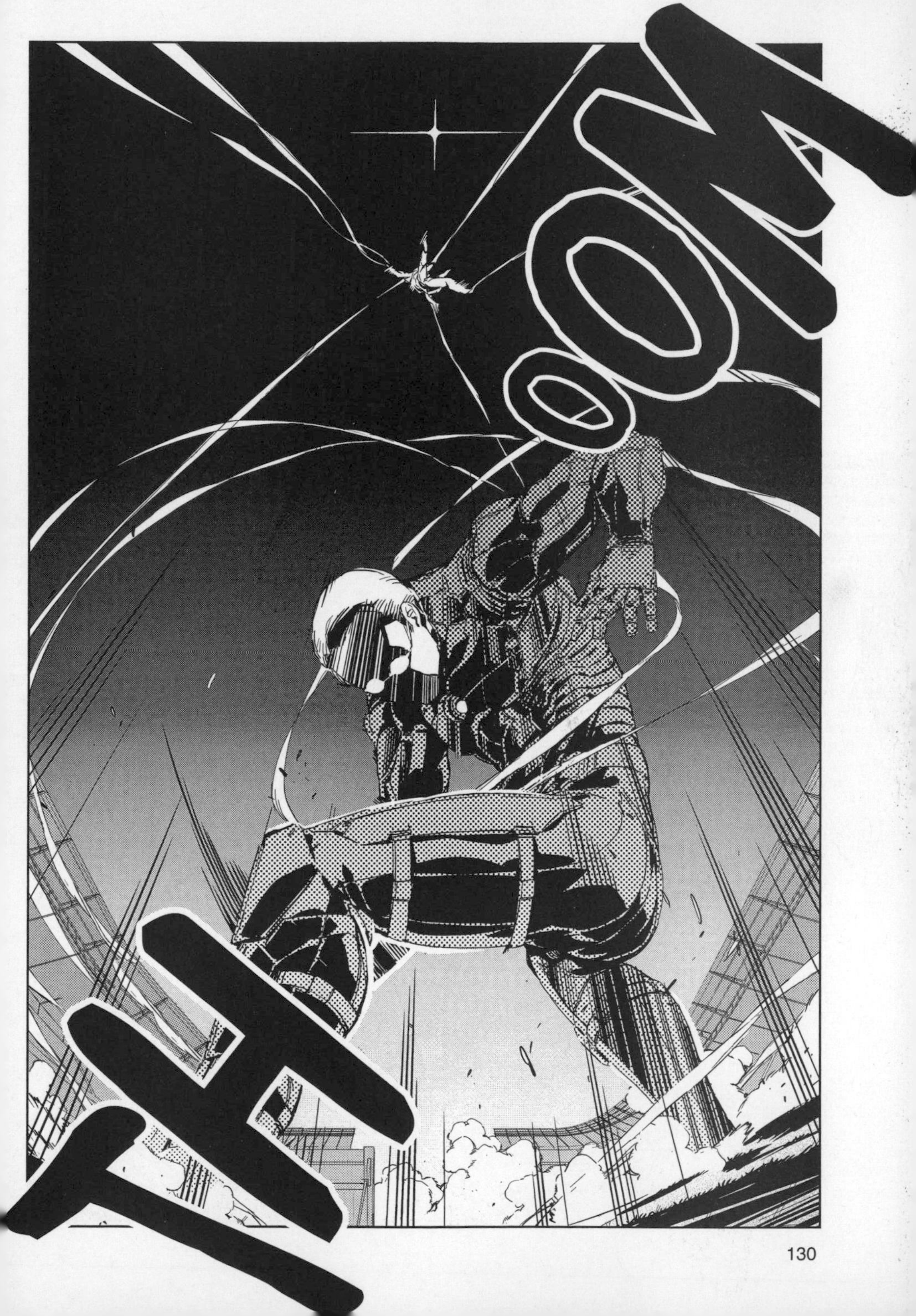
THOOM

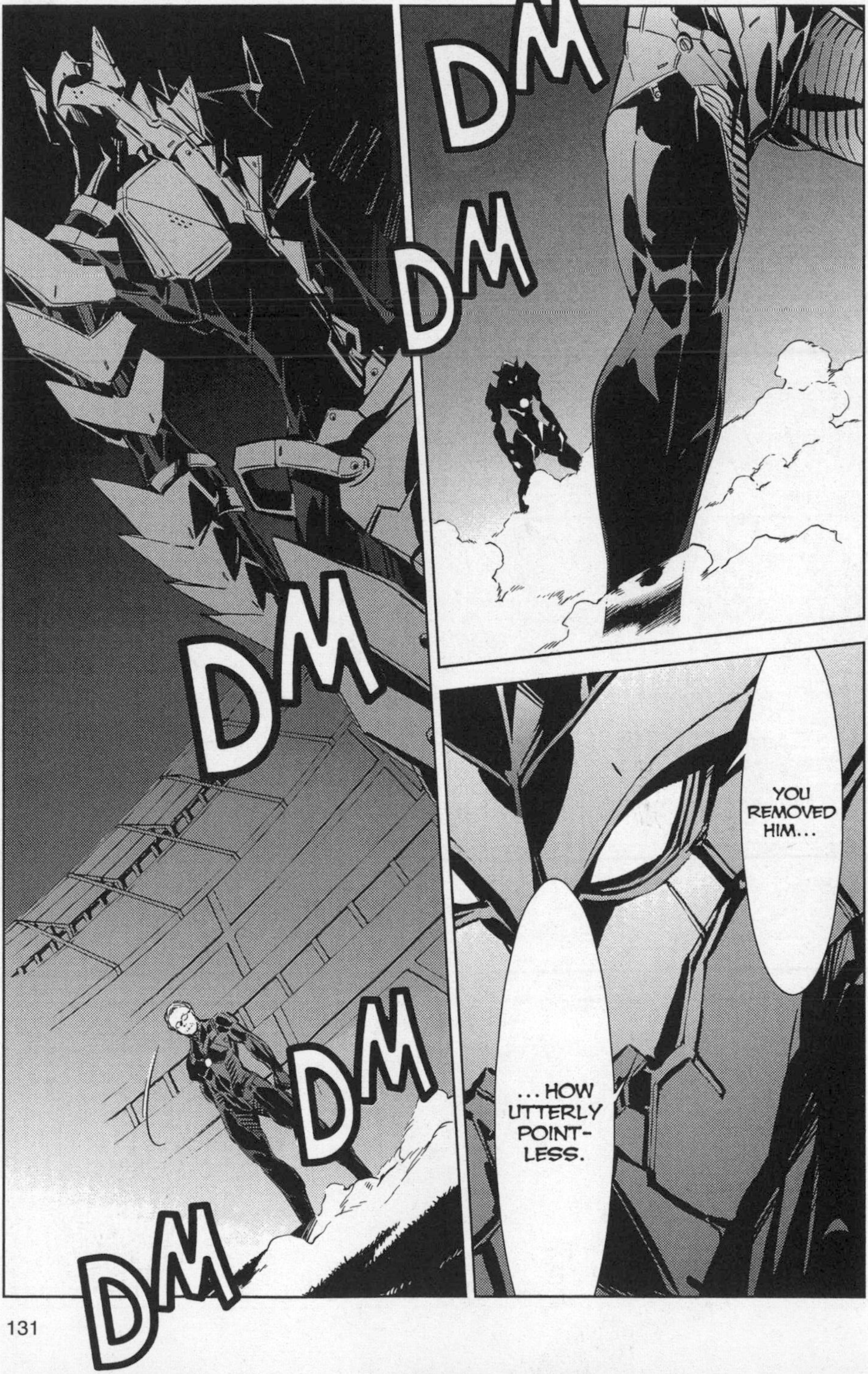
DM
DM
YOU REMOVED HIM...
...HOW UTTERLY POINT-LESS.
DM
DM
DM

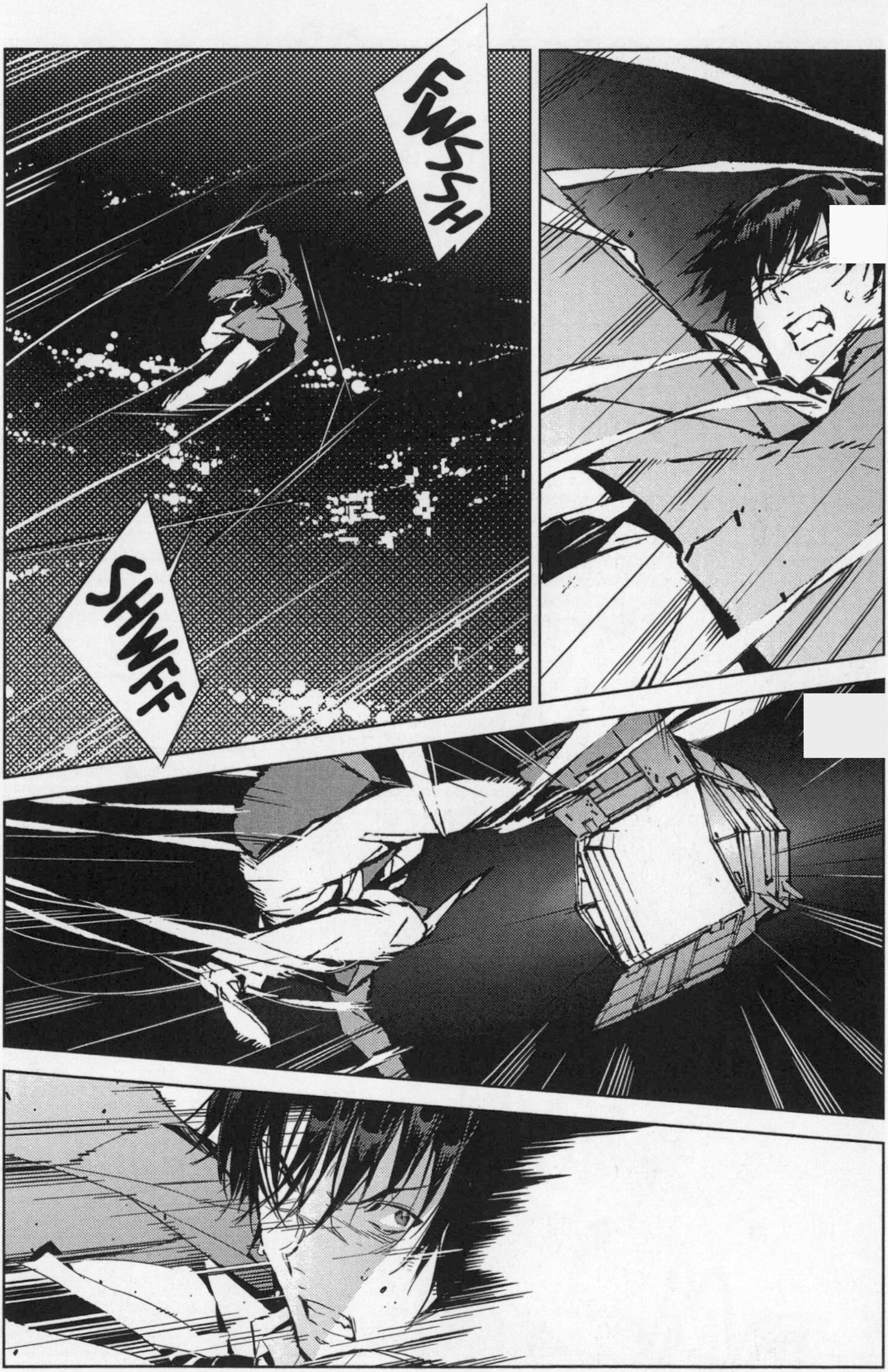
FWSSH
SHWFF

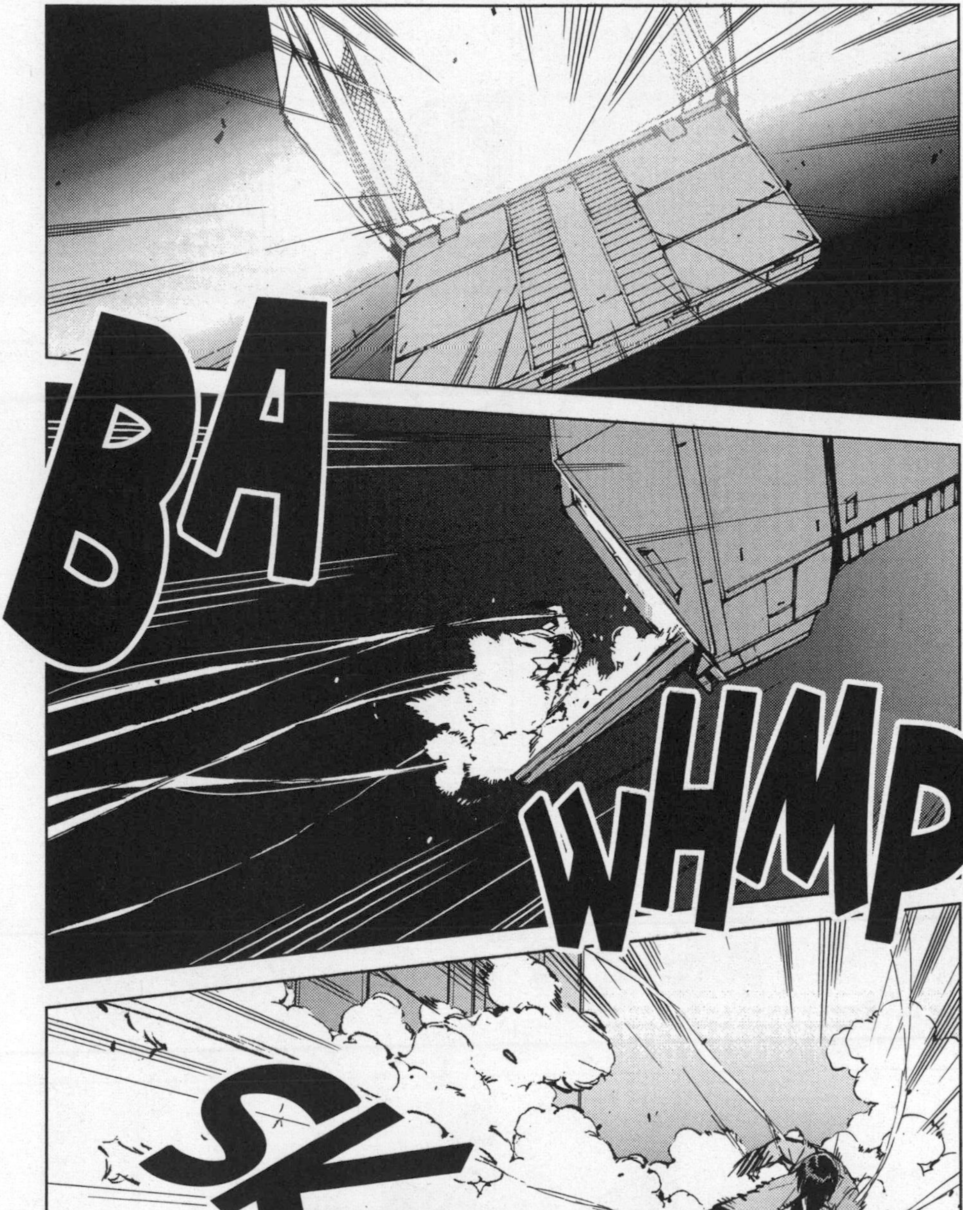
BA
WHMP
SKFF

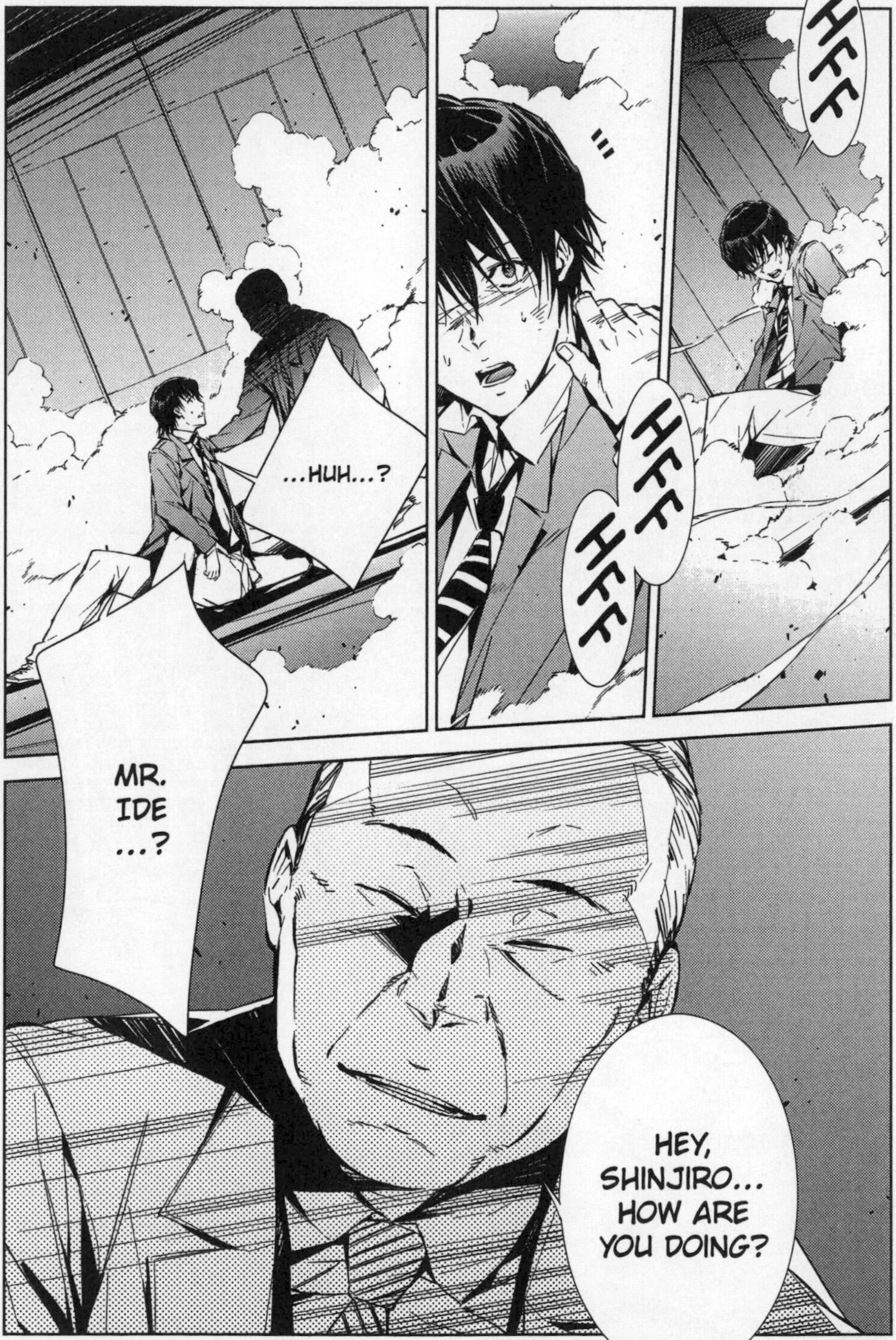
HFFF
...
HFFF
HFFF
...HUH...?
MR. IDE ...?
HEY, SHINJIRO... HOW ARE YOU DOING?

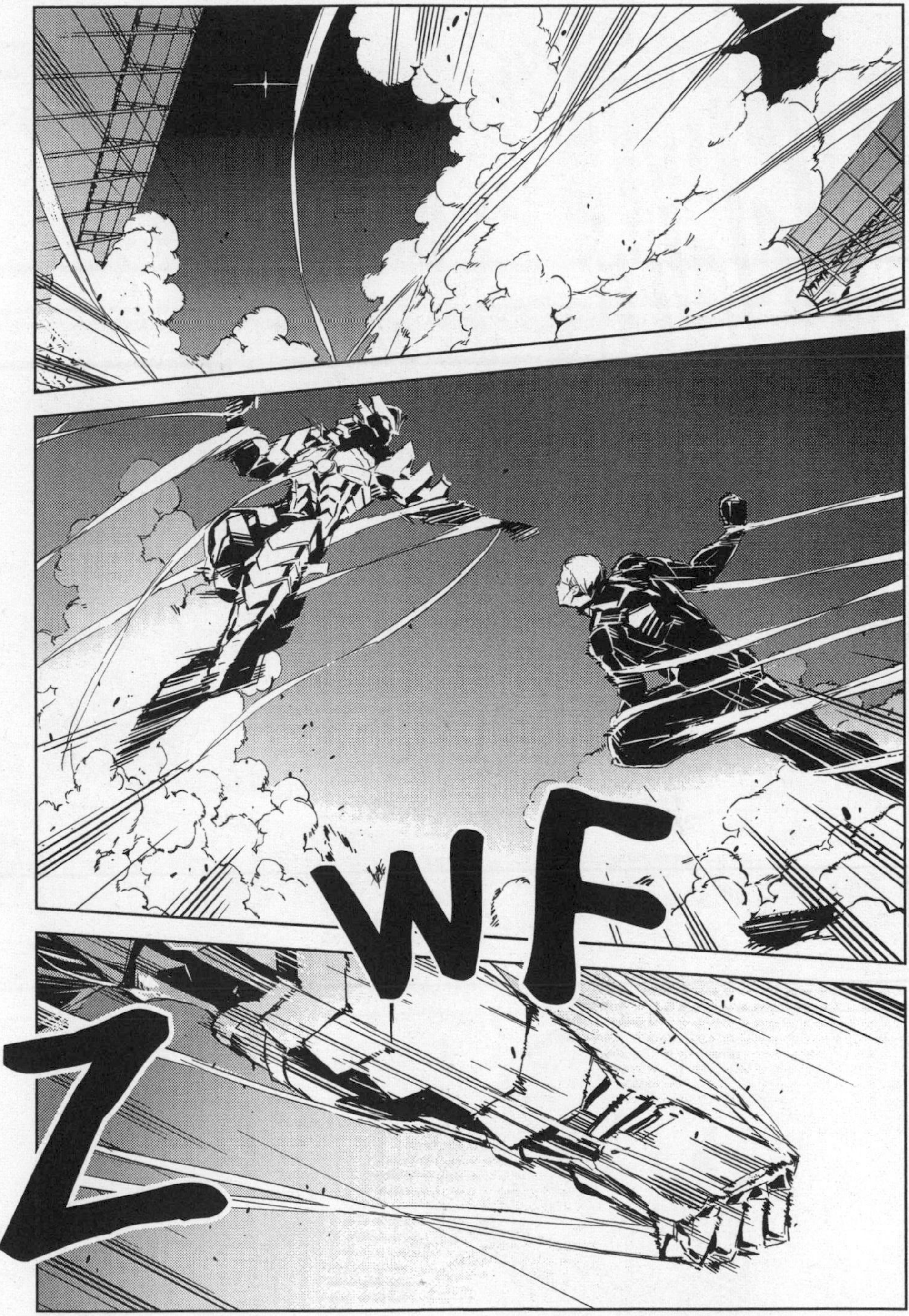
ZWF

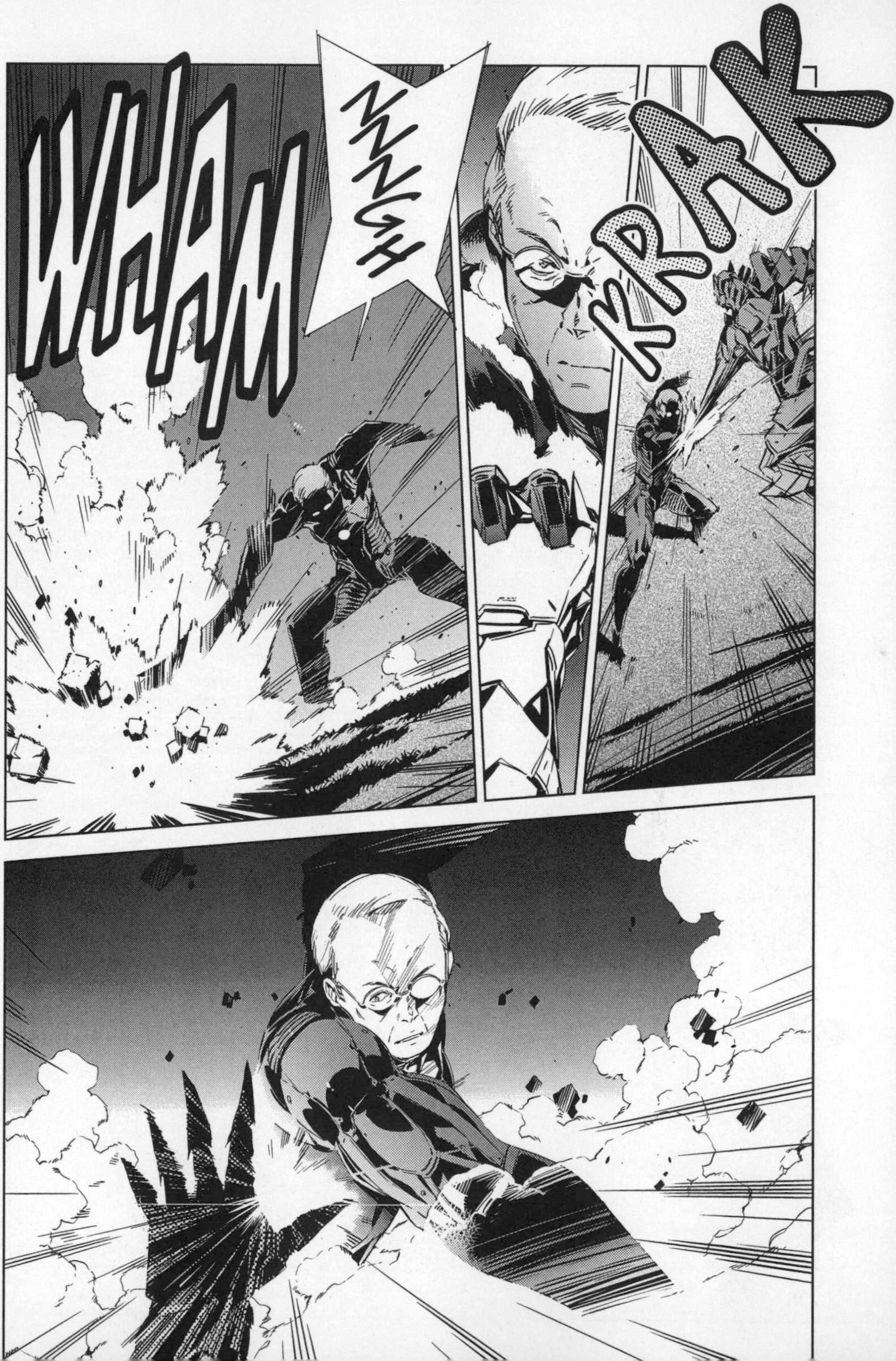
KRAK
ZZZNGH
WHAM

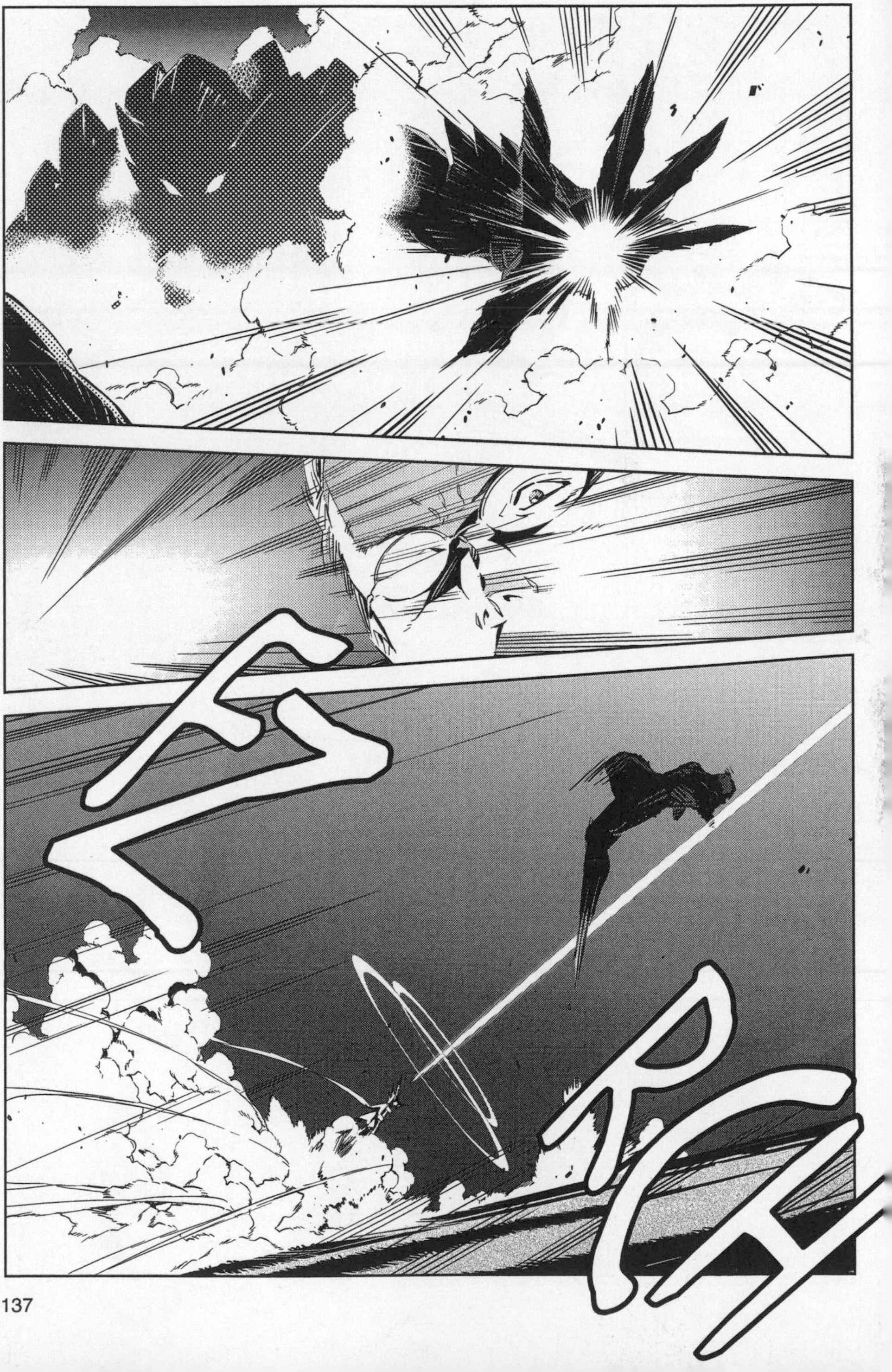
KRCH

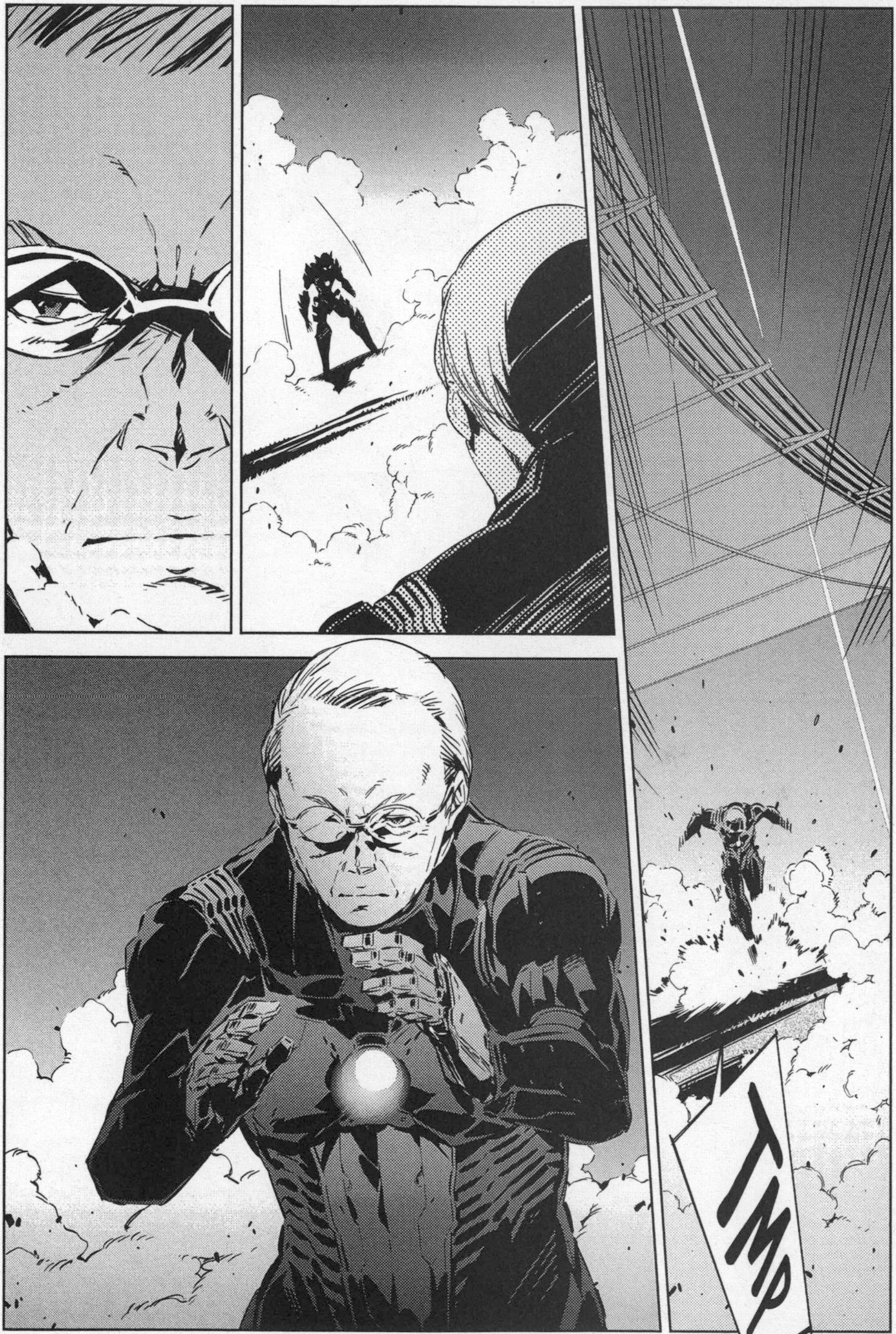
TMP

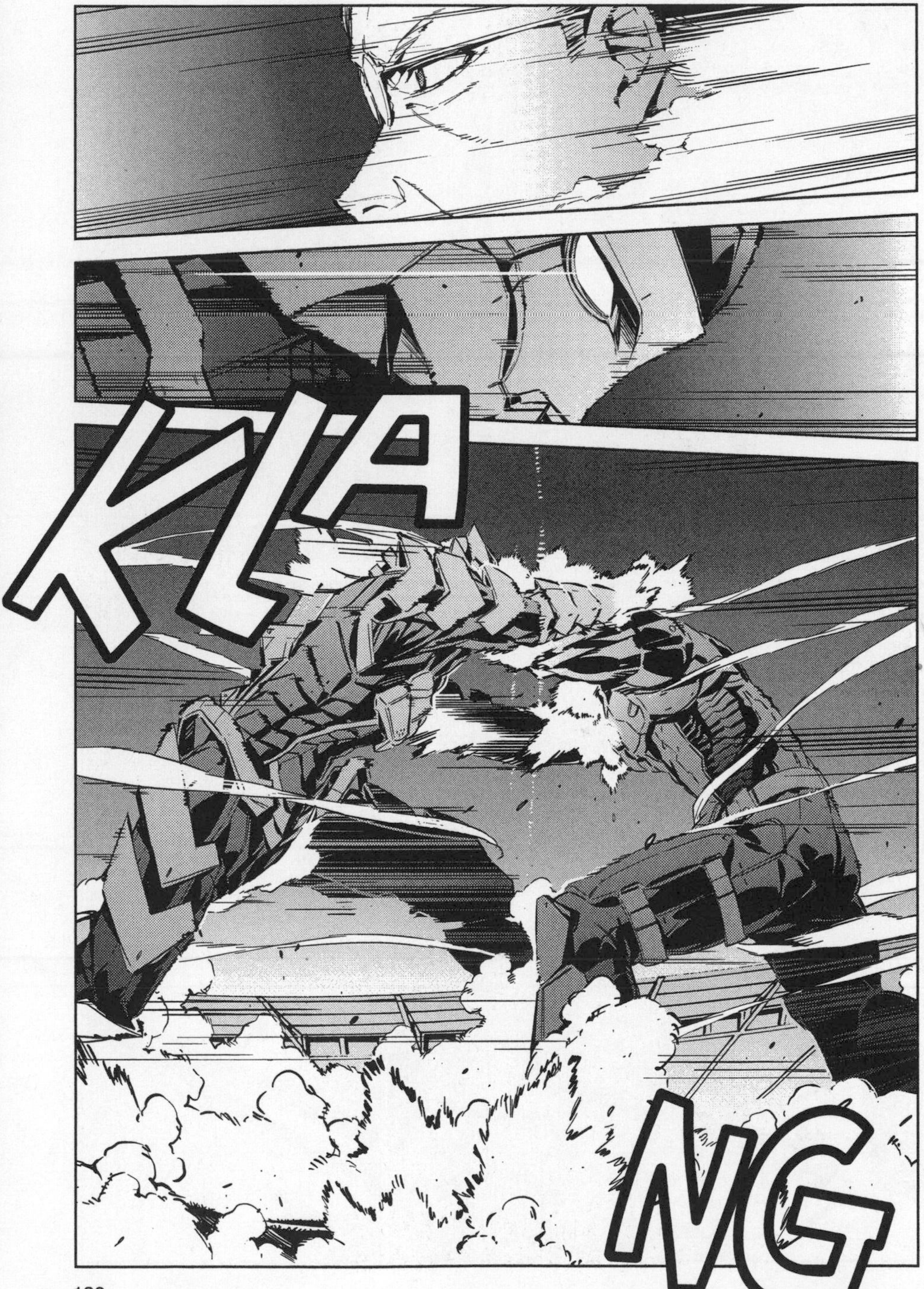
KI'A
NG

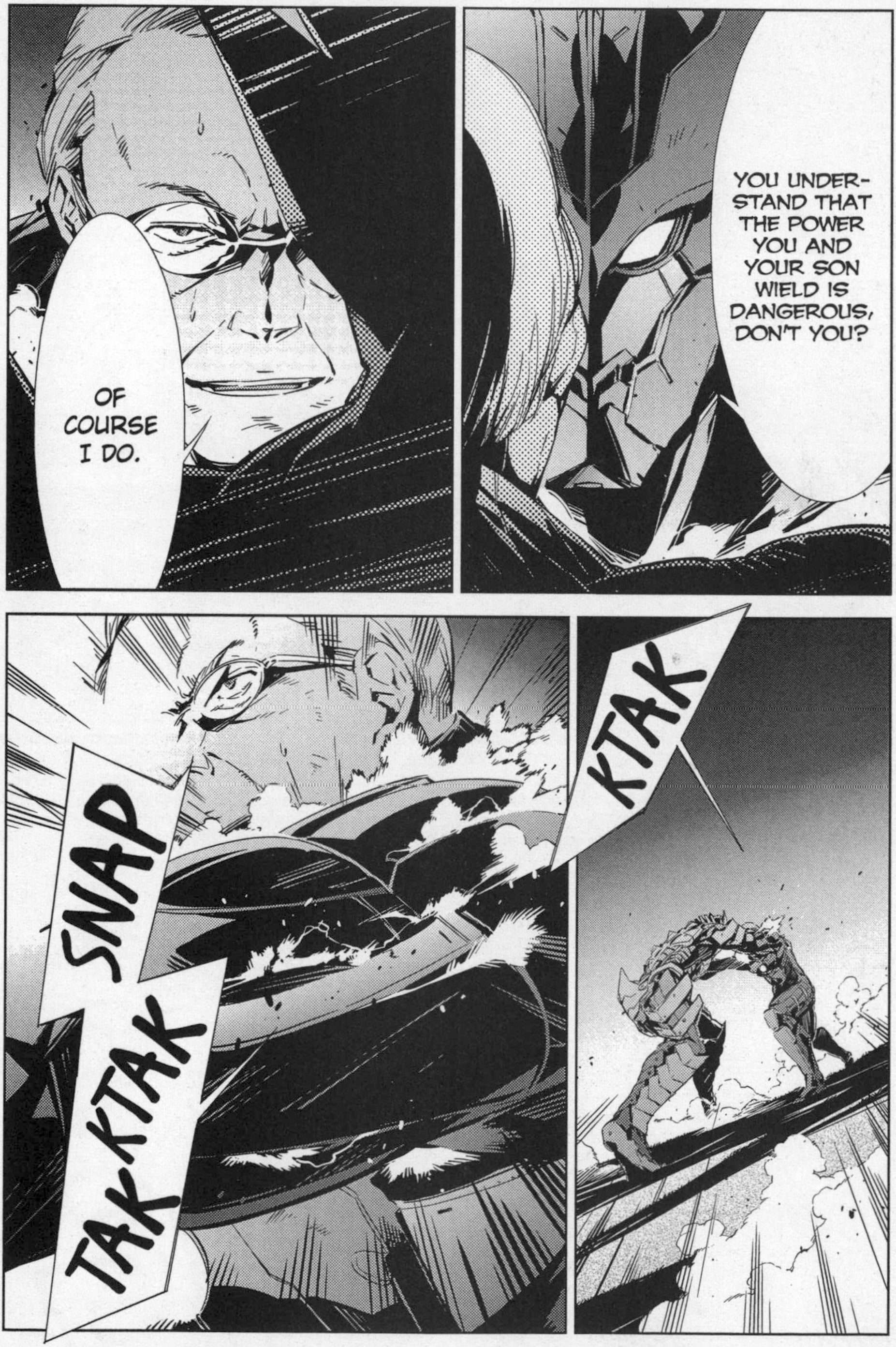
YOU UNDER-STAND THAT THE POWER YOU AND YOUR SON WIELD IS DANGEROUS, DON'T YOU?
OF COURSE I DO.
KTAK
SNAP
TAKKTAK

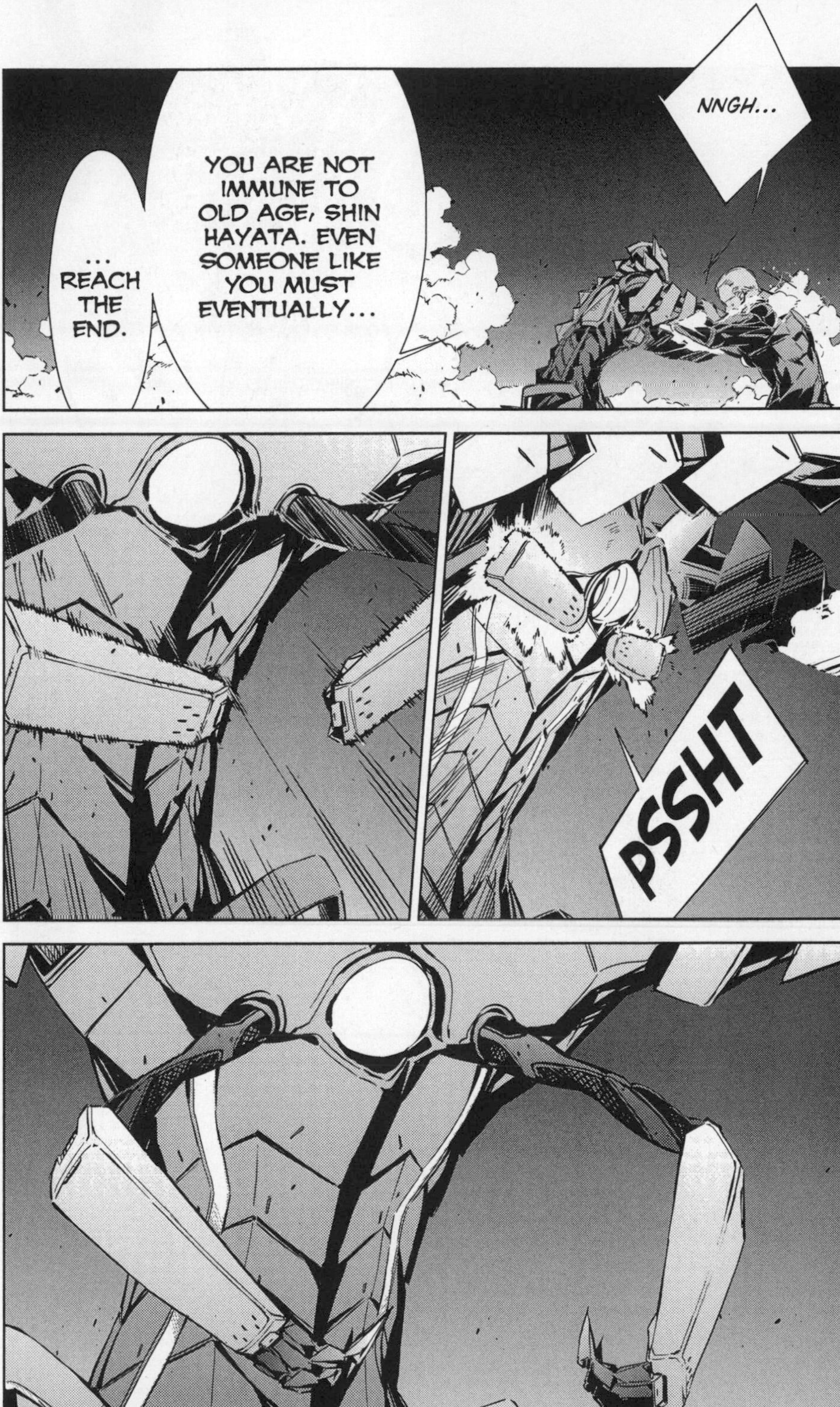
NNGH...
YOU ARE NOT IMMUNE TO OLD AGE, SHIN HAYATA. EVEN SOMEONE LIKE YOU MUST EVENTUALLY...
... REACH THE END.
PSSHT

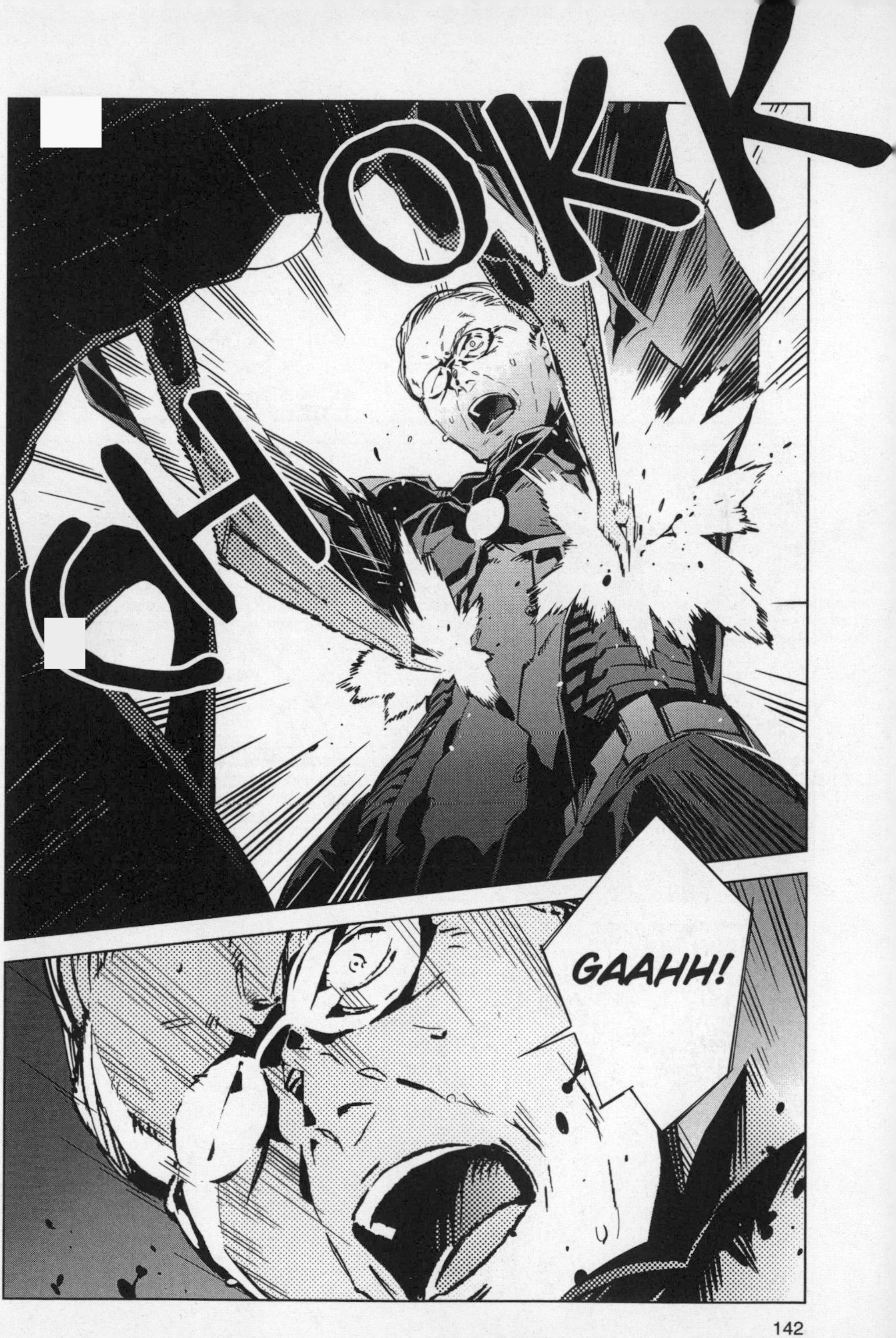
CHOKK
GAAHH!

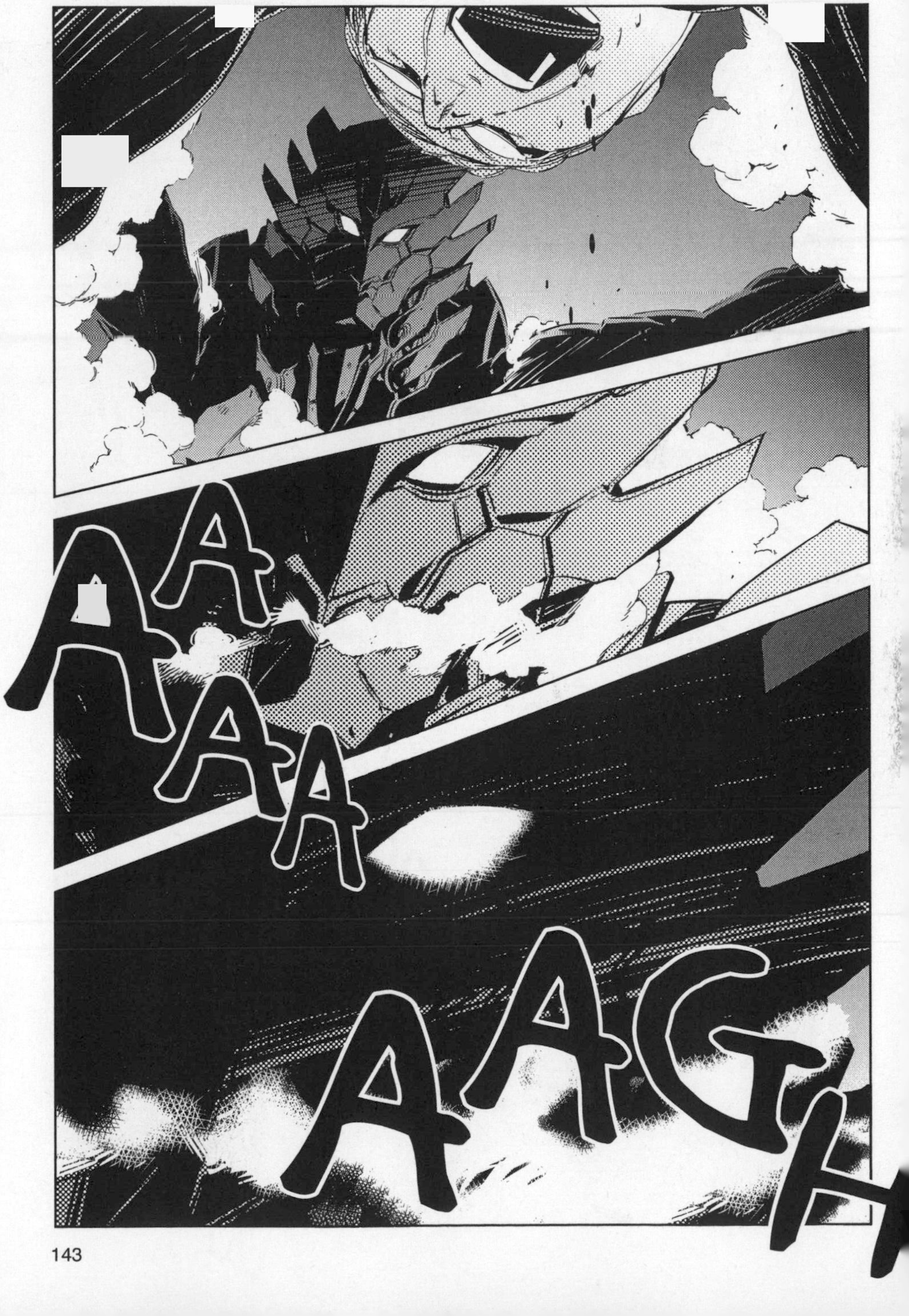
AAAAAA
AAAGH

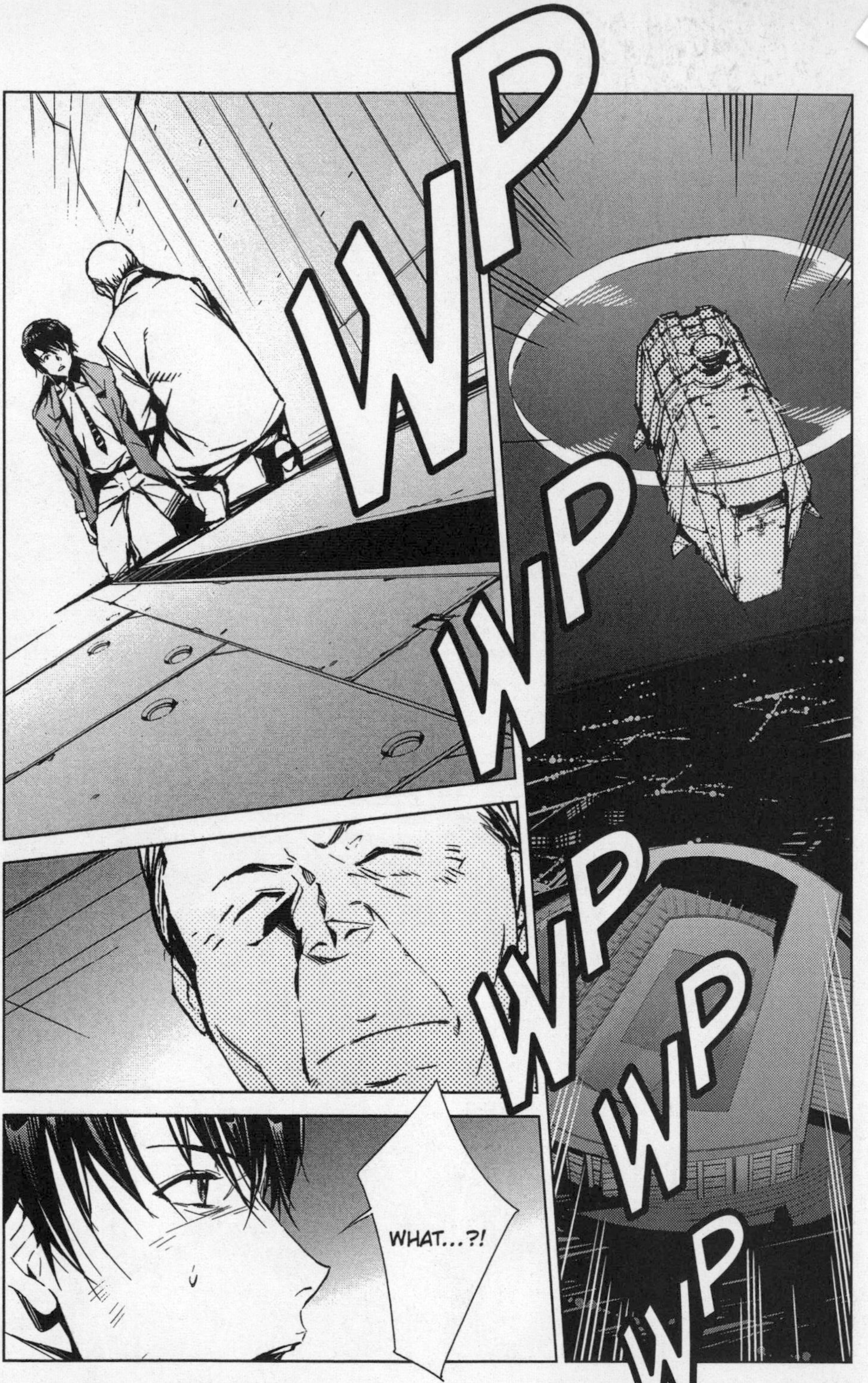
WP
WP
WP
WP
WP
WHAT...?!

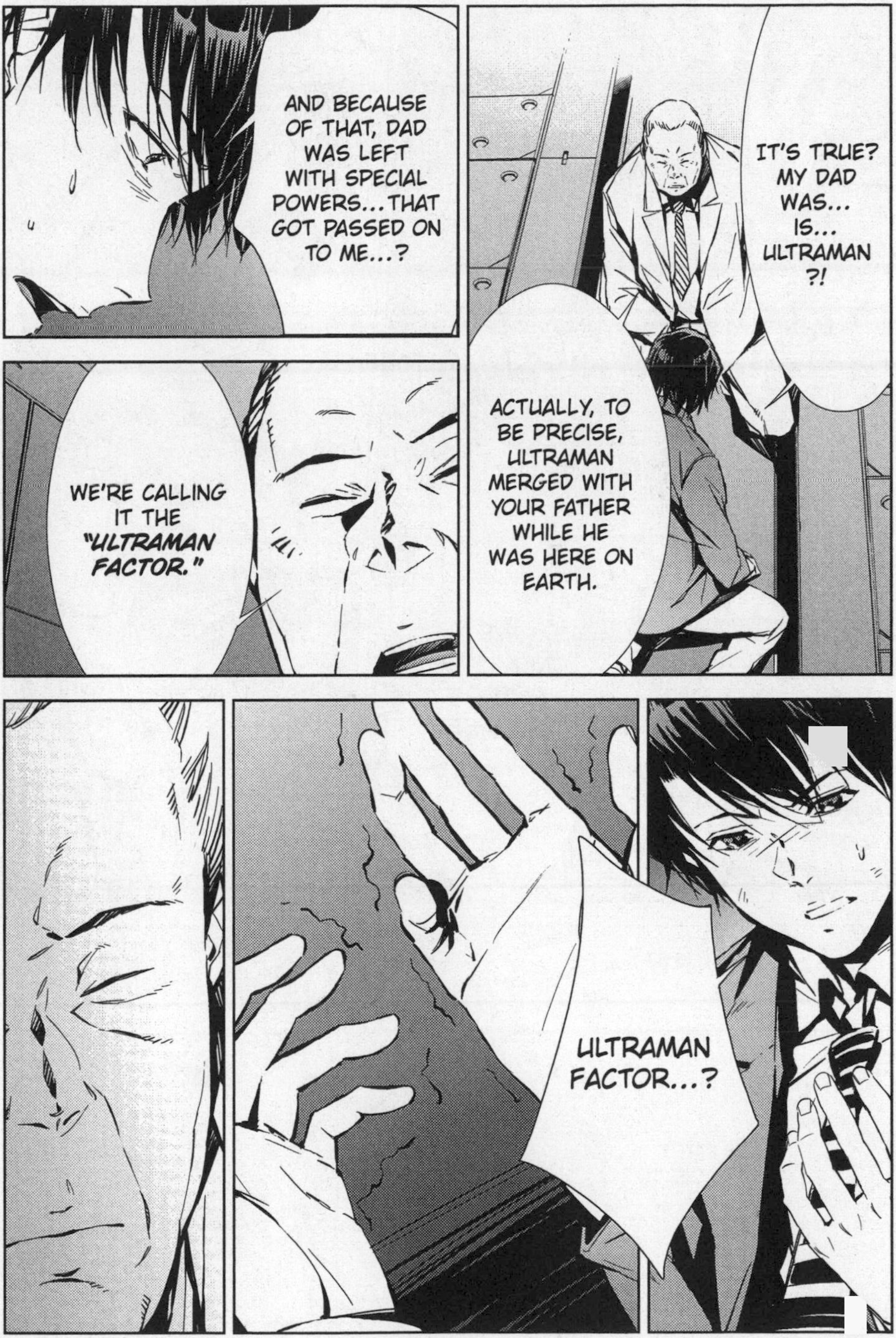
IT'S TRUE? MY DAD WAS... IS... ULTRAMAN?!
ACTUALLY, TO BE PRECISE, ULTRAMAN MERGED WITH YOUR FATHER WHILE HE WAS HERE ON EARTH.
AND BECAUSE OF THAT, DAD WAS LEFT WITH SPECIAL POWERS...THAT GOT PASSED ON TO ME...?
WE'RE CALLING IT THE *"ULTRAMAN FACTOR."*
ULTRAMAN FACTOR...?

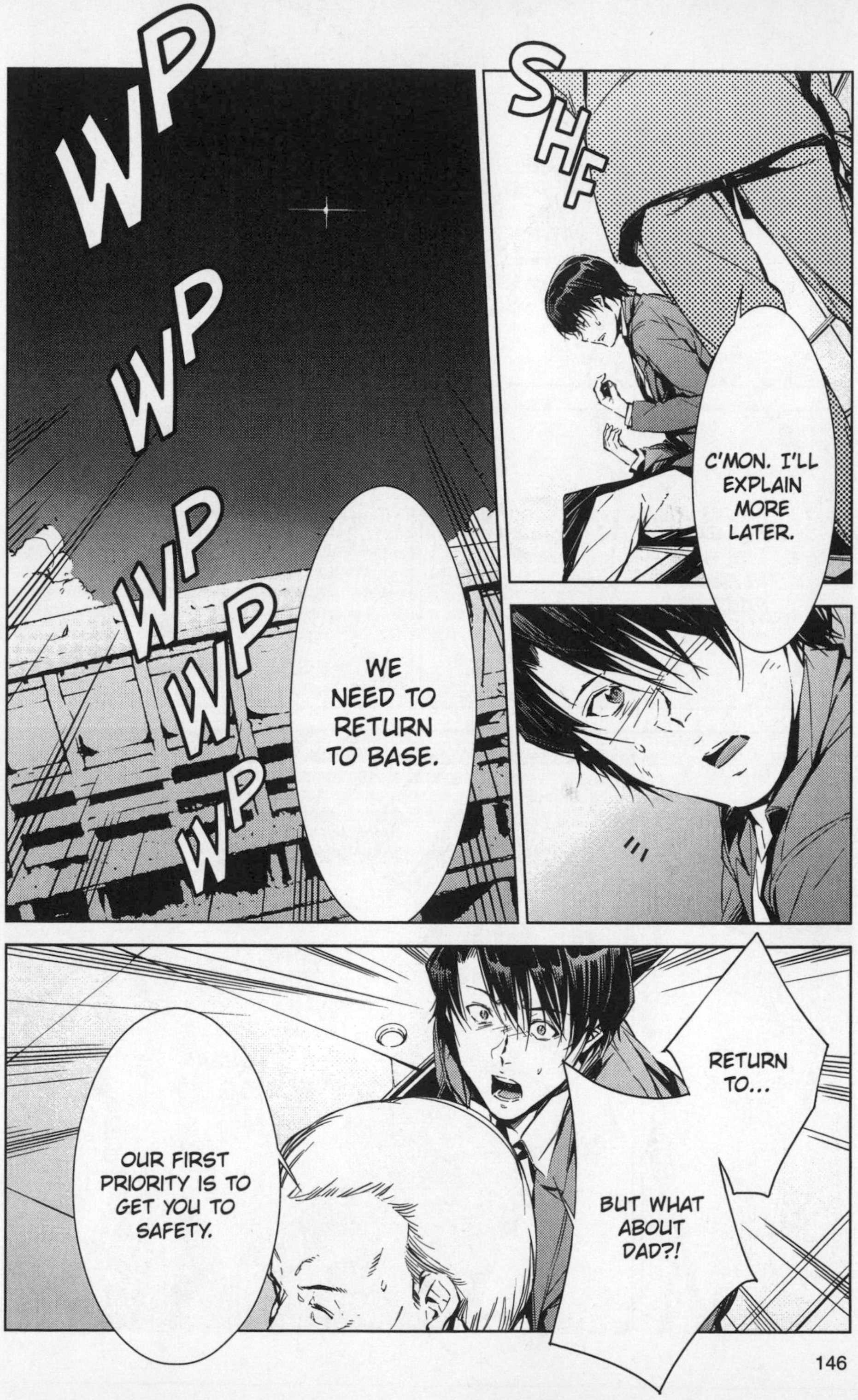
SHF
C'MON. I'LL EXPLAIN MORE LATER.
WP WP WP WP WP WP
WE NEED TO RETURN TO BASE.
RETURN TO...
BUT WHAT ABOUT DAD?!
OUR FIRST PRIORITY IS TO GET YOU TO SAFETY.

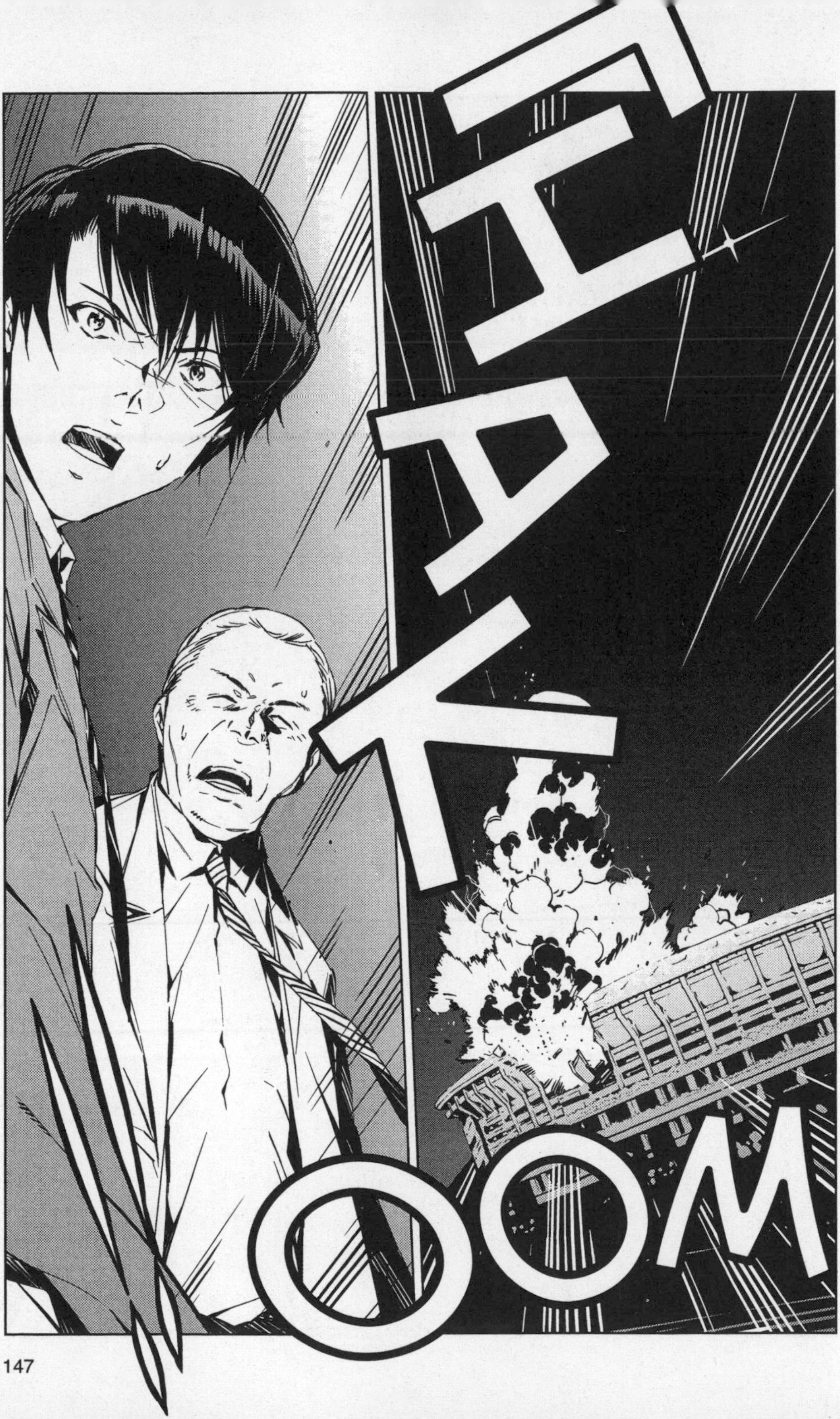
HAKOOM

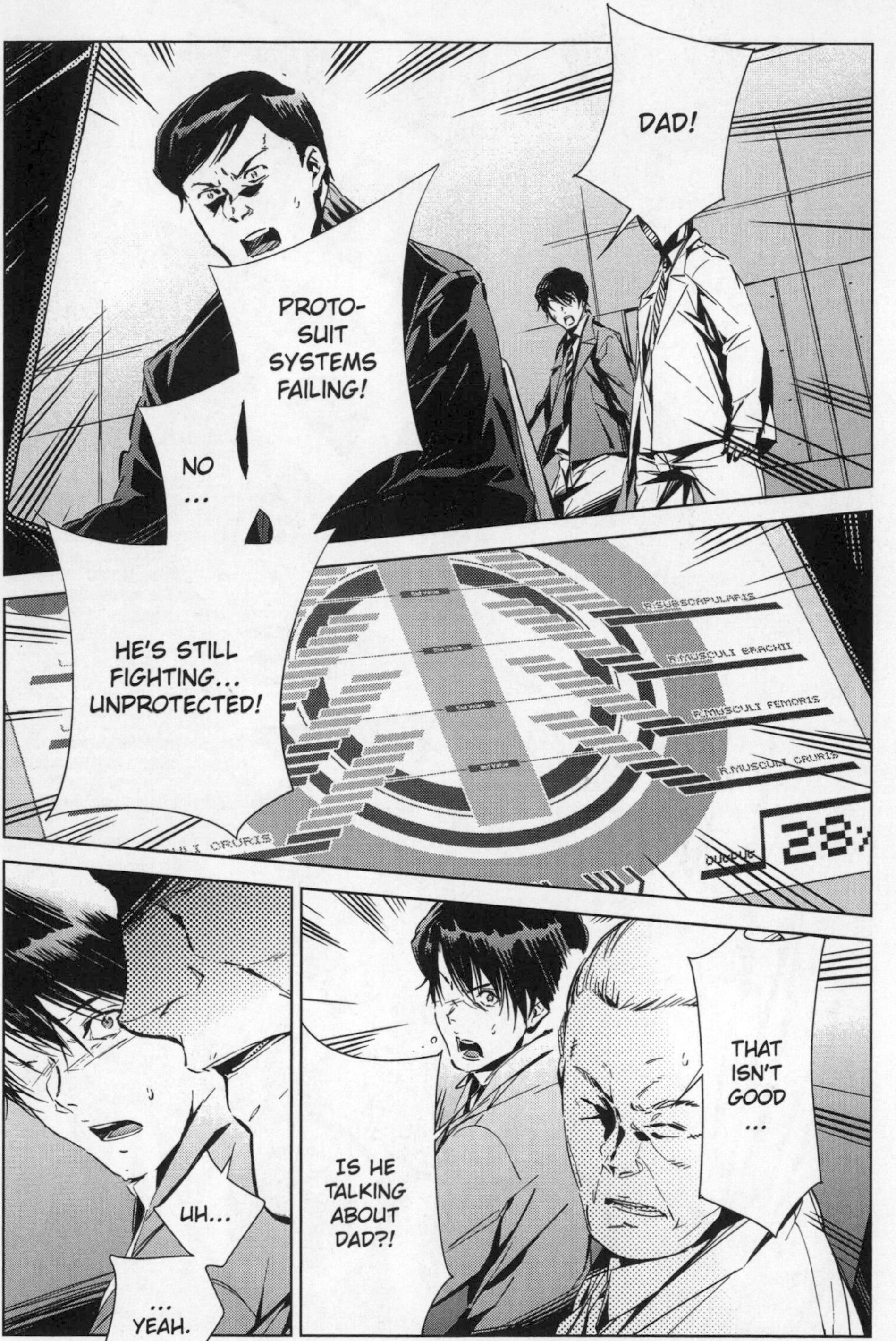
DAD!
PROTO-SUIT SYSTEMS FAILING!
NO ...
HE'S STILL FIGHTING... UNPROTECTED!
R.SUBSCAPULARIS
R.MUSCULI BRACHII
R.MUSCULI FEMORIS
R.MUSCULI CRURIS
THAT ISN'T GOOD ...
IS HE TALKING ABOUT DAD?!
UH...
... YEAH.

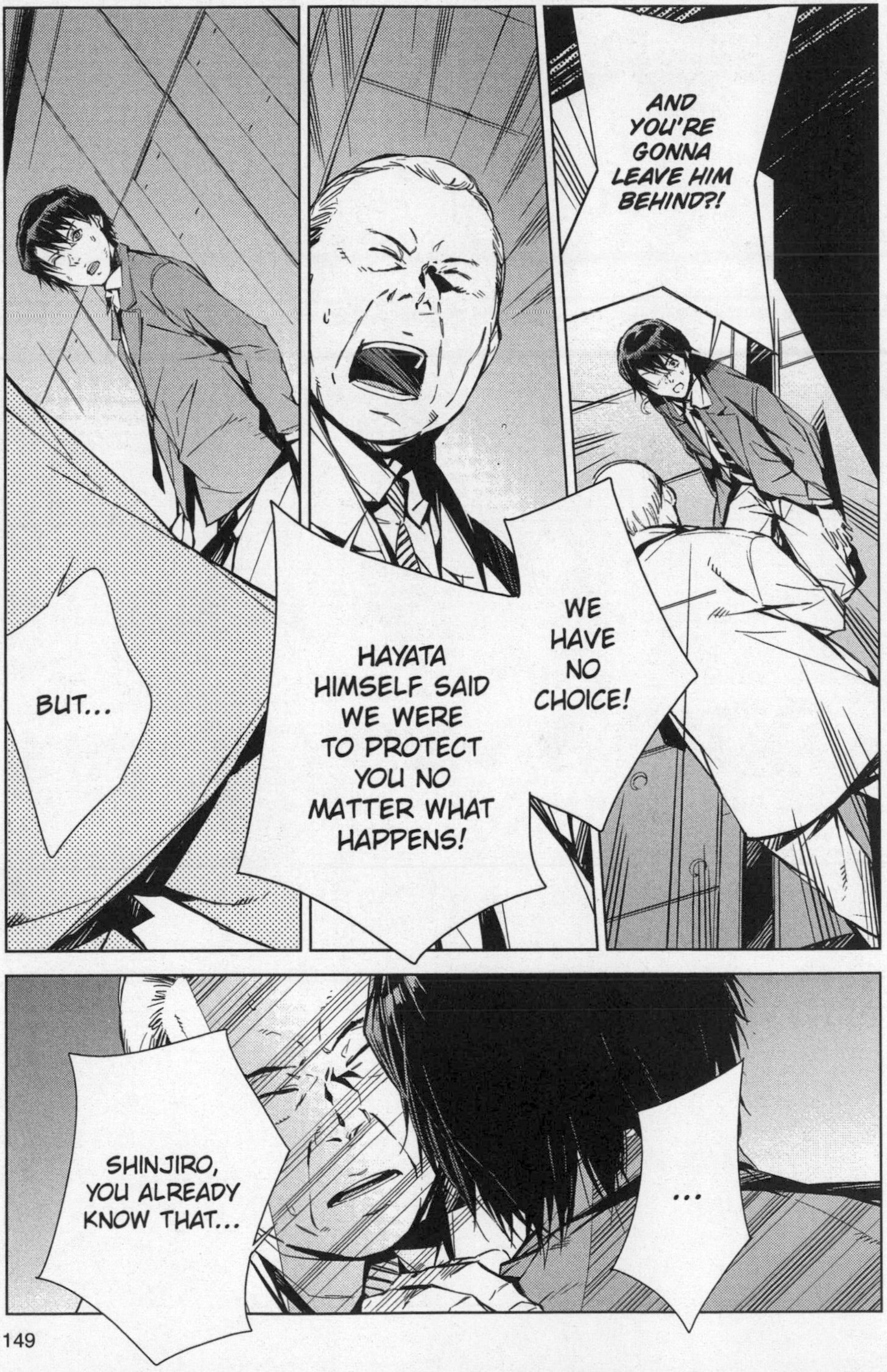
AND YOU'RE GONNA LEAVE HIM BEHIND?!
WE HAVE NO CHOICE!
HAYATA HIMSELF SAID WE WERE TO PROTECT YOU NO MATTER WHAT HAPPENS!
BUT...
...
SHINJIRO, YOU ALREADY KNOW THAT...

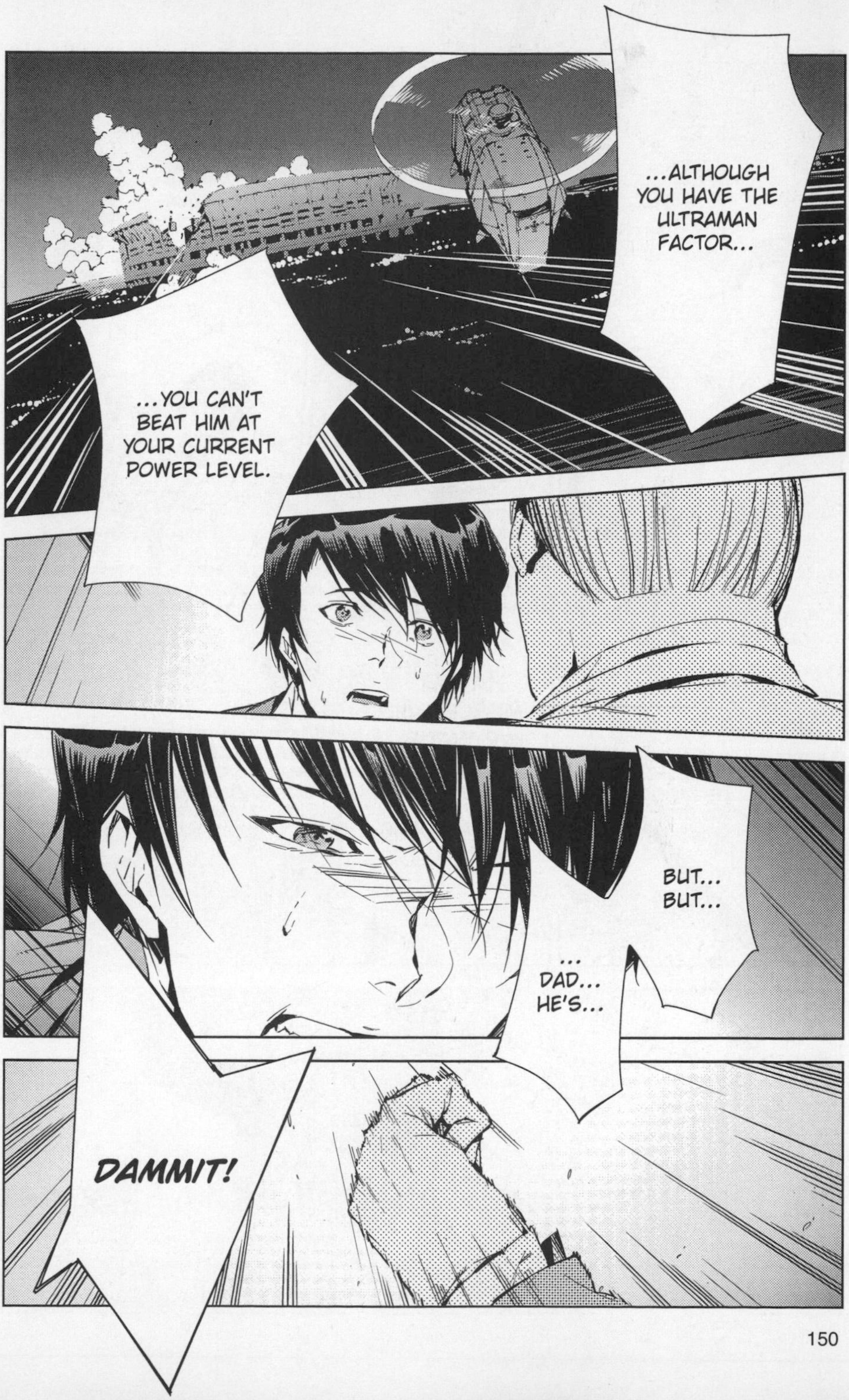
...ALTHOUGH YOU HAVE THE ULTRAMAN FACTOR...
...YOU CAN'T BEAT HIM AT YOUR CURRENT POWER LEVEL.
BUT... BUT...
... DAD... HE'S...
DAMMIT!

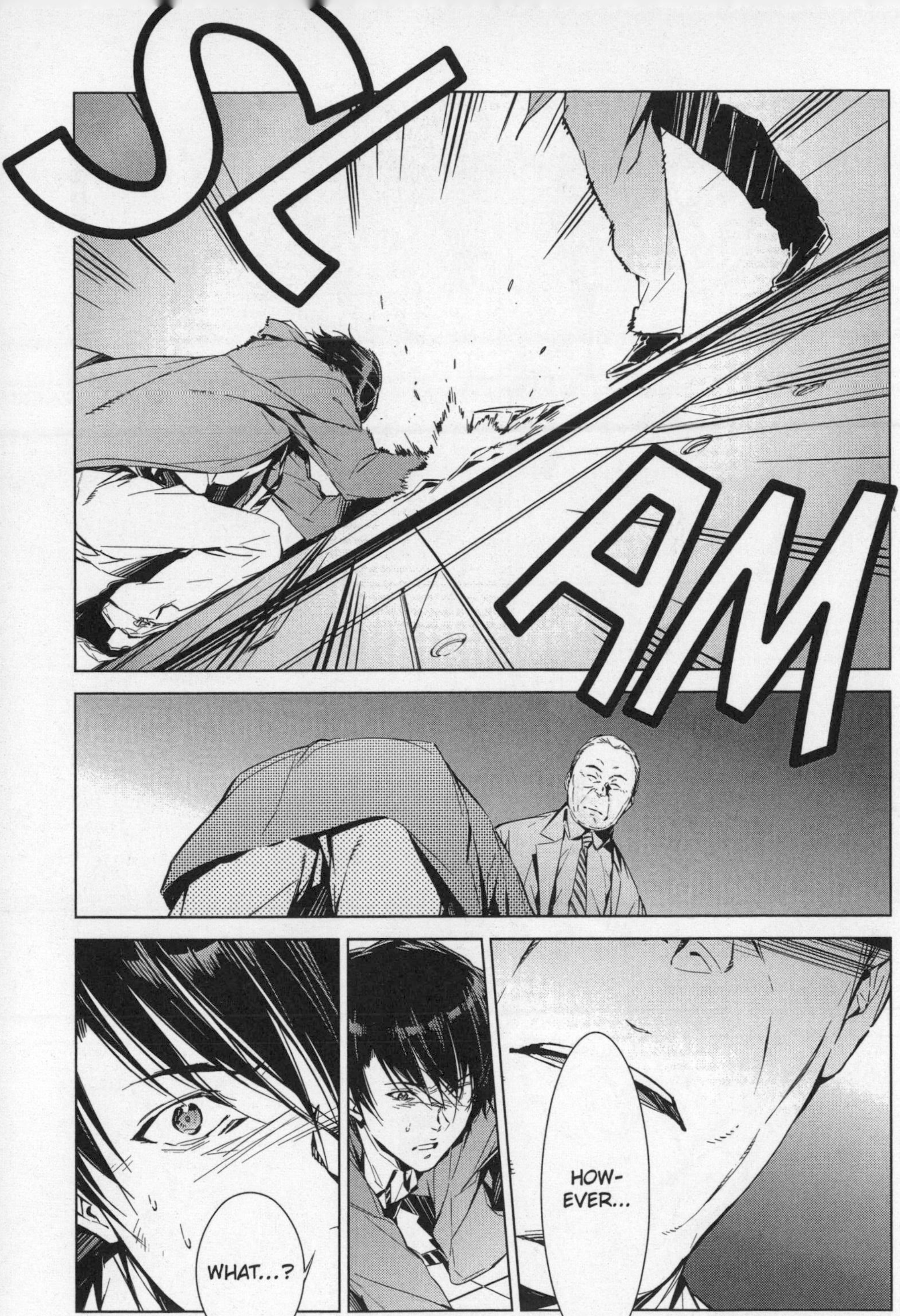
SLAM
HOW-EVER...
WHAT...?

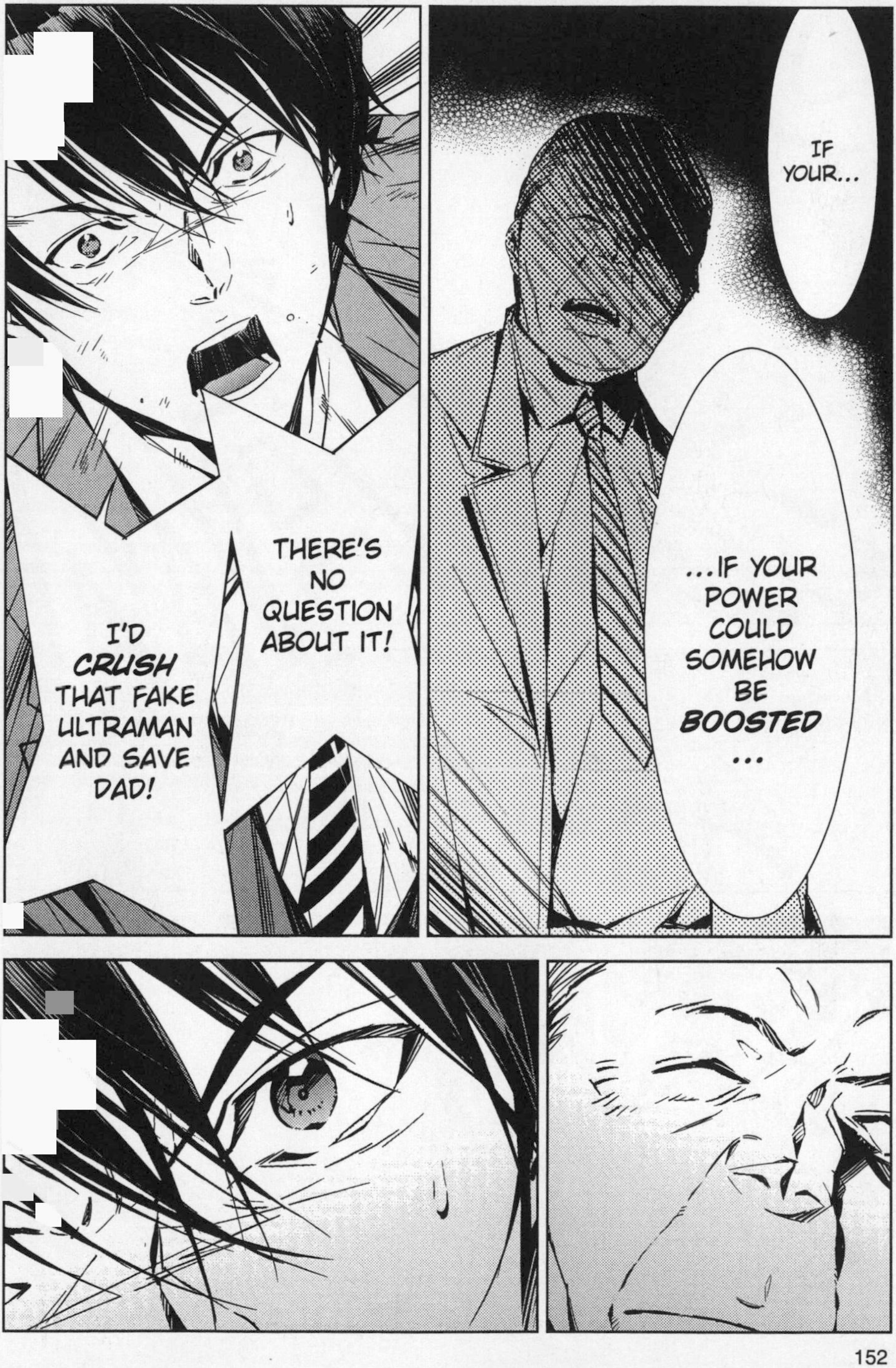
IF YOUR...
...IF YOUR POWER COULD SOMEHOW BE BOOSTED...
THERE'S NO QUESTION ABOUT IT!
I'D CRUSH THAT FAKE ULTRAMAN AND SAVE DAD!

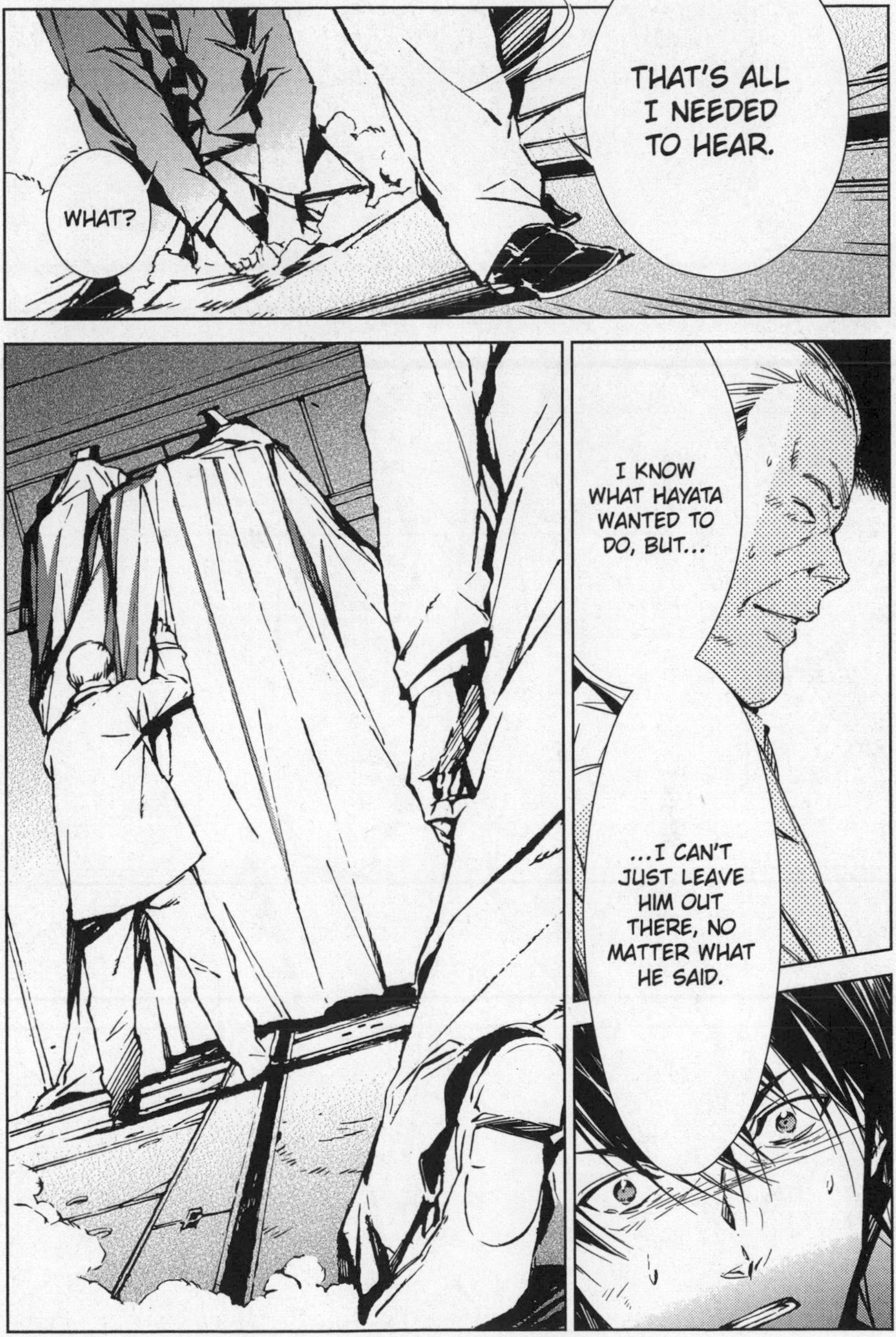
THAT'S ALL I NEEDED TO HEAR.
WHAT?
I KNOW WHAT HAYATA WANTED TO DO, BUT...
...I CAN'T JUST LEAVE HIM OUT THERE, NO MATTER WHAT HE SAID.

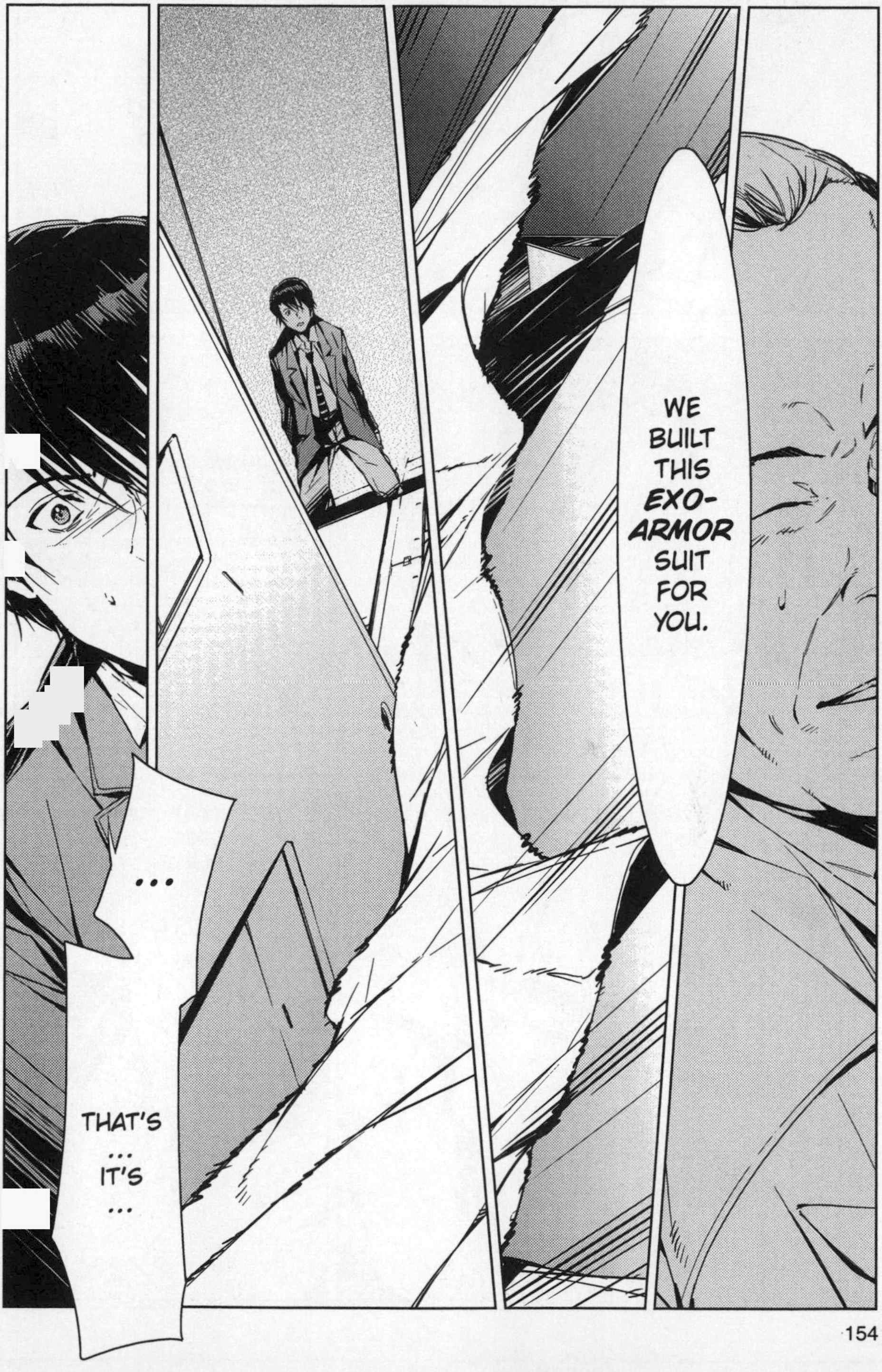
WE BUILT THIS EXO-ARMOR SUIT FOR YOU.
...
THAT'S ... IT'S ...

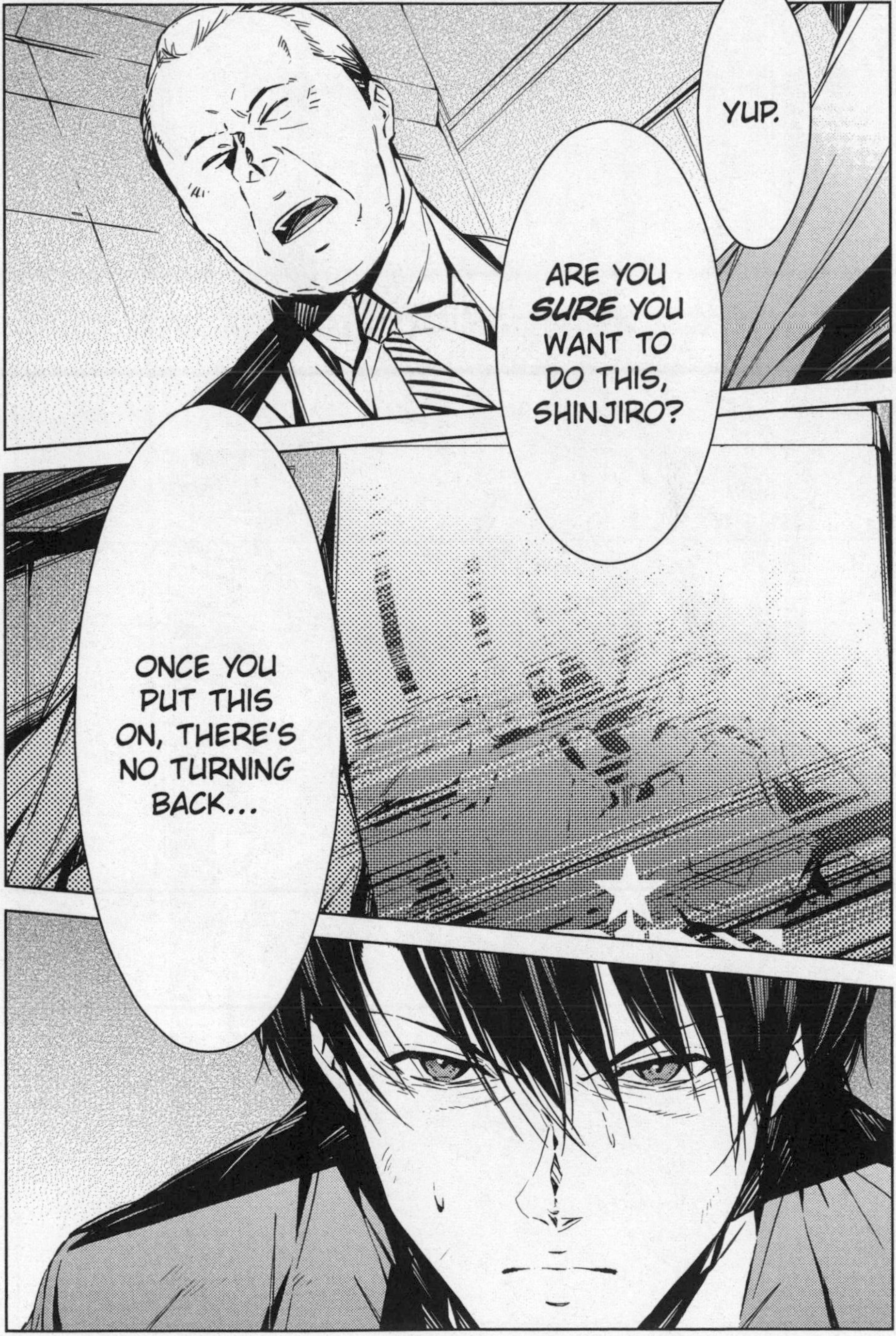
YUP.
ARE YOU SURE YOU WANT TO DO THIS, SHINJIRO?
ONCE YOU PUT THIS ON, THERE'S NO TURNING BACK...

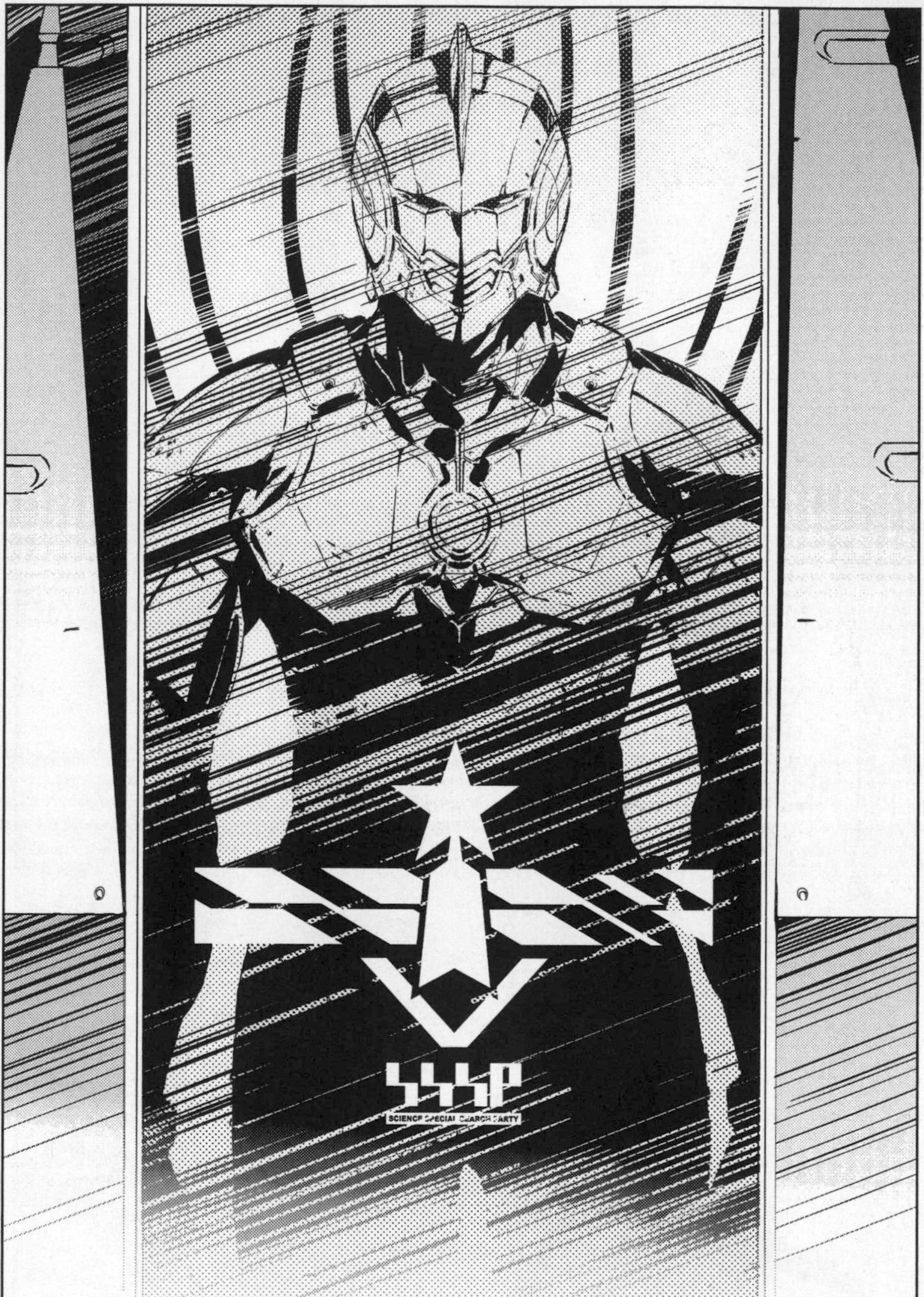

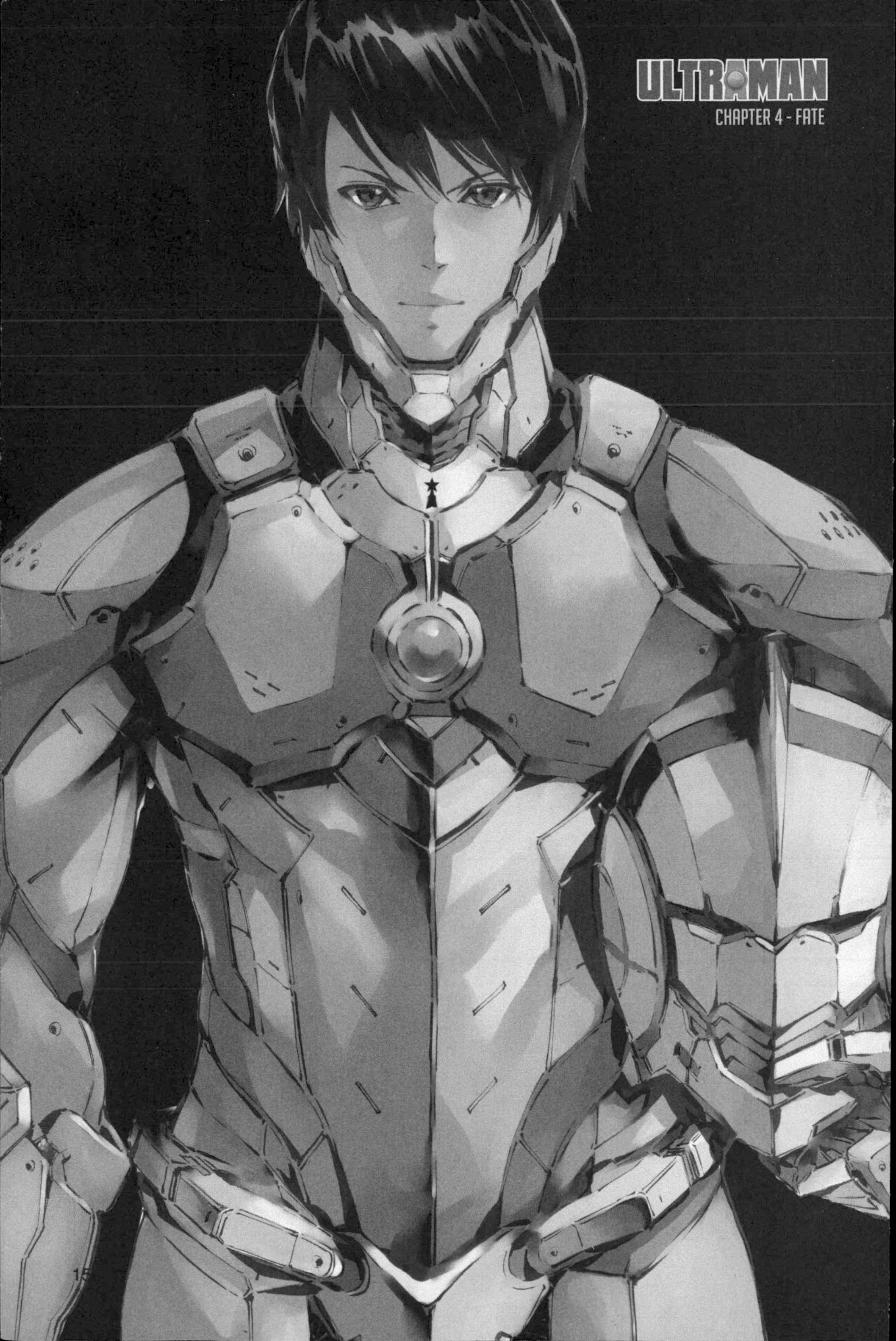
ULTRAMAN
CHAPTER 4 - FATE

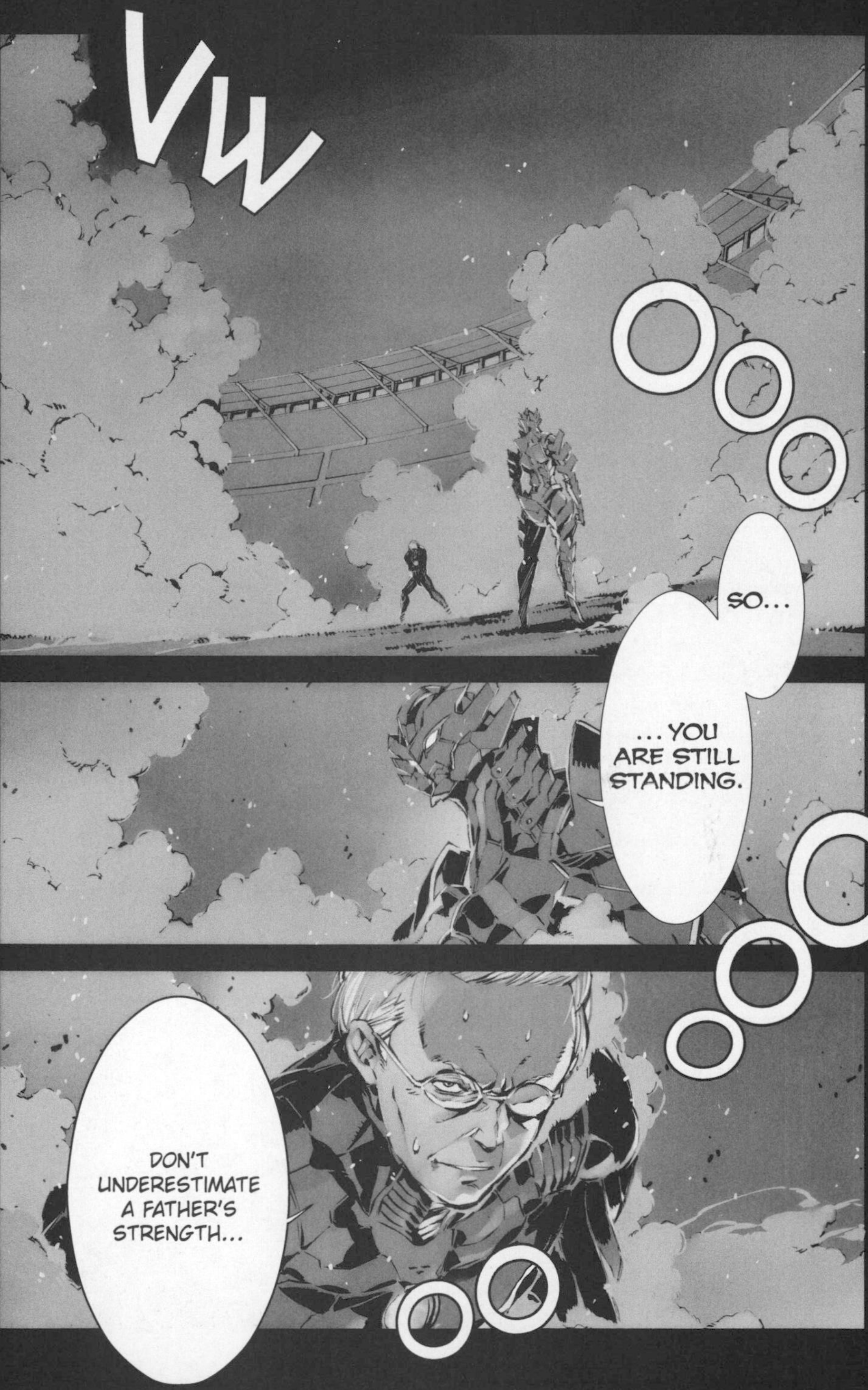
VW
SO...
...YOU ARE STILL STANDING.
DON'T UNDERESTIMATE A FATHER'S STRENGTH...

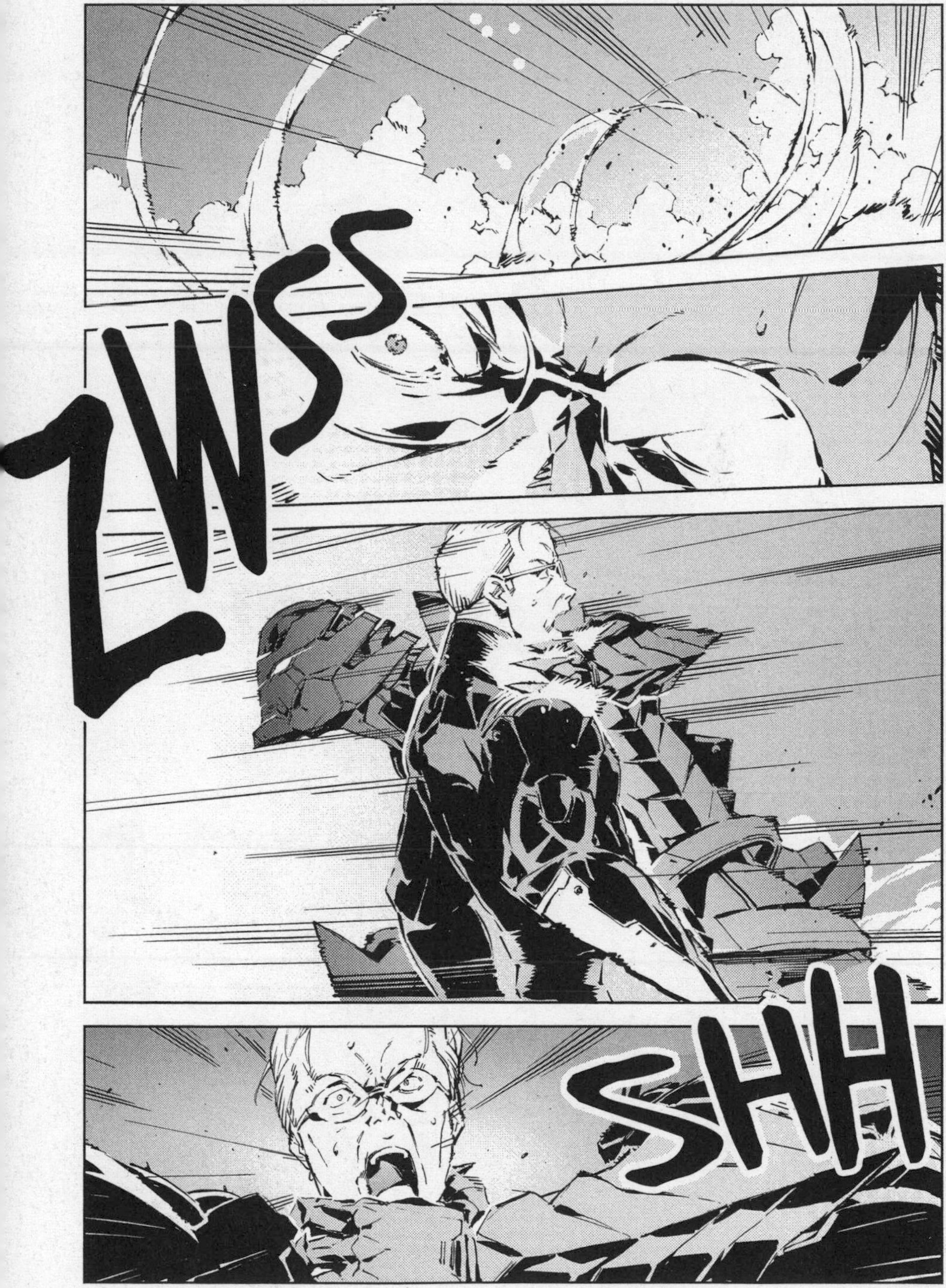
ZWSS
SHH

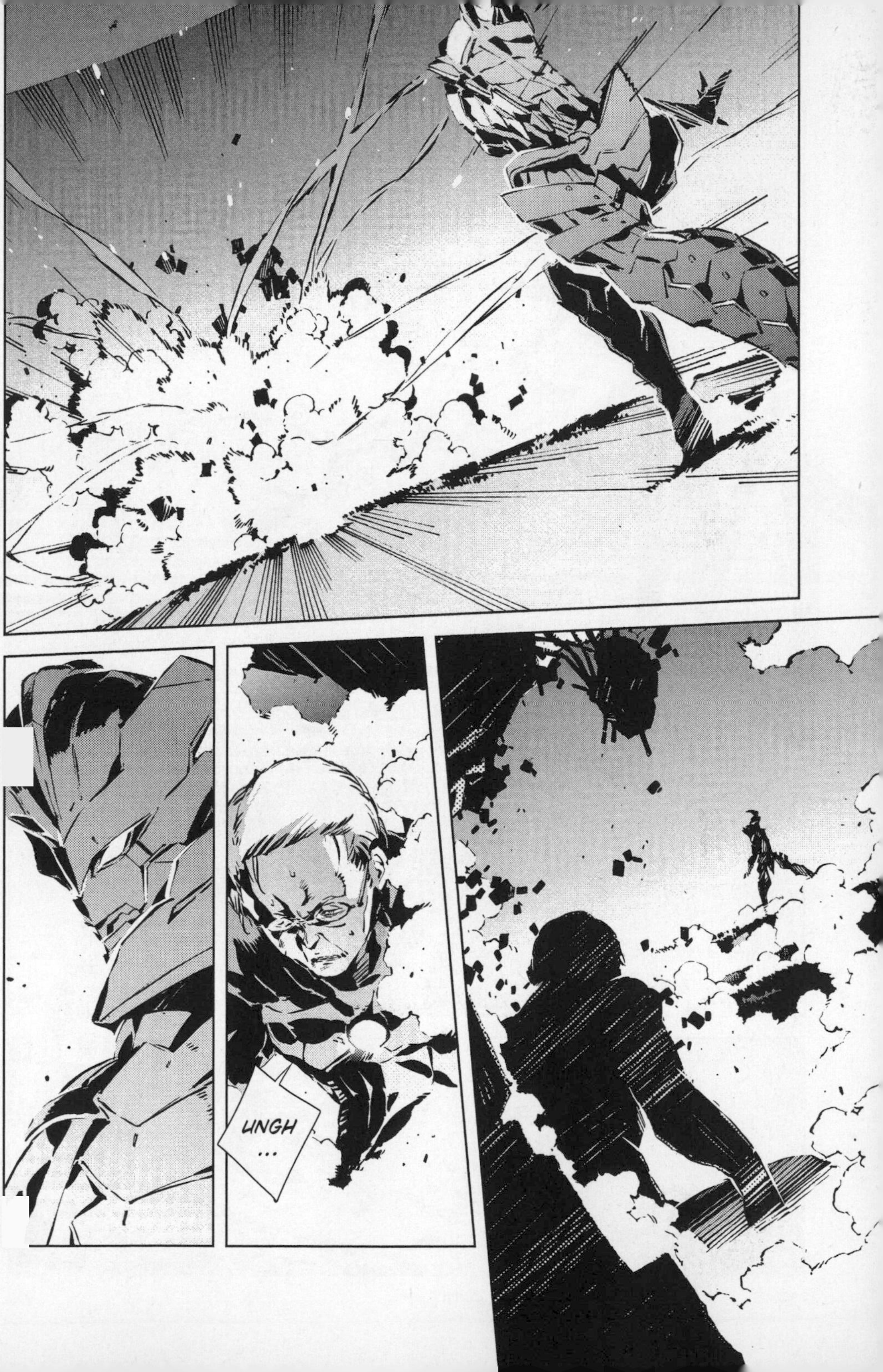
UNGH ...

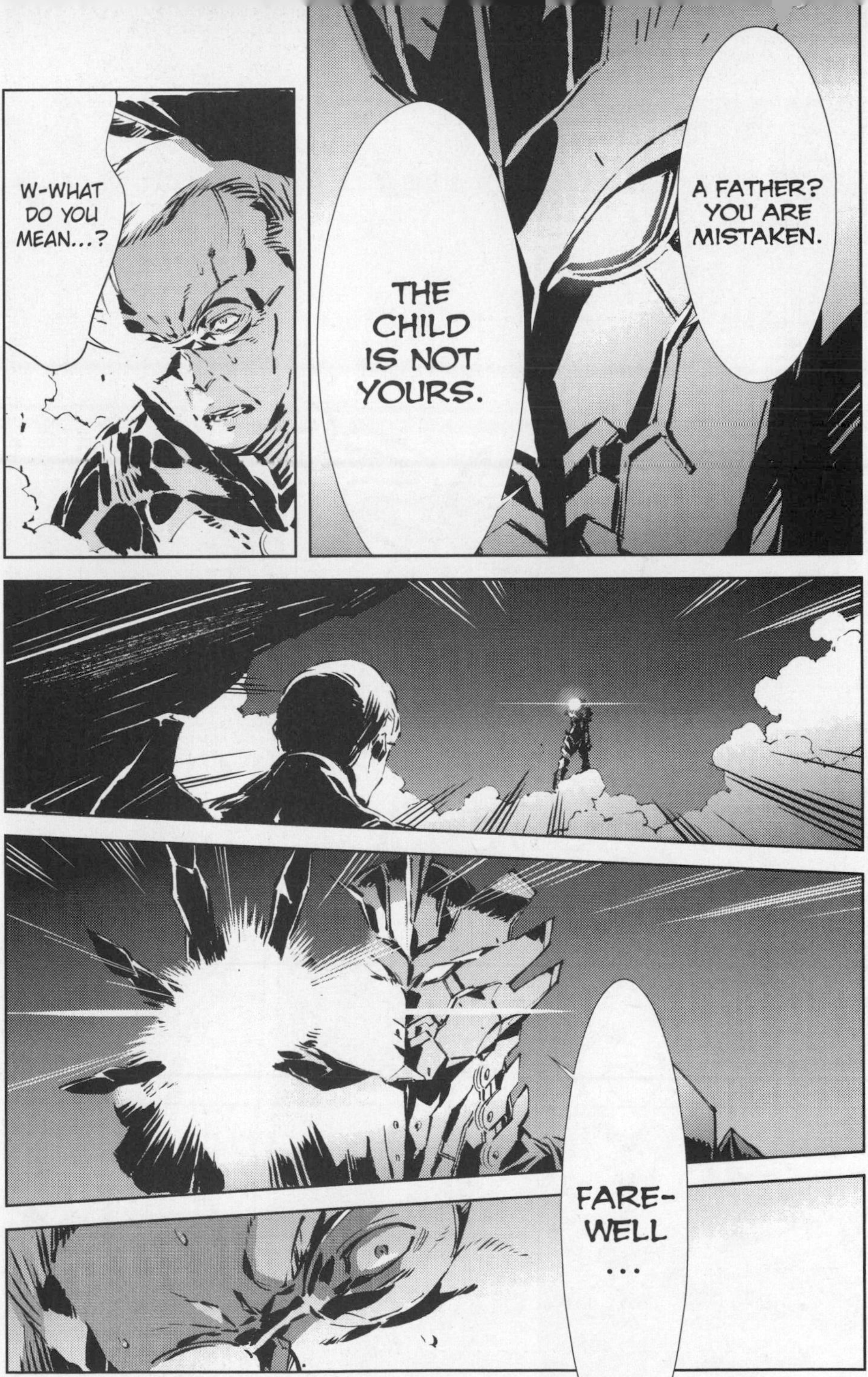
A FATHER? YOU ARE MISTAKEN.
THE CHILD IS NOT YOURS.
W-WHAT DO YOU MEAN...?
FARE-WELL...

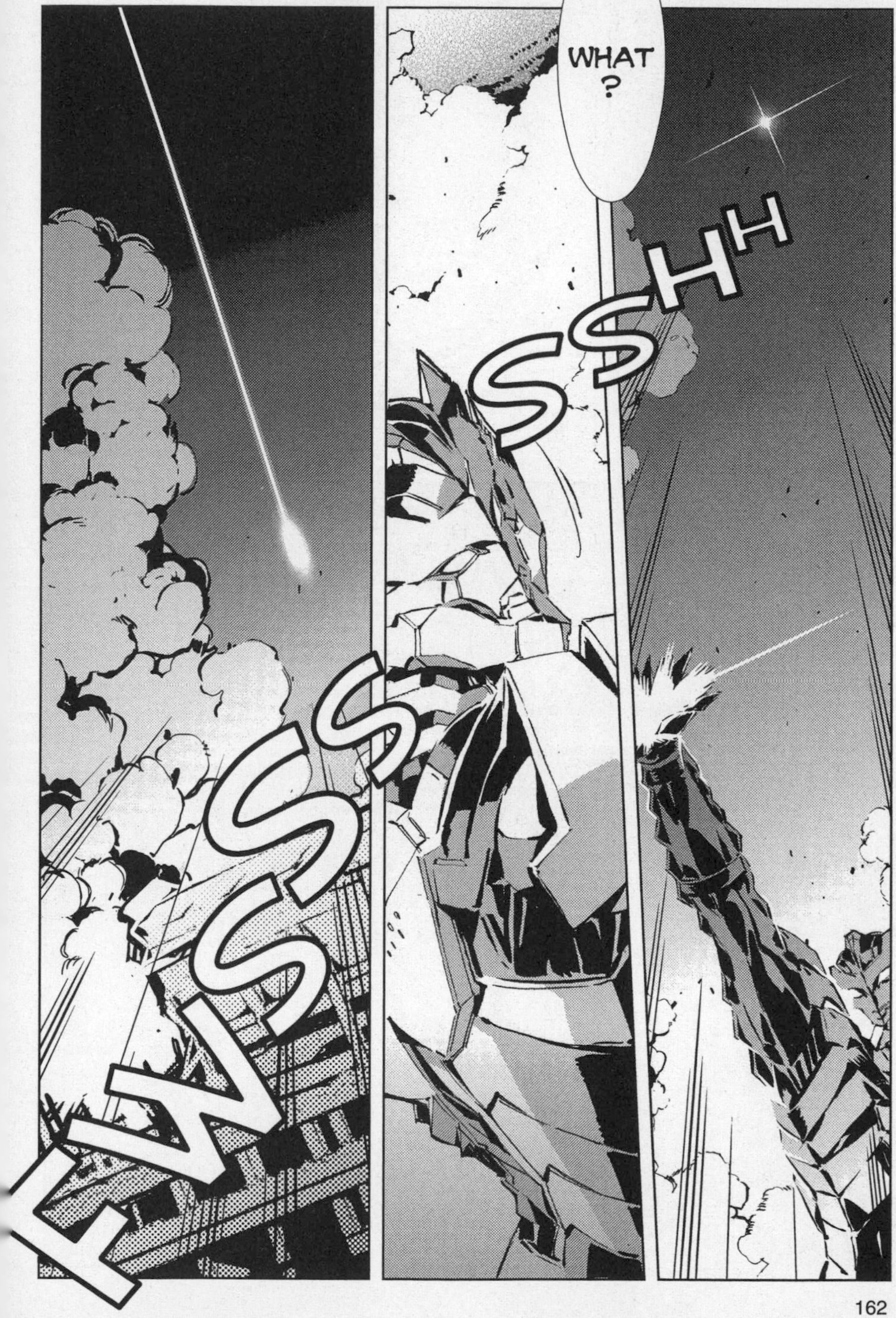
WHAT ?
FWSSSSSHH

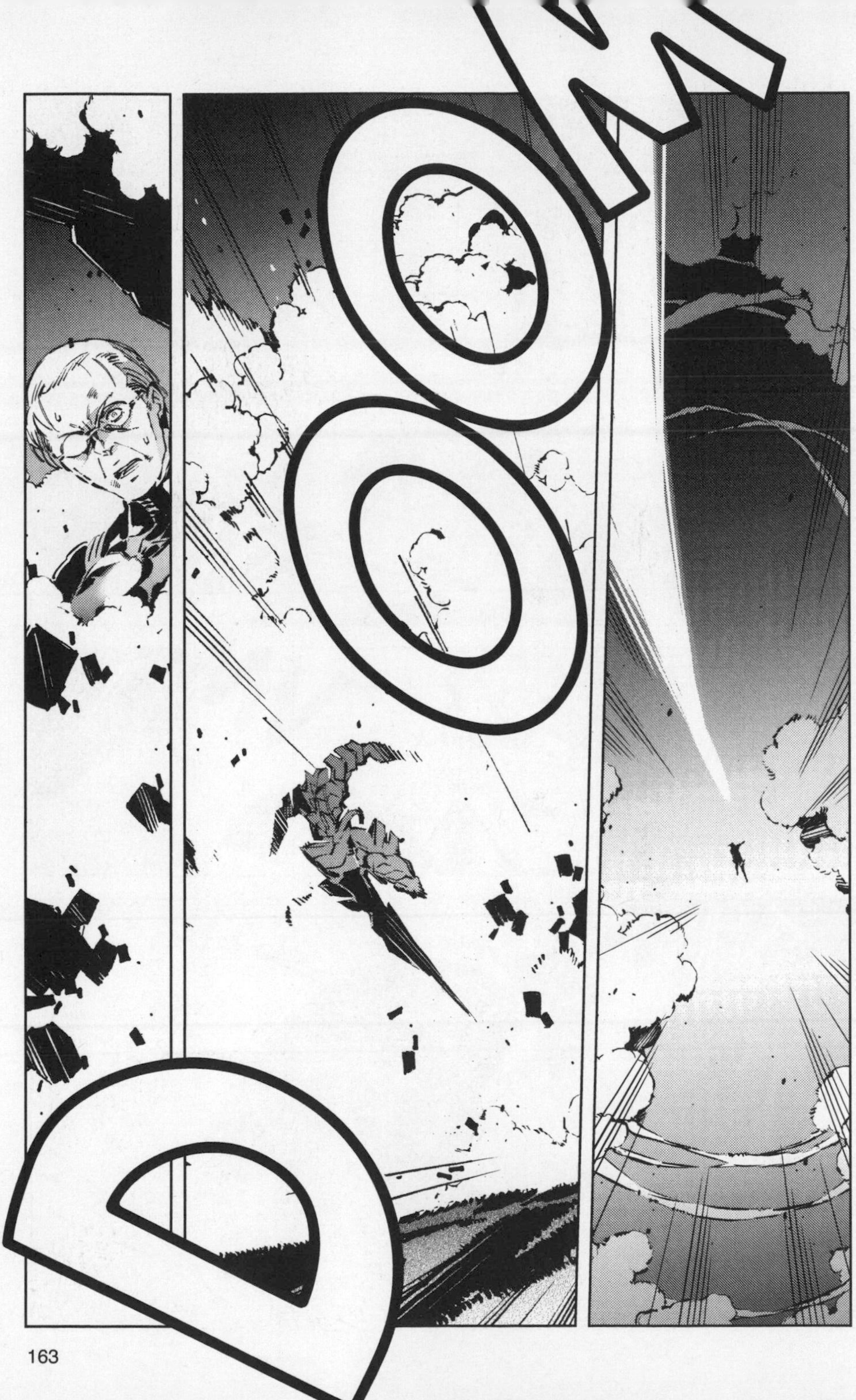
DOOM

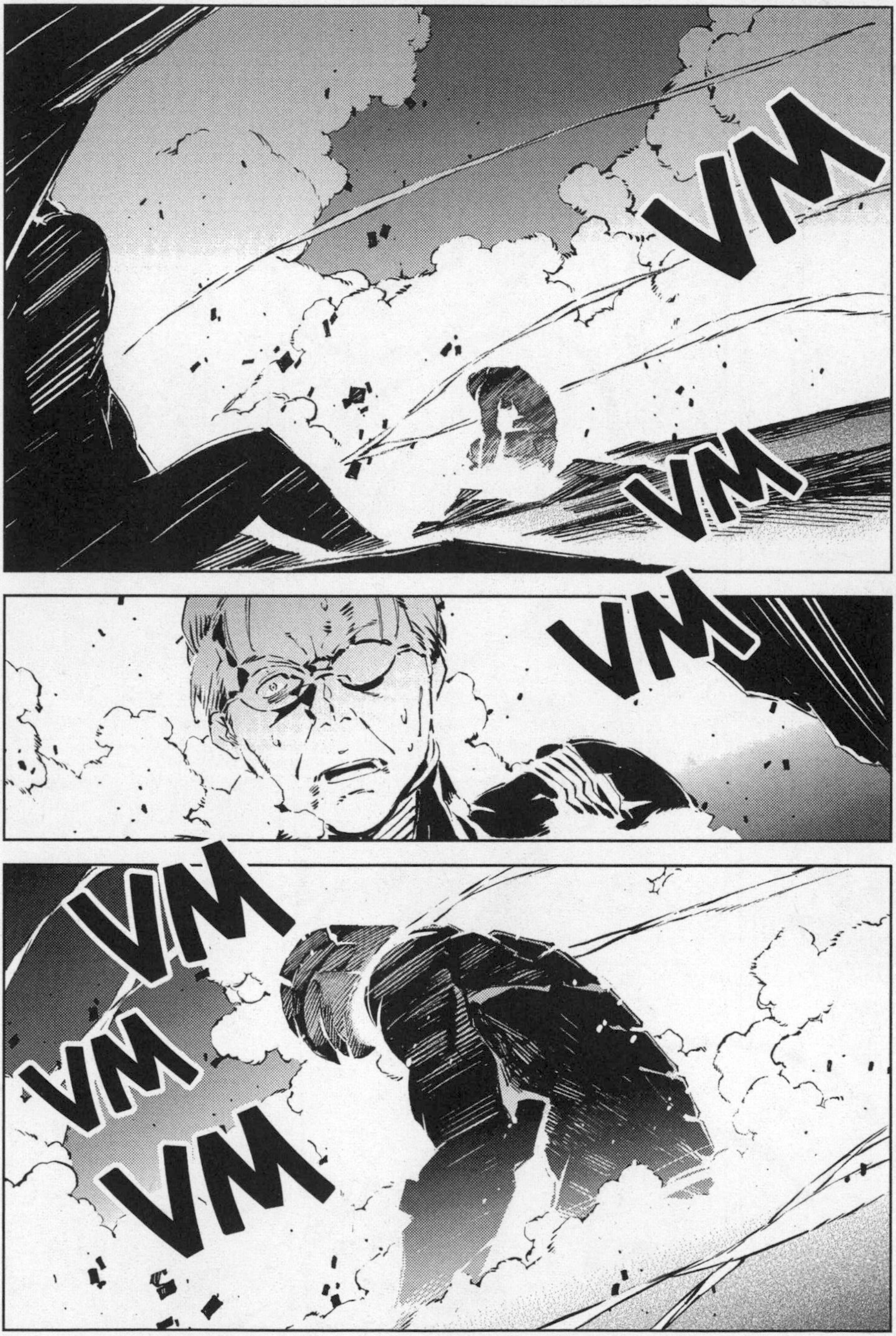
VM
VM
VM
VM
VM
VM

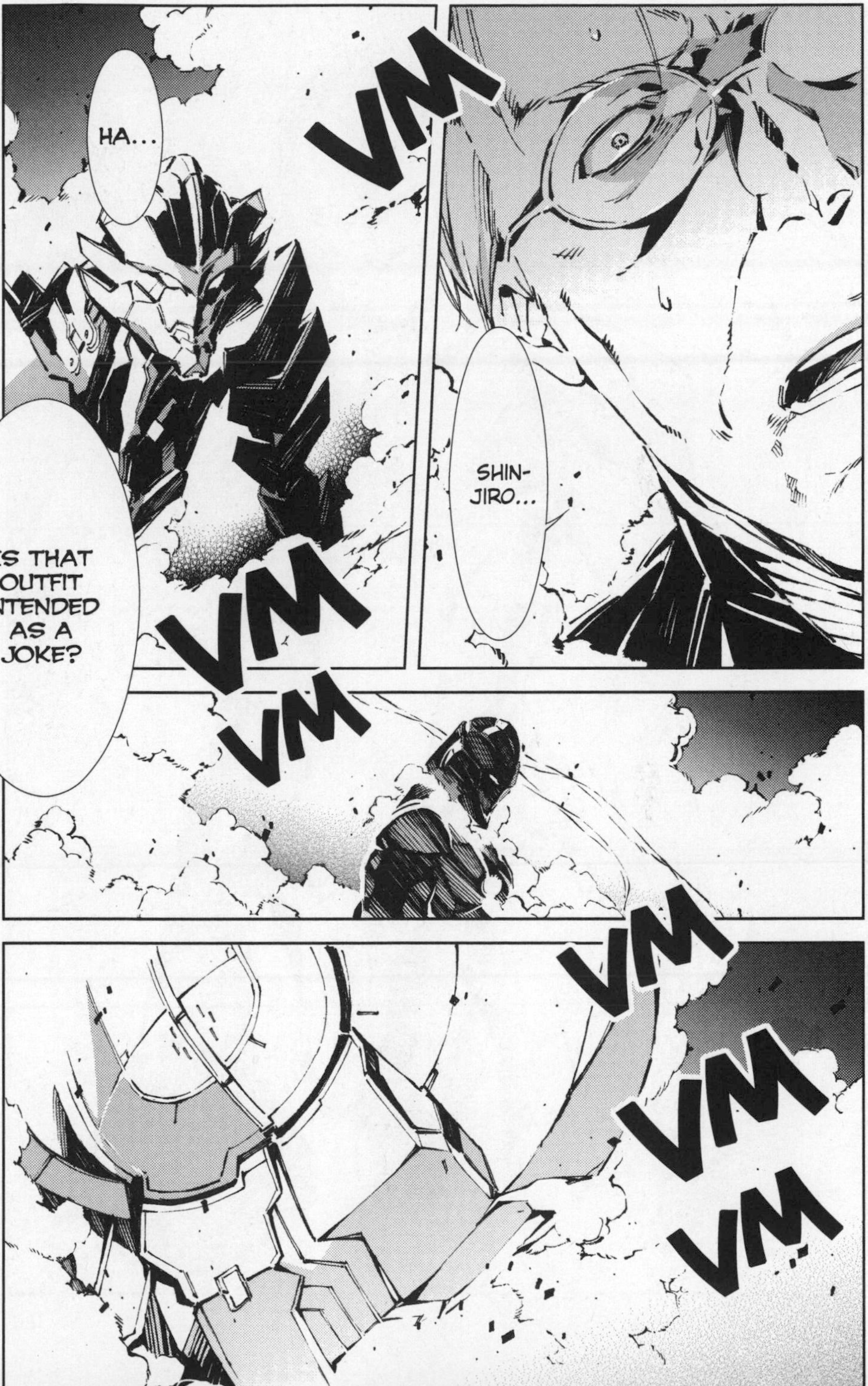
SHIN-JIRO...
VM
HA...
IS THAT OUTFIT INTENDED AS A JOKE?
VM
VM
VM
VM
VM

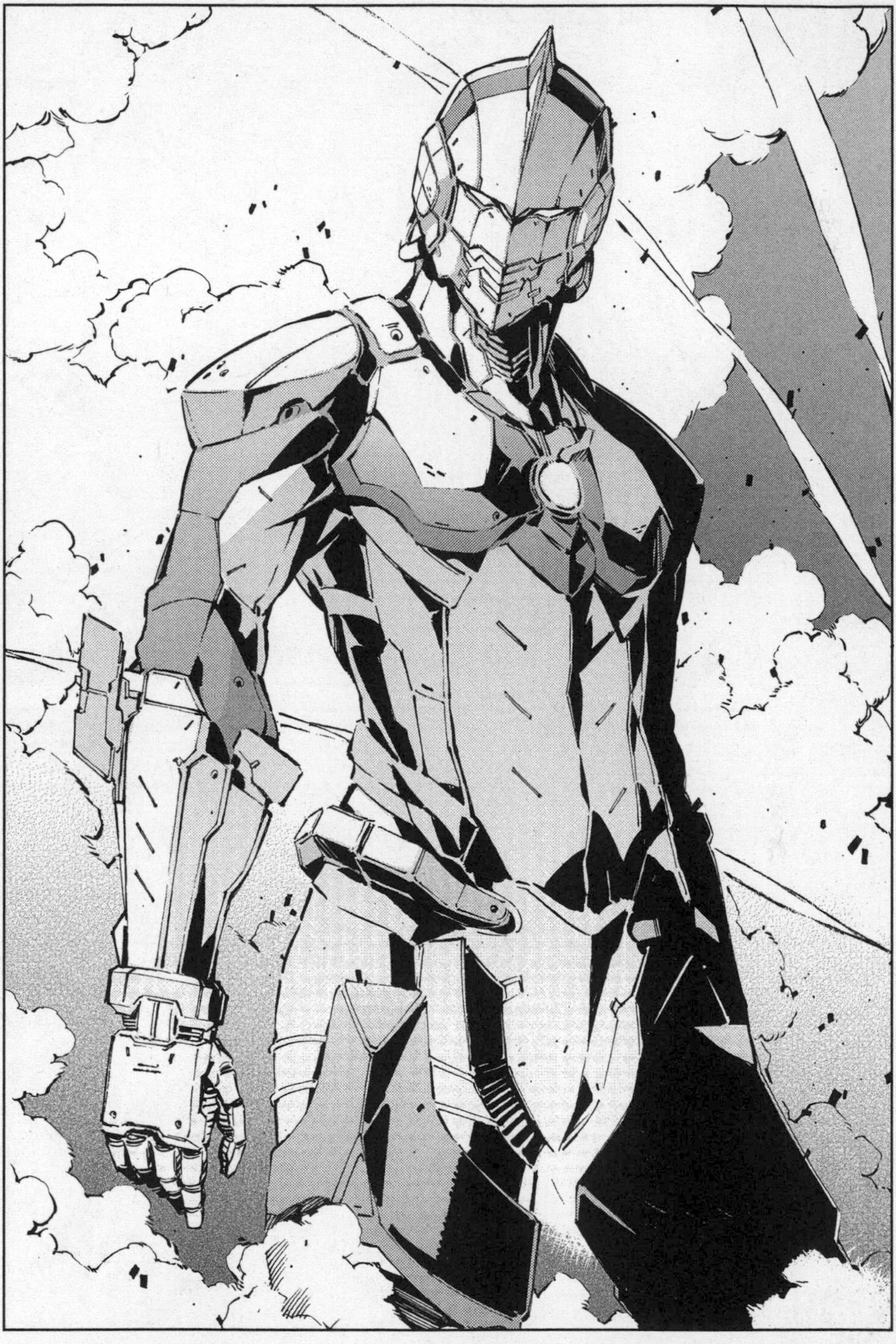

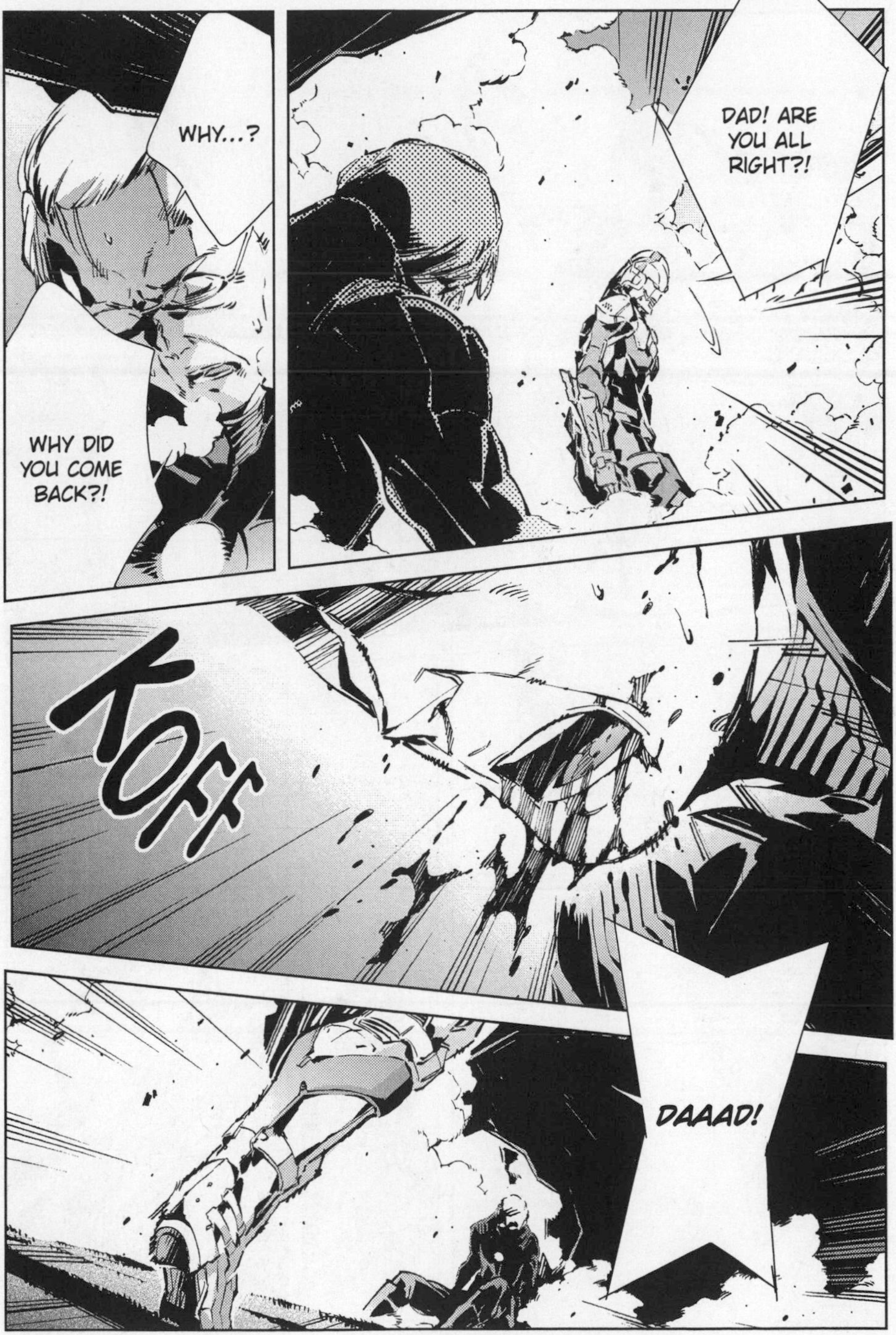
DAD! ARE YOU ALL RIGHT?!
WHY...?
WHY DID YOU COME BACK?!
KOFF
DAAAD!

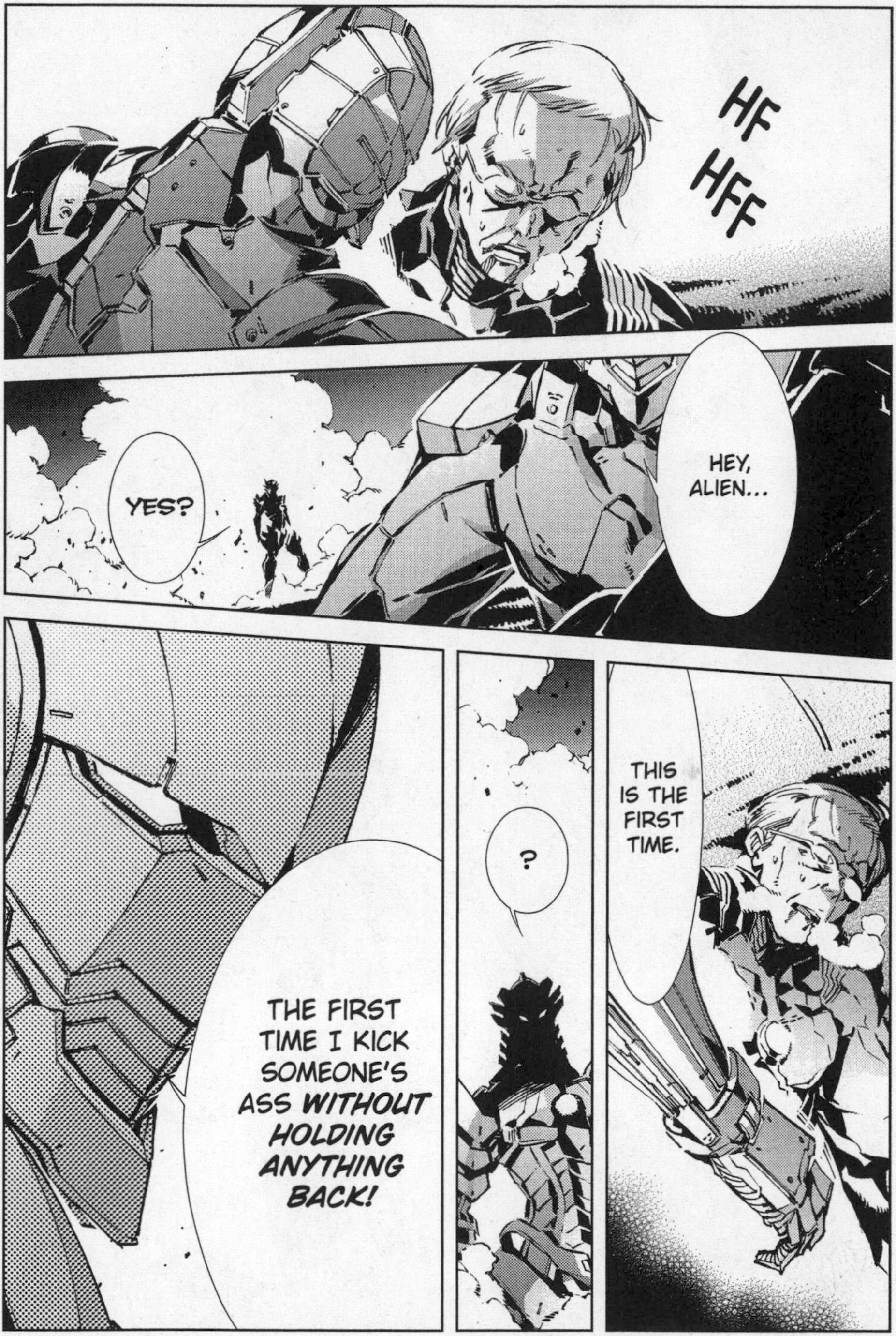
HF HFF
HEY, ALIEN...
YES?
THIS IS THE FIRST TIME.
?
THE FIRST TIME I KICK SOMEONE'S ASS *WITHOUT HOLDING ANYTHING BACK!*

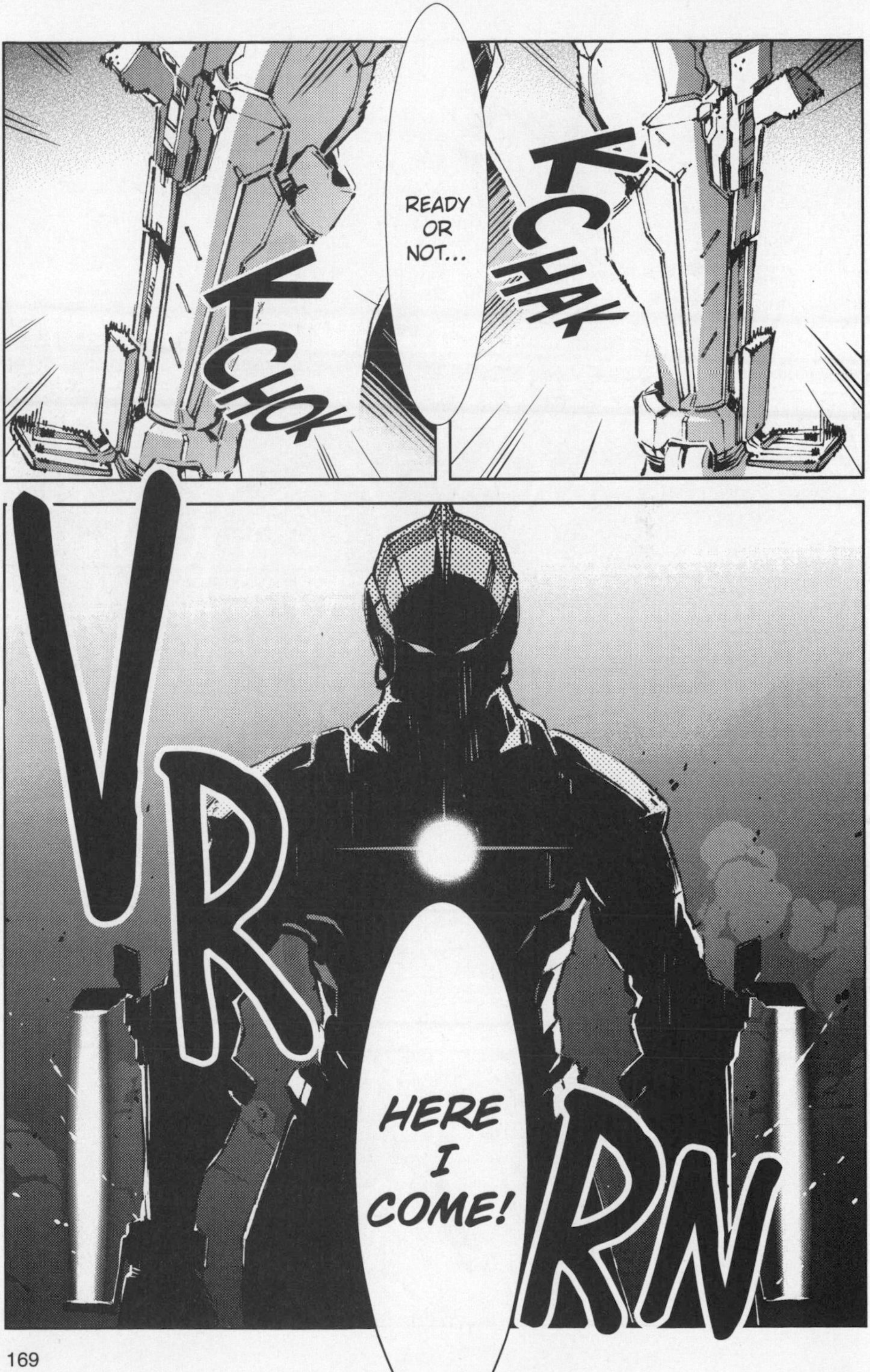
READY OR NOT...
KCHAK
KCHOK
VRRM
HERE I COME!

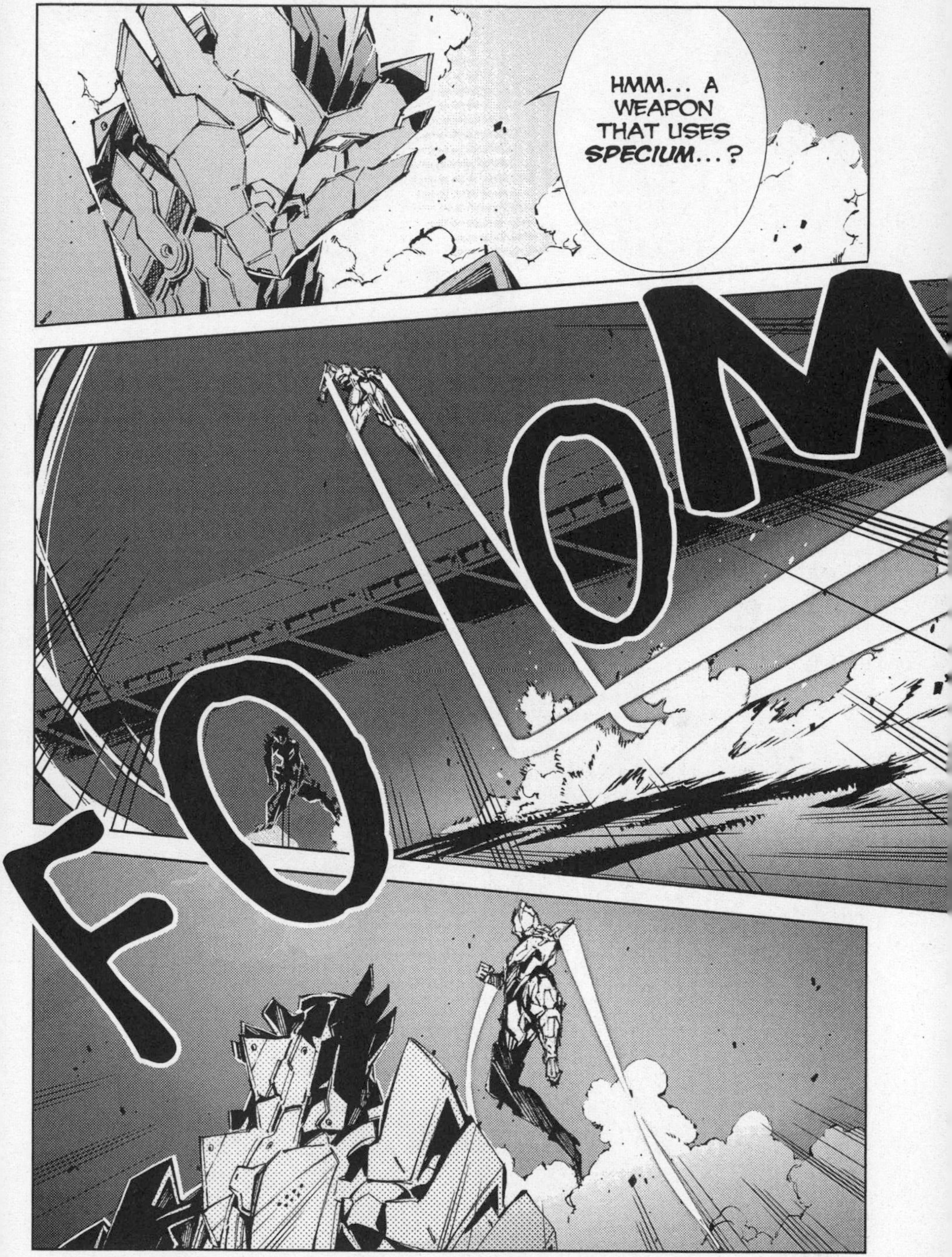
HMM... A WEAPON THAT USES *SPECIUM*...?
FOOM

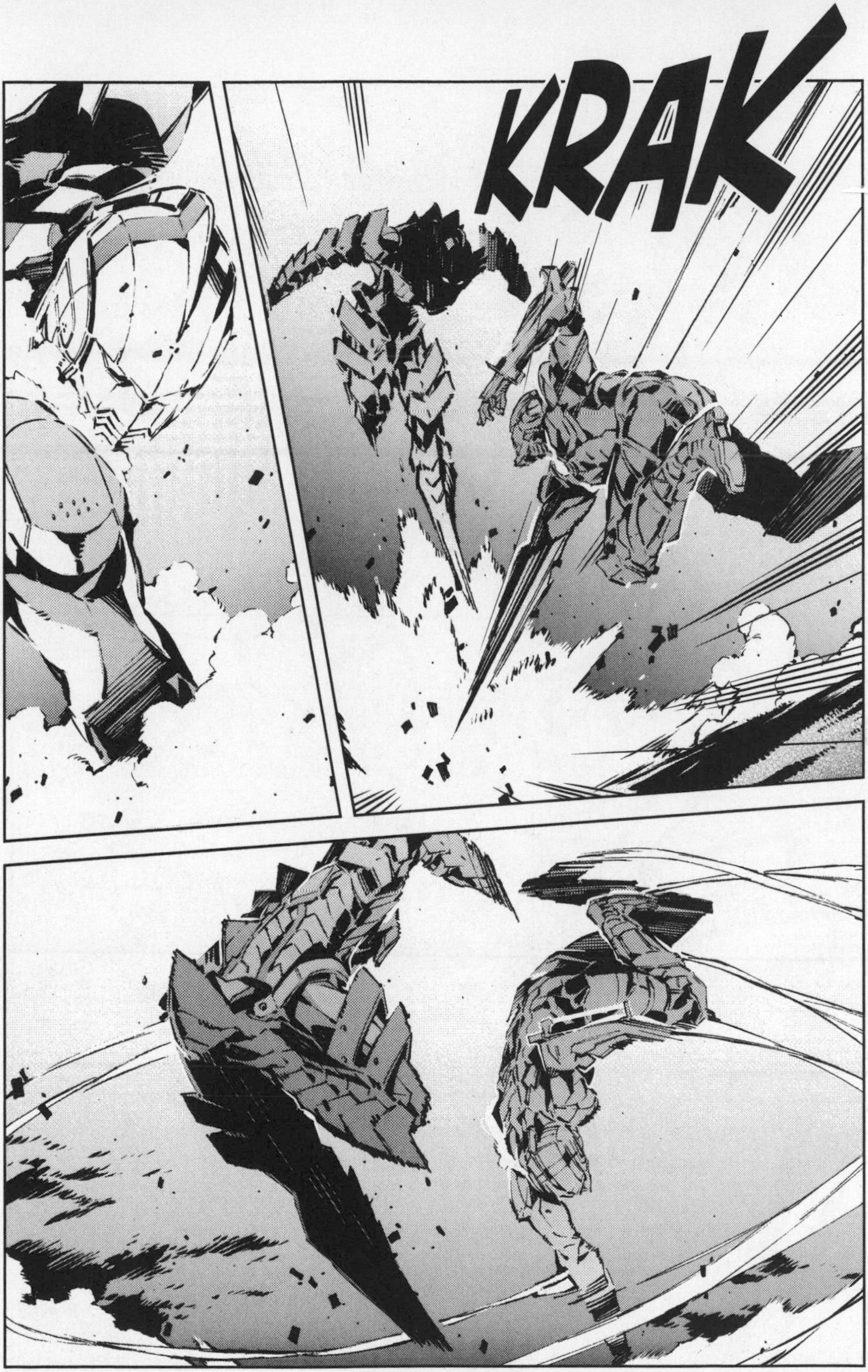
KRAK

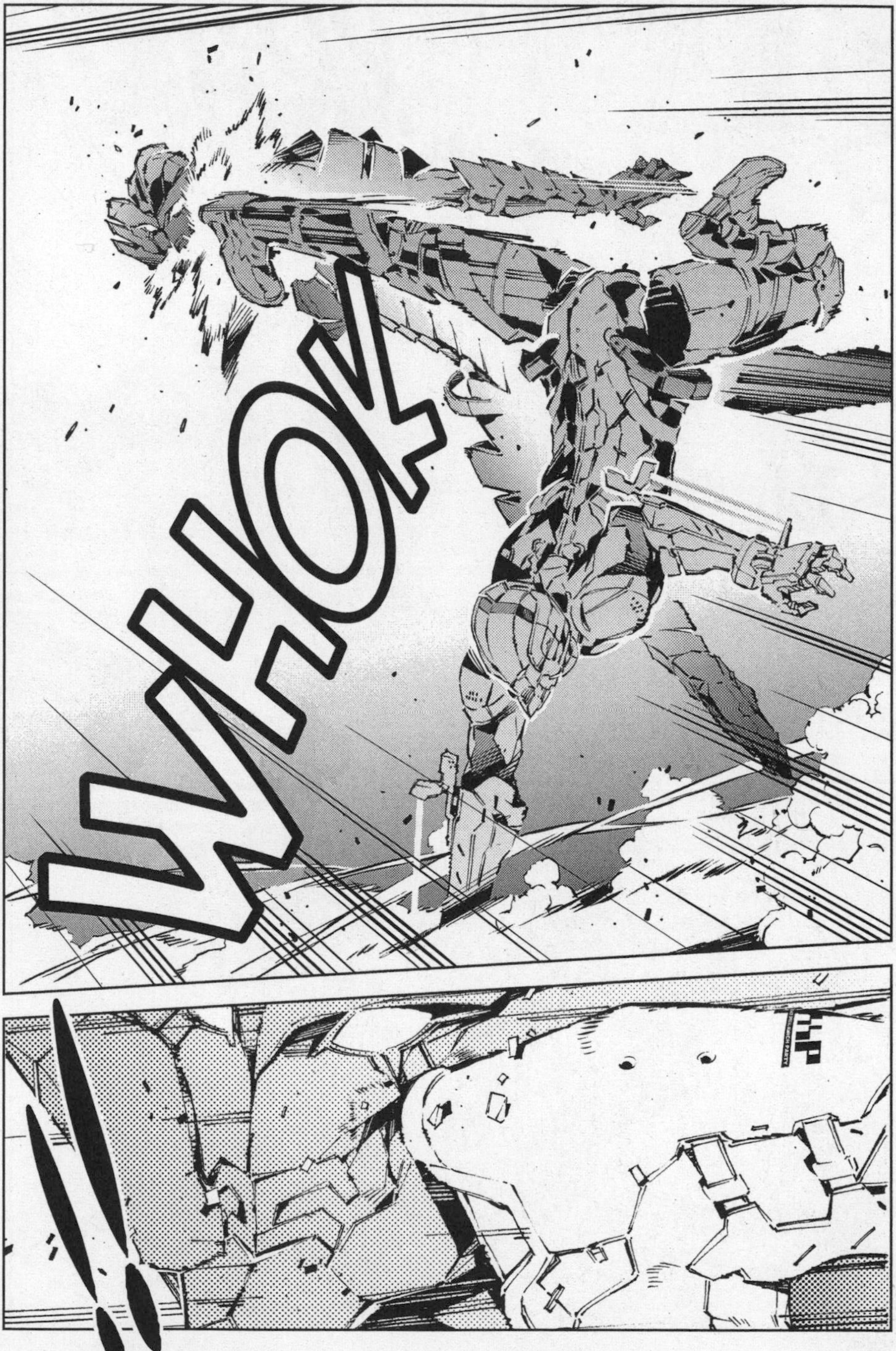
WHOK
!!

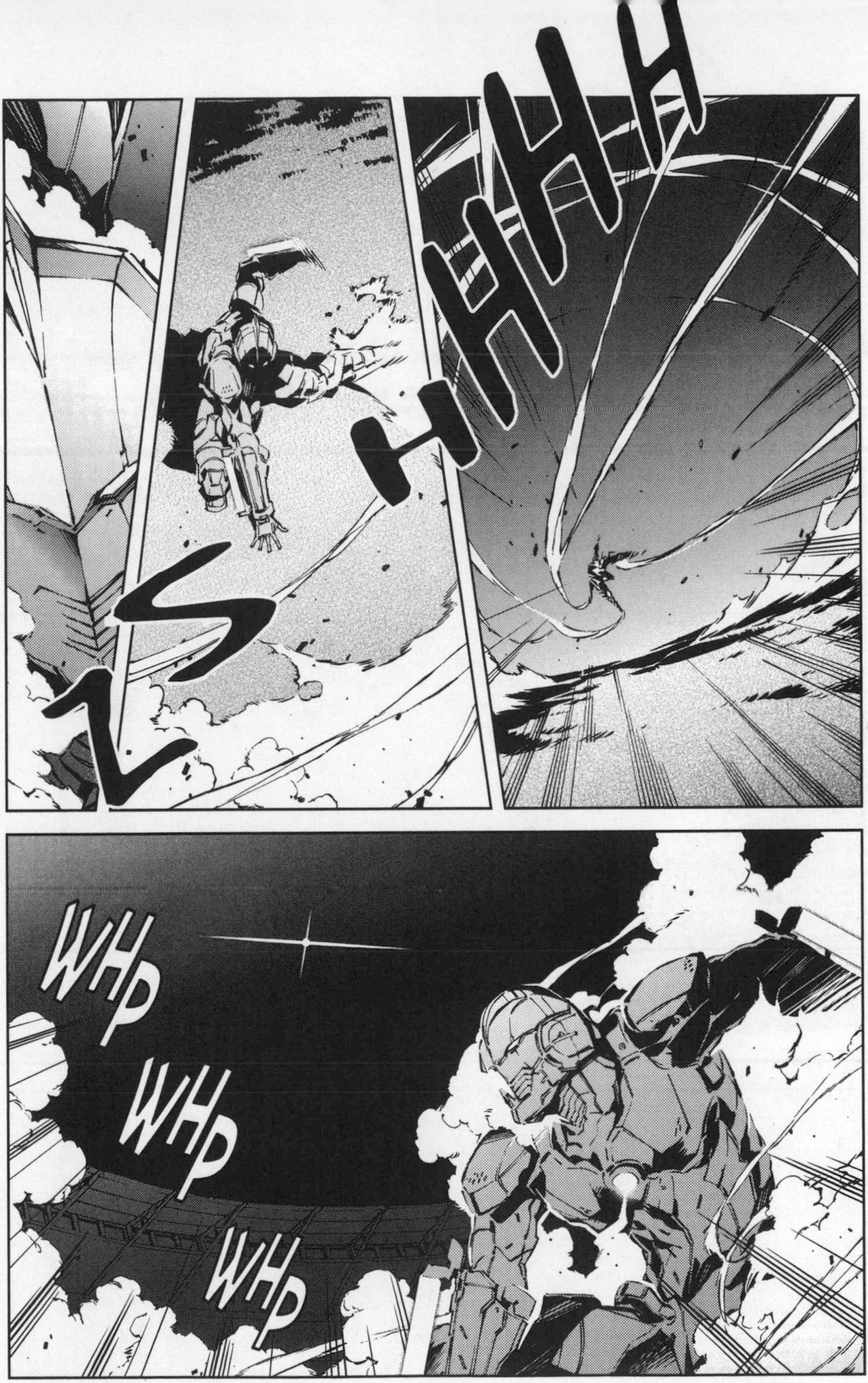
WHP
WHP
WHP

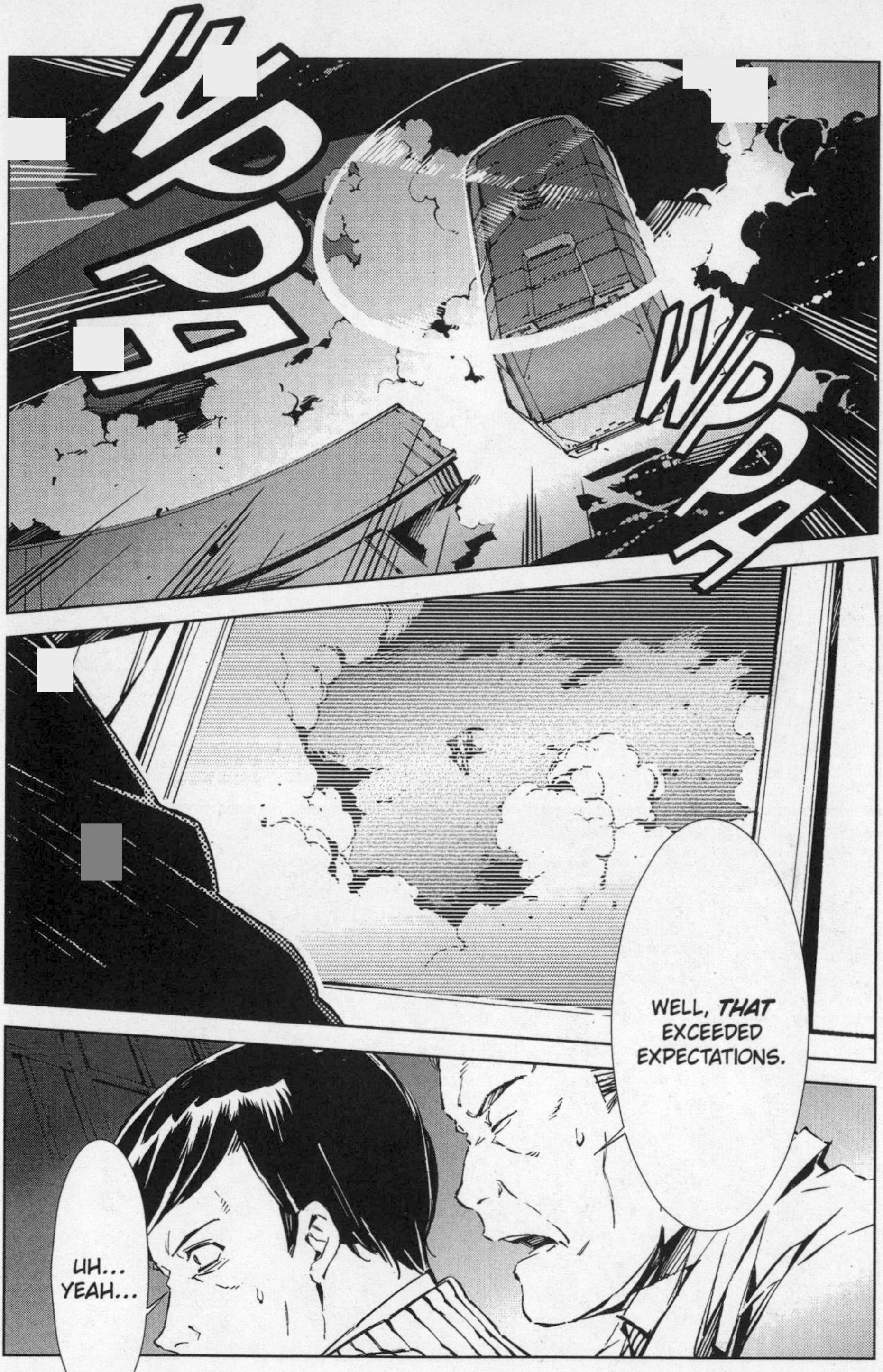
WPPA
WPPA
WELL, *THAT* EXCEEDED EXPECTATIONS.
UH... YEAH...

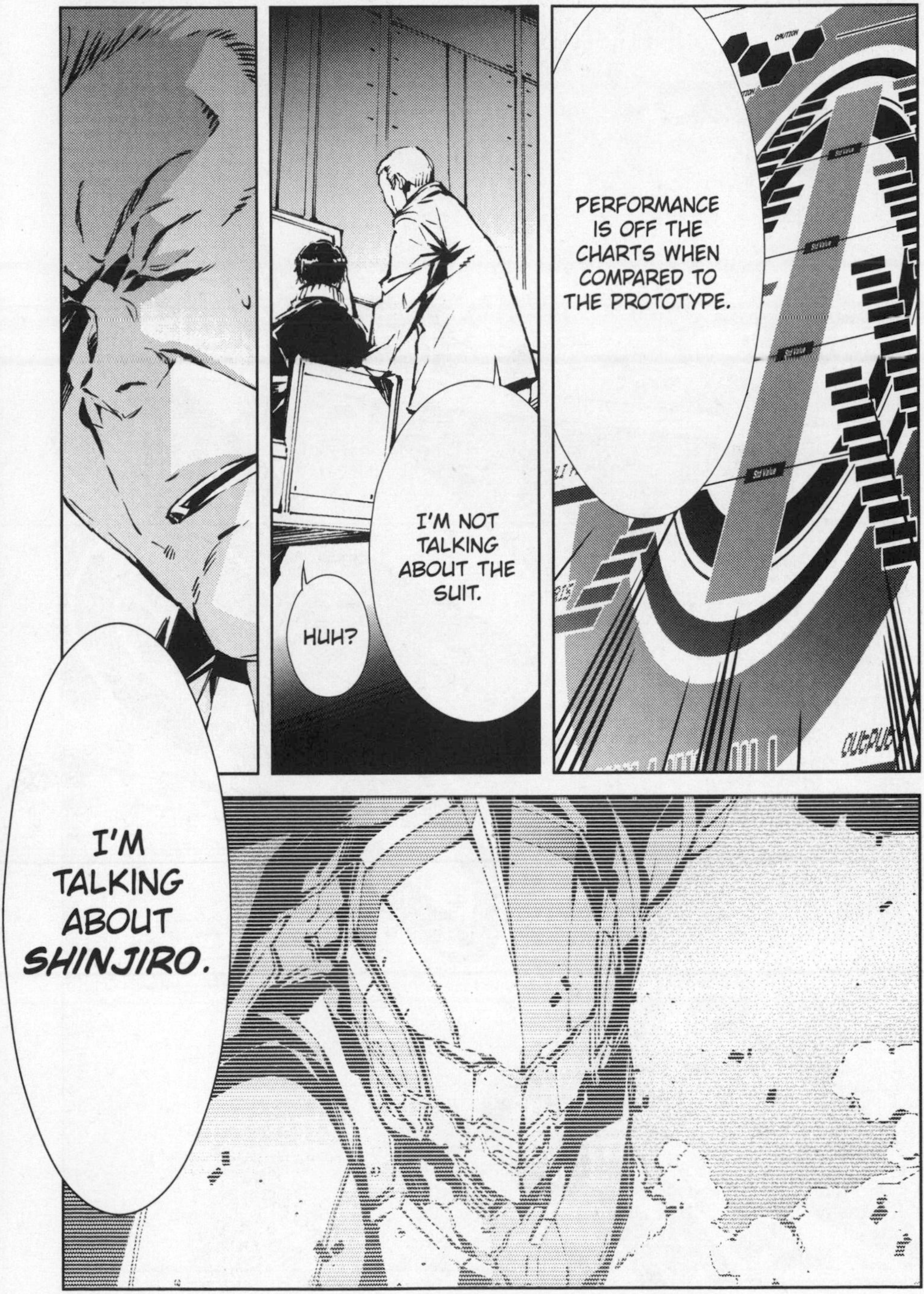
PERFORMANCE IS OFF THE CHARTS WHEN COMPARED TO THE PROTOTYPE.
I'M NOT TALKING ABOUT THE SUIT.
HUH?
I'M TALKING ABOUT *SHINJIRO*.

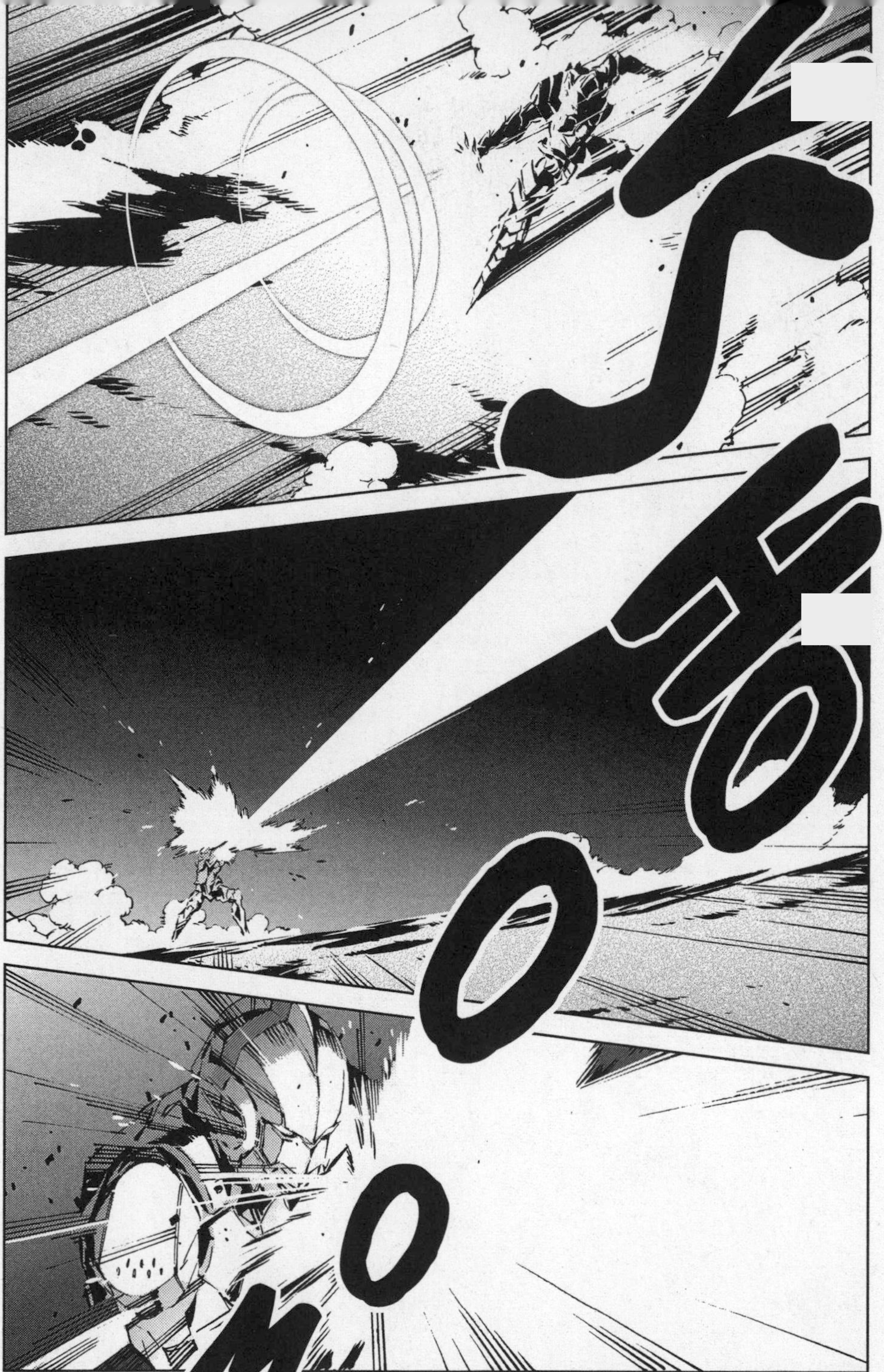
SHOOOM

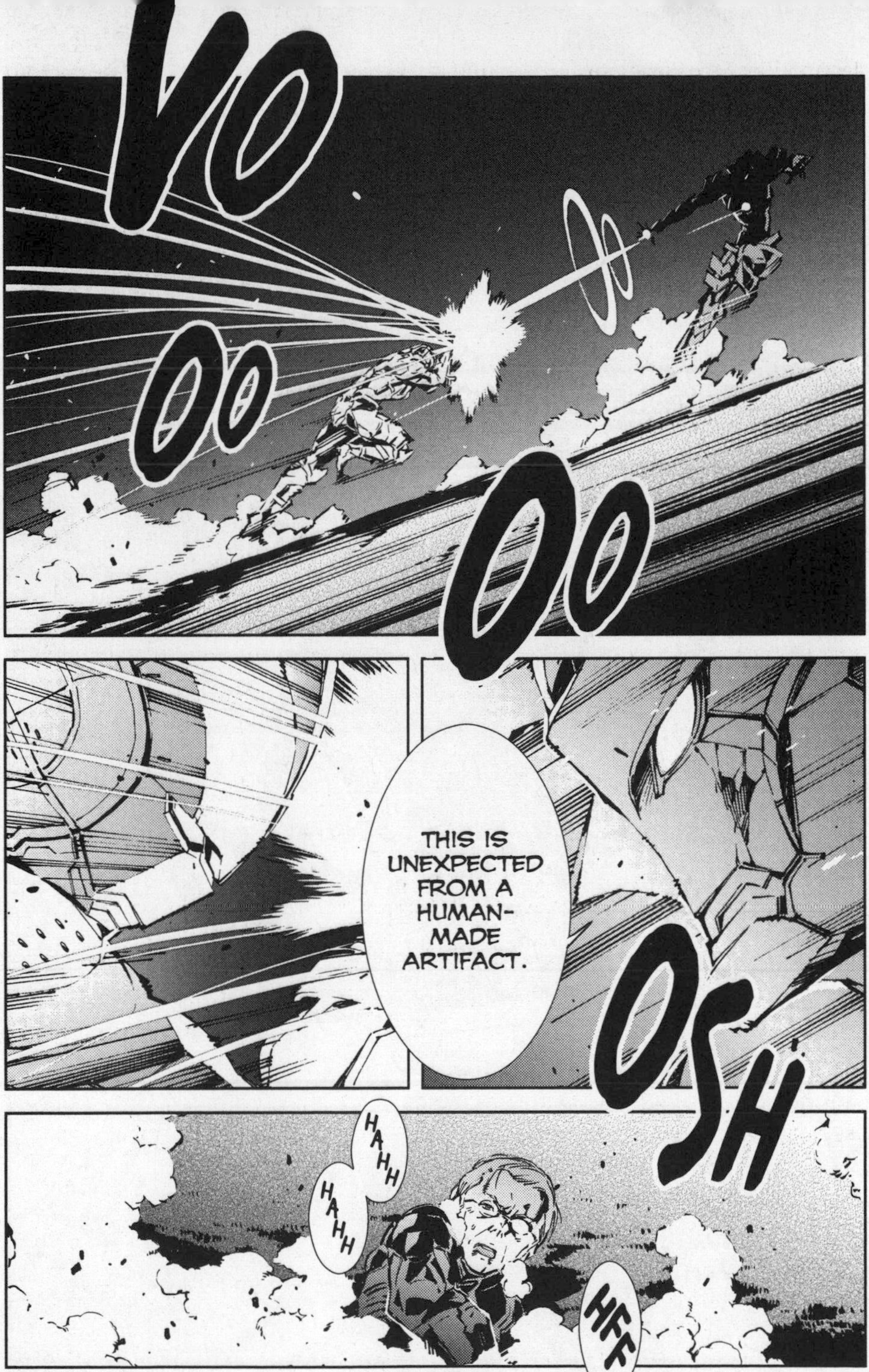
VOOOOO
THIS IS UNEXPECTED FROM A HUMAN-MADE ARTIFACT.
OOSH
HAHH
HAHH
HFF

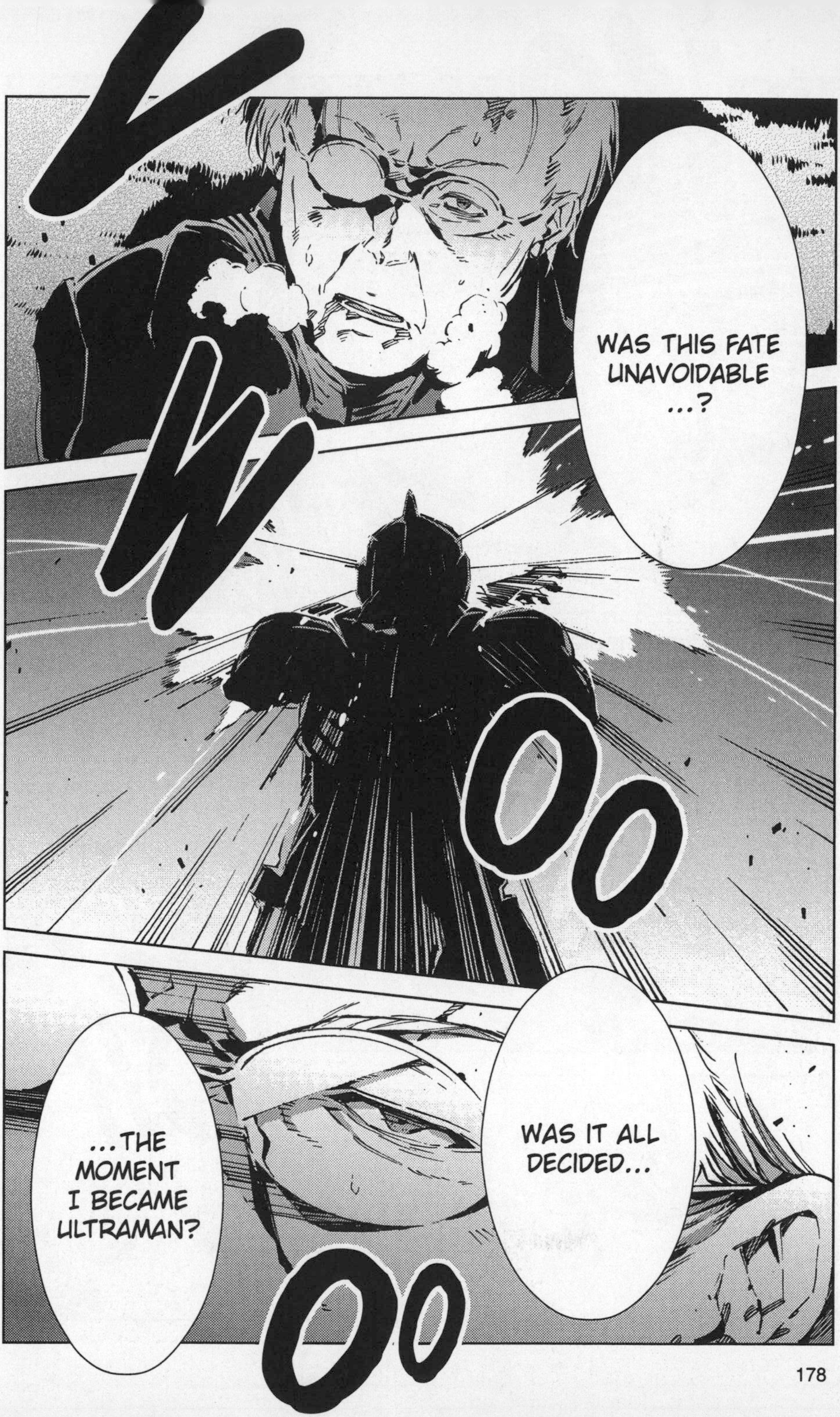
V
WAS THIS FATE UNAVOIDABLE ...?
W
OO
WAS IT ALL DECIDED...
...THE MOMENT I BECAME ULTRAMAN?
OO

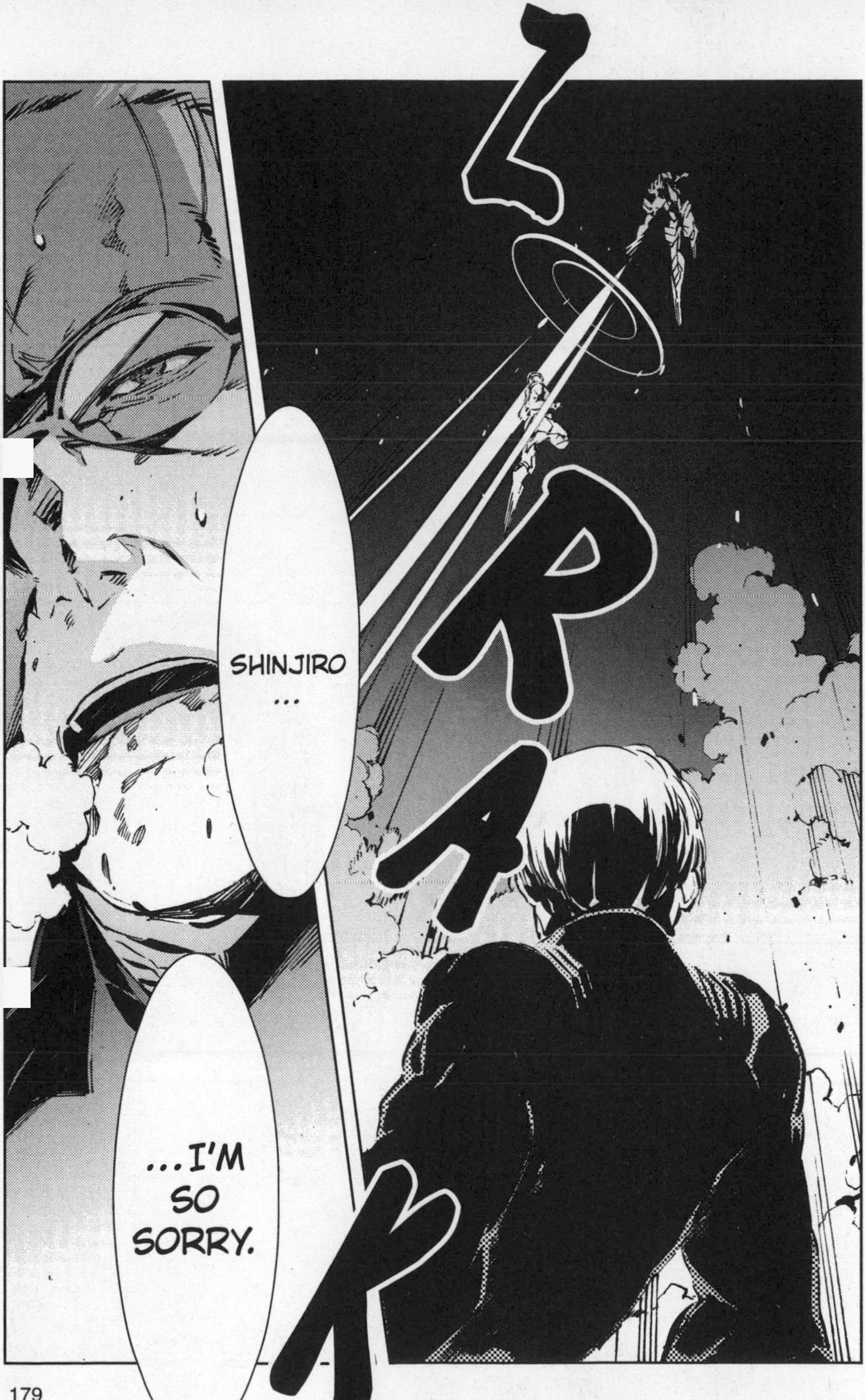
SHINJIRO ...
...I'M SO SORRY.

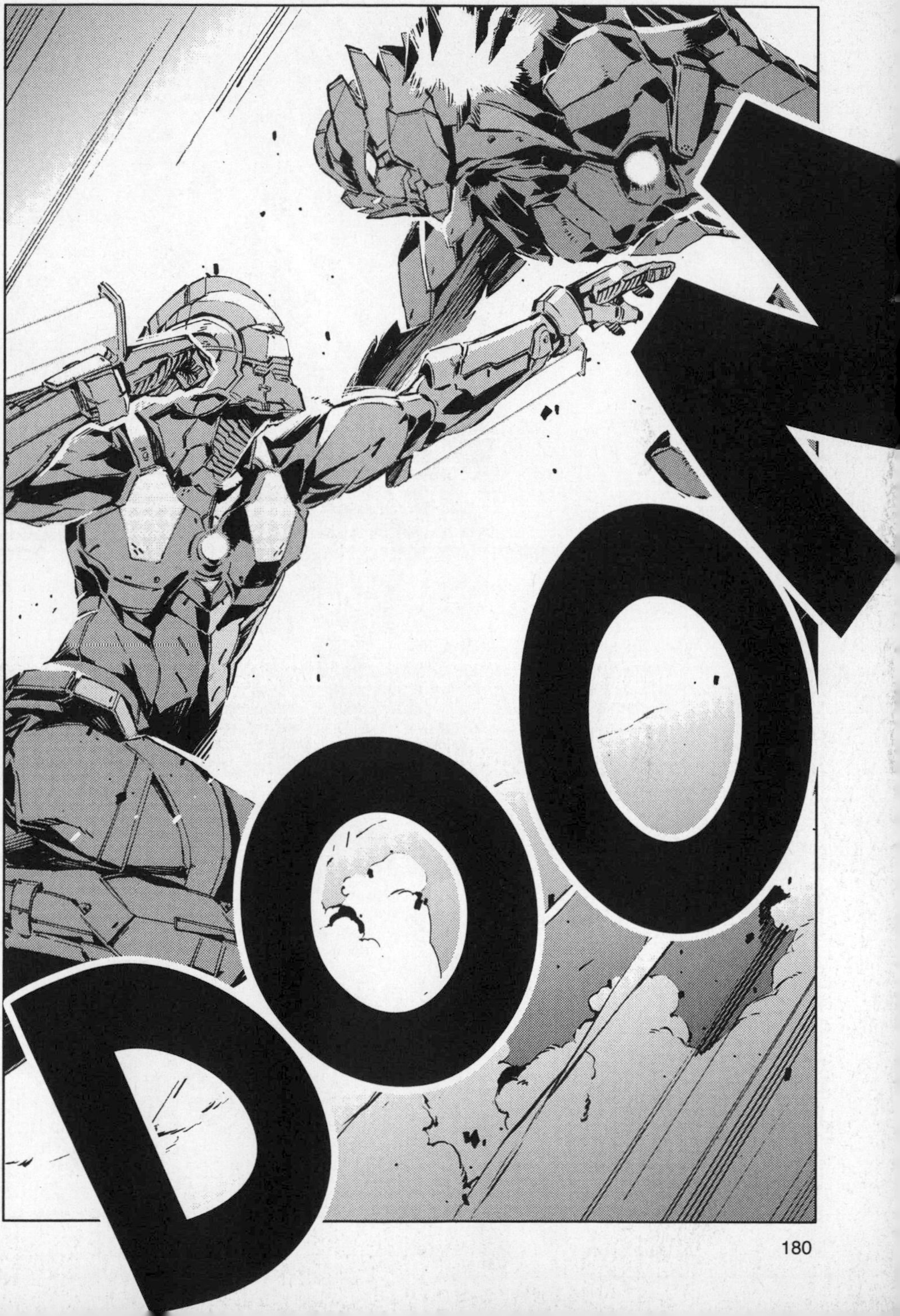
DOOM

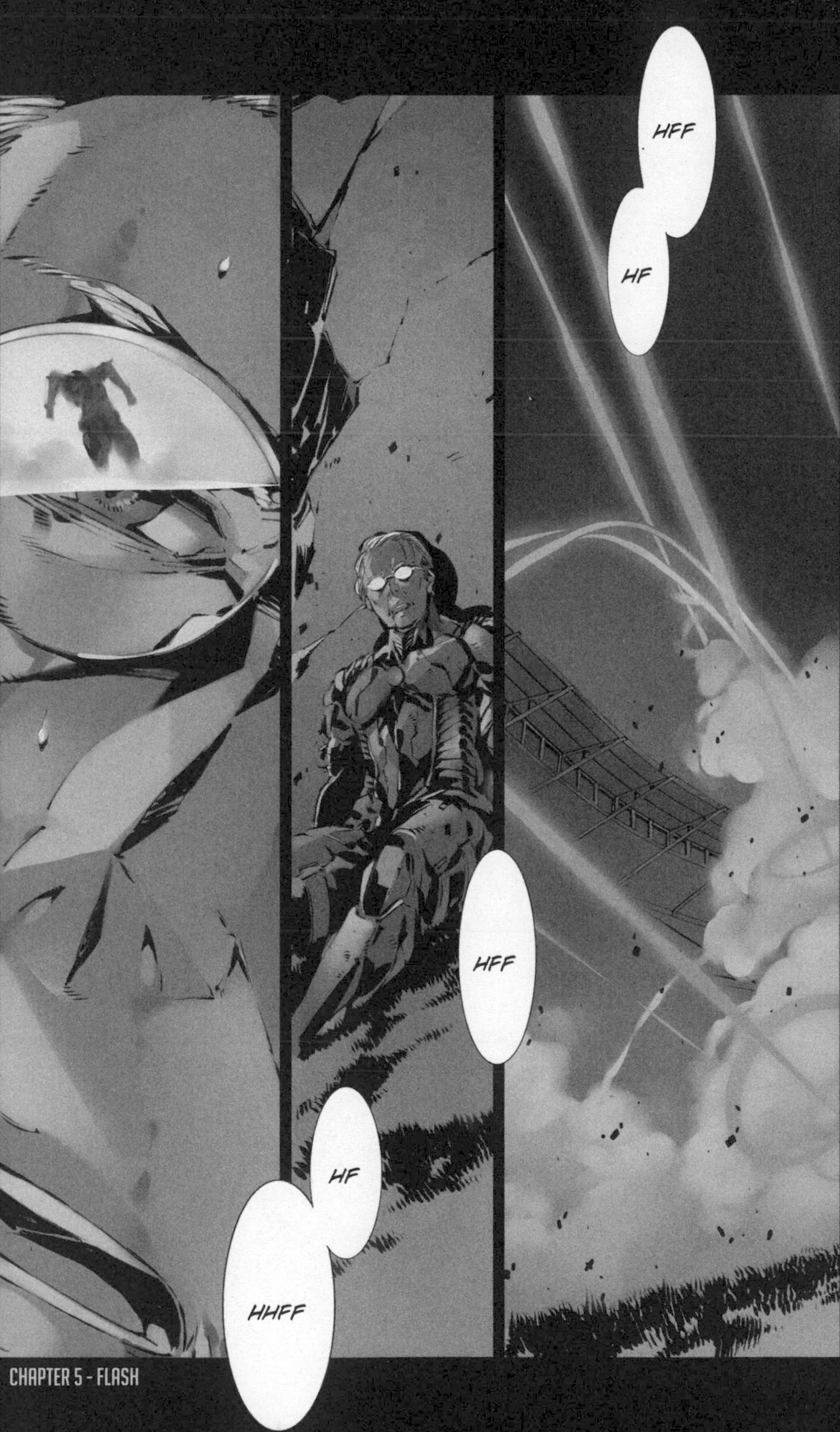
HFF
HF
HFF
HF
HHFF

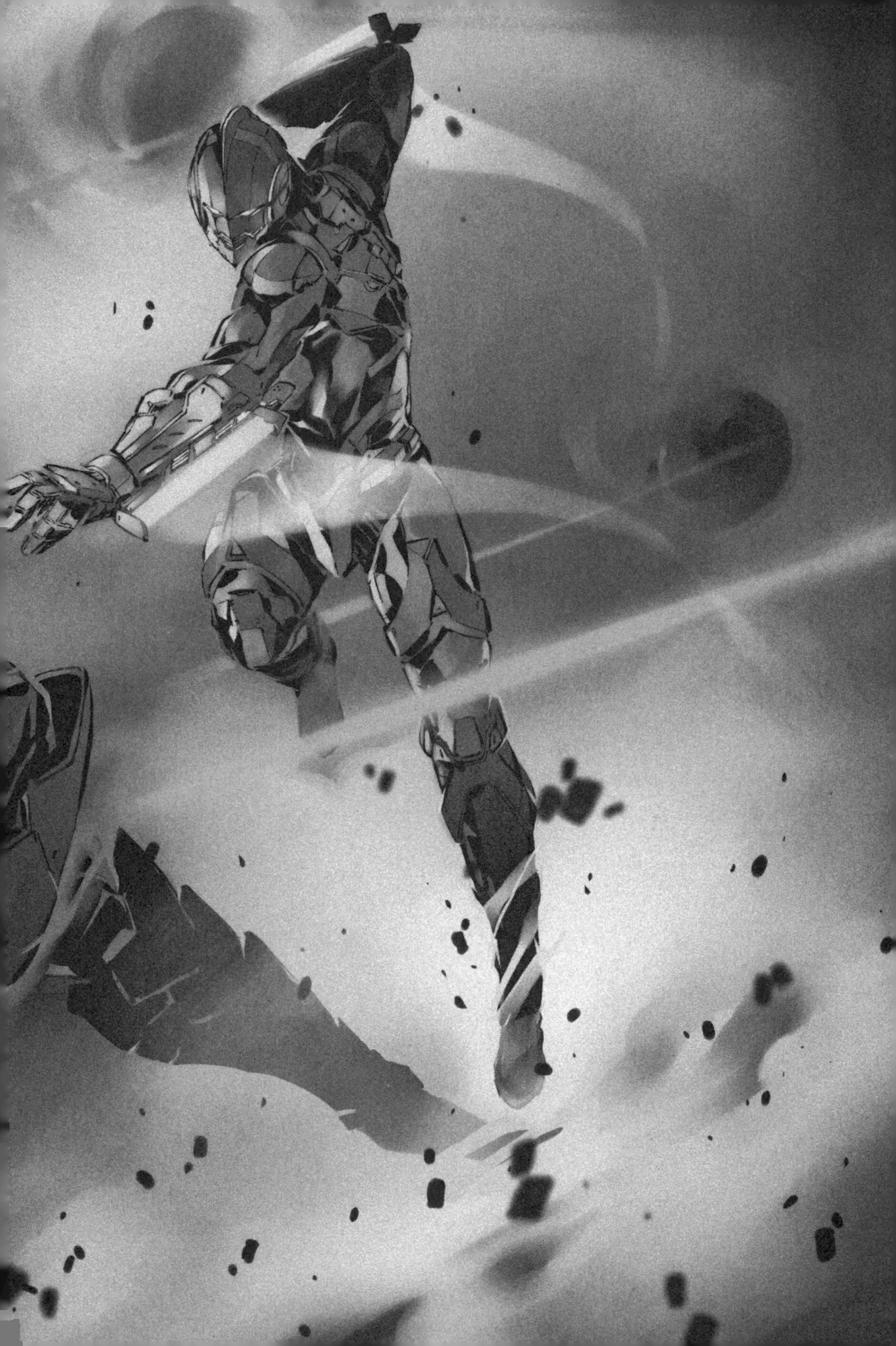

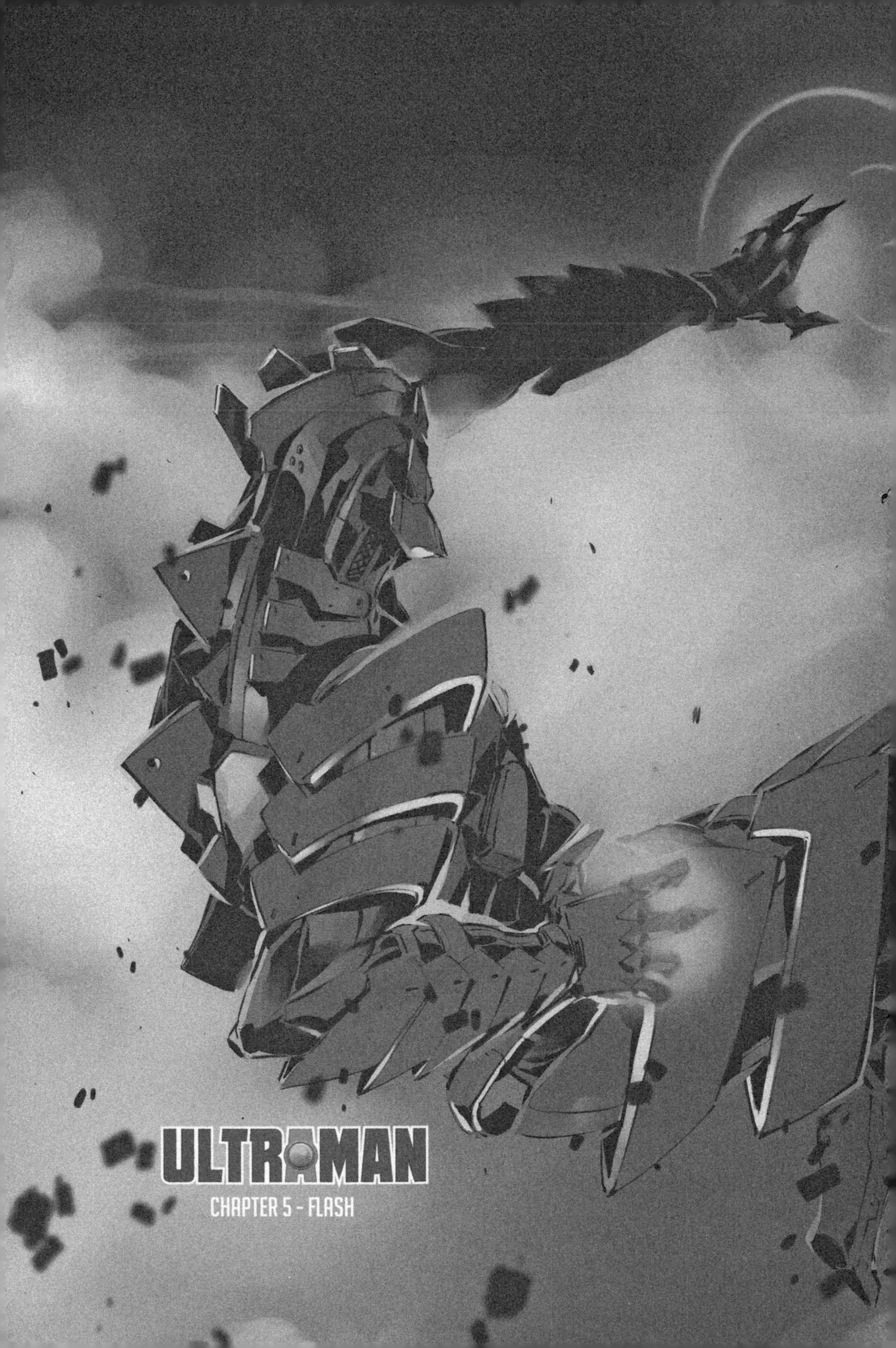
ULTRAMAN
CHAPTER 5 - FLASH

SSS
PARTY

SCIENCE SPECIAL
SEARCH PARTY

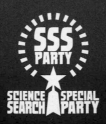

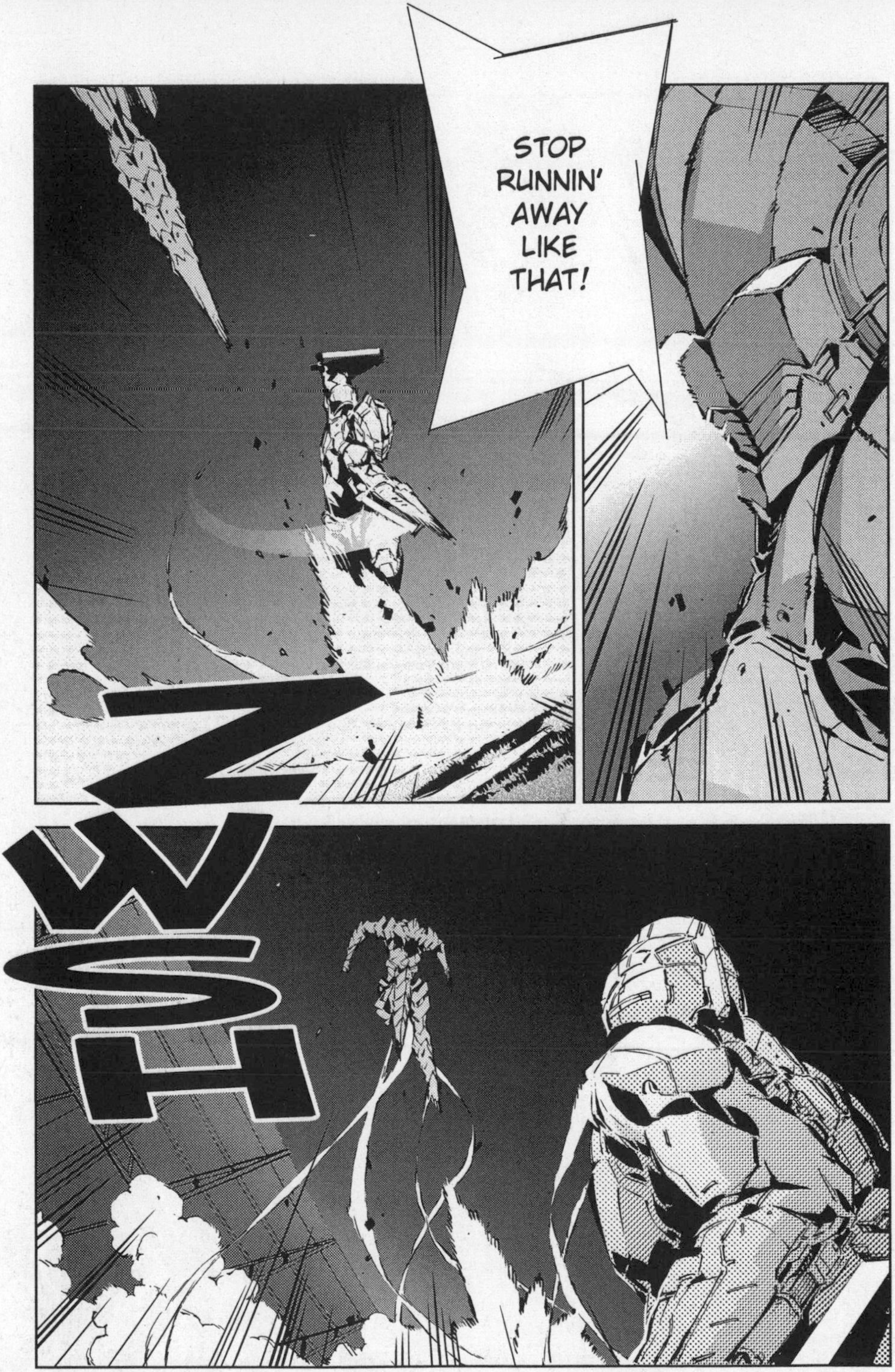
STOP RUNNIN' AWAY LIKE THAT!

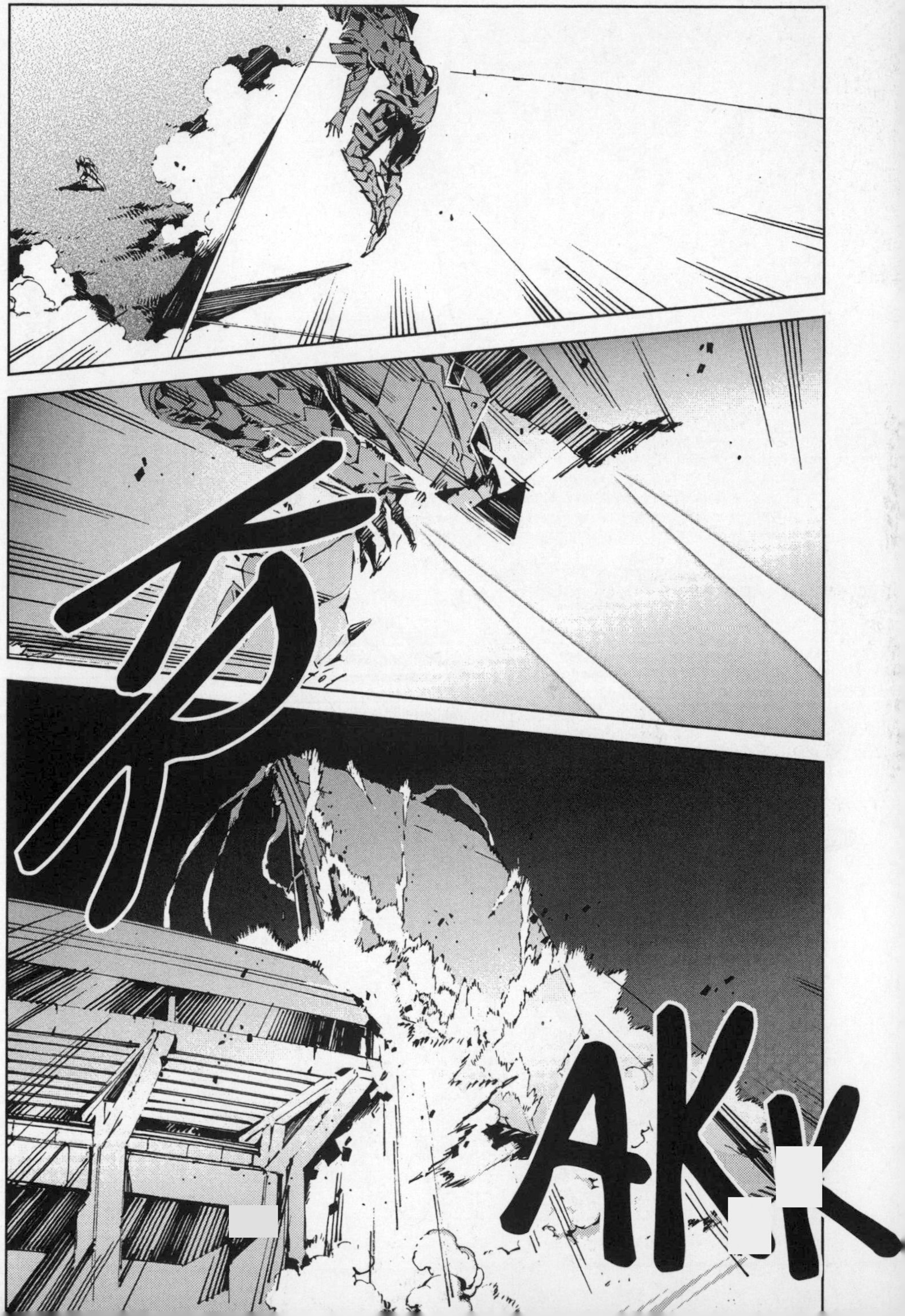
AKK

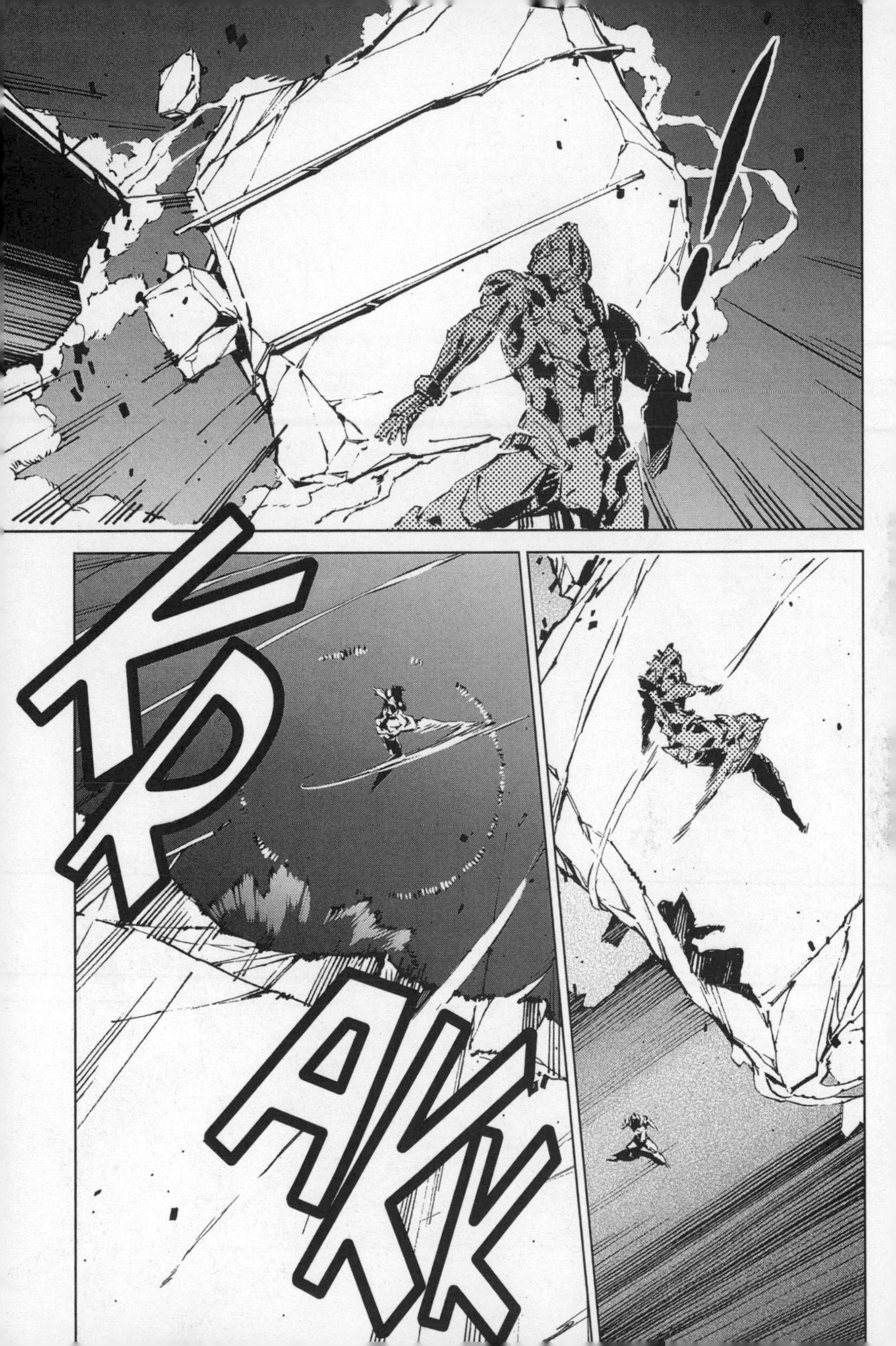
KRAKK

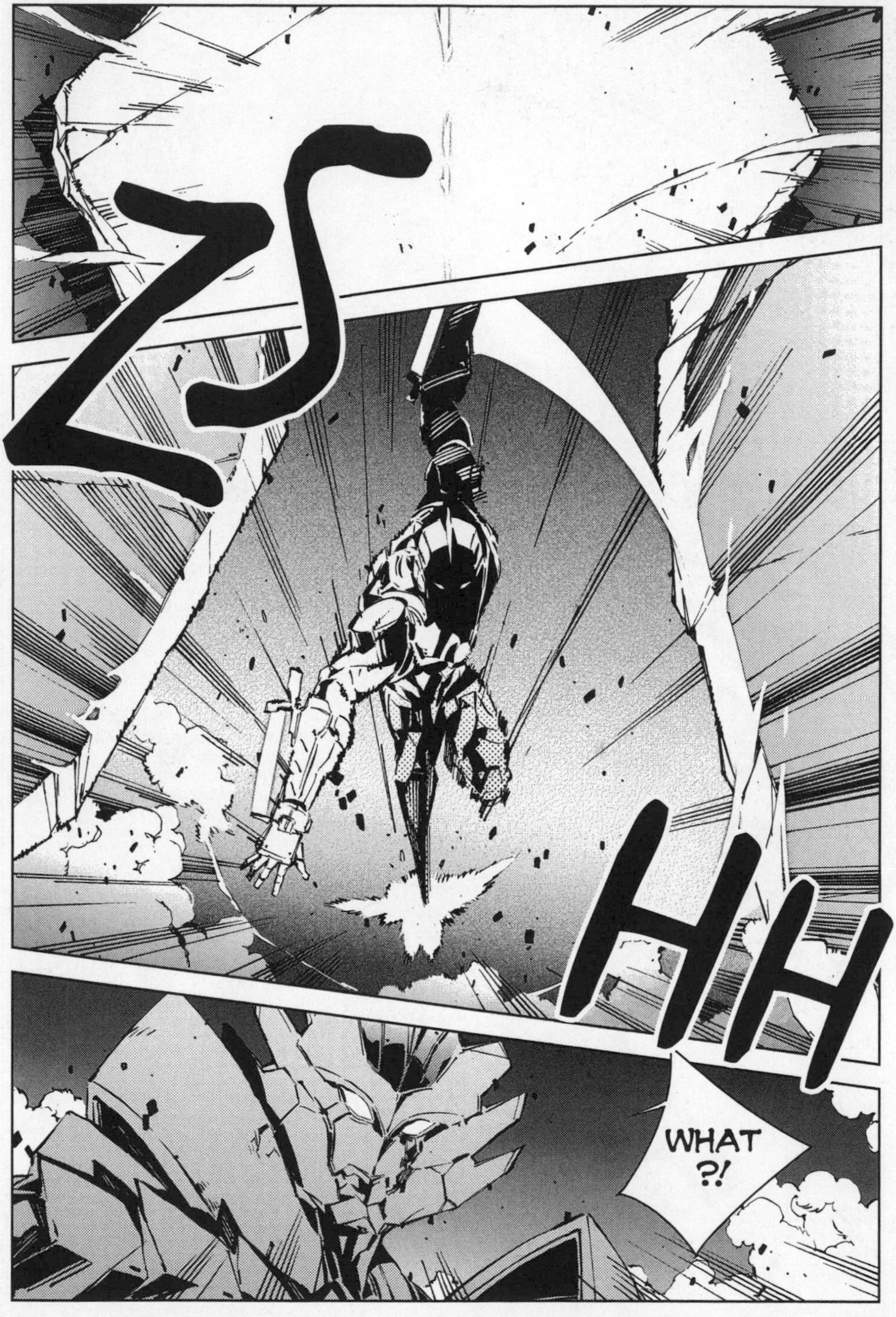
ZS
HH
WHAT ?!

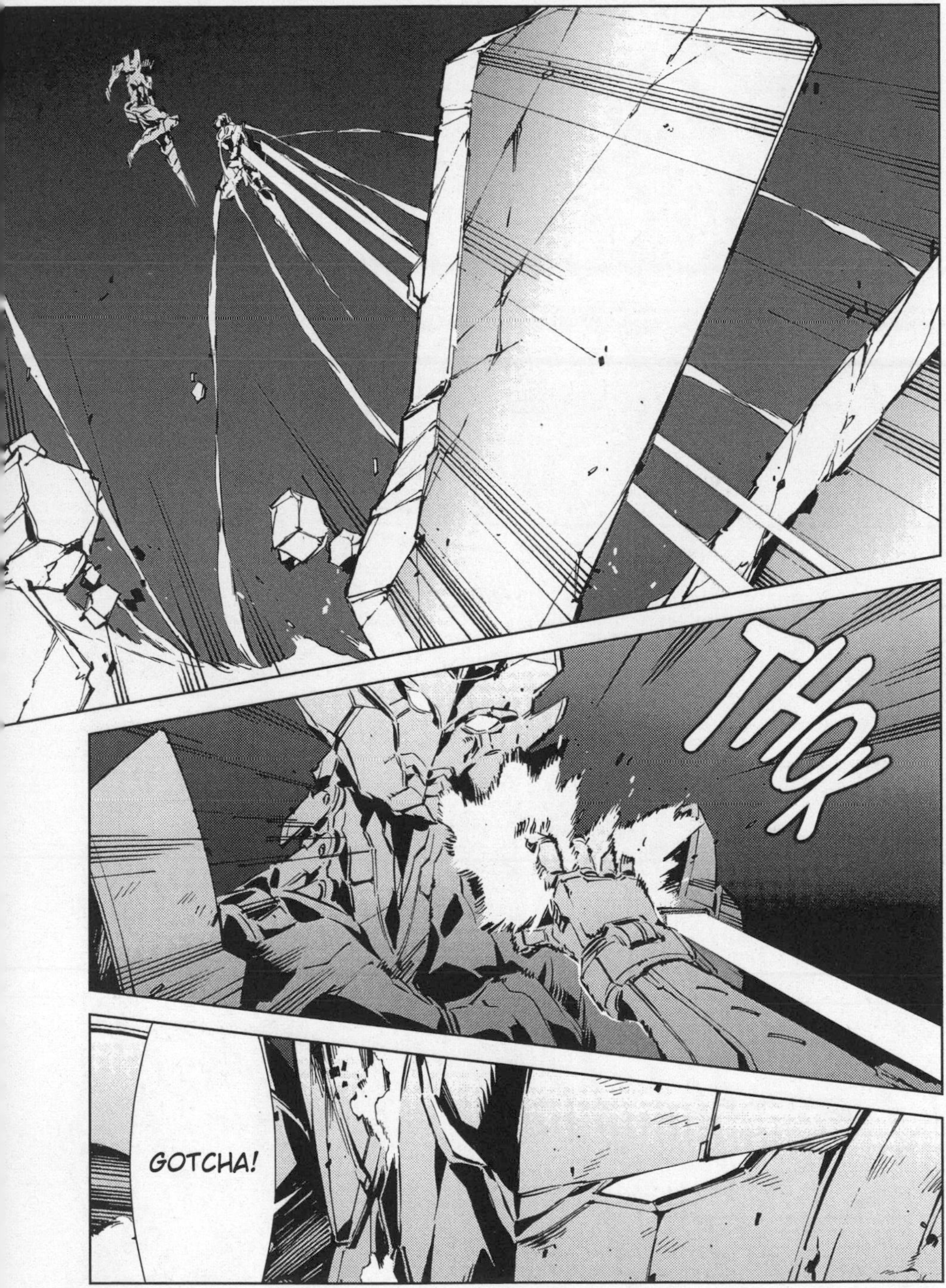
THOK
GOTCHA!

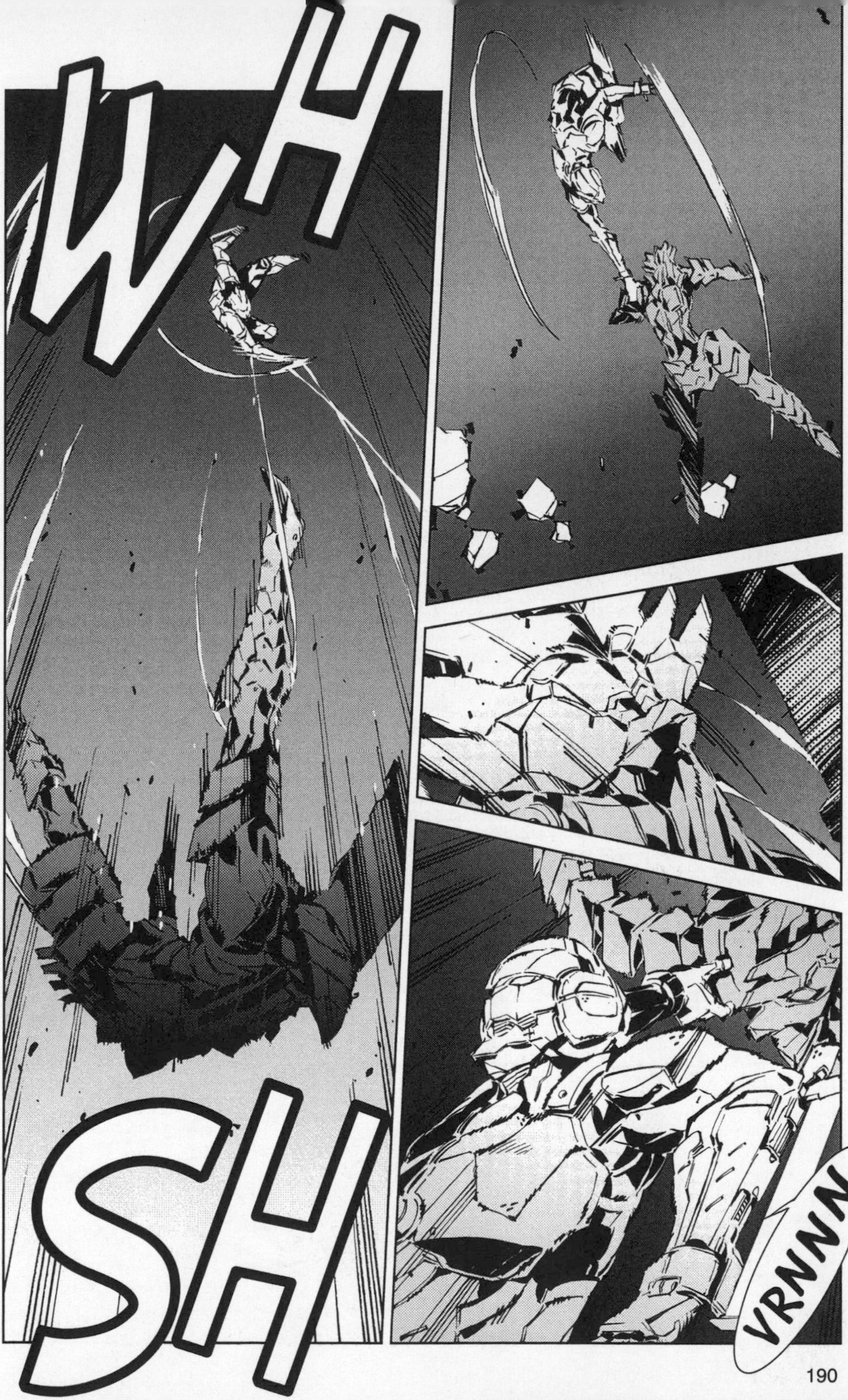
VRNNN
WHSH

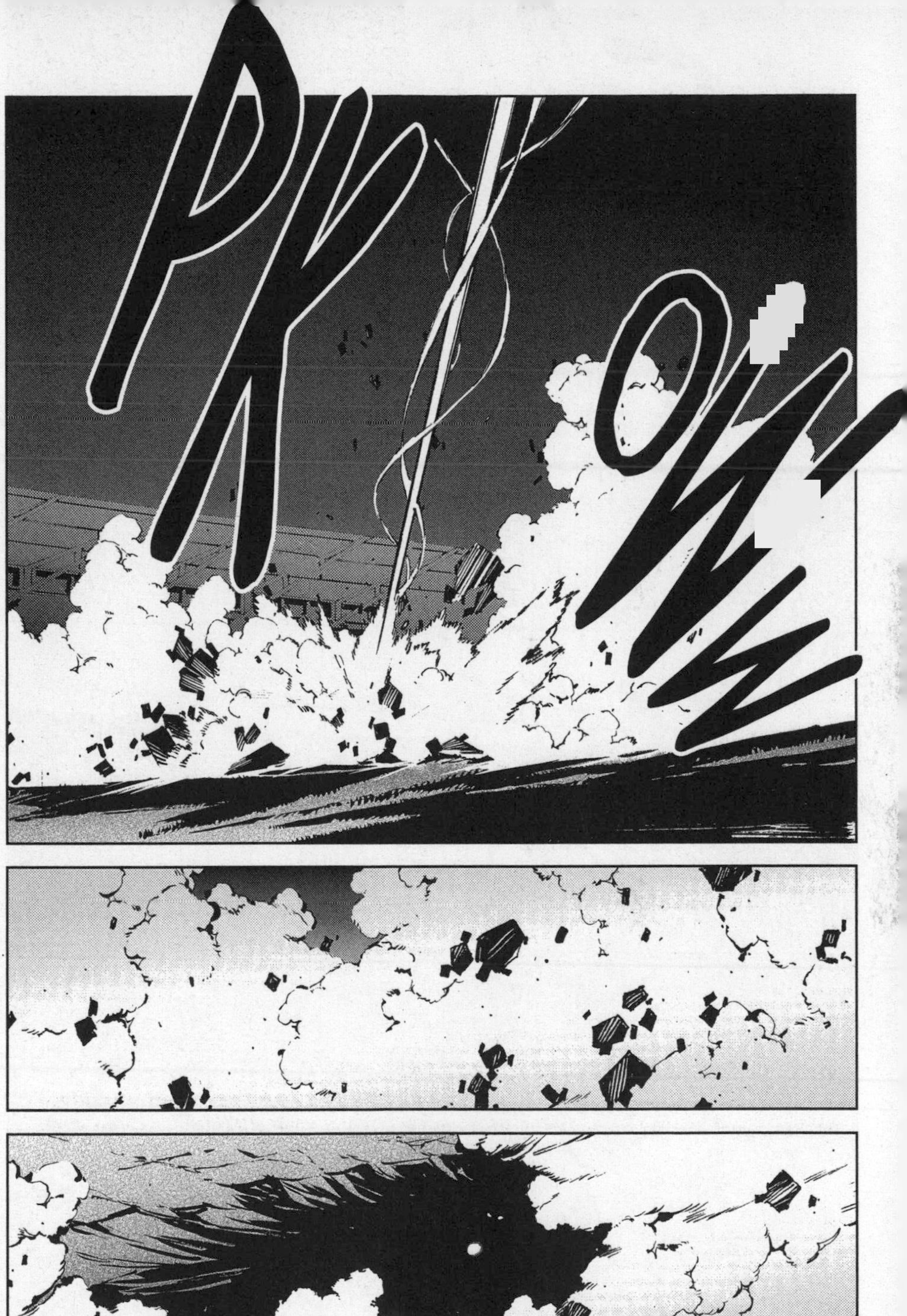
PKOWW

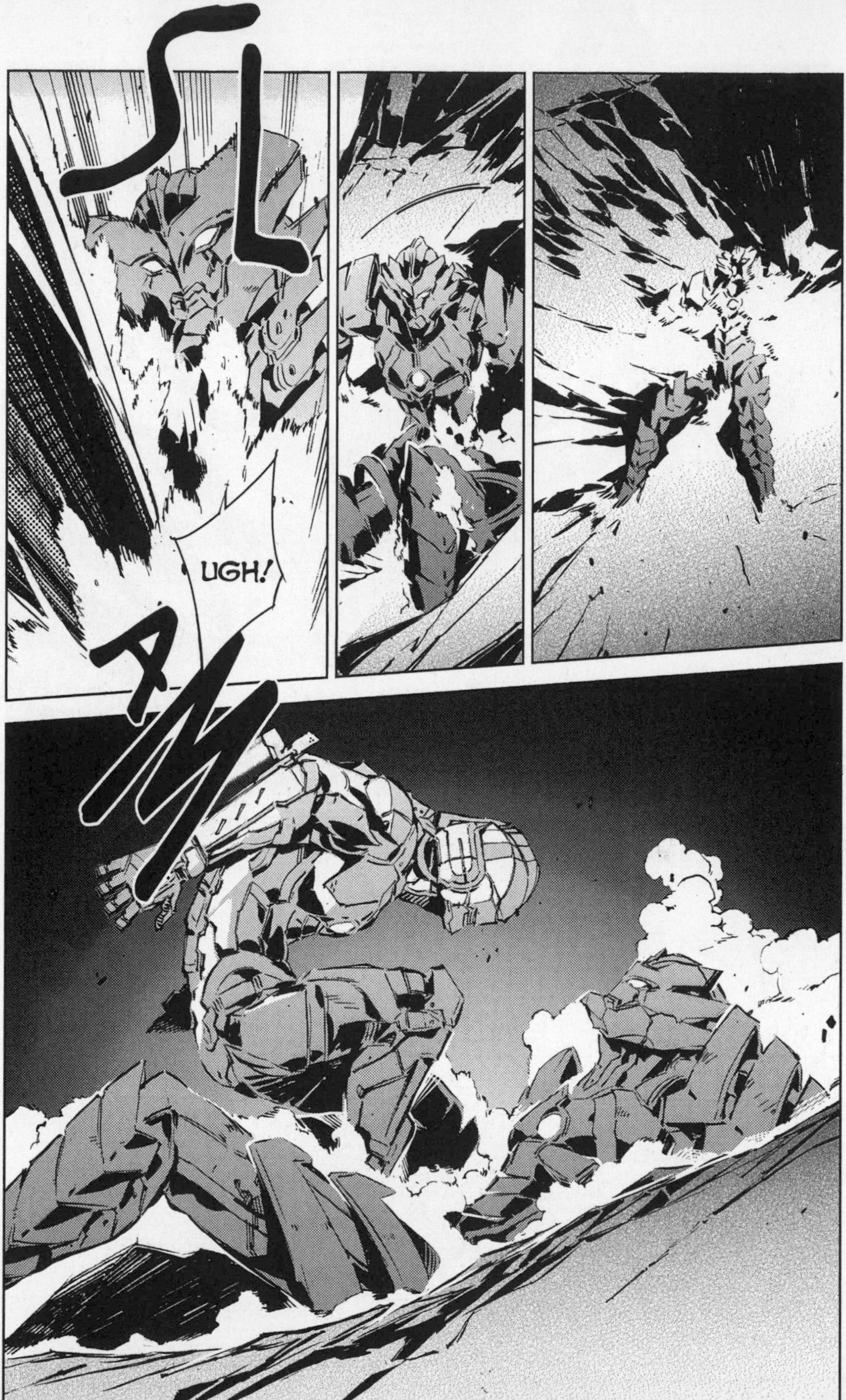
SLAM
UGH!

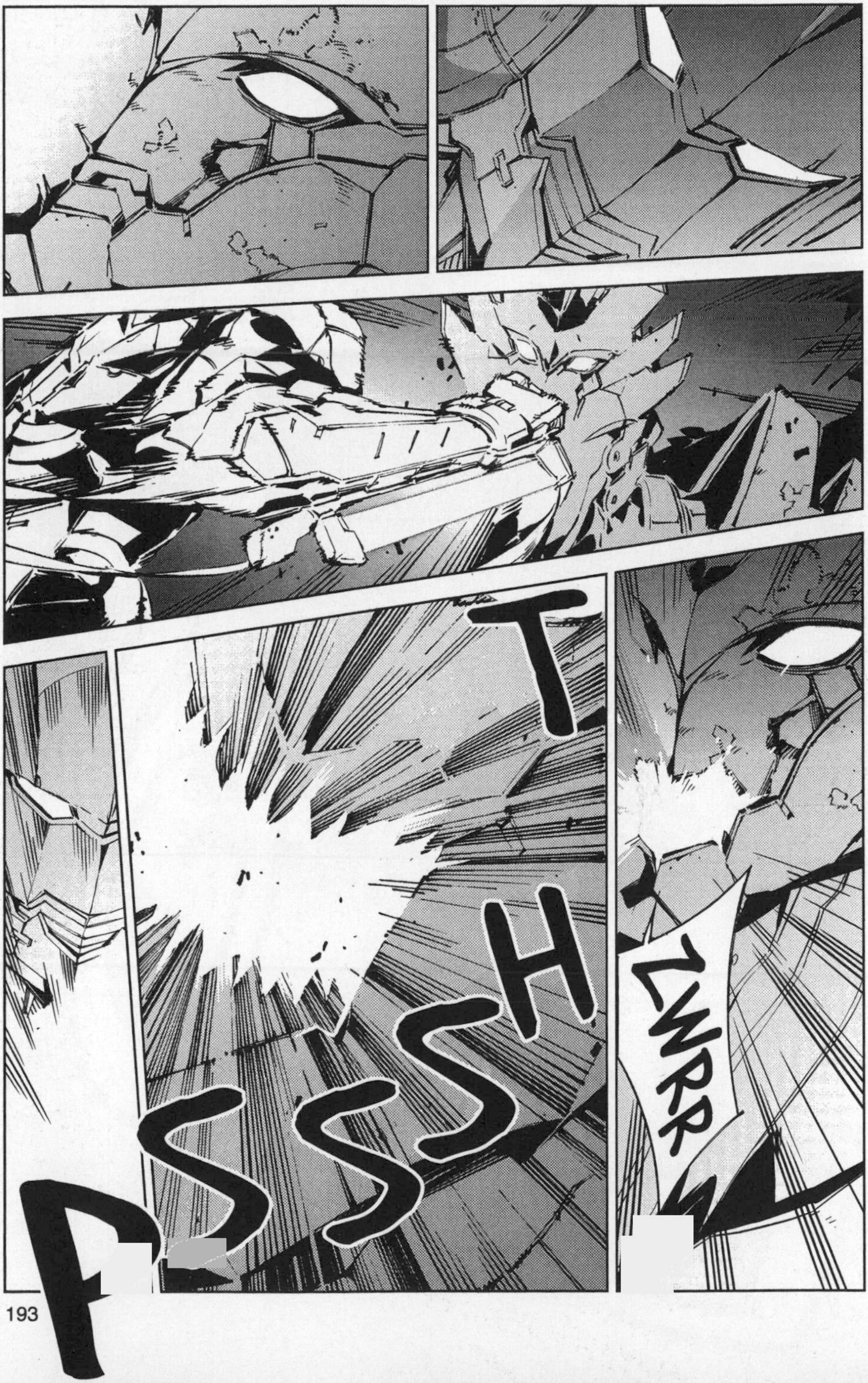
ZWRR
PSSSHT

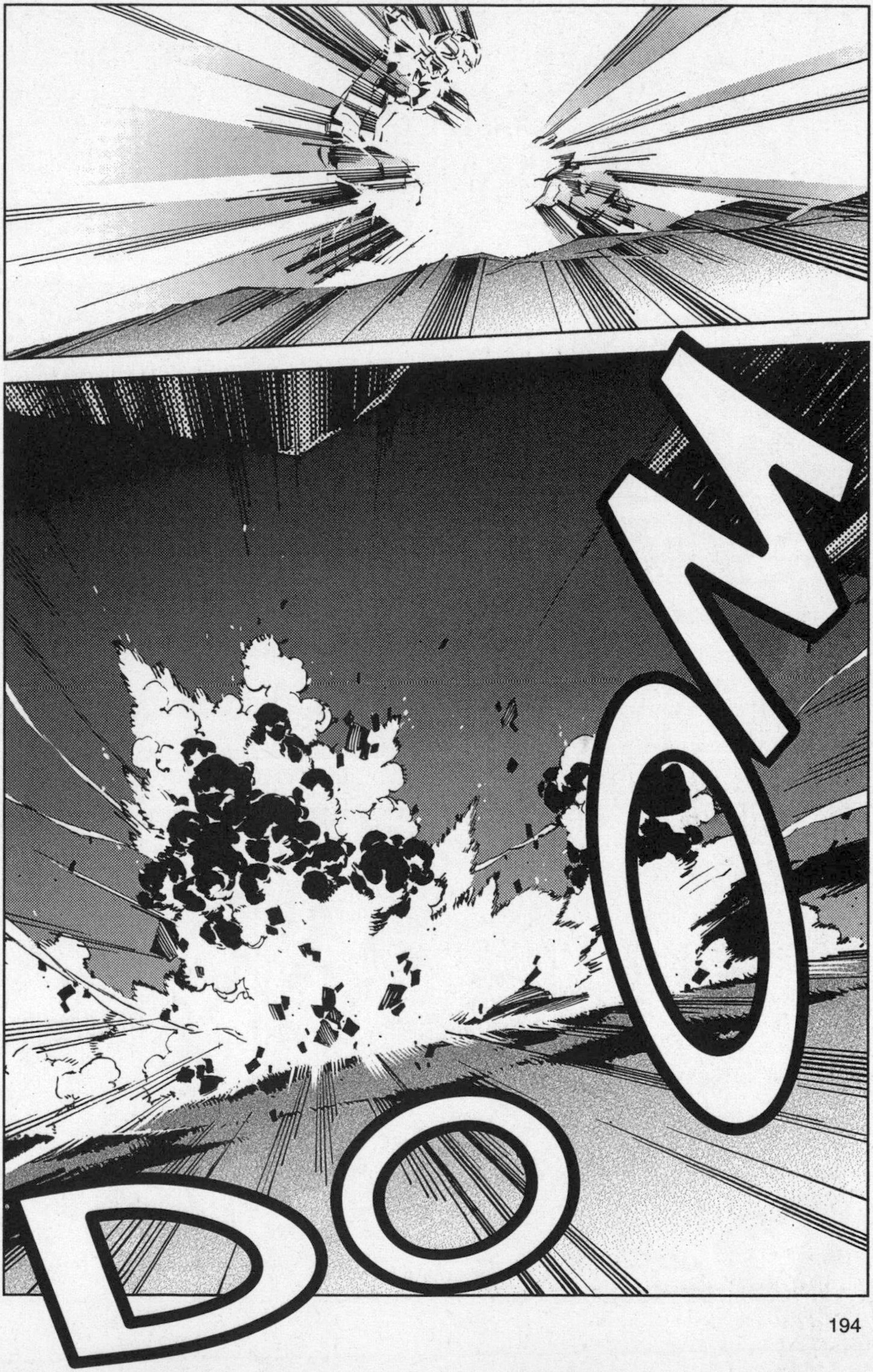
DOOM

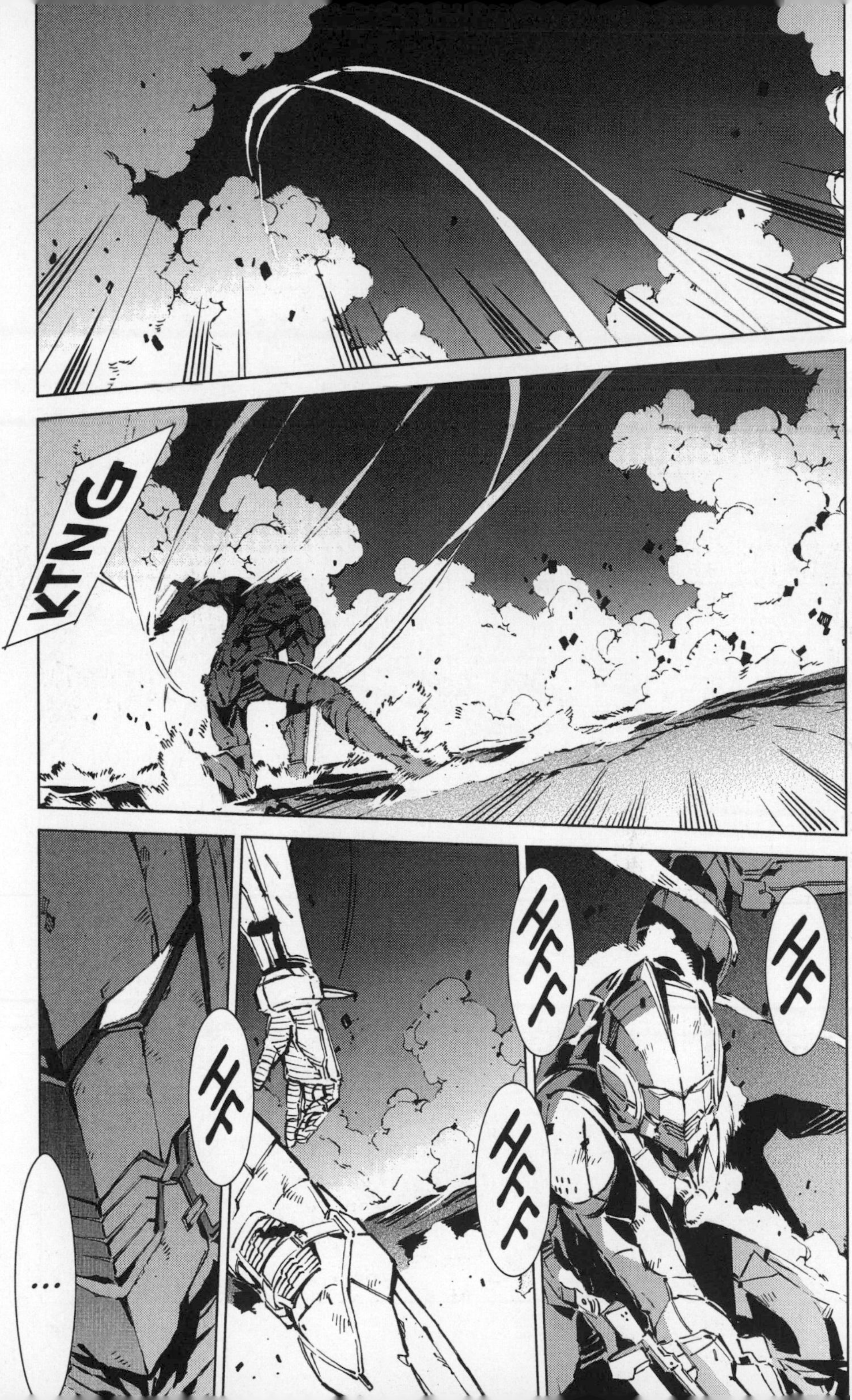
KTNG
HFF
HFFF
HFFF
HFF
...

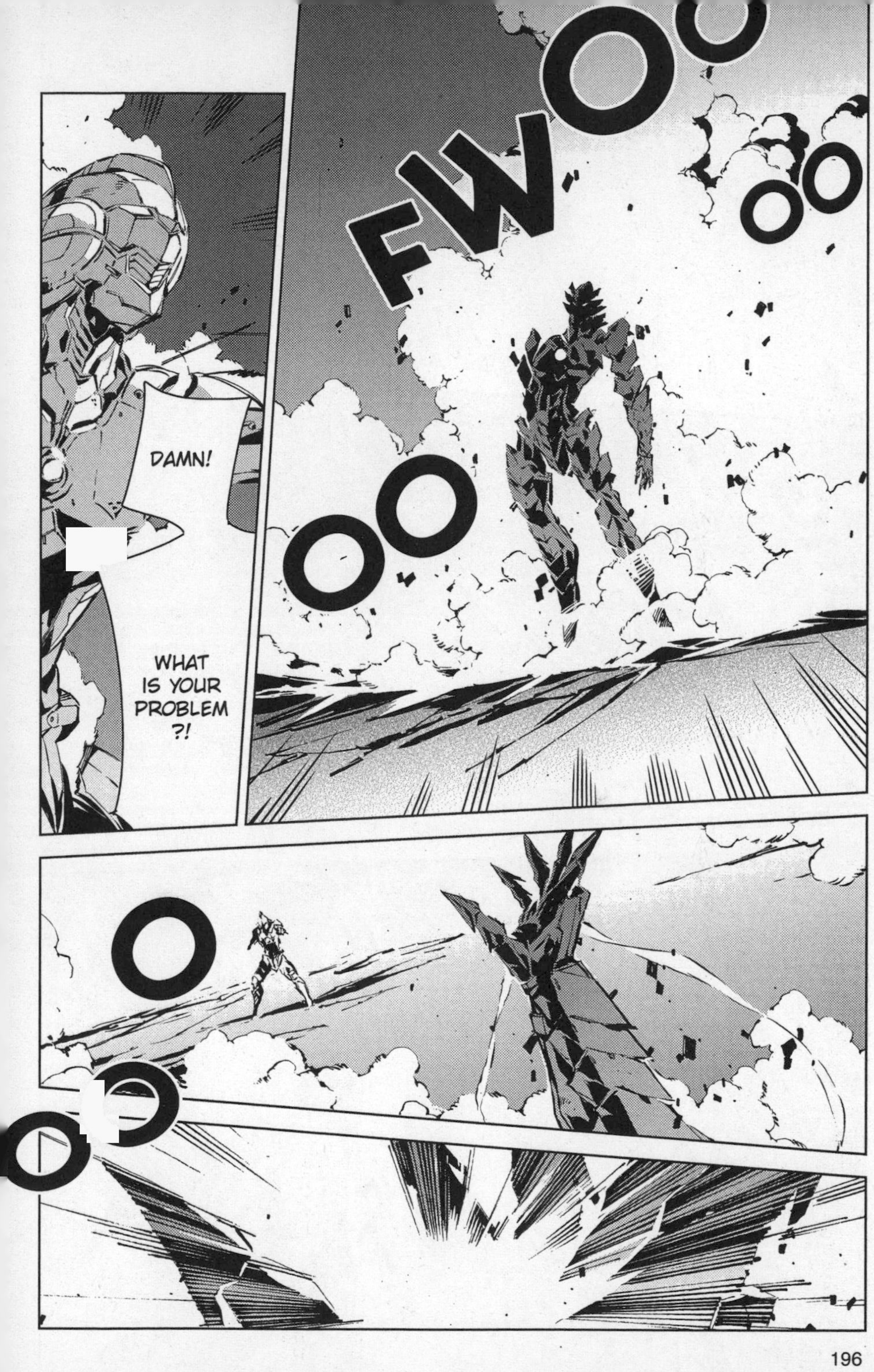
FWOOOOOO
DAMN!
WHAT IS YOUR PROBLEM ?!
OOO

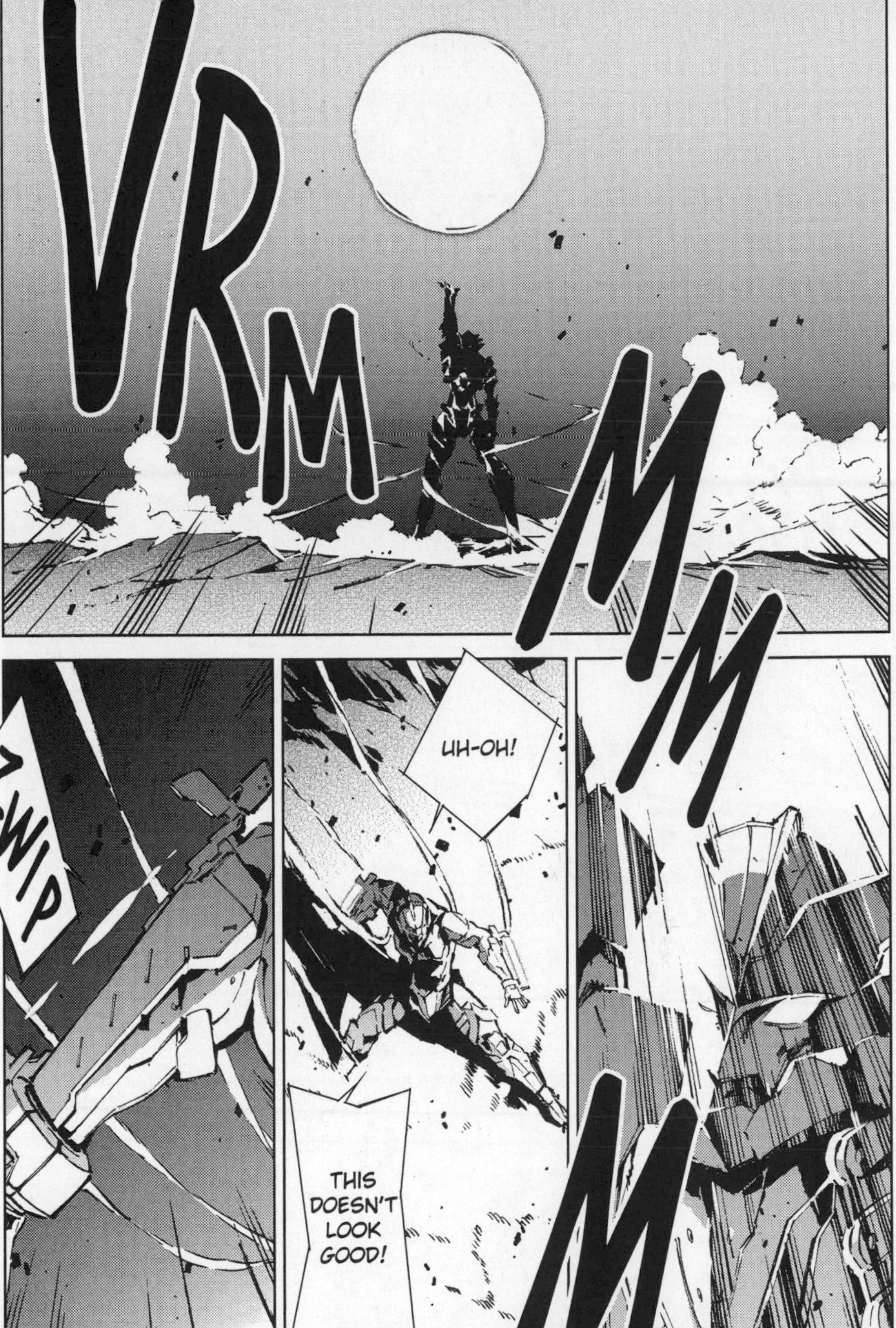
VRMMMM
UH-OH!
THIS DOESN'T LOOK GOOD!
ZWIP

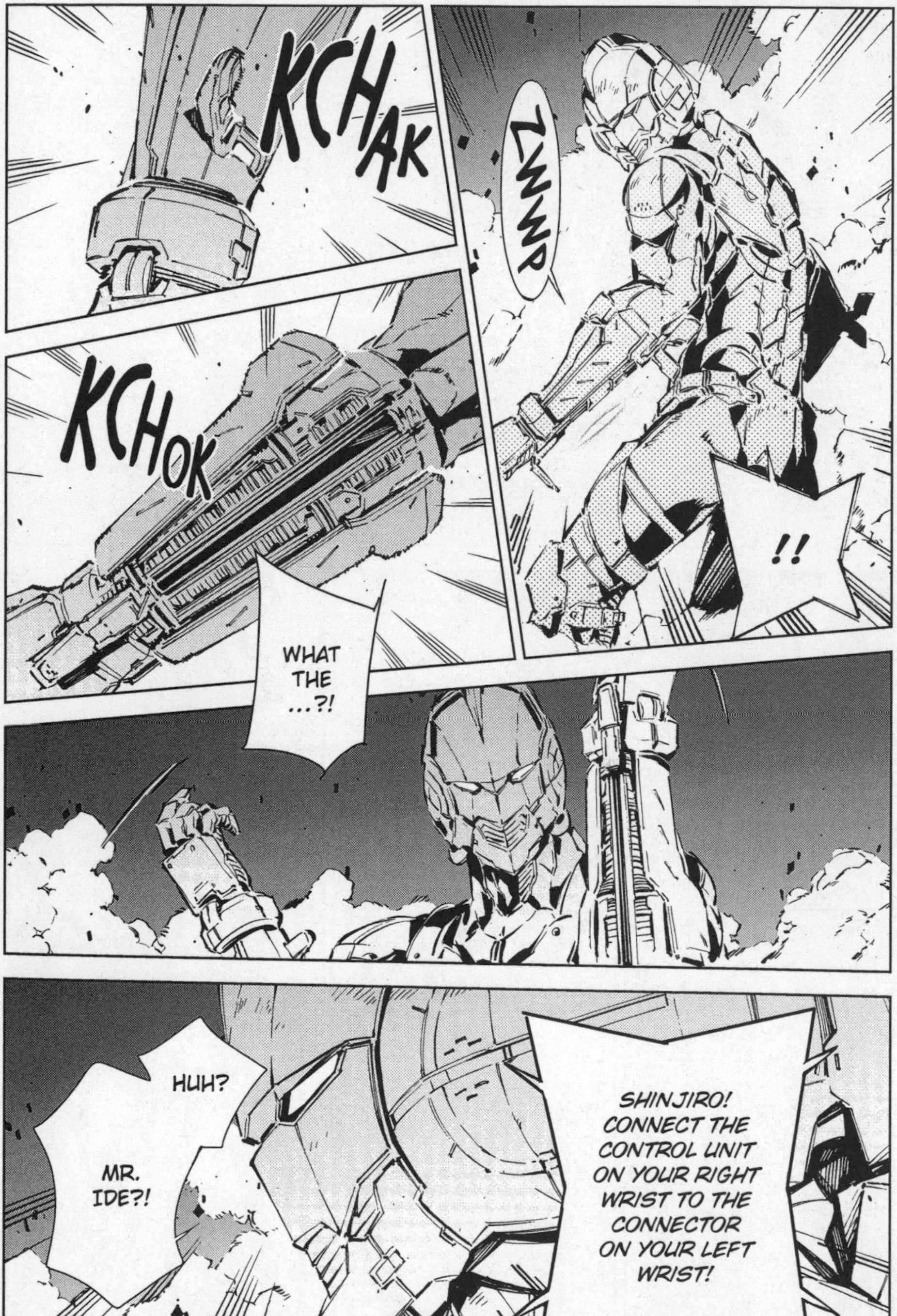
ZWWP
!!
KCHAK
KCHOK
WHAT THE ...?!
SHINJIRO! CONNECT THE CONTROL UNIT ON YOUR RIGHT WRIST TO THE CONNECTOR ON YOUR LEFT WRIST!
HUH?
MR. IDE?!

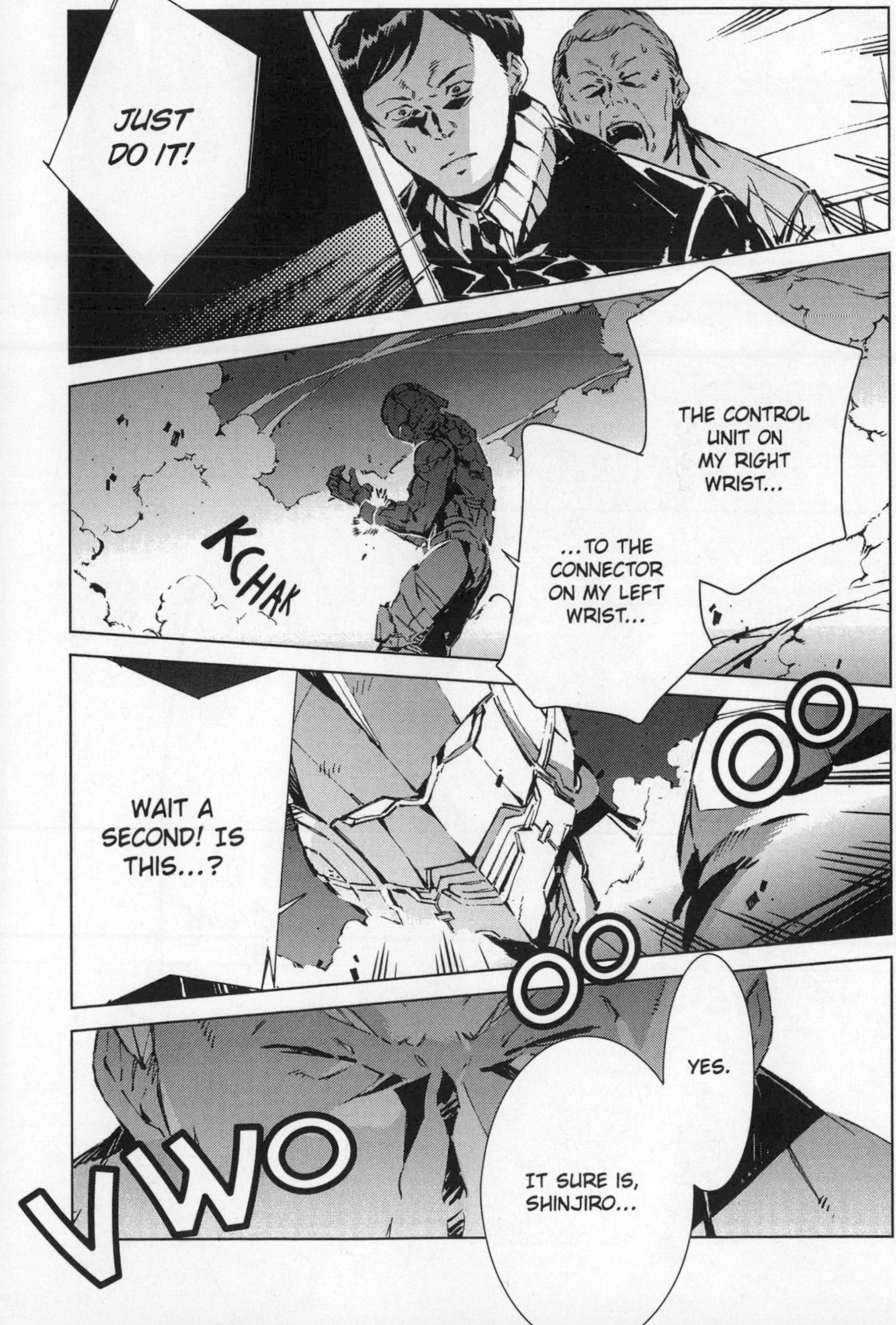
JUST DO IT!
THE CONTROL UNIT ON MY RIGHT WRIST...
...TO THE CONNECTOR ON MY LEFT WRIST...
KCHAK
WAIT A SECOND! IS THIS...?
YES.
IT SURE IS, SHINJIRO...
VWOOOOO

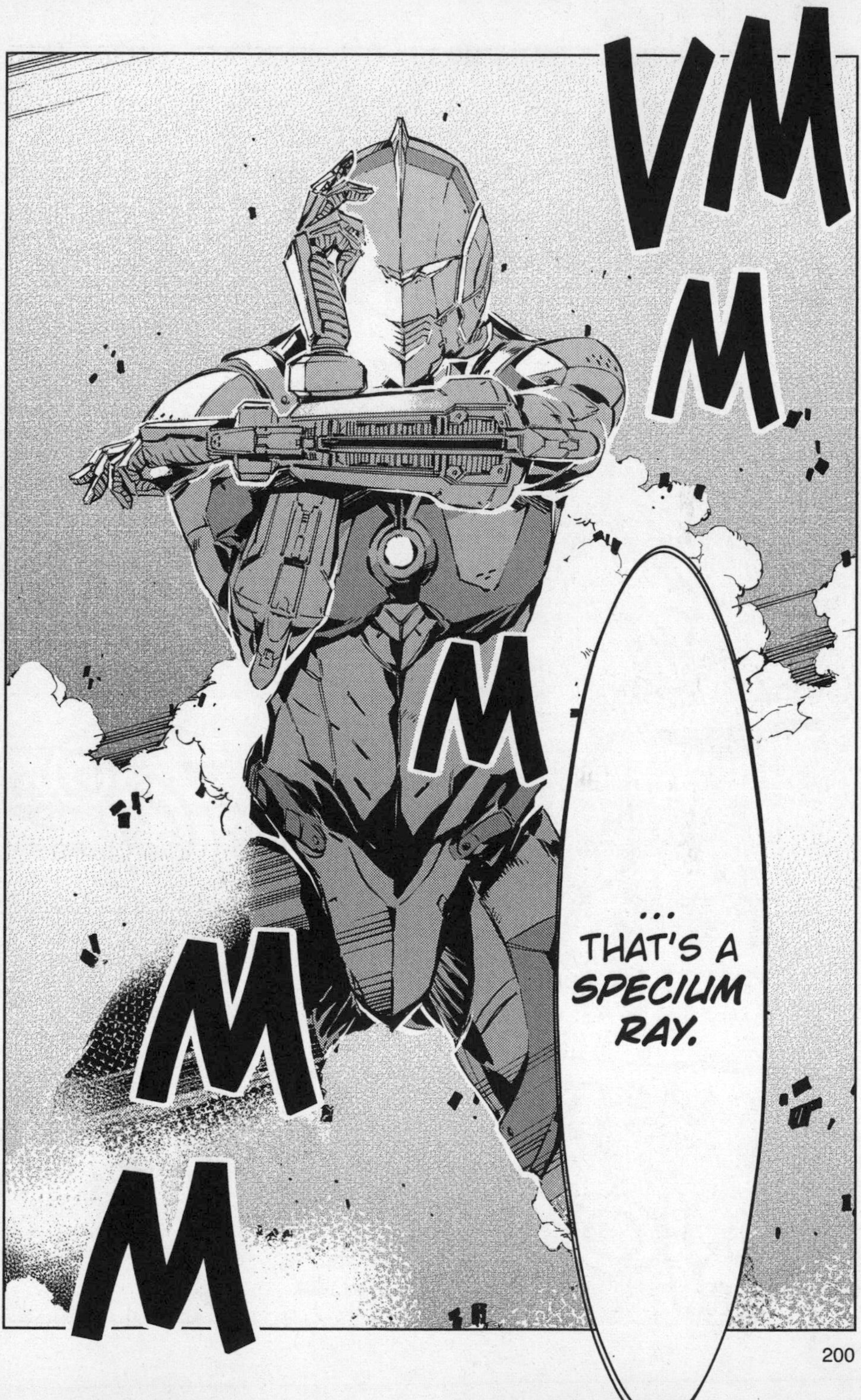
VM
M
M
M
M
... THAT'S A SPECIUM RAY.

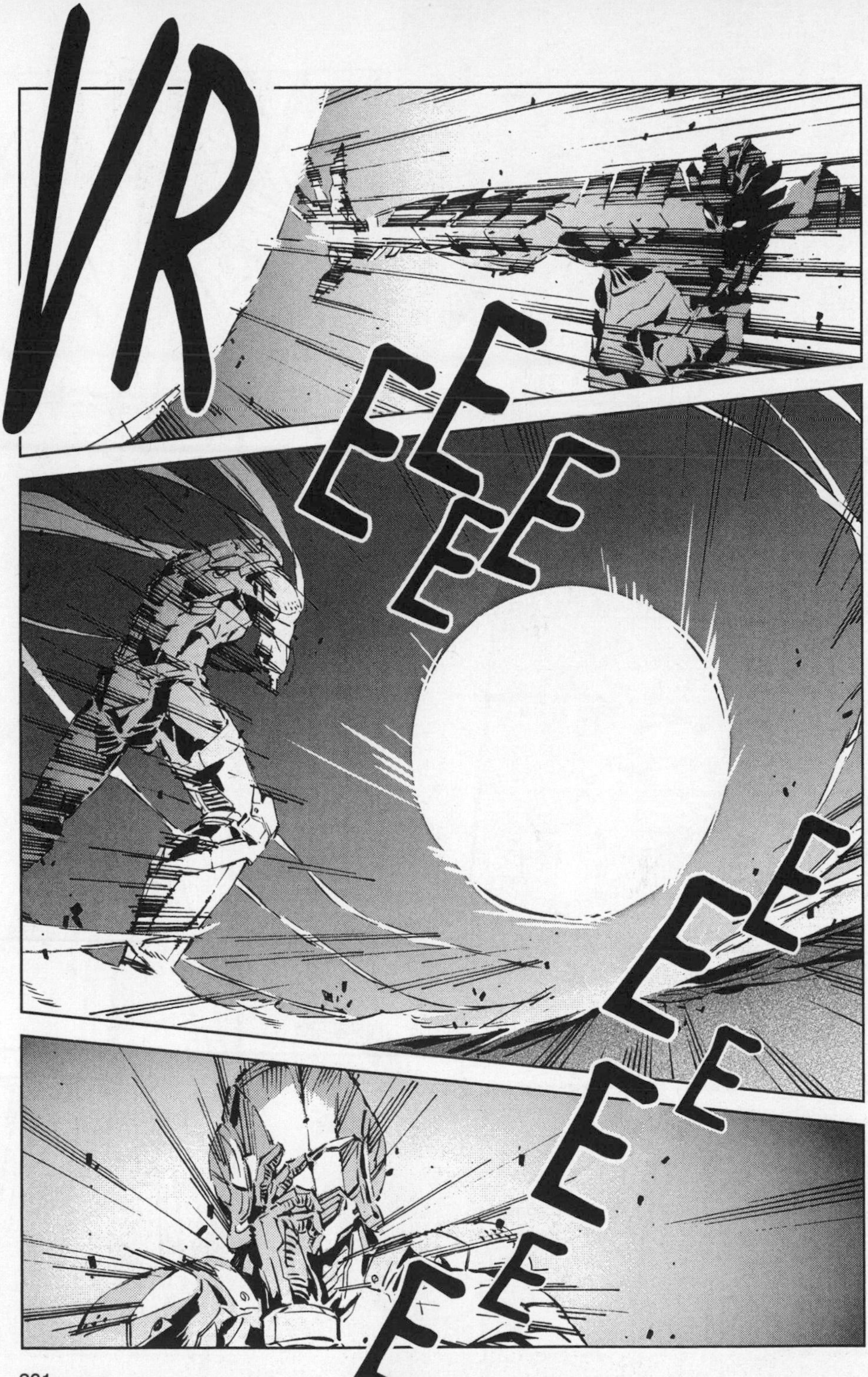
VREEEEEEEEEEEEEEEE

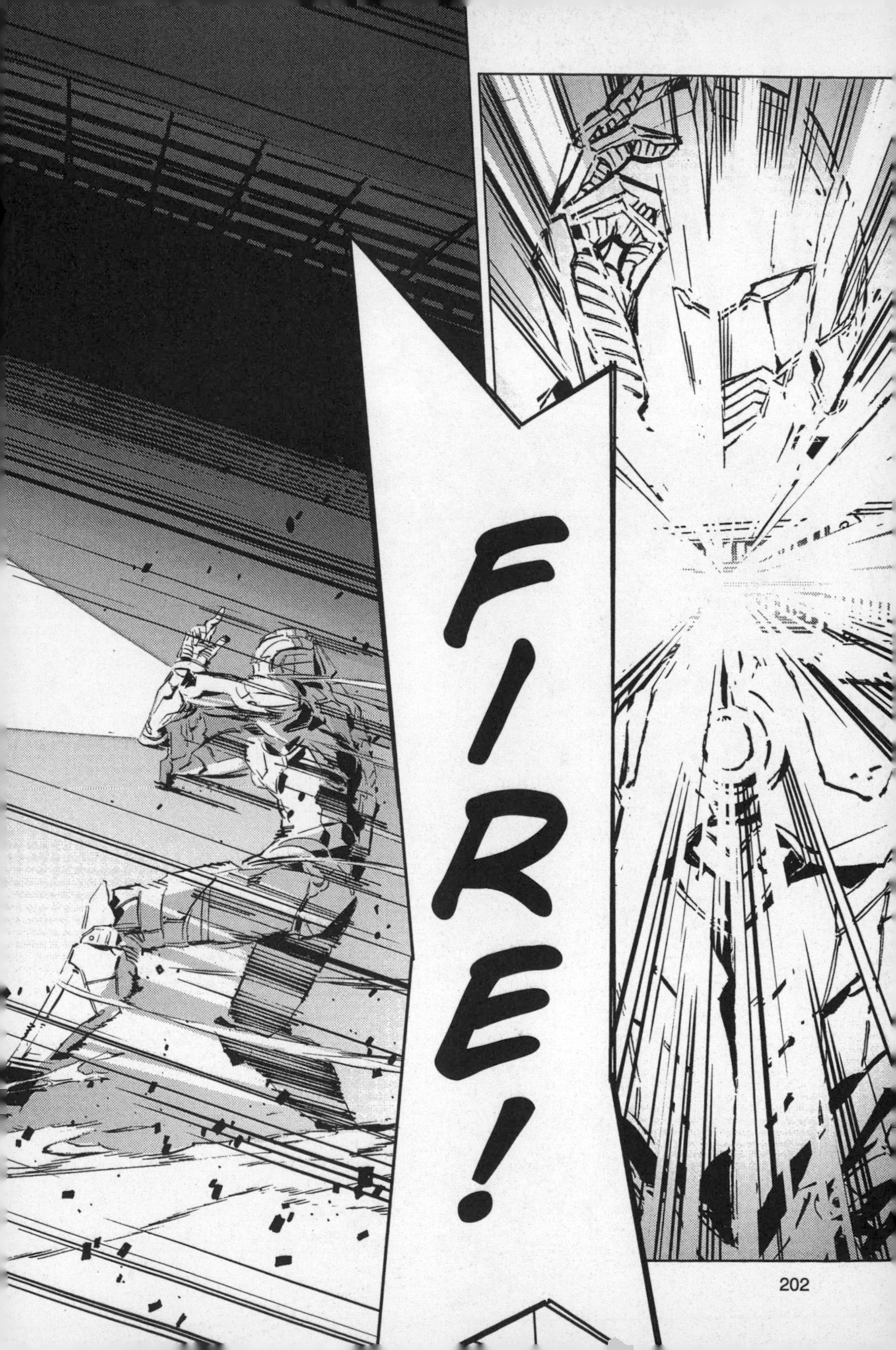
FIRE!

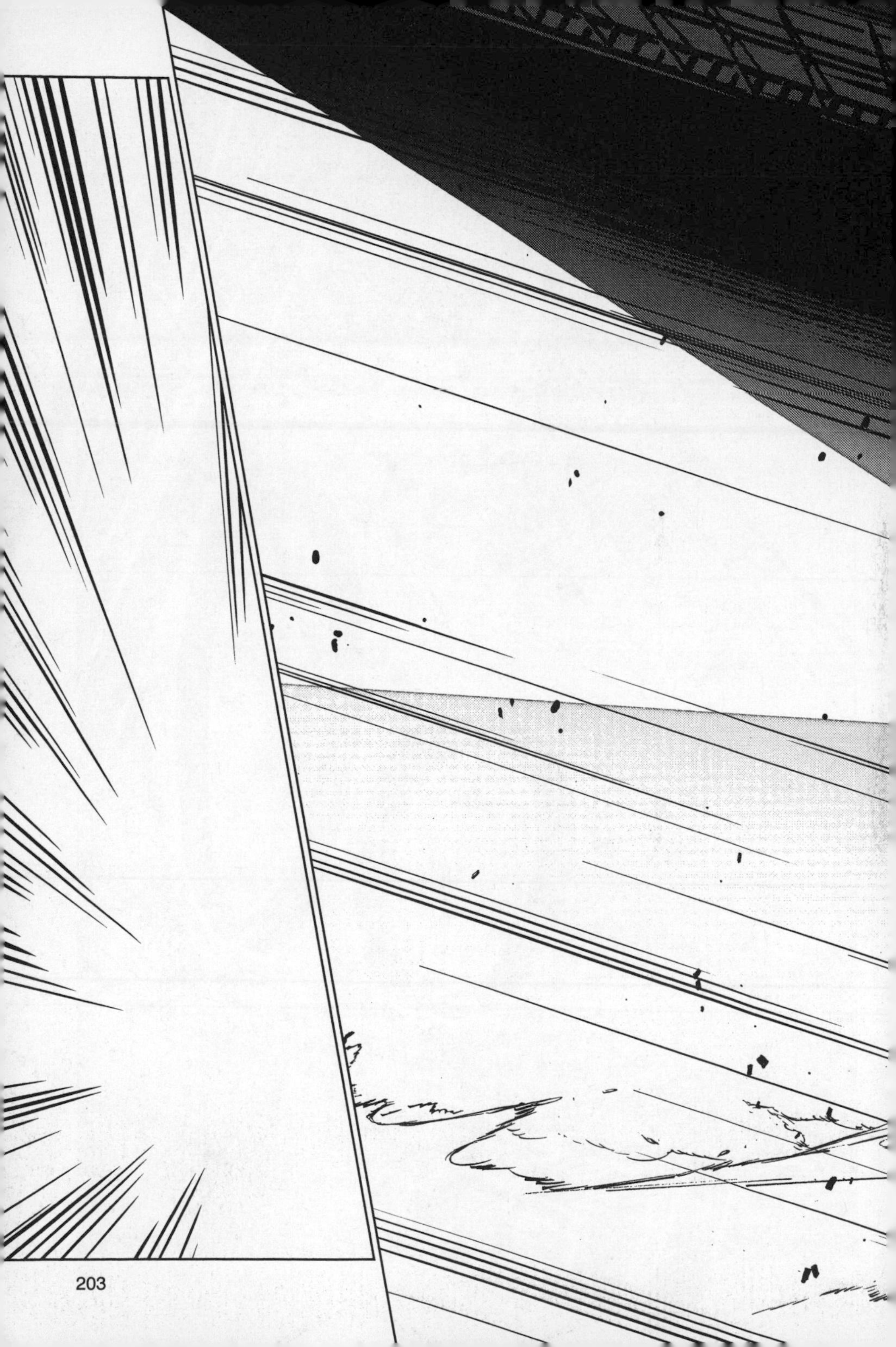

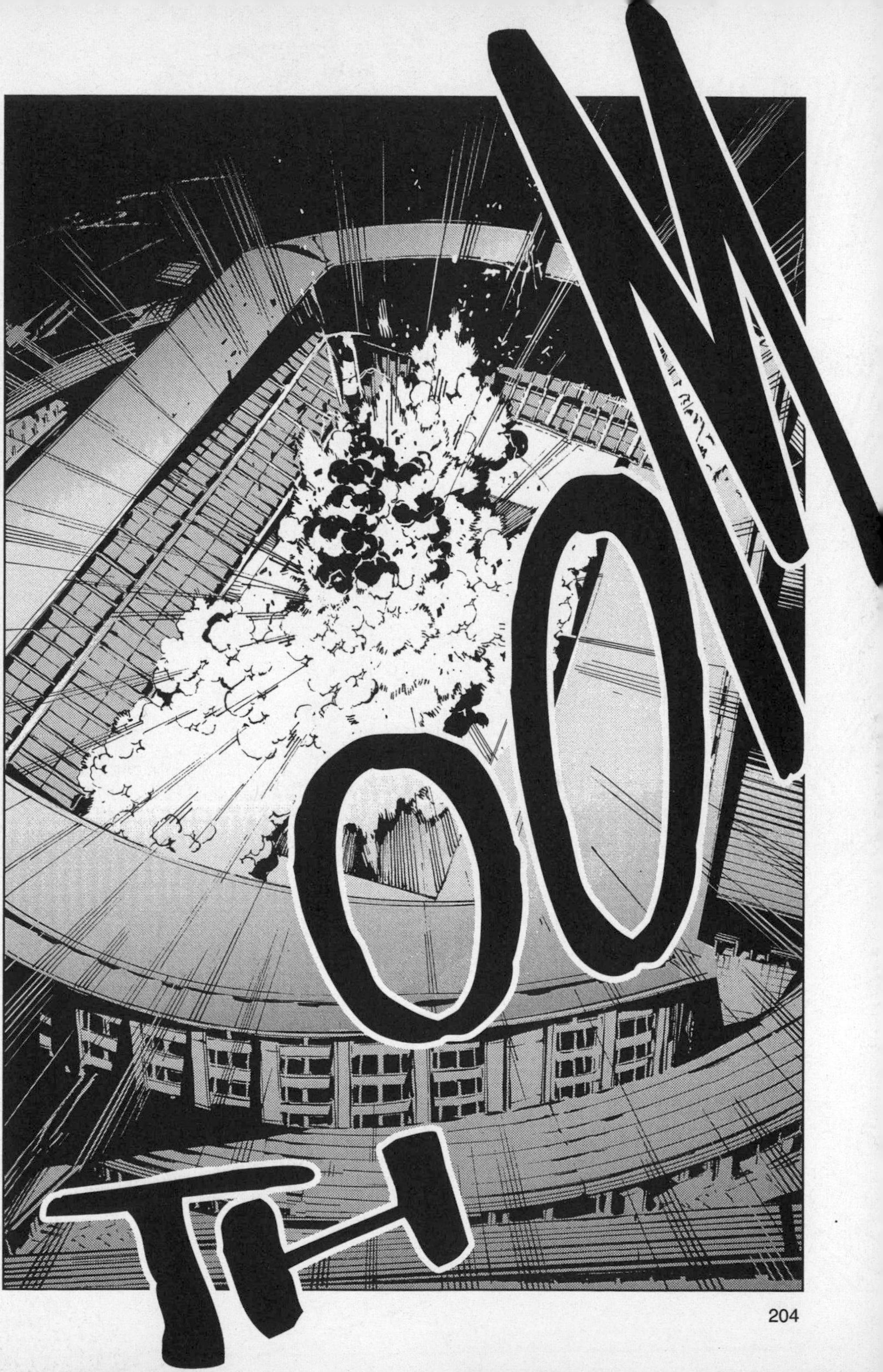
TOOM

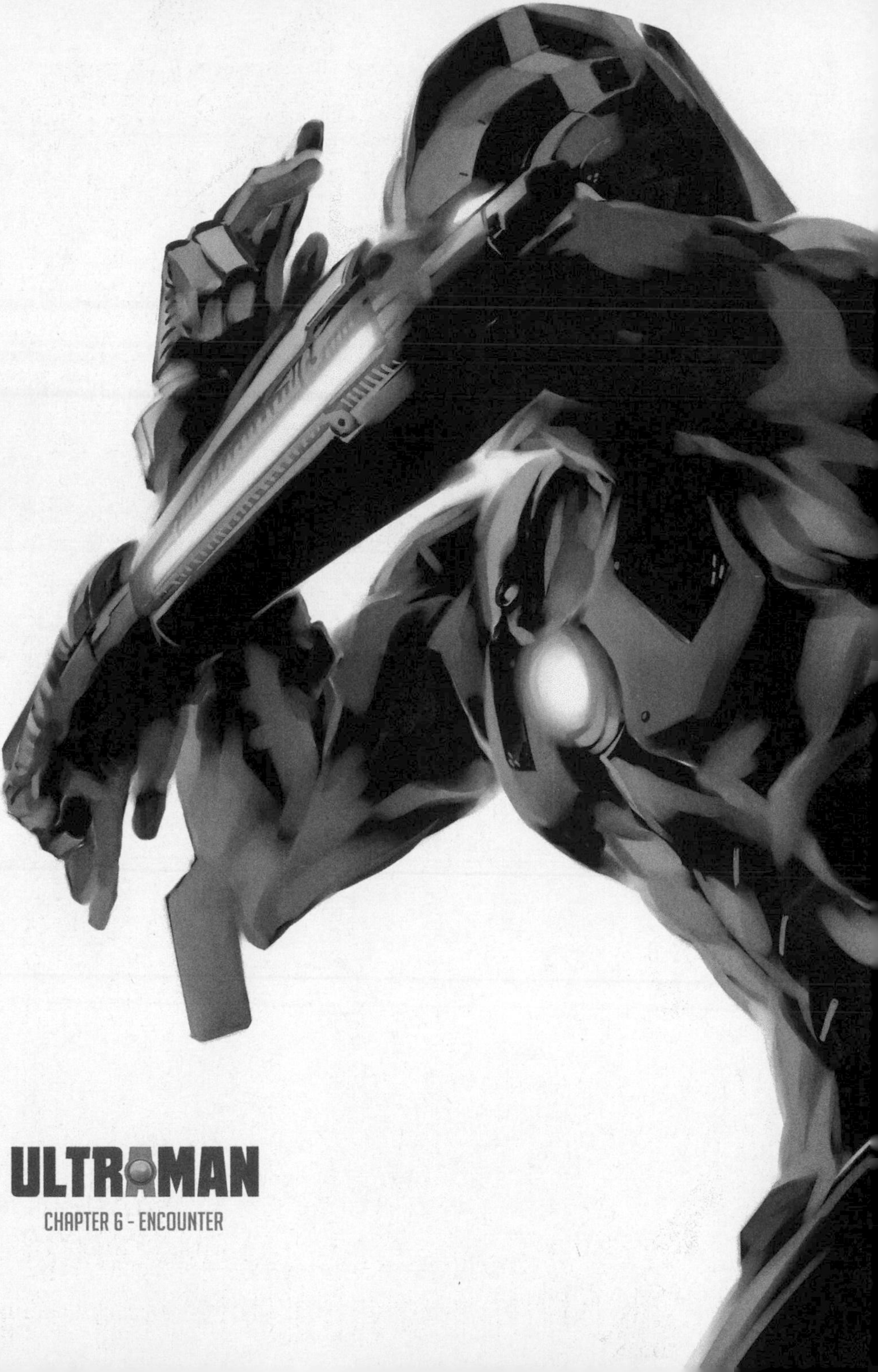

ULTRAMAN

CHAPTER 6 - ENCOUNTER

ULTRAMAN

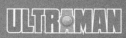

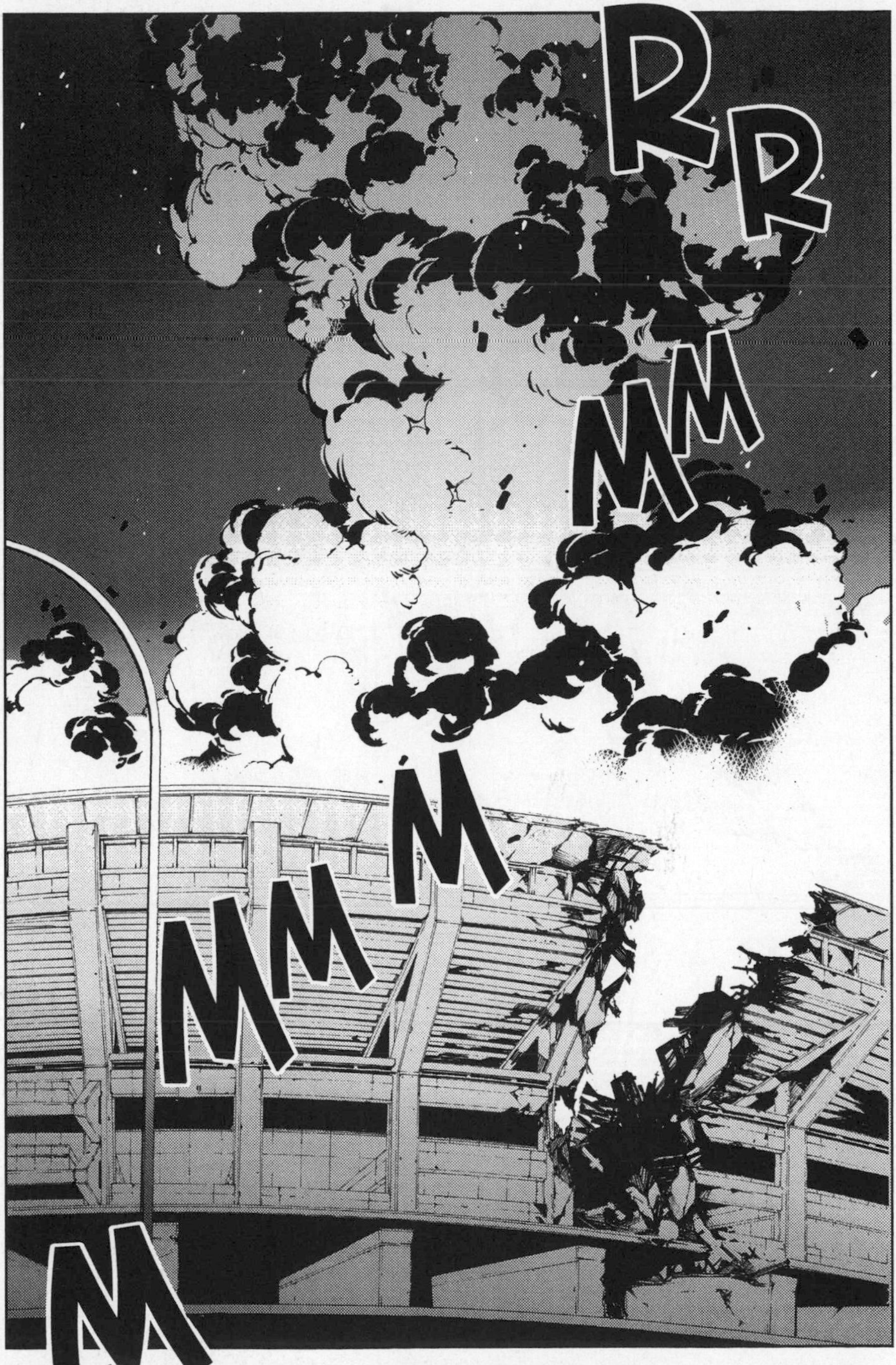
RRMMMMMM

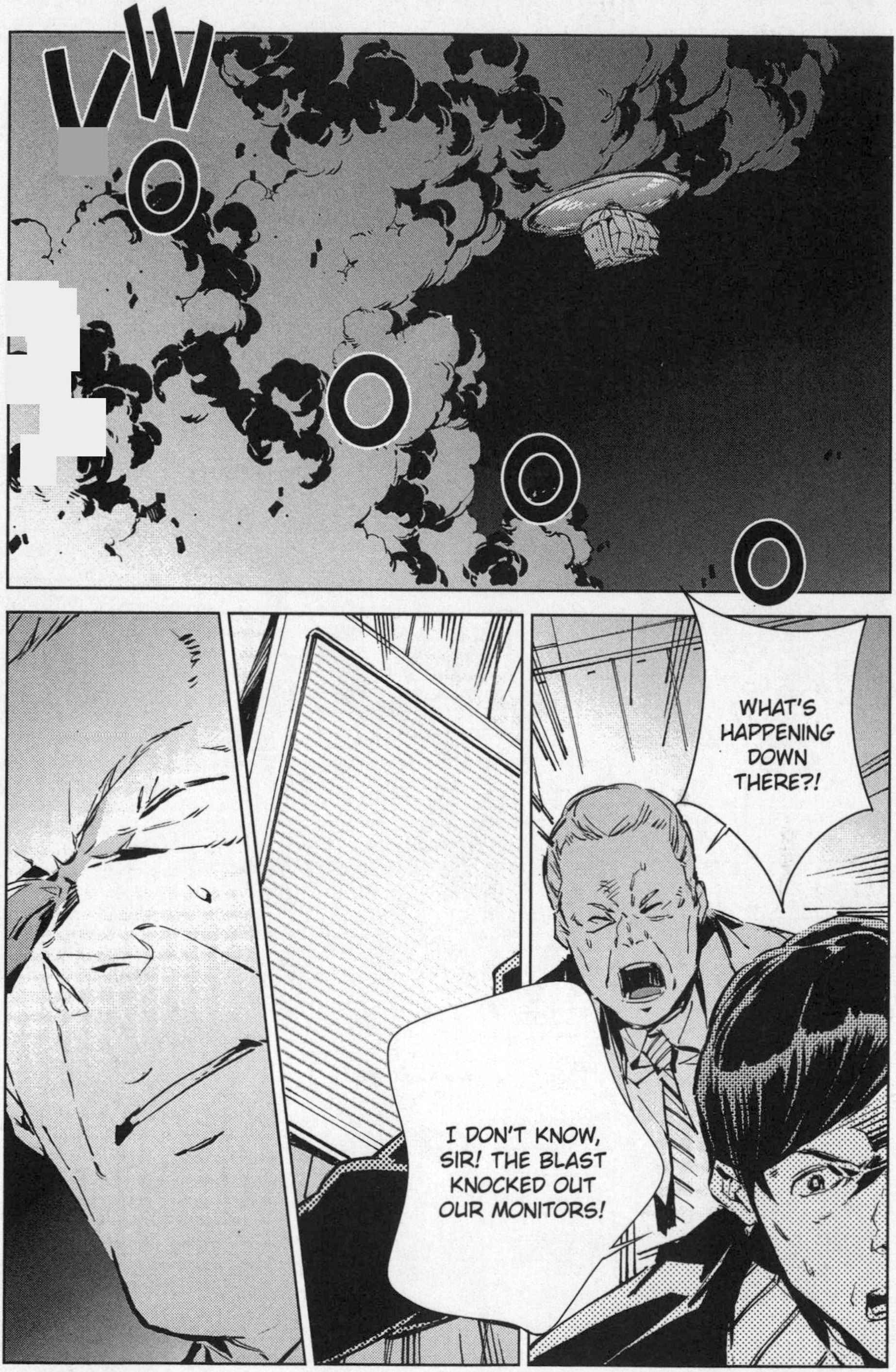
VWOOOO
WHAT'S HAPPENING DOWN THERE?!
I DON'T KNOW, SIR! THE BLAST KNOCKED OUT OUR MONITORS!

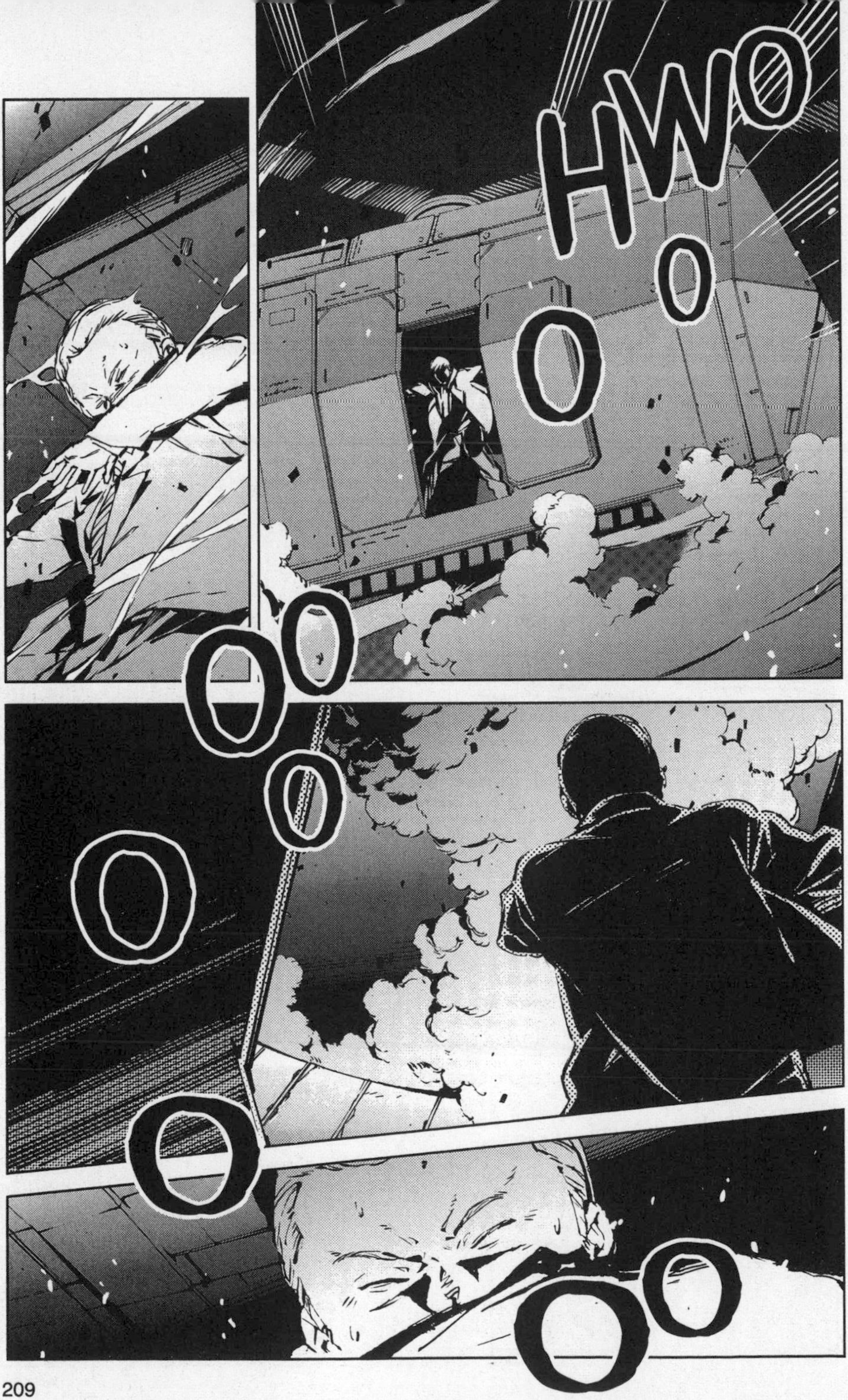
HWOOOOOOOOOO

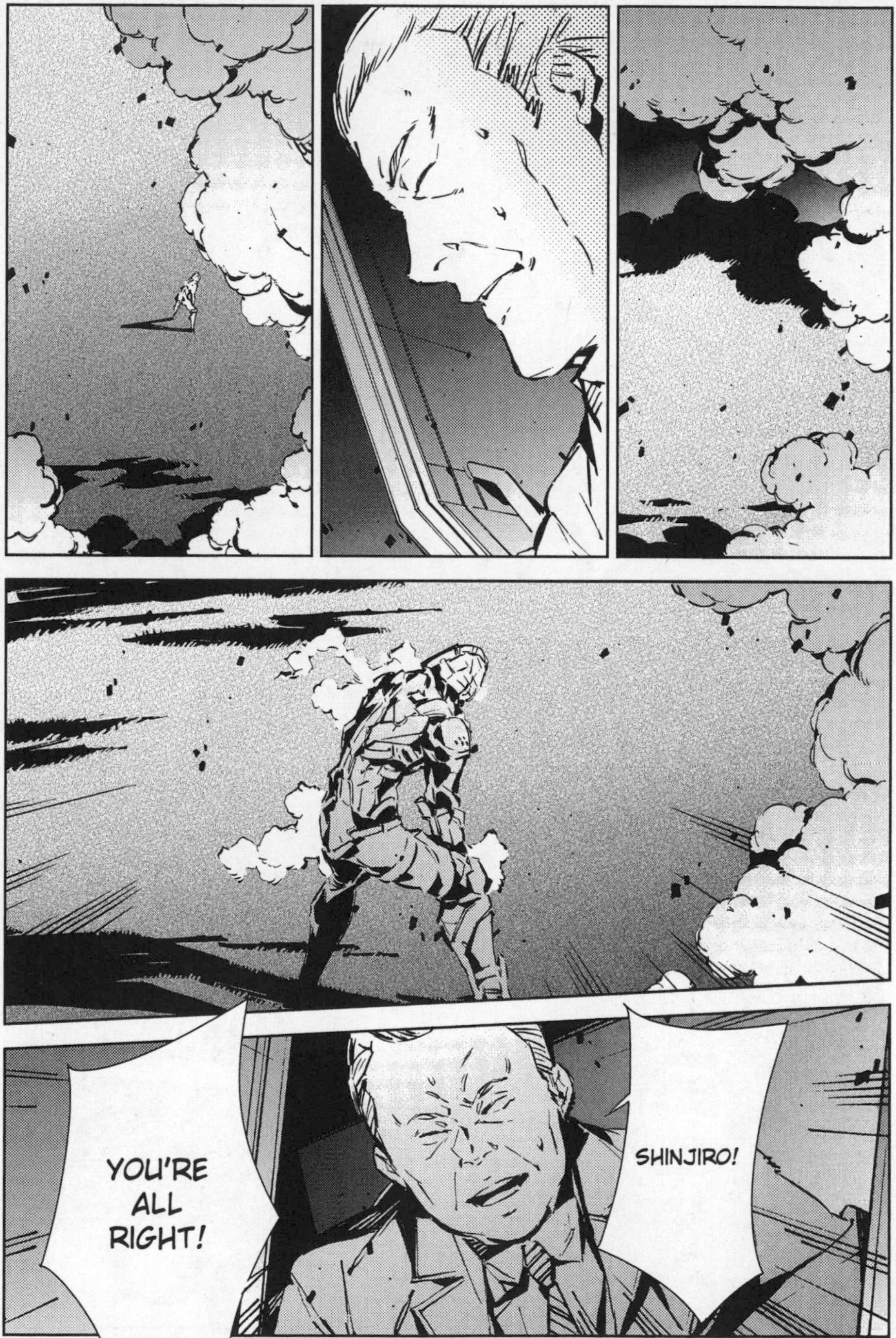
SHINJIRO!
YOU'RE ALL RIGHT!

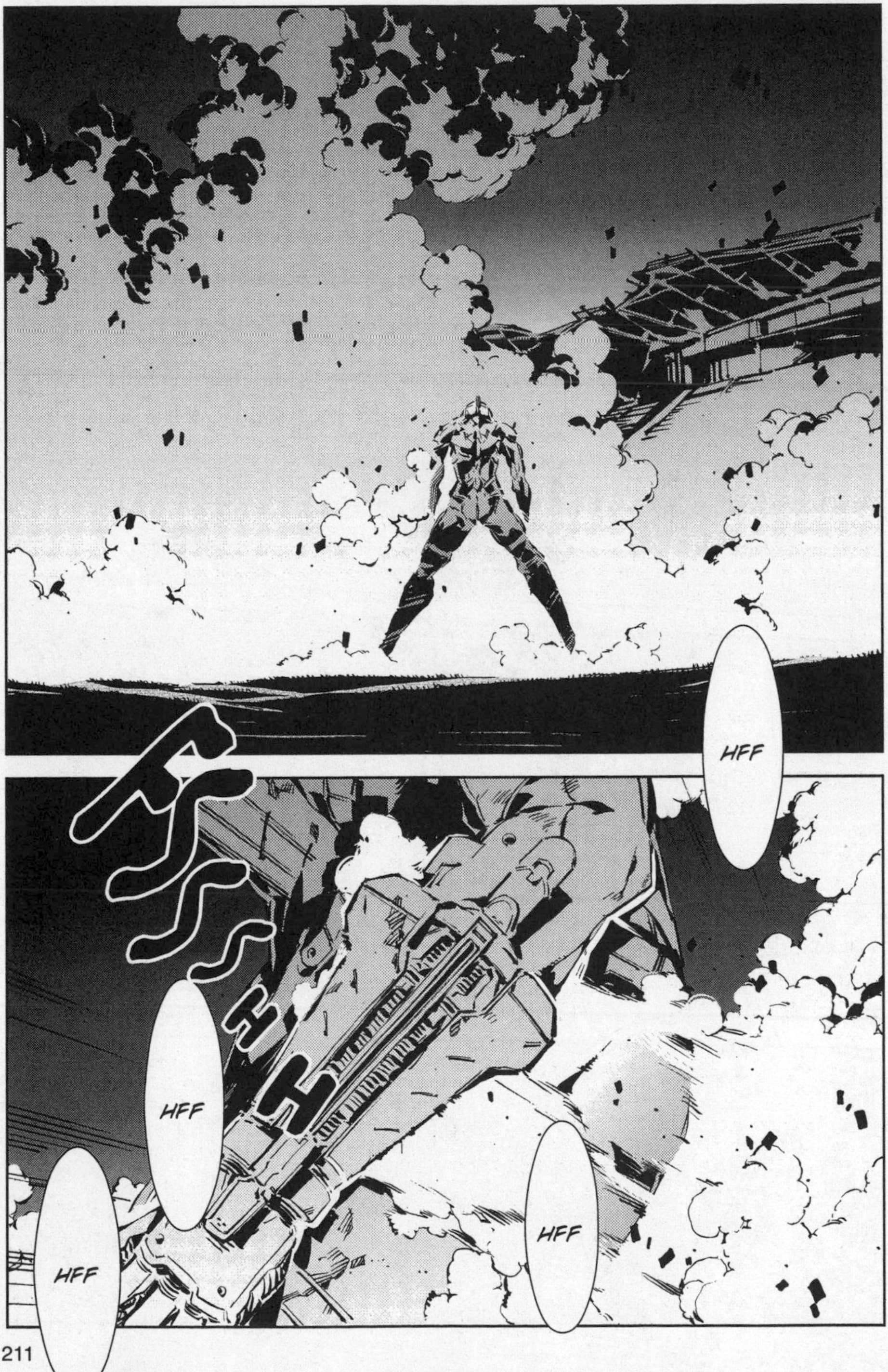
HFF
FSSSHH
HFF
HFF
HFF

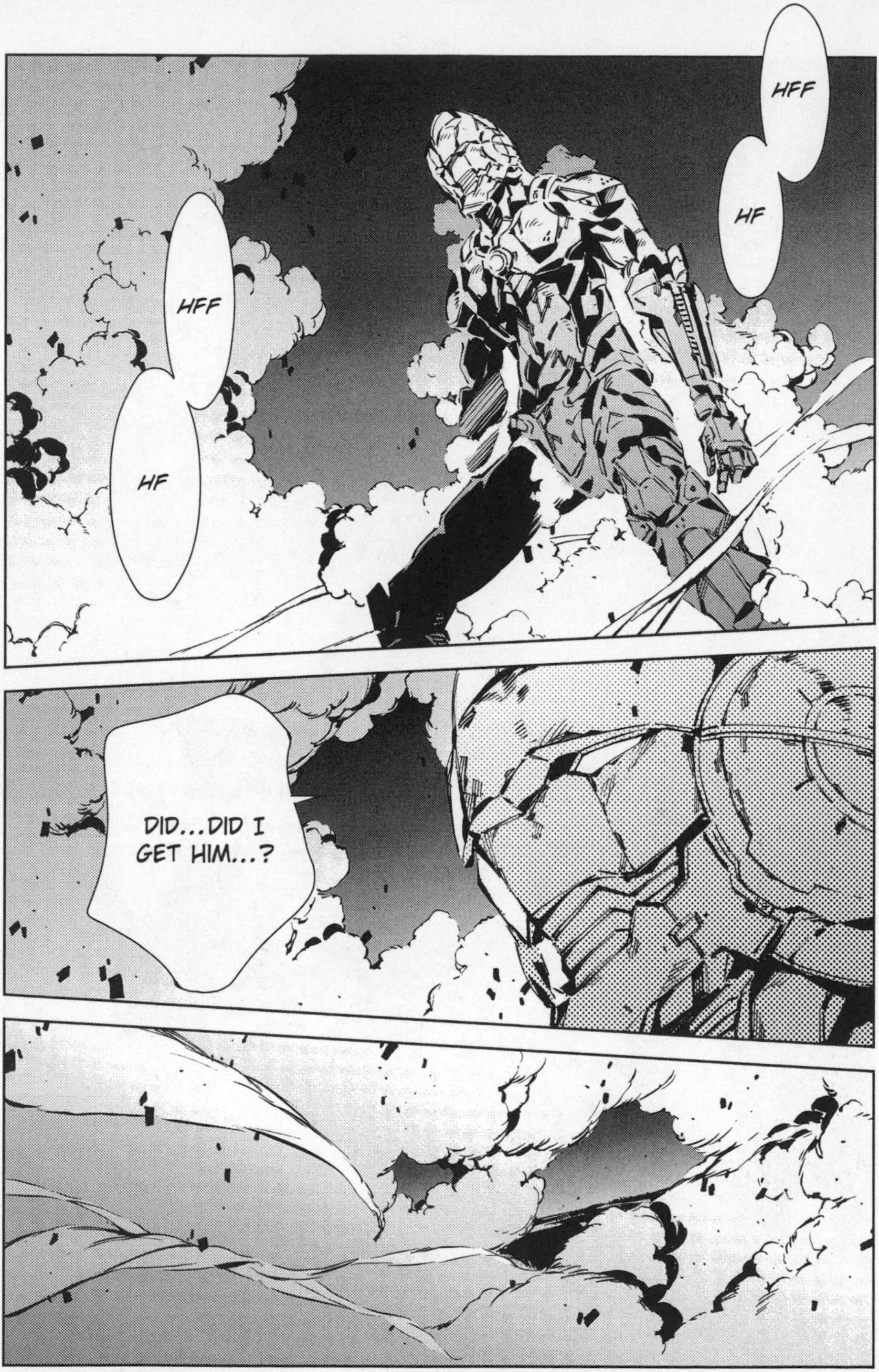
HFF
HF
HFF
HF
DID...DID I GET HIM...?

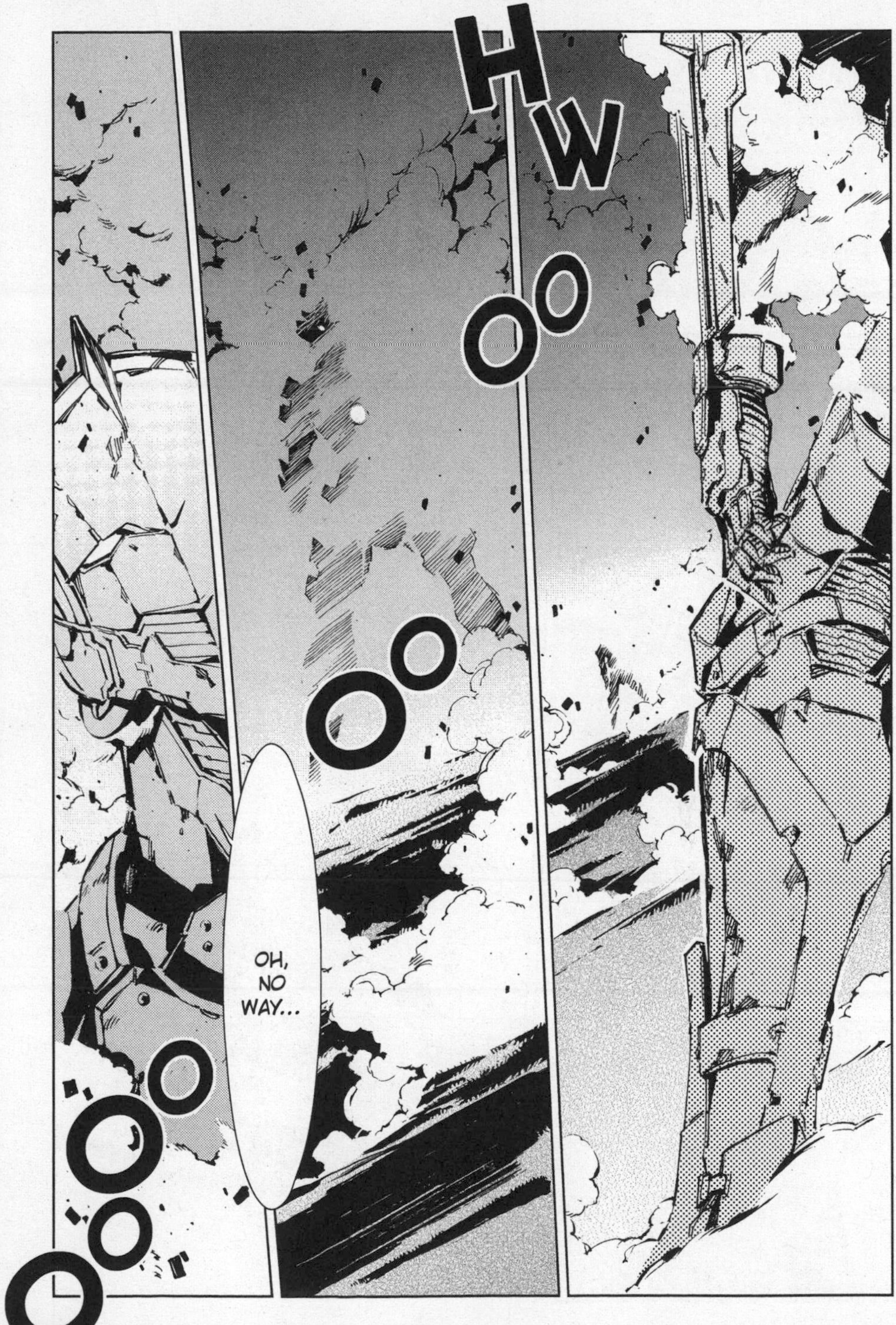
HWOOOOOOOO
OH, NO WAY...

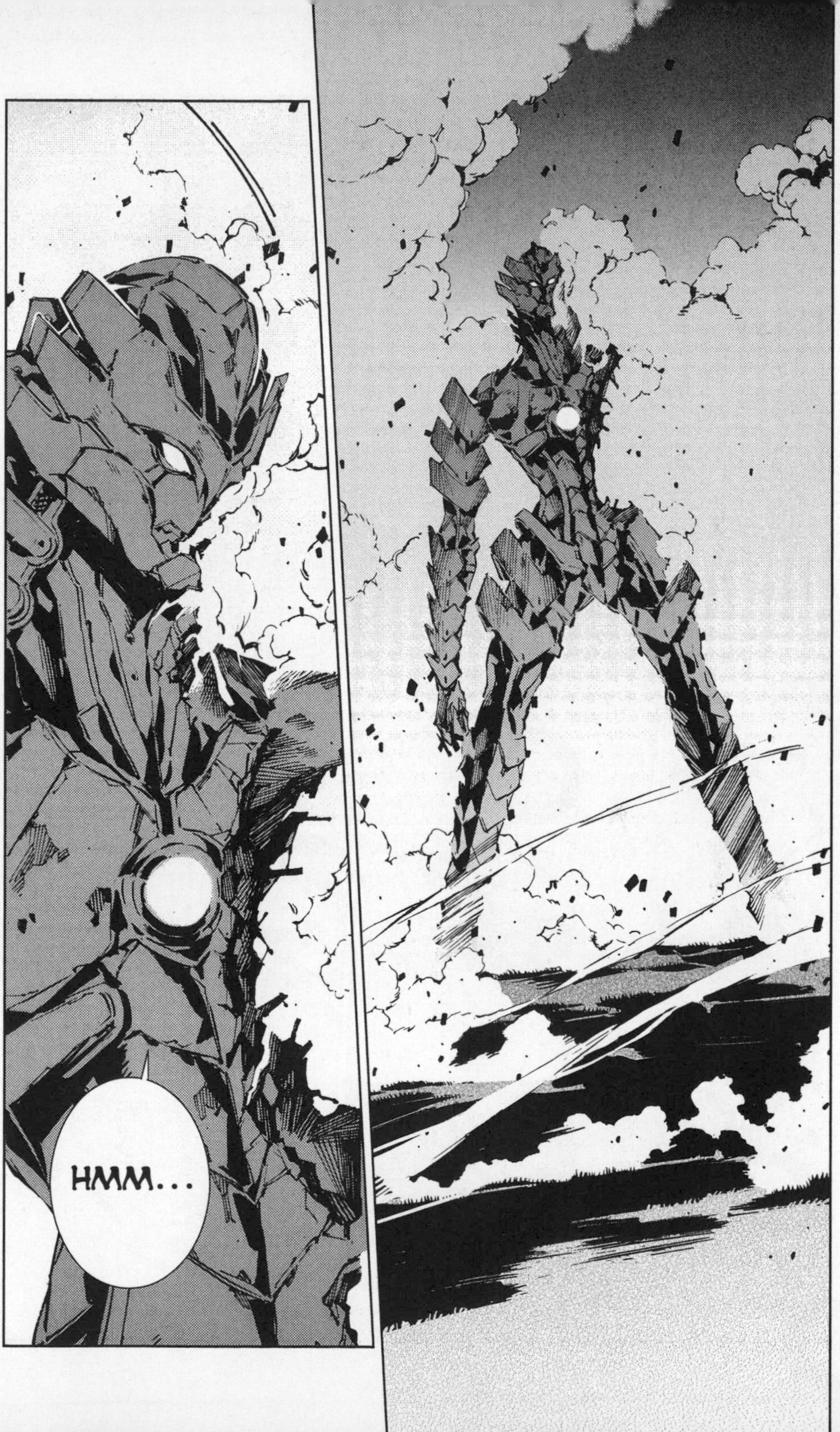
HMM...

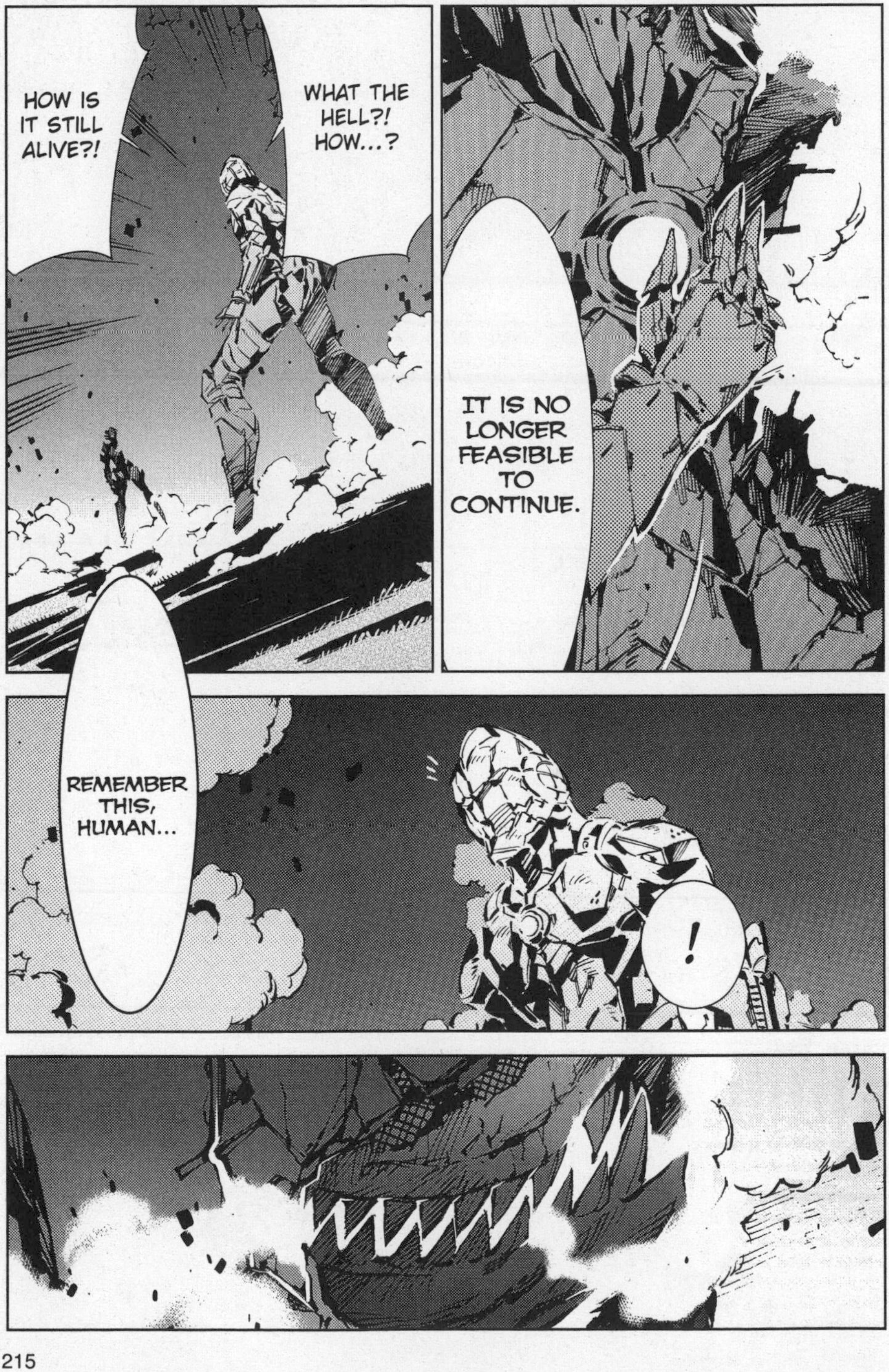
IT IS NO LONGER FEASIBLE TO CONTINUE.
WHAT THE HELL?! HOW...?
HOW IS IT STILL ALIVE?!
REMEMBER THIS, HUMAN...
!

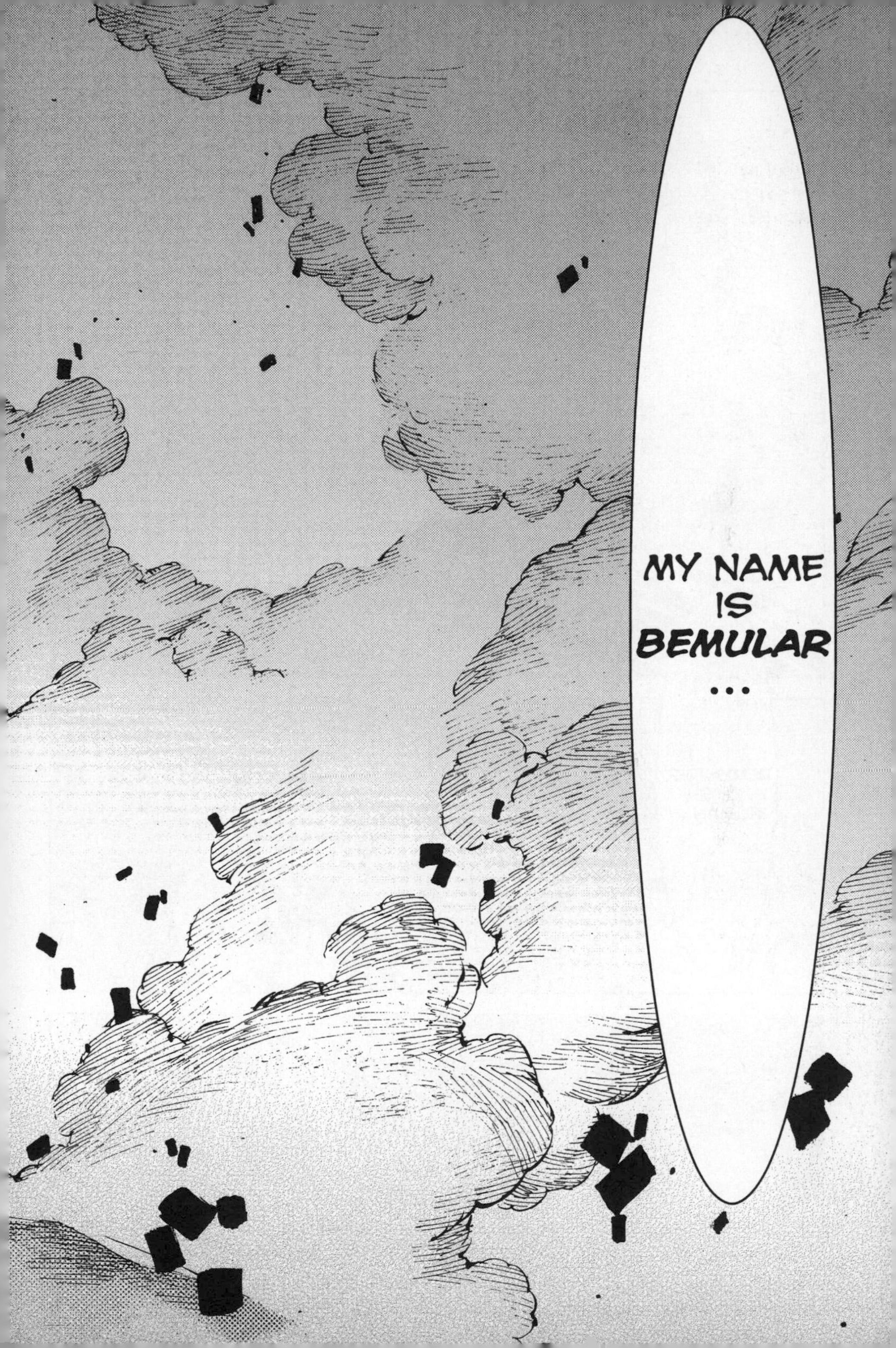
MY NAME IS BEMULAR...

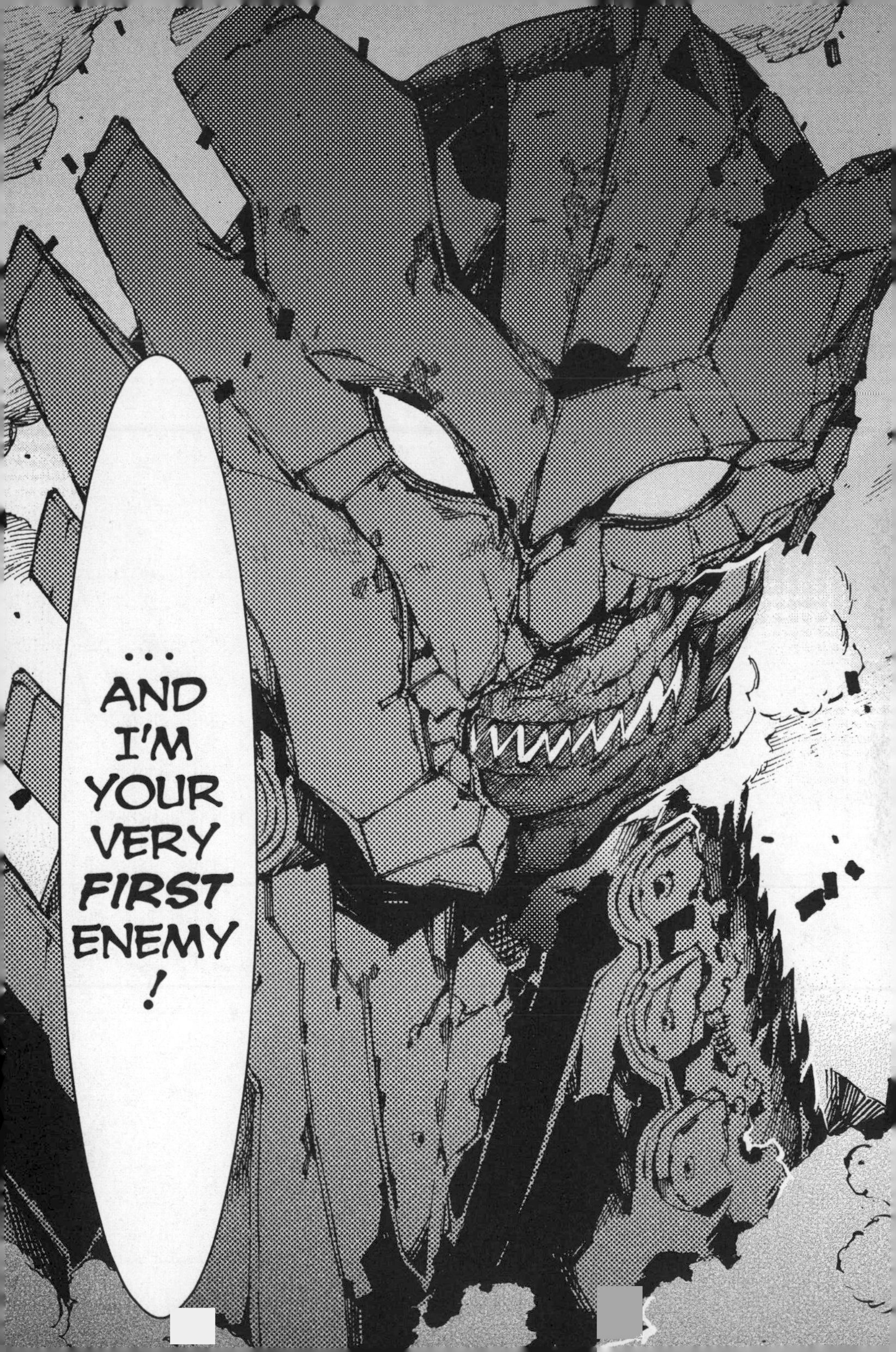
... AND I'M YOUR VERY FIRST ENEMY!

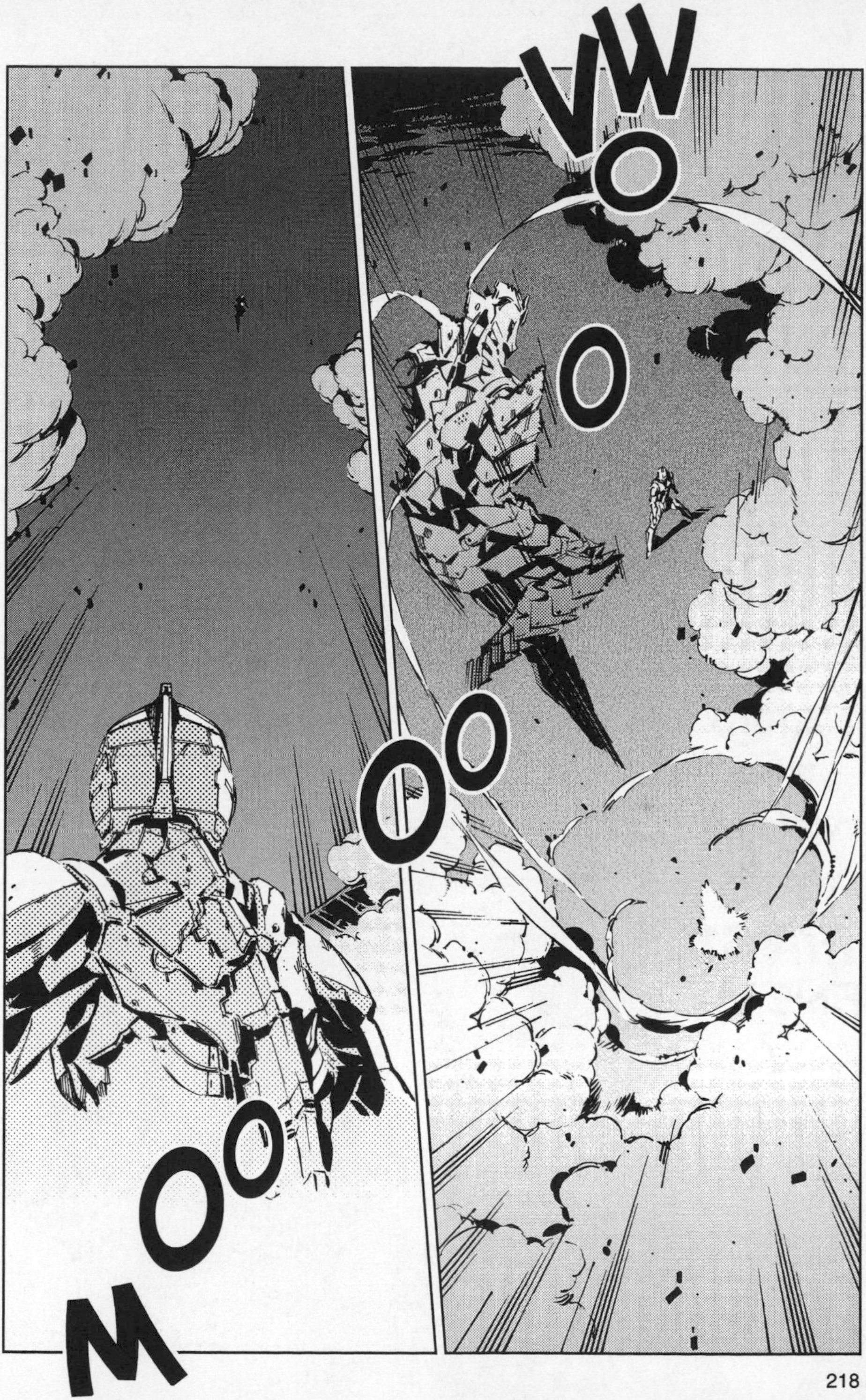
VWOOOOOOM

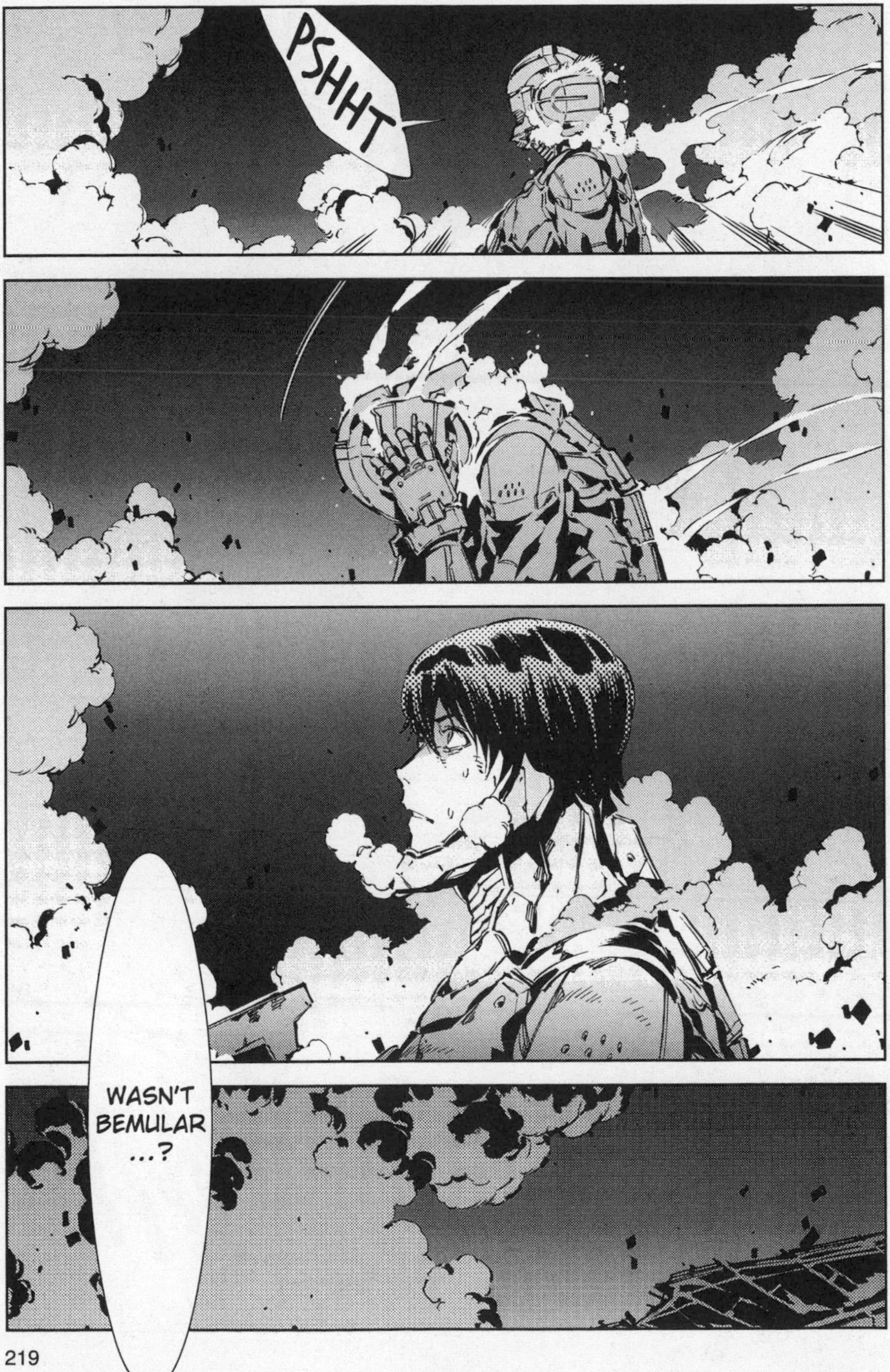
PSHHT
WASN'T BEMULAR ...?

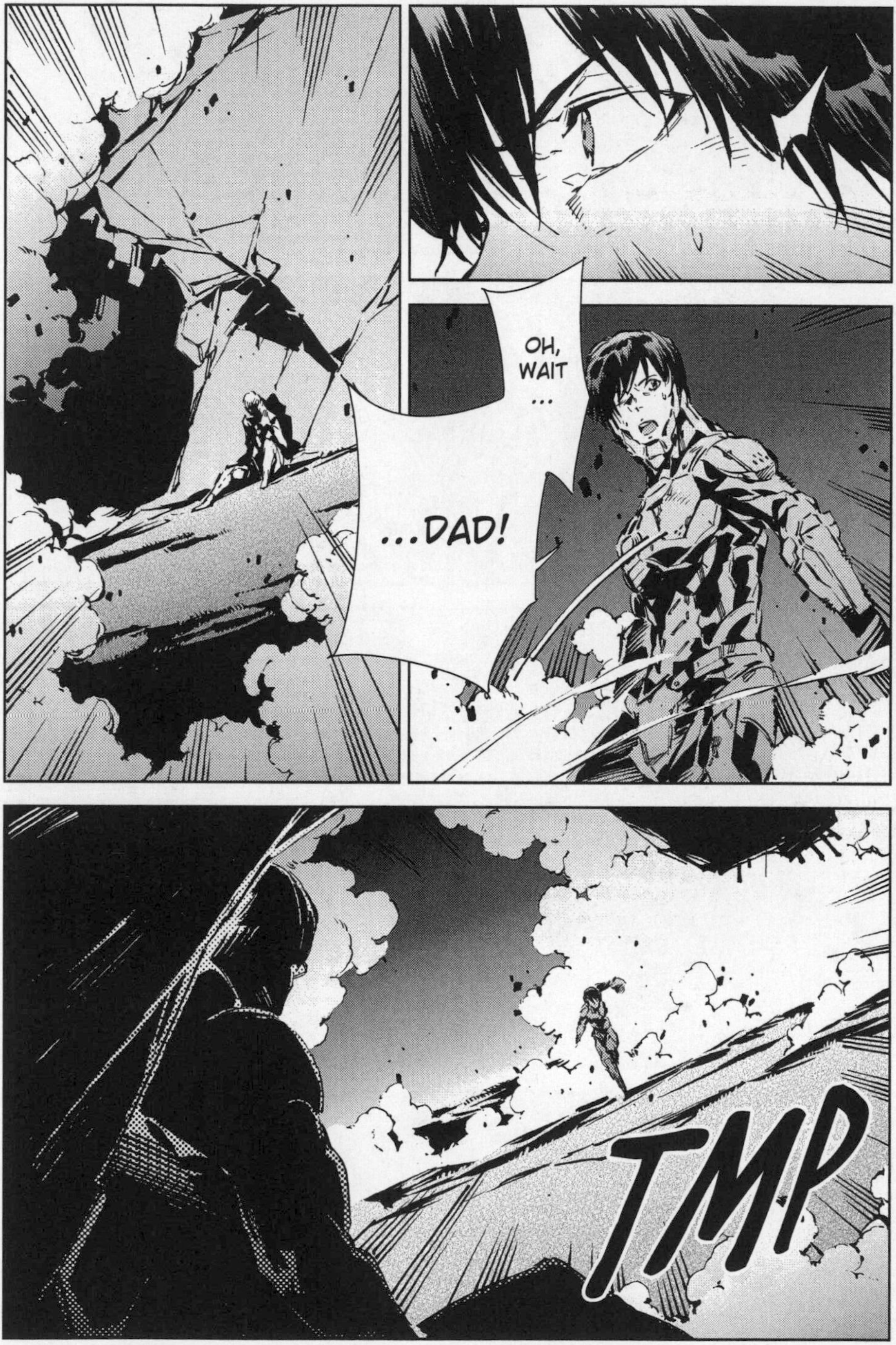

OH, WAIT ...
...DAD!
TMP

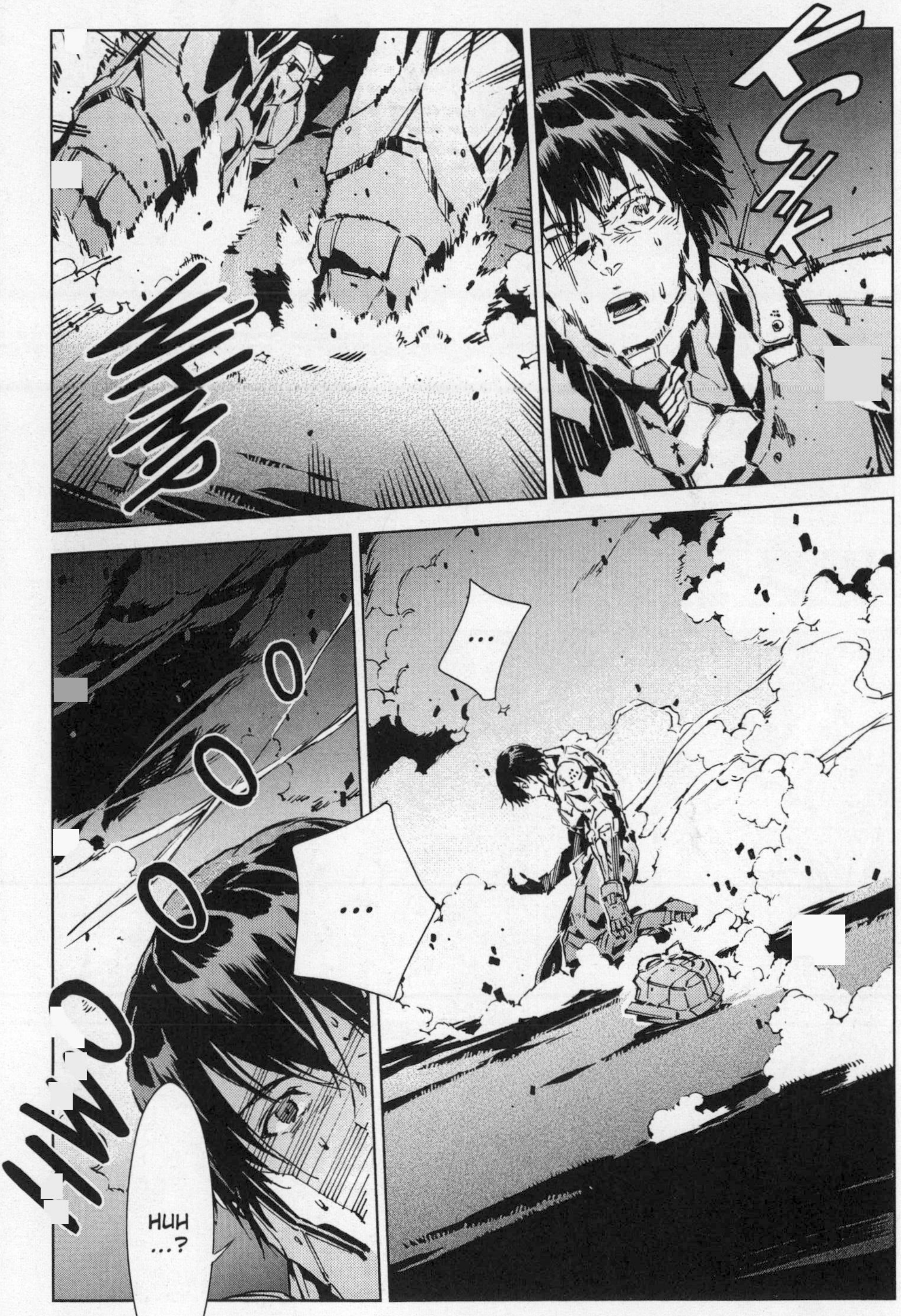
KCHK
WHUMP
...
...
HUH ...?

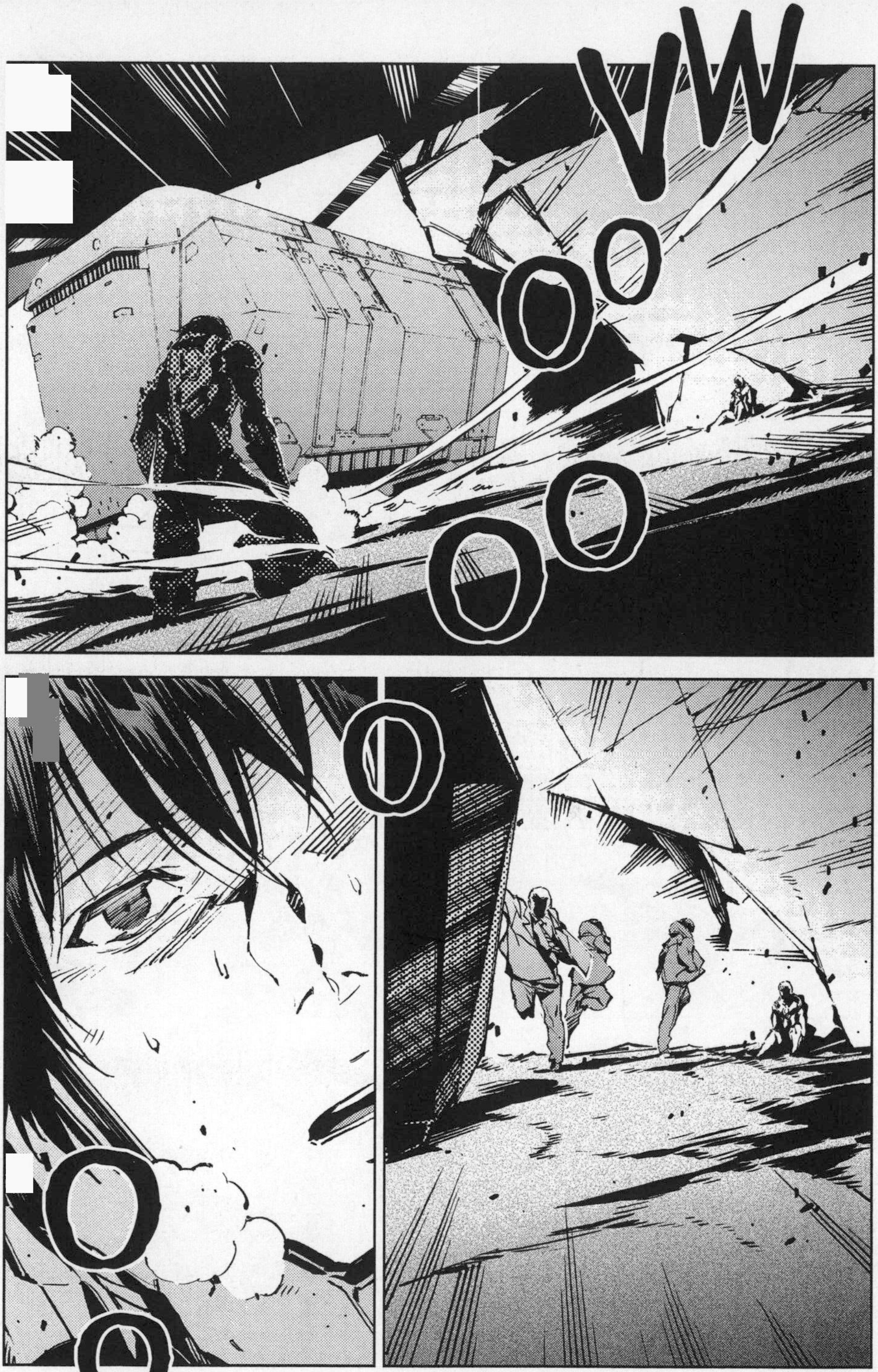
VWOOOOOOO

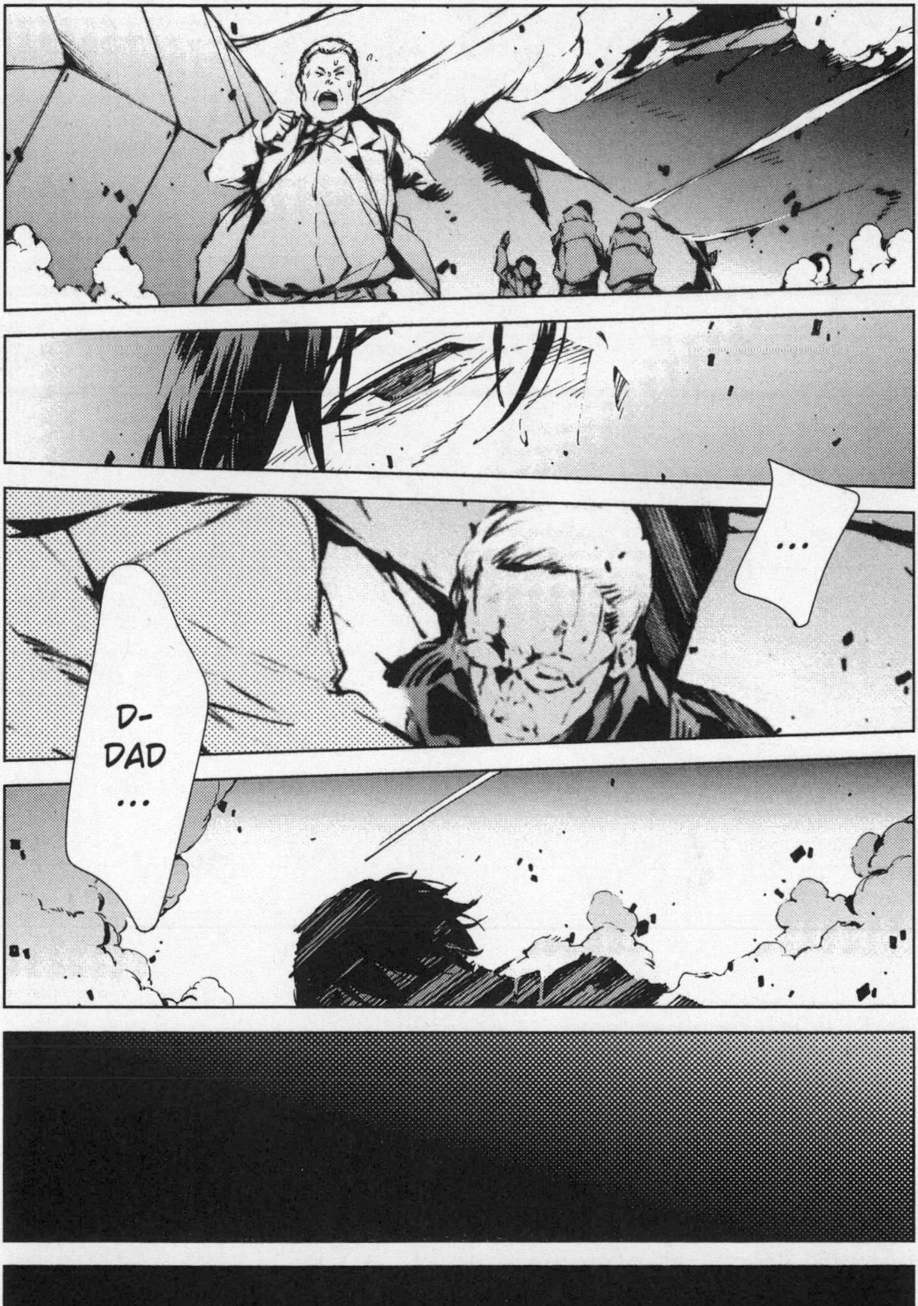
...
D-DAD ...

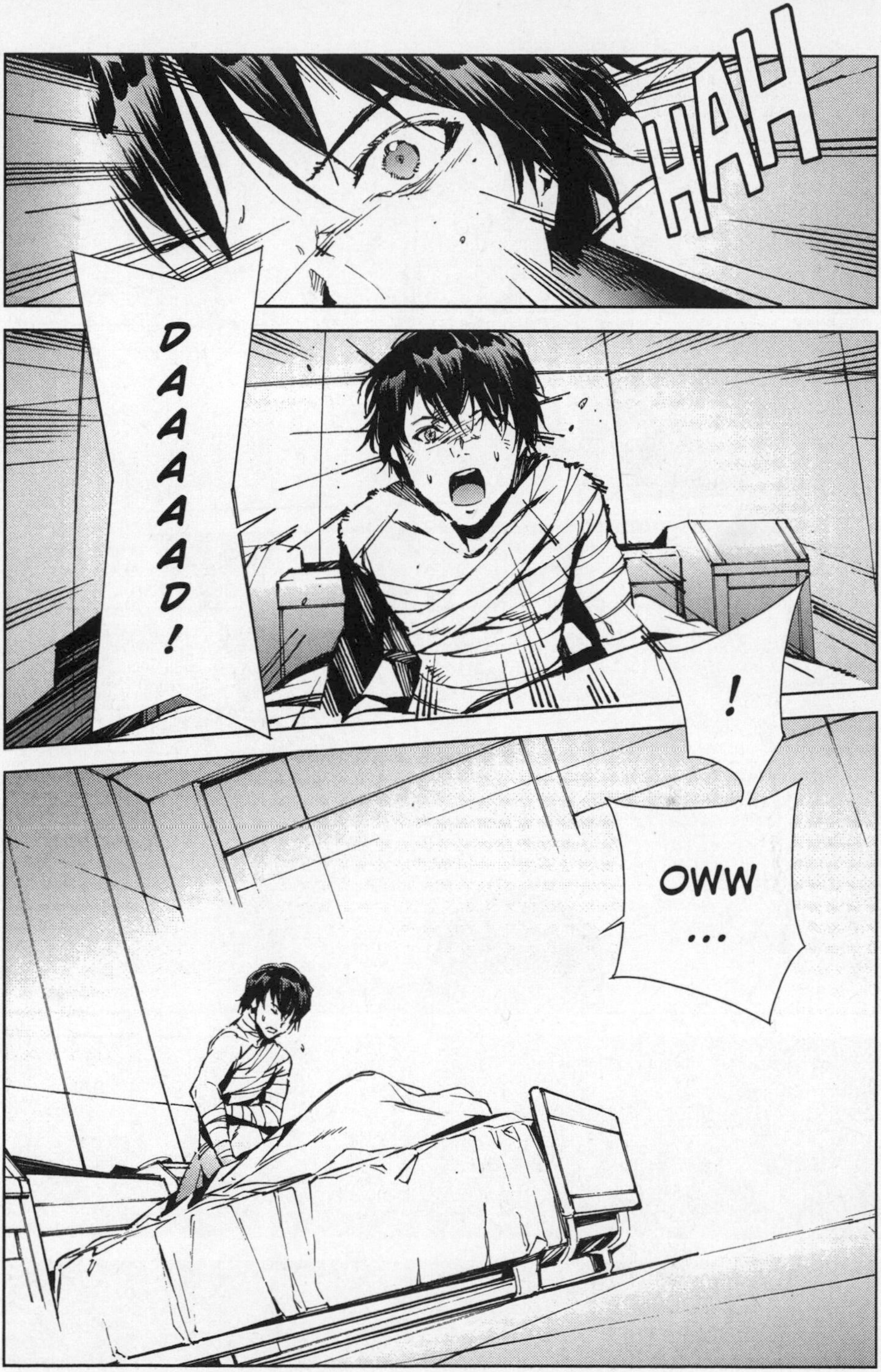
HAH
DAAAAAD!
!
OWW ...

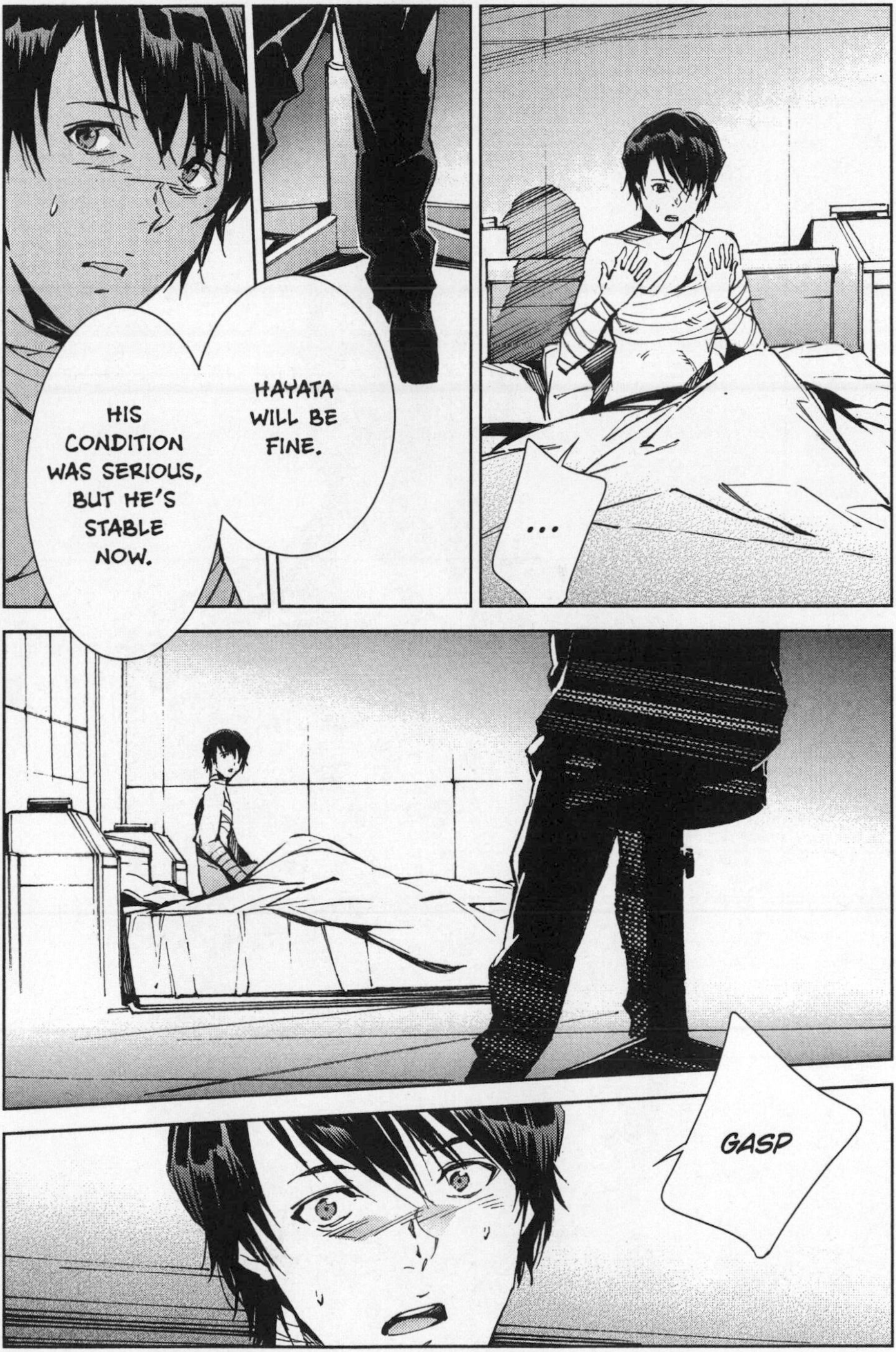
...
HAYATA WILL BE FINE.
HIS CONDITION WAS SERIOUS, BUT HE'S STABLE NOW.
GASP

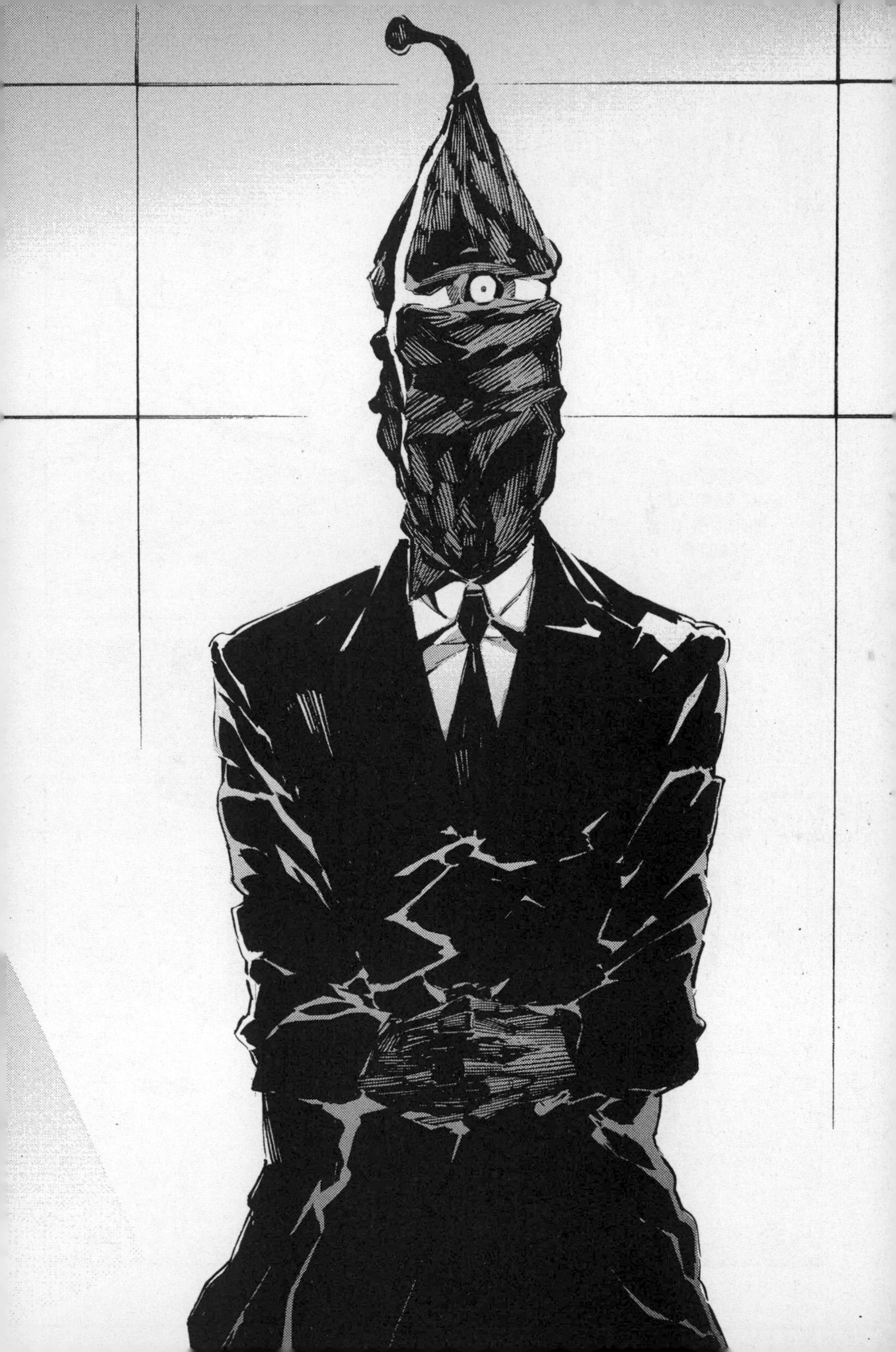

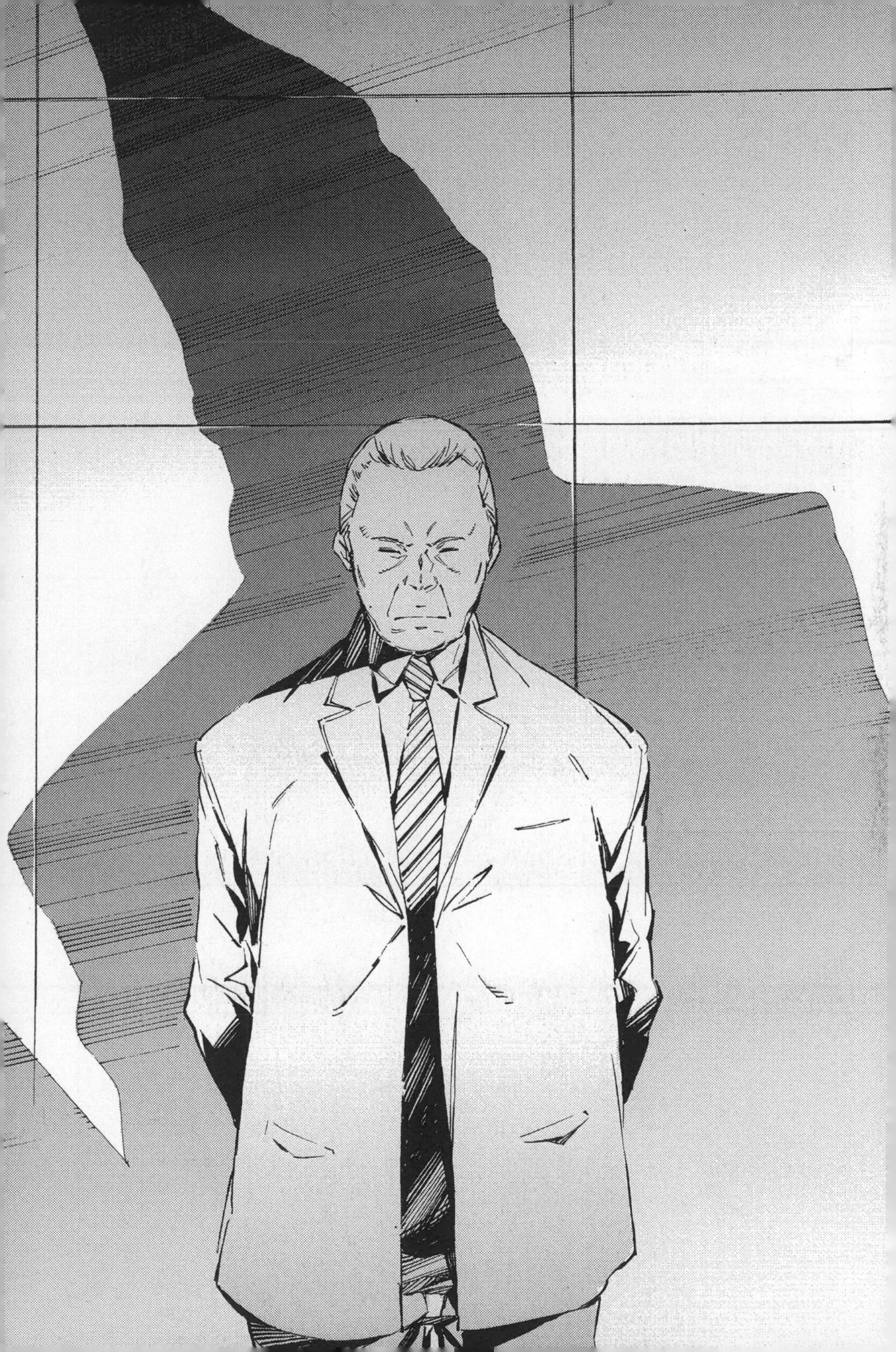

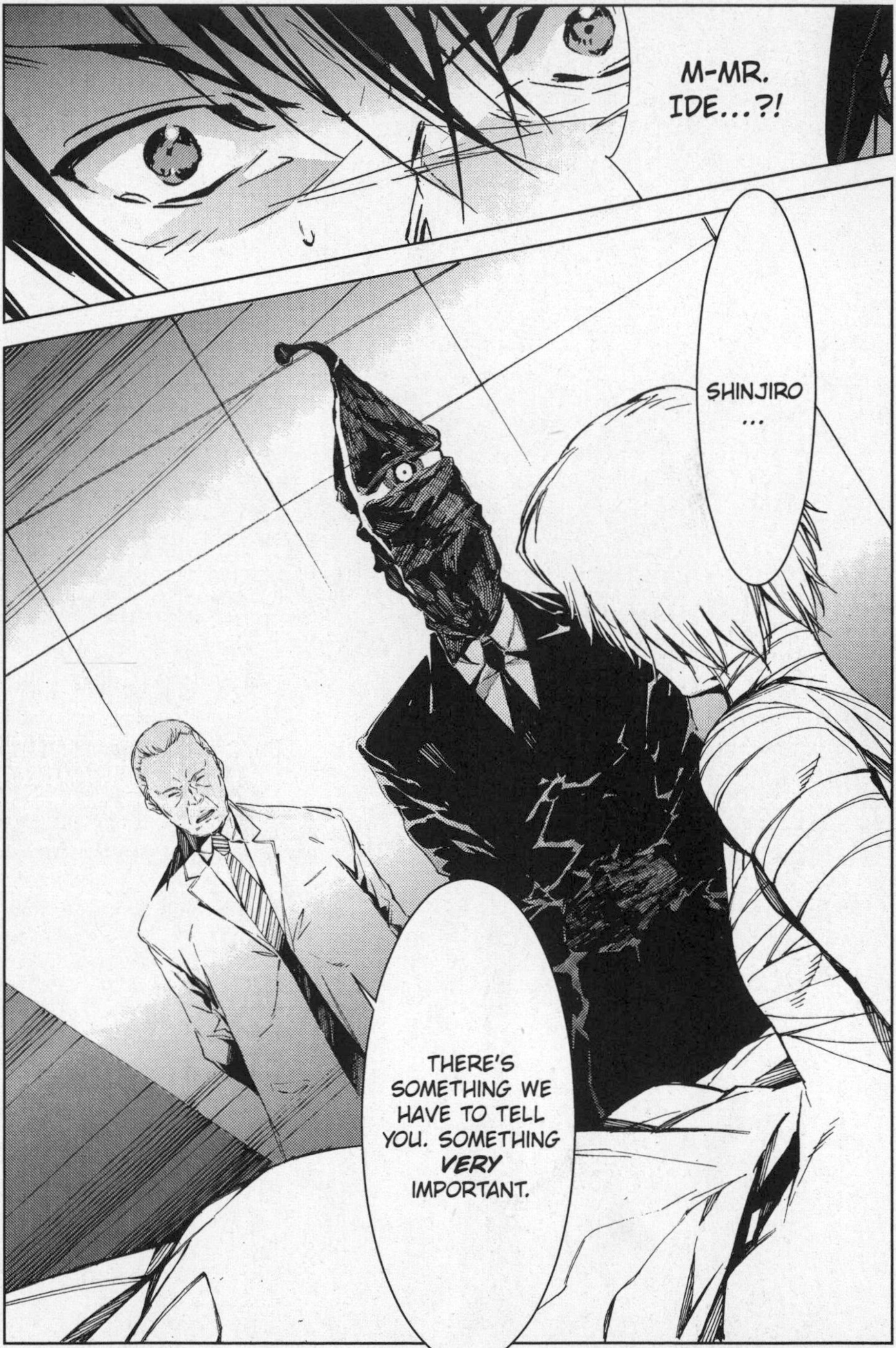
M-MR. IDE...?!
SHINJIRO ...
THERE'S SOMETHING WE HAVE TO TELL YOU. SOMETHING VERY IMPORTANT.

ULTRAMAN 1 - END

THIS IS THE BEGINNING OF A NEW AGE.

An Ultraman-type exo-armor suit built specifically for Shinjiro Hayata. Created by the Technological Development Team (led by Mitsuhiro Ide) for Shinjiro, who possesses the Ultraman Factor and physical abilities far beyond ordinary humans. Each arm is equipped with a weapon that uses Specium as an energy source. Exo-armor for normal humans is currently in development.

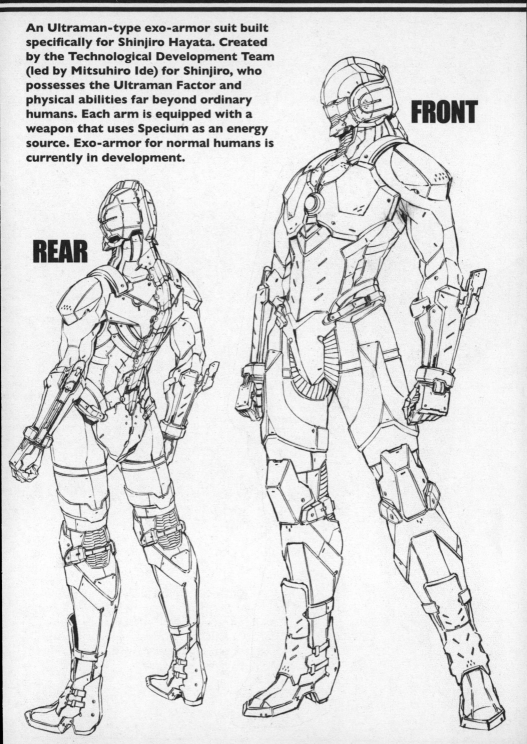

FRONT

REAR

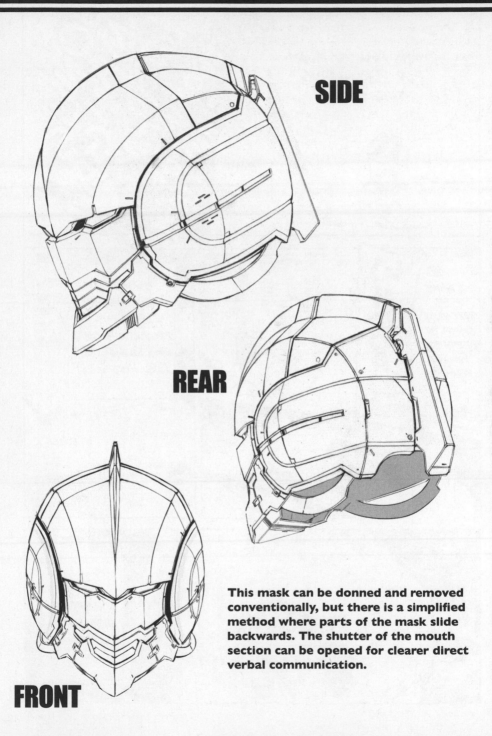

SIDE

REAR

FRONT

This mask can be donned and removed conventionally, but there is a simplified method where parts of the mask slide backwards. The shutter of the mouth section can be opened for clearer direct verbal communication.

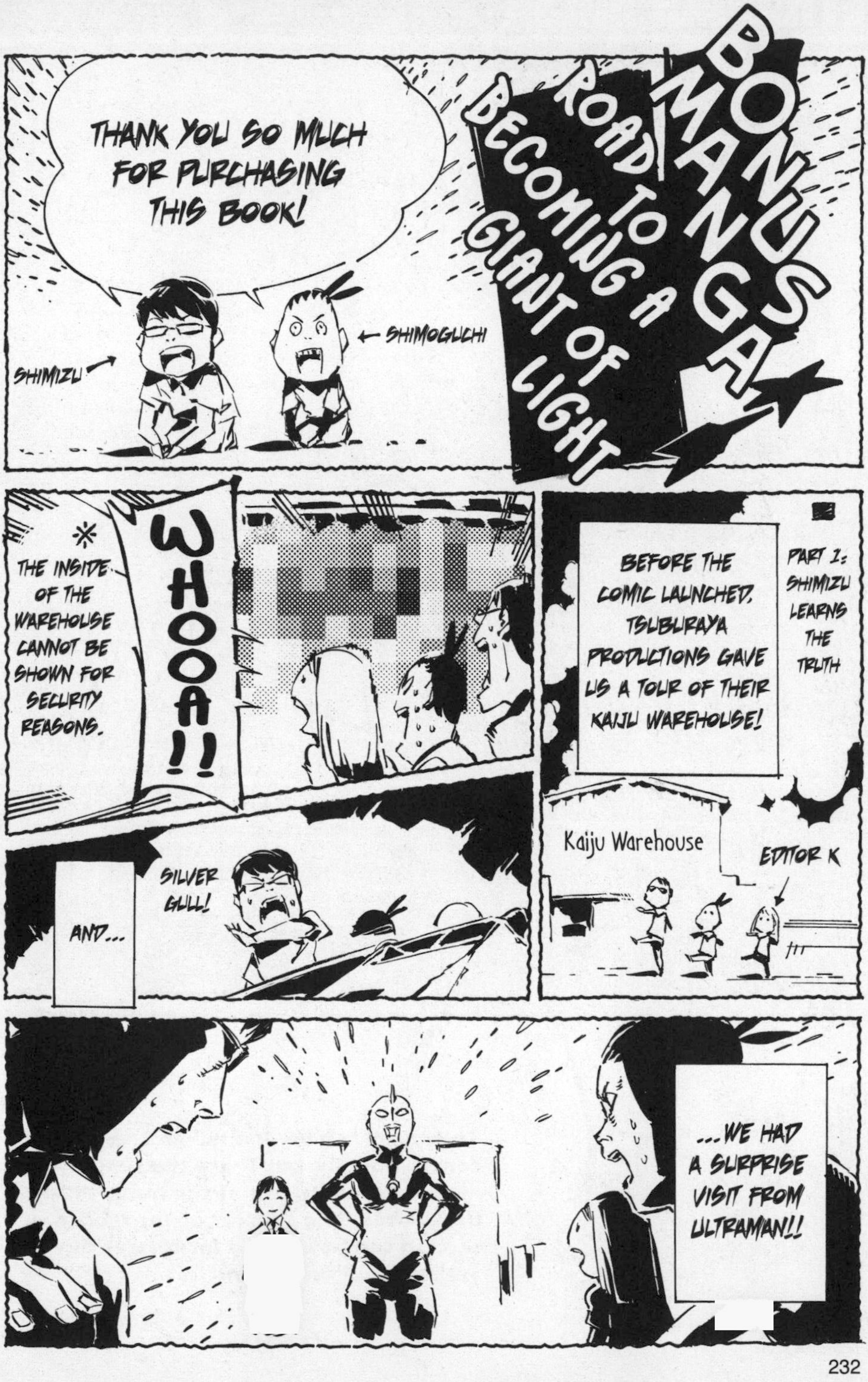
BONUS MANGA
ROAD TO BECOMING A GIANT OF LIGHT
THANK YOU SO MUCH FOR PURCHASING THIS BOOK!
SHIMOGUCHI
SHIMIZU
PART 1: SHIMIZU LEARNS THE TRUTH
BEFORE THE COMIC LAUNCHED, TSUBURAYA PRODUCTIONS GAVE US A TOUR OF THEIR KAIJU WAREHOUSE!
Kaiju Warehouse
EDITOR K
WHOOA!!
※ THE INSIDE OF THE WAREHOUSE CANNOT BE SHOWN FOR SECURITY REASONS.
SILVER GULL!
AND...
...WE HAD A SURPRISE VISIT FROM ULTRAMAN!!

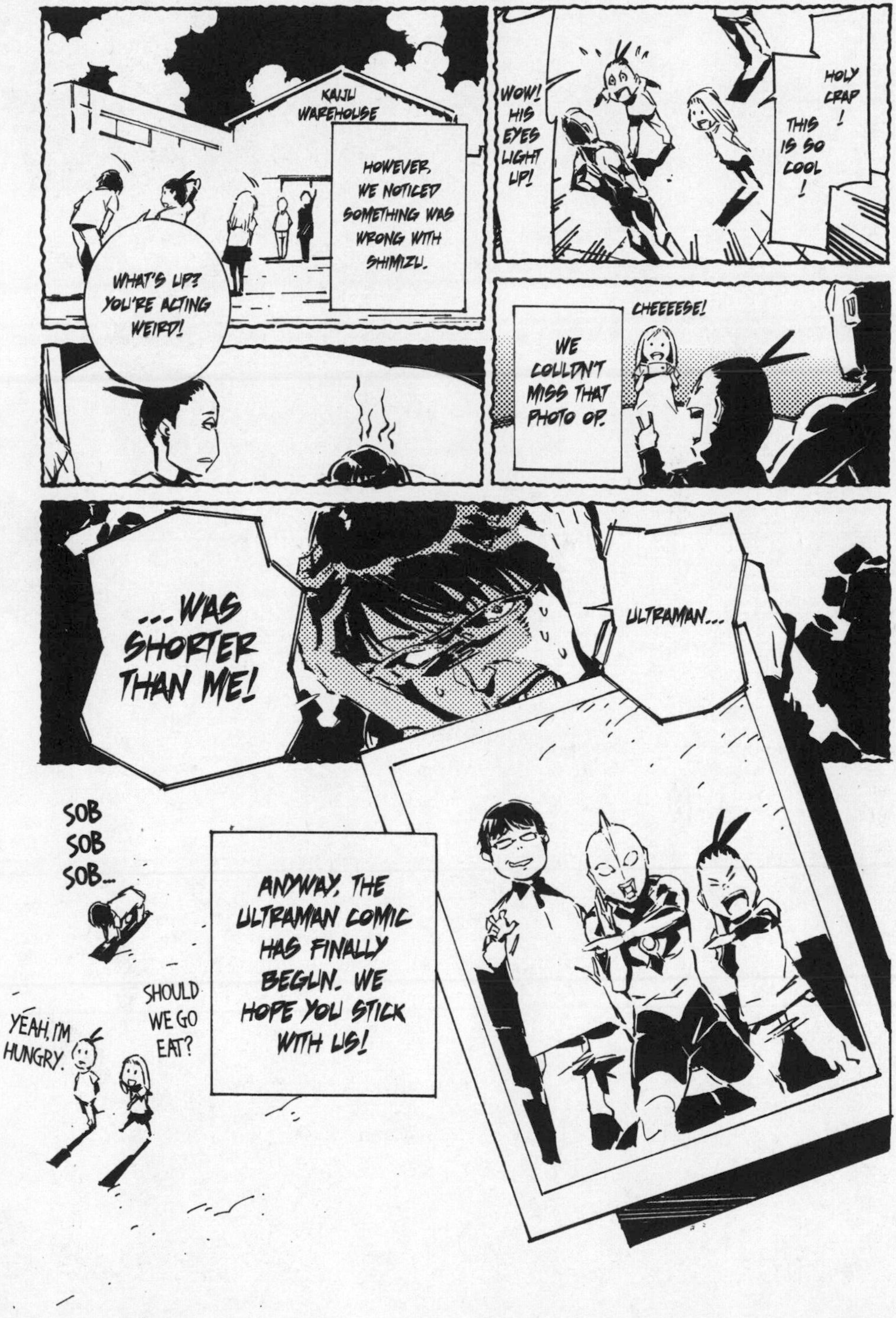
HOLY CRAP! THIS IS SO COOL!
WOW! HIS EYES LIGHT UP!
KAIJU WAREHOUSE
HOWEVER, WE NOTICED SOMETHING WAS WRONG WITH SHIMIZU.
WHAT'S UP? YOU'RE ACTING WEIRD!
CHEEEEESE!
WE COULDN'T MISS THAT PHOTO OP.
ULTRAMAN...
...WAS SHORTER THAN ME!
ANYWAY, THE ULTRAMAN COMIC HAS FINALLY BEGUN. WE HOPE YOU STICK WITH US!
SOB SOB SOB...
SHOULD WE GO EAT?
YEAH, I'M HUNGRY.

EIICHI SHIMIZU ✕ **TOMOHIRO SHIMOGUCHI**

We used to fanatically watch reruns of *Ultraman* as kids. We never dreamed we would be working on an *Ultraman* manga several decades later. So we offer *Ultraman* to you, packed with several decades' worth of love. We hope you enjoy it.

ULTRAMAN

VOLUME 1
VIZ SIGNATURE EDITION

STORY/ART BY **EIICHI SHIMIZU** AND **TOMOHIRO SHIMOGUCHI**

©2012 Eiichi Shimizu and Tomohiro Shimoguchi / TSUBURAYA PROD.
Originally published by HERO'S INC.

TRANSLATION **JOE YAMAZAKI**
ENGLISH ADAPTATION **STAN!**
TOUCH-UP ART & LETTERING **EVAN WALDINGER**
DESIGN **FAWN LAU**
EDITOR **MIKE MONTESA**

Printed in the U.S.A

Published by VIZ Media, LLC
P.O. Box 77010
San Francisco, CA 94107

10 9 8 7 6 5 4 3 2 1
First printing, August 2015

VIZ SIGNATURE

www.viz.com

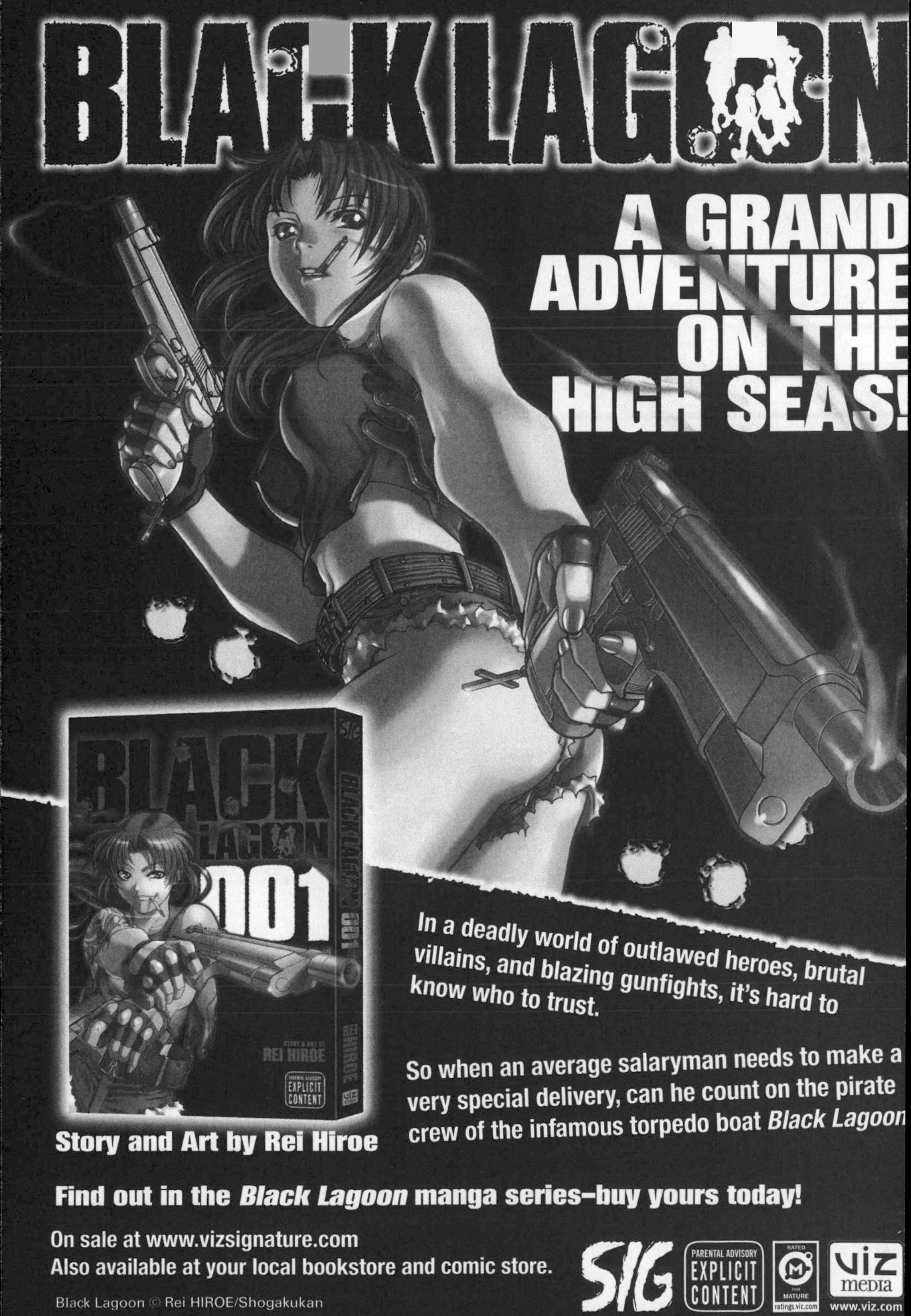
BLACK LAGOON
A GRAND ADVENTURE ON THE HIGH SEAS!
BLACK LAGOON 001
STORY & ART BY REI HIROE
PARENTAL ADVISORY EXPLICIT CONTENT
Story and Art by Rei Hiroe
In a deadly world of outlawed heroes, brutal villains, and blazing gunfights, it's hard to know who to trust.
So when an average salaryman needs to make a very special delivery, can he count on the pirate crew of the infamous torpedo boat *Black Lagoon*?
Find out in the *Black Lagoon* manga series–buy yours today!
On sale at www.vizsignature.com
Also available at your local bookstore and comic store.
SIG
PARENTAL ADVISORY EXPLICIT CONTENT
RATED M FOR MATURE ratings.viz.com
VIZ media
www.viz.com
Black Lagoon © Rei HIROE/Shogakukan

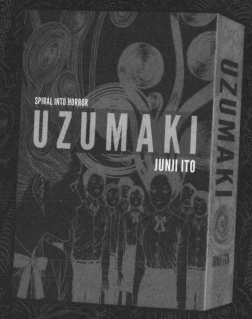

HEY! YOU'RE READING IN THE WRONG DIRECTION!

This is the END of the graphic novel

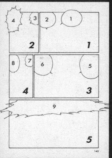

Follow the action this way

To properly enjoy this VIZ graphic novel, please turn it around and begin reading from RIGHT TO LEFT. Unlike English, Japanese is read right to left, so Japanese comics are read in reverse order from the way English comics are typically read.

This book has been printed in the original Japanese format in order to preserve the orientation of the original artwork.

HAVE FUN WITH IT!